The Basic Principles of the Business Rule Approach

- *Rules should be written and made explicit.*
- *Rules should be expressed in plain language.*
- *Rules should exist independent of procedures and workflows.*
- *Rules should build on facts, and facts should build on concepts as represented by terms.*
- *Rules should guide or influence behavior in desired ways.*

- *Rules should be motivated by identifiable and important business factors.*
- *Rules should be accessible to authorized parties.*
- *Rules should be single-sourced.*
- *Rules should be specified directly by those people who have relevant knowledge.*
- *Rules should be managed.*

Principles of
the Business
Rule Approach

Addison-Wesley Information Technology Series
Capers Jones and David S. Linthicum, Consulting Editors

The information technology (IT) industry is in the public eye now more than ever before because of a number of major issues in which software technology and national policies are closely related. As the use of software expands, there is a continuing need for business and software professionals to stay current with the state of the art in software methodologies and technologies. The goal of the Addison-Wesley Information Technology Series is to cover any and all topics that affect the IT community. These books illustrate and explore how information technology can be aligned with business practices to achieve business goals and support business imperatives. Addison-Wesley has created this innovative series to empower you with the benefits of the industry experts' experience.

For more information point your browser to http://www.awprofessional.com/itseries

Sid Adelman, Larissa Terpeluk Moss, *Data Warehouse Project Management*. ISBN: 0-201-61635-1

Sid Adelman, Joyce Bischoff, Jill Dyché, Douglas Hackney, Sean Ivoghli, Chuck Kelley, David Marco, Larissa Moss, and Clay Rehm, *Impossible Data Warehouse Situations: Solutions from the Experts*. ISBN: 0-201-76033-9

Wayne Applehans, Alden Globe, and Greg Laugero, *Managing Knowledge: A Practical Web-Based Approach*. ISBN: 0-201-43315-X

David Leon Clark, *Enterprise Security: The Manager's Defense Guide*. ISBN: 0-201-71972-X

Frank P. Coyle, *XML, Web Services, and the Data Revolution*. ISBN: 0-201-77641-3

Kevin Dick, *XML, Second Edition: A Manager's Guide*. ISBN: 0-201-77006-7

Jill Dyché, *e-Data: Turning Data into Information with Data Warehousing*. ISBN: 0-201-65780-5

Jill Dyché, *The CRM Handbook: A Business Guide to Customer Relationship Management*. ISBN: 0-201-73062-6

Patricia L. Ferdinandi, *A Requirements Pattern: Succeeding in the Internet Economy*. ISBN: 0-201-73826-0

Nick V. Flor, *Web Business Engineering: Using Offline Activites to Drive Internet Strategies*. ISBN: 0-201-60468-X

David Garmus and David Herron, *Function Point Analysis: Measurement Practices for Successful Software Projects*. ISBN: 0-201-69944-3

John Harney, *Application Service Providers (ASPs): A Manager's Guide*. ISBN: 0-201-72659-9

International Function Point Users Group, *IT Measurement: Practical Advice from the Experts*. ISBN: 0-201-74158-X

Capers Jones, *Software Assessments, Benchmarks, and Best Practices*. ISBN: 0-201-48542-7

Ravi Kalakota and Marcia Robinson, *e-Business 2.0: Roadmap for Success*. ISBN: 0-201-72165-1

Greg Laugero and Alden Globe, *Enterprise Content Services: Connecting Information and Profitability*. ISBN: 0-201-73016-2

David S. Linthicum, *Enterprise Application Integration*. ISBN: 0-201-61583-5

David S. Linthicum, *B2B Application Integration: e-Business-Enable Your Enterprise*. ISBN: 0-201-70936-8

Sergio Lozinsky, *Enterprise-Wide Software Solutions: Integration Strategies and Practices*. ISBN: 0-201-30971-8

Larissa T. Moss and Shaku Atre, *Business Intelligence Roadmap: The Complete Project Lifecycle for Decision-Support Applications*. ISBN: 0-201-78420-3

Bud Porter-Roth, *Request for Proposal: A Guide to Effective RFP Development*. ISBN: 0-201-77575-1

Ronald G. Ross, *Principles of the Business Rule Approach*. ISBN: 0-201-78893-4

Mai-lan Tomsen, *Killer Content: Strategies for Web Content and E-Commerce*. ISBN: 0-201-65786-4

Karl E. Wiegers, *Peer Reviews in Software: A Practical Guide*. ISBN: 0-201-73485-0

Ralph R. Young, *Effective Requirements Practices*. ISBN: 0-201-70912-0

Bill Zoellick, *CyberRegs: A Business Guide to Web Property, Privacy, and Patents*. ISBN: 0-201-72230-5

Principles of
the Business
Rule Approach

Ronald G. Ross

✦ Addison-Wesley

Boston • San Francisco • New York • Toronto • Montreal
London • Munich • Paris • Madrid
Capetown • Sydney • Tokyo • Singapore • Mexico City

The publisher offers discounts on this book when ordered in quantity for bulk purchases and special sales. For more information, please contact:

U.S. Corporate and Government Sales
(800) 382-3419
corpsales@pearsontechgroup.com

For sales outside of the U.S., please contact:
International Sales
(317) 581-3793
international@pearsontechgroup.com

Visit Addison-Wesley on the Web: www.awprofessional.com

Library of Congress Cataloging-in-Publication Data

Ross, Ronald G.
    Principles of the business rules approach / Ronald G. Ross.
        p. cm.
    Includes bibliographical references and index.
    ISBN 0-201-78893-4 (pbk. : alk. paper)
    1. Business—Databases—Management.   2. Database management.   3. Management information systems.   4. Information technology—Management.   I. Title: Business rules approach.   II. Title.

HD30.2 .R673 2003
658.4'013—dc21   2002151451

ISBN: 0-201-78893-4
Text printed on recycled paper
1 2 3 4 5 6 7 8 9 10—MA—0706050403
First printing, February 2003

To Gladys S.W. Lam, business colleague and friend,
and originator of many of the applied ideas in this book.

Contents

CHAPTER 10   Functional Categories of Rules: The BRS Rule Classification Scheme   141

CHAPTER 11   Sentence Patterns for Rule Statements: The RuleSpeak Templates   145

CHAPTER 12   Expressing Business Logic by Using Decision Tables: The RuleSpeak Approach   161

Preface

The driver for business systems should always be business need. Business workers should be involved in expressing this need in very direct, concrete ways. Applying these principles in practice means taking a fresh approach to business systems that will profoundly affect the roles of both business professionals and information technology (IT) professionals.

This fresh approach can be called *business analysis* and its basic deliverable a *business model*. Unfortunately, these terms are often used very loosely. Many system developers think their deliverables qualify as business models, but they do not. Rather than try to explain here (it does require some background), I will leave that topic for Part I. For now, let's simply call the fresh approach *business-driven* and move on.

A basic ingredient of the business-driven approach—a very exciting one—is *business rules*. Before continuing, let me clarify something. We could certainly talk about business rules without necessarily discussing everything else needed for a business-driven approach. In other words, we *could* discuss business rules separately.

But why would we want to? If business need is the driving factor for business systems, then both the business-driven approach and business rules should be put on the table and served together. That way the business can achieve the very best business solutions to the challenges it faces in the 21st century. In a nutshell, that describes the basic mind-set of this book.

That brings me to the audience, or more accurately the audiences, for this book. In general terms, there are three audiences: business professionals, IT professionals, and academics. In today's world, there are significant gaps between these three communities—and that in itself is part of the problem. To create the best business solutions possible, these three communities must come closer together in common purpose and approach. This book helps show the way.

About Technology

I will say a few words to each of these three communities in a moment, but first let me say a word about technology. Because I believe so strongly that business systems should be driven by business need, I have purposely avoided discussing technology (with some difficulty!) throughout the book. But the topic certainly does deserve comment, so let me talk about it briefly.

We are on the verge of a huge new wave of technological innovation focused on the knowledge capabilities of the business. Think of business rules (which I collectively call *business logic*) as a first—and in many respects relatively modest—step in that direction.

The plain truth is that such technology has never been a significant part of mainstream business IT. Expert systems made a minor foray into that realm in the 1980s but had very little impact. There were many reasons why, but perhaps the most important was technological. Computing architectures then (and since then until recently) were basically monolithic, and they provided no easy way to accommodate "outside" services.

Without going into detail, that fundamental barrier is now being eliminated, and plug-in services are becoming easier and easier to incorporate. And what better service to incorporate than direct knowledge support?

Knowledge support does sound a bit abstract. There are several terms in current usage for such a service, including *rule engine* and *decision management platform*. In Part V of this book, I suggest *business logic server*. By whatever name, I predict without hesitation that such services will be part of all major business software platforms within a mere matter of years.

To many, this technology will seem like a tidal wave from nowhere. But that's not really true. In fact, the theoretical foundations of this new technology go back many, many years, again as discussed in Part V. Commercial offerings date to the mid-1980s; applied research goes back well before that. Refer to the special boxed item for a brief review of where this technology stands at present.

> **Business Logic Technology: Near-Term Directions**
>
> In the near future, commercial technology servicing business logic is likely to be offered in several different ways, including the following.
>
> - *Supported as a stand-alone component:* In this case, the business can acquire a best-fit or best-of-breed package and incorporate it into its computing architecture as appropriate.
> - *Coupled with a workflow engine:* This powerful combination features automated process management with coordination and decision making provided by the business logic technology. The result permits not only more sophisticated workflow control but automation of selected decision-making tasks as well.
> - *Bundled into other packaged software:* Many other kinds of software capabilities, including customer relationship management (CRM) and enterprise resource planning (ERP), provide natural niches for business logic technology, which will undoubtedly be exploited to the full extent their architectures permit.
>
> And the list goes on. A big question mark for the future concerns database management systems (DBMSs). In Part V, I argue that in the long run, database support should be integrated within a business logic server.

Again, our focus in this book is not technology, but rather where do the business rules *come from?* That brings us to the business rule approach.

About the Business Rule Approach

Like the technology, the business rule approach did not suddenly appear from nowhere. In fact, the core concepts (as described in Part II) date to the early to mid-1990s, and many of the related techniques and methodologies (including those in Part III) have been thoroughly battle-tested by pioneering organizations during the late 1990s and early 2000s. (The same is true, incidentally, about business-driven approaches.) So what I talk about in this book is not unproven theory or academic conjecture but pragmatic, real-world stuff.

The interesting and perhaps unique thing about the business rule approach is that it did *not* arise as a response to any emerging new class of software tools—knowledge-oriented or otherwise. (Again, the same is true for business-driven approaches.)

Rather, the business rule approach is a real-world, grassroots movement whose driving force is business success, not technology. It arose from the vision of dedicated professionals with many years of experience in the trials and challenges of business software. Their goal: to offer companies the best possible approach to developing business solutions involving automated systems.

To Business Professionals

For that reason, it is appropriate that I address members of the business community first. To repeat, this is not a book about technology, but rather one about business opportunity. The key question should therefore be why knowing about business rules is important as a business proposition.

So exactly what is the value proposition of business rules? Part I provides the answer, but let me give you a short version here, then invite you to read on. Refer to the special boxed item.

What Problems Does the Business Rule Approach Address?

Ad hoc rules: Most businesses have no logical approach for defining their business rules. As a result, business workers often make up the rules as they go along. This leads to confusion, contradiction, and operational inefficiency. After-the-fact resolution of these problems wastes time and resources and causes frustration for customers and staff alike. The larger the organization, the bigger the problem. Also, since many business rules involve monetary transactions (for example, whether a customer should be given a discount, and if so, how much), this problem can also directly affect the bottom line.

Business rule solution: A structured approach helps you think through rules before the fact.

Miscommunication: Misunderstanding of key business concepts inevitably results in miscommunication. Does *preferred customer discount* mean the same across all departments? If not, what are the differences? What rules apply? Do these rules differ for different areas of the business? Are the rules consistent?

Business rule solution: A clear set of concepts provides a foundation on which rules can be directly based.

Inaccessible rules: Finding out what rules apply to a given business situation often involves an open-ended search through multiple sources. It is not uncommon in the end to resort to the application source code. Pursuing rules in this fashion is time-consuming, inefficient, inaccurate, and frustrating.

Business rule solution: A way to manage business rules provides direct accessibility.

Massive differentiation: Many businesses seek to support highly individualized relationships with growing numbers of customers and other partners for ever more complex products or services. How can businesses massively differentiate between business parties and, at the very same time, conduct each business transaction faster, more accurately, and at ever lower costs?

Business rule solution: A rule-based approach featuring rapid development and deployment of rules supports differentiation.

The need to keep up to speed: Rapid change, at an ever faster pace, is a fact of life. In the Internet age, people expect almost instantaneous implementation of changes. How can line workers consumed with day-to-day activities ever hope to keep up?

Business rule solution: Real-time delivery of business logic to knowledge workers as errors actually occur creates a seamless, never-ending, self-training environment.

Knowledge walking out the door: By and large, baby boomers created much of the operational business capacity and operational systems we see in place in larger organizations today. Much of the related knowledge still sits in their heads—and nowhere else. What will happen when they retire? On a smaller scale, people with vital operational knowledge walk out the door almost every day.

> *Business rule solution:* A systematic way of capturing, documenting, and retaining the business rules prevents the loss of knowledge when people leave.

Part I also discusses what business-driven approaches are about. From a business perspective, the business rule approach fits hand-in-glove with them. Combined, they are potent indeed. I hope Part I will prove so compelling in this regard that you will read on. I have tried to use a readable, nontechnical style throughout the book, so there is much to be gained from going as deep into the book as you care to read.

Part II explains the basic ideas of the business rule approach using a broad analogy to the human body. Continuing from there (or skipping ahead if you choose), Part III provides a comprehensive language, called *BRS RuleSpeak*, to capture and express your business rules. You will find that material informative and in places perhaps entertaining.

Part IV is officially directed toward IT professionals, but it is actually a continuation of, or more accurately a different perspective on, the material in Part I. I believe it is very important for business professionals and IT professionals to speak with the same voice; this material should help your organization achieve it. By the way, the first chapter of Part IV is the only other place in the book where I talk about business-driven approaches directly.

To IT Professionals

Just a word about business-driven approaches first: I believe they are closely aligned with the architecture-based or model-based development strategies now emerging in the industry. In particular, a business-driven approach provides an excellent front end for these strategies in the form of the business model. A business model represents a top-down, multi-aspect blueprint of the business whose contents are driven by business professionals. That's a great starting point for system design and development of an application system (or deployment of an application package). These ideas are developed in Parts I and IV of the book.

If your interest centers specifically on business rules, you can concentrate on Parts II and III. You will also not want to miss important portions of Part IV devoted to rule management, rule capture, and data design.

The main objective for all this material is to help you gain a deep understanding of what business rules are about and to enable you to make them a comfortable part of your professional toolkit. I think you will be quite excited by the powerful ideas and techniques that await you.

To Academics

By *academics,* I do not mean only those readers who happen to be in universities or research labs. I mean any serious student of logical systems—*systems* here in the sense of theory, not applications. I also mean those who are just plain intellectually curious. Part V is aimed toward all such readers.

Part V provides answers to some of the big questions of business rules, such as their basis in formal theory—the predicate logic. You should not let that intimidate you. Part V is written as a tutorial so that the ideas are as accessible as possible to everyone. At the same time, I anticipate that this material will provide the basis for continuing research, some of which has already commenced.

The bottom line is this: You know you are on to something really powerful when good theory and successful practices converge. That convergence is exactly what has happened with business rules, and it is a very exciting time to be in the field!

PART I

The Business Problem: Why Business Rules?

Readings for Business Professionals

Overview

I will keep this Overview of Part I brief. If you have just finished reading the Preface, you already know where we are headed. If not, the content presented here will speak largely for itself.

The material in this part appears as a set of informal readings, each packaging a key insight about the business rule approach. These readings are organized into the following chapters.[1]

- Chapter 1 presents just enough information about the basic ideas of business rules so that we can move quickly into discussion of their business application in the chapters that follow.
- Chapter 2 discusses how business rules are key to many of the most exciting trends in business today. Indeed, I believe business rules make certain changes in the business landscape inevitable. This chapter identifies what these opportunities are and how you can stay on top of them.
- Chapter 3 revisits the idea presented in the Preface that automated knowledge (business logic) services will rapidly become part of mainstream information technology (IT) practices. This chapter provides a quick look at the role business rules will play in that change.

---

1. In some places in these chapters I describe practices and experiences shared by my colleagues and myself. In such instances, *we* refers to the Principals of Business Rule Solutions, LLC.

- Chapter 4 discusses the business-driven approach (mentioned in the Preface) for building better business solutions. Business rules are just one element of that approach. If you are interested in pragmatic yet innovative ways in which IT projects can be aligned more directly with business goals, be sure to have a look at Chapter 4.

CHAPTER ONE

What's This about Business Rules?

The Problem and the Fix in a Nutshell

A Telltale E-Mail Trail

The Case for Business Rules

The brief series of e-mails reproduced here illustrates some of the snarls in day-to-day tactical decision making that plague most organizations today. The overall problem is so pervasive—*so* big—that it can be difficult even to see at first. It is so much part of our everyday way of doing business that we tend to accept it as a given and simply work around it. (The exchange presented here is a real one, altered only to disguise the identities of those involved.)

As illustrated in the exchange, we often discover holes in operational policy only *after* it is too late to do much about them, at least without significant expense or loss of face. Is there a solution? Yes, there is—the business rule approach.

What are *business rules*? You probably have a pretty good intuitive sense of them already, at least from a business perspective. For now, let's simply characterize a business rule as follows.

Business Rule

A directive intended to influence or guide business behavior.

Re: The GenTech Sale

The parties involved in the following e-mail exchange:

Tracy, accounting staff member
Ken, the product manager
Glenda, the sales manager

At 08:52 AM July 8 Ken wrote:

Tracy,

Yesterday we received the 2nd Qtr Sales Report and Income Statement. You listed the revenue from our 6/5 sale to GenTech as $14,358.00. How was this amount determined?

I know GenTech attended our annual conference, and since they initially saw the product there, they got the special 20% conference discount. Since they purchased two copies, shouldn't the total be $15,587.00 ($9,592 for the first copy under the special 20% discount, and $5,995 for the second copy)?

Ken

At 10:32 AM July 8 Tracy wrote:

Ken,

Since GenTech attended the conference, we extended them the special 20% conference discount on *both* copies. So the total was $14,358.00 ($9,592 for the first copy under the special 20% discount, and $4,796 for the second copy under the special 20% discount). Hope you don't have a problem with this(?).

Tracy

At 03:25 PM July 8 Ken wrote:

Tracy,

My understanding was that only the *first* copy of any sale was to be offered at the special conference discount. Subsequent copies are already being deeply discounted a full 50%!!

Unfortunately, this is now water under the bridge as far as these first two copies for GenTech goes. However, they have already committed to buying another 8 or 9 copies. THERE IS TO BE NO FURTHER DISCOUNT ON THESE COPIES. Have you received their new purchase order yet? Unfortunately, they are probably under the impression that they will get the conference discount on these additional copies too. I'll have to touch base with Glenda so she can straighten all this out with them.

We need to get our act together before closing more new sales. What is the specific intent of offering a discount to conference attendees? It gets a little nebulous when we say "conference attendees receive a discount." Does the discount extend to any organization/person the attendee is associated with? Does the purchase need to be made on the spot to qualify? Does the discount have an expiration date? Are the discounted purchases limited to one per person?

These are just some of the questions that come to mind. If some rules aren't established here this is going to bite us again. GenTech placed the order more than 3 months *after* the conference. Since they are buying a relatively expensive product, it isn't reasonable to expect them to purchase it on the spot. Having said that, there should be an EXPIRATION DATE for the conference discount. I would suggest 30 to 60 days after the conference. And in the future we should make it clear the discount applies only to the first copy, *not* to subsequent copies.

Let's establish some good guidelines so we are all on the same page. We want to avoid any future misunderstandings and maintain the good will of our customers.

Ken

At 05:15 PM July 8 Glenda wrote:

Ken,

I've been going back and forth with GenTech over this for a good while, but after making a few other concessions, I think the fires are out on this one for now.

I agree fully with your concerns. Next time we offer something like this, let's spend a few minutes thinking it through first. Shouldn't take all that long—you came up with a great list of questions to consider. I'm *sure* that would take a lot less time than all this has!

Glenda

We need not dwell on more precise definitions for now—there is plenty of opportunity for that in the rest of the book.[1] More important is why your business should focus on business rules. I will answer that question in this part of the book.

---

1. For an in-depth discussion of definitions for *business rule*, refer to What Is a Business Rule? in Chapter 13.

When Is a Door Not a Door?

The Business Rule Difference

One of the interesting things about consulting with different organizations on business rules and publishing a journal[2] on that subject is that a lot of really silly rules cross my desk. I think you might enjoy some of these, so I have included several small selections in Part III.

One reader recently forwarded a rule that raises some interesting questions. He observed that in his apartment building the doors to the stairwells all have signs on them that say, "Doors must be kept closed at all times." His question was, "Is a door you must never open really a door?" If the rule is followed religiously, he noted, the door might as well be considered part of the wall.

DOORS MUST
BE KEPT
CLOSED AT
ALL TIMES

---

2. *Business Rules Journal*; see the Web site at *http://www.BRCommunity.com.*

Before addressing that tongue-in-cheek question, let's do some analysis on this rule. I think we can safely assume that the rule as stated is actually a shorthand form. A more complete and accurate version might be, "You may use this door for entry and exit, but it must be closed behind you." If we wanted to be very complete, we might explain the basic motivation for the rule by adding, "This is a fire door."

Further analysis of this simple rule reveals some fundamental ideas of the business rule approach.

- The rule was posted, that is, written down. Why? The answer lies in the motivation for the rule. Its purpose is to protect the inhabitants of the building against the dangers of fire. *When a rule becomes important enough, it is always written down.*

- The rule was written in plain English. If the rule were difficult to understand or encoded in such a way that many of the inhabitants could not readily interpret it, the rule would not serve its purpose very well. *A rule important enough to write down is worth writing plainly.*

- A procedure for this situation is not really needed. We could write one, of course, but in this case it would probably be trivial. ("Approach door; grasp doorknob with hand; twist doorknob in clockwise direction; pull/push carefully. . . .") Nonetheless, the rule is still crucial. *Rules can exist independent of procedures.*

- This rule—like all rules—serves to shape behavior. The posting of the rule reminds inhabitants, staff, and others to close the door, and presumably they are therefore less likely to forget or perhaps even block the door open. *The purpose of a rule is always to guide or influence behavior in desired ways.*

- The rule serves a purpose. It is neither frivolous nor arbitrary. Fire is a deadly risk, and all reasonable measures must be taken to protect against it. *Business rules never arise in a vacuum; there are always identifiable and important business factors motivating them.*

- The rule was posted right where the action is—that is, where actual use of the door occurs. This proximity to the action helps ensure that people follow the rule as events actually unfold. *The best way to ensure rules are followed is to get them right in front of people at the exact point where the guidance is relevant.*

- The rule is undoubtedly part of a larger body of regulatory fire code rules for buildings. Even though the rule might be posted thousands of times for enforcement purposes, these postings arise from a single source. This ensures consistency. *If rules are important enough to be enforced, they are important enough to be single-sourced.*

- The body of fire codes was undoubtedly produced by experts experienced in the field and is backed by the political authority of the city or state. The regulations were *not* produced or mandated by an IT department! *Business logic should always be specified directly by those people who have relevant knowledge.*

- Because of the importance of the regulations to the well-being of the community, any and all changes to them must be reviewed, approved, incorporated, and disseminated carefully. Because new dangers and liabilities can be discovered at any time, this process should be as streamlined and efficient as possible. On the other hand, over time some rules may become obsolete and even dangerous. The bottom line: *Rules must be managed.*

The Basic Principles of the Business Rule Approach

- *Rules should be written and made explicit.*
- *Rules should be expressed in plain language.*
- *Rules should exist independent of procedures and workflows.*
- *Rules should build on facts, and facts should build on concepts as represented by terms.*
- *Rules should guide or influence behavior in desired ways.*

- *Rules should be motivated by identifiable and important business factors.*
- *Rules should be accessible to authorized parties.*
- *Rules should be single-sourced.*
- *Rules should be specified directly by those people who have relevant knowledge.*
- *Rules should be managed.*

These commonsense observations represent basic principles of the business rule approach. Your business undoubtedly has literally hundreds or thousands of such rules guiding its various business processes. Yet in practice, these basic principles are seldom followed. In many organizations, the problem is so severe that the overall guidance process has just about broken down.

Can you do something about it? *Yes!* This book will guide you toward solutions.

Now back to that question, "Is a door you must never open really a door?" The answer is obvious—yes, of course it is. A wall *without* a door will always just be a wall. If you need a door sometime in the future, you must re-model, and that means time and money (not to mention disruption for the inhabitants). If you have ever remodeled your home, you know exactly what I mean.

The wall *with* a door acts like just a wall until such time that the "must remain closed" rule is discontinued. Then, with relatively little delay, expense, or disruption, the wall can become a wall with a *functional* door.

Think of the business rule approach as a relatively inexpensive way to build potential doors for your business for all those many cases when they might one day be needed. That way you can avoid walling yourself off from best-fit solutions and quick-response opportunities. In a world of constant and accelerating change, *adaptability* is the name of the game. This is why your company should focus on business rules today!

CHAPTER TWO

Areas of Opportunity

Changing the Face of Business

Where Does the Business Rule Approach Apply?

The "Re's" of Business Rules

In my experience, business rule projects generally fall into one of the following major categories. Without exaggeration, I suspect one or more of these categories apply to virtually every organization of any size worldwide—including *your* organization!

Reengineering

The first category involves projects to reengineer business processes. The focus here is on a top-down, business-driven requirements process. Business rule development—especially for *core* business rules—is a critical part of such an approach for at least two reasons.

1. Business rules play a central role in strategizing, that is, in rethinking the business problem and in developing a full and optimal business solution up front. I will have more to say on that point later (see Chapter 4).
2. Business rules sharpen and complement other, more traditional deliverables (for example, workflow models). In short, business rules handle the *business logic* portion of redevelopment efforts.

Revitalization

At more or less the opposite extreme are projects with no intent to reengineer any business process. Instead, their focus is on the day-to-day problem of how to implement changing policies and directives coming down from above (and/or from outside regulatory or governmental bodies) into existing processes. This needs to be done in a timely and efficient manner.

Typically, these organizations currently lack any effective means to trace the higher-level policies and rules to their actual implementation in legacy environments and related procedures. Because the connections are lost, impact assessment and modification can be performed only slowly and painfully. These projects view the business rule approach as a way to *reestablish lost connections* by reinventing their rule management environments.

Redeployment

Just about every company these days is eyeing the Web as an environment for redeploying basic business services. To do that, a company must identify and encode the business logic that governs those services (that is, the business rules).

This type of project actually represents the larger problem of how to exploit new hardware/software environments more quickly and cheaply—in other words, how to rearchitect the technical environment. By no means is this problem limited to organizations that have been around for a good while. For example, I recently talked with the staff members of a dot.com company (still alive and kicking as of this writing). They were looking for a way to escape their "unlivable" *five-year-old* legacy hardware/software environment. Legacy time frames are continuously shrinking, so the business must find new ways to become ever more nimble about *migrating* business logic from one environment to another.

Recapture

There are actually several related "Re's" in this category—*reverse engineering*, *retention*, and *redocumentation*. This type of project is really motivated by fear (or risk avoidance, to put a more positive spin on it). The issue is how to avoid losing your business rules. Many business rules, for example, are buried deep in undocumented legacy systems. Here, the focus is on reverse engineering of the program code to get at the business rules—that is, on *rule mining*.

Other projects focus more on knowledge retention: identifying those workers who know the business practices, sitting them down in a room together, and extracting the rules on a facilitated basis. The objective is to record this knowledge before the workers are lost to retirement—or to the competition. I will have more to say on this point later (see Chapter 3).

Whichever way you choose to recapture the rules (whether by rule mining or by undertaking facilitated retention sessions), the objective is to *redocument your rules.*

Reempowerment

This is perhaps the most exciting area of business rule activity. Initially, this category focused on customer relationship management (CRM). (This focus is currently expanding—I'll say more about this later in this chapter.) Companies are using the business rule approach to handle highly individualized customer relationships on a huge scale.

For that, you must do three things.

1. You must record and manage the rules of engagement. (Many companies are so out of touch with their customers you could probably call this an attempt at *re*engagement.)
2. You must "operationalize" new or modified rules of engagement quickly—weeks or months of delay in programming is unacceptable.
3. You must manage the rules of engagement on the business side, not the IT side. In other words, you must *reempower* business users to manage the rules directly.

This area is clearly target-rich for business rules. As an idea of great potential for your business, it is worth examining more closely.

Let's Make a Deal

A Killer App for Business Rules

Let's take a closer look at the *reempowerment* category of business rule activity mentioned above. This type of project often focuses on opportunities in the general area of CRM—in particular, on making deals. Deals (or, more precisely, contracts and agreements) are how the company formalizes the "rules of engagement" with each customer.

Just about every company these days, of course, wants more and more customers—and highly individualized relationships with each and every one of them. Making the situation even more challenging is the fact that products and services in today's economy are also increasingly complex and/or differentiated. So the question becomes, how can you manage highly individualized or even one-of-a-kind agreements for increasingly complex and differentiated products with increasingly large numbers of customers? And, by the way, how can you do it economically, flexibly, and quickly?

One thing is for sure: you can't do it successfully the way it has been done in the past. The traditional approach might be summarized as follows. A manager, marketing representative, and/or lawyer comes to some agreement with a customer. Such agreement might be about the acquisition of a product or service as a whole (including options, timing, pricing, delivery, and so on) or about some specific aspect thereof (for example, discounts). Once formalized (for example, in a contract or letter of understanding), the agreement is then handed over to the programming staff (or, if simpler, to the operational staff) to implement and operationalize. Depending on the complexity and availability of resources, this might take weeks or months—a virtual lifetime at this crucial juncture in building the customer relationship.

There are at least three things fundamentally wrong with this approach.

1. *It is far too slow.* These days, operationalizing an agreement needs to take place in hours or days, not weeks or months.
2. *It cannot be effectively managed.* Even if the programming and/or implementation is done correctly (a very big if), the resulting code is far removed—almost completely disconnected—from the original agreement. Any resemblance in form is vague at best. Subsequent changes in the rules (inevitable these days) become slow, painful, and expensive affairs.
3. *The approach is deeply flawed from an organizational viewpoint.* Those workers in actual contact with the customers are displaced from those workers who have the skills to adjust the implemented rules of engagement. This leads to gaps, inefficiency, and frustration all around.

The business rule approach offers a potent two-part solution. First, deals are viewed as nothing more than collections of high-level business rules. (We call these *governing rules*.) The business rule approach has already evolved effective techniques to interpret and manage such rules.

Second, the programming of deals clearly must be *eliminated*. Business logic technology[1] addresses that problem by allowing the rules of engagement to be implemented much more directly.

This approach produces a huge additional advantage—much of the business rule activity can now go outboard. By this I mean it can be removed from the IT department and distributed to those directly in contact with the customers. This will empower those users to manage the rules of engagement directly. Now the deal making (and deal remaking) is done directly, through what I call *eDeals*. I believe enabling these power users for eDeals will prove a killer app for business rules—and, more importantly, for the business!

Reempowerment for the Company's Provisioning Processes

There's a Lot More to Reference Data Than Just Data!

A high-level manager at a large, well-established high-tech company recently summarized his company's operational problems in two succinct statements:

"We can't always deliver the products we announce correctly."

"We don't always know exactly who our customers are."

These problems posed serious risks to the company's ability to remain competitive.

A quick look at the company's fulfillment process revealed two obvious signs of trouble. First, the rate of complaints from the company's best customers was significant. Second, at several points in the process growing pools of workers had formed, focusing almost exclusively on problem resolution.

The manager's first impulse was to consider reengineering the fulfillment process itself. That course of action was a daunting one, however, because of the size, complexity, and distribution of the operation. It also promised only incremental improvements at relatively high cost.

Probing deeper, it became apparent that the real source of problems did not lie within the fulfillment process at all. The fulfillment process was highly

---

1. By *business logic technology*, I mean *rule engines*, *decision management platforms*, *business logic servers*, and so on. Since this discussion is nontechnical, I will not use any of these more technical terms in this part of the book.

dependent on other aspects of business operations, and these other aspects were simply not well organized.

In IT terms, applications supporting the fulfillment process were dependent on data feeds from other operational systems. IT therefore viewed the issue as a data quality problem and proposed a technical solution. From the business perspective, however, the real problem did not lie with the data but rather with the business processes that produced the data.

There were basically two such processes. First was the company's product release process. This process, which for more complex products typically stretched over many months, involved establishing valid product configurations based on a significant number of technical, packaging, and marketing guidelines (business rules). It also orchestrated the timing of releases across the large number of worldwide geographical areas of company operations. Each geographical area, of course, had its own local rules for releases, based on law, market factors, and customs. Also important was coordinating the ongoing review and approval process, which involves many levels of staff in different parts of the organization. The product release process had evolved in an ad hoc manner over many years' time and was highly fragmented. This produced flawed product and release data before even reaching the fulfillment process.

The second business process supporting the fulfillment process was the company's customer process—or, rather, the *lack* of one. The company had never evolved a global view of the customer base (at least at the operational level), and consequently the company had no focal point for managing the complexities of customer data (for example, subsidiary versus parent company, account versus customer, and so on). Rules about customer identification and data could not be effectively enforced at the source (that is, at the point of origin). Although the company's data warehouse did support a consolidated version of customer information, this data was aimed for *business intelligence* (that is, customer profiles, trending, competitive strategy, and so on) rather than for operational needs.

As a result of this analysis, the company began to focus more and more on the two upstream business processes: the product release process and the customer process. Its motto became the following.

 "Do it once, right at the source."

Doing it right at the source is another basic principle of the business rule approach. As the above case study illustrates, it means reexamining the business processes that provide essential business inputs (for example, product release information and customer information) for day-to-day operational processes. My name for these upstream support business processes is *provisioning processes.*

Provisioning processes present a high-yield opportunity to apply business logic technology. They are inevitably rule-intensive but are not themselves highly dependent on *incoming* data feeds. Also, they inevitably offer substantial opportunities for direct specification of rules by business-side workers.

From an IT perspective, provisioning processes produce what has traditionally been called *reference data*—data that historically often appears as codes and/or in look-up tables. Typical kinds of reference data, as suggested by the case study above, include *product configurations, product families, customers, geographical areas,* and so on. This is obviously just the tip of the iceberg. A more complete list is presented in Table 2–1. For each there is an associated provisioning process and a likely candidate for a business rule project.

The term *reference data,* unfortunately, does not do justice either to the problem or to the core issue of provisioning processes. From a business perspective, provisioning processes are critical to the effectiveness of operational activities. For example, in the case study above, at stake was no less

Table 2–1   Examples of Provisioning Processes

A provisioning process and the associated business rules might focus on . . .

- *Customers:* including segmentation
- *Companies:* suppliers, outlets, channels, and so on
- *Part types:* including substitution options
- *Product configurations:* often in the form of technical templates
- *Product types:* including option selections
- *Facilities:* including capacity and usage restrictions
- *Agreements:* any kind of service contract
- *Charts of accounts:* including currency conversions
- *Organizational charts:* including titles, ranks, and so on
- *Personnel base:* not limited to employees
- *Skill sets:* including certification requirements
- *Calendar:* including categorizations of time periods
- *Jurisdictions:* geographies, political units, and so on
- *Connections:* routes, links, networks, and so on
- *Diagnostic sets:* including sets of inspection criteria

than correct product configuration. This capacity, by the way, encompasses support for fast product *re*configuration—increasingly a must in today's competitive business environment.

From a business rule perspective, the core issue lies in standard business *vocabulary*—the terms the business uses to communicate (and potentially to automate) fundamental aspects of its knowledge.[2] It turns out there is a whole lot more to "reference data" than just data!

Business Rules as Customer Interface

New Ways to Link Up

The business rule approach is profoundly changing the way we think about supporting business-to-business and business-to-customer interfaces. The concept of *eDeals* (any kind of agreement automated as business rules) mentioned earlier is just one way in which this is happening. Here are several more.

- *Supporting the supply chain:* A parts supplier must package its goods for the convenience of the finished-goods manufacturers who use them. Convenience is naturally different for each manufacturer. How does each customer define convenience? Business rules!

- *Integrating support services:* An international package delivery service seeks to integrate its services seamlessly within the automated workstation environments of its customers worldwide. Imagine all the differences across (a) national and subnational boundaries, (b) hardware/software platforms, and (c) customized user interfaces. What approach is the delivery service using to establish a standard baseline? Business rules!

- *Setting customer expectations:* Local walk-in betting offices in a certain European country are required by law to make available to customers all the rules governing the placing of bets. These rules must cover every possible contingency. For example, what happens if your bet on a horse race includes some horse to show (come in third), but only two horses finish the race? (I am not really sure, but you probably end up losing your money somehow.) Basically, the betting rules let the customer know what treatment he or she can expect. By making transactions more transparent, you build trust. In general, how do you make business transactions transparent? Business rules!

---

2. Refer to Chapter 14 for more on this topic.

What about Web-Based Commerce?

Harnessing the Dynamics of an Open Rule Marketplace

Over the past several years, companies have asked us to apply business rule techniques to the relatively new area of *Web content management*. (I use *content* here in the sense of what information Web pages hold.) These are typically larger organizations, with many sources of product and pricing content and many Web-based channels (eChannels) through which that information needs to be published. And, as you might guess, these organizations also have large numbers of business rules.

What have we found in these cases? You might think that the problems we diagnosed were all essentially new ones and therefore that all our solutions would be new ones as well. Not unreasonable, but *wrong*!

The first thing we discovered was a classic case of out-of-control bridges and interfaces (data feeds). I say *classic* because this problem has been recognized as a fundamental problem in business systems for at least a quarter century [Ross 1978]. The Web environment does put a new face on the problem, but underneath, it is the same as ever.

This problem can be addressed by introducing a *universal content repository* to keep the total number of bridges and interfaces to a manageable level. For more about this rather simple classic solution, refer to the boxed item, The "Old" Issue of Scalability.

Does the business rule approach also support the new challenges of organizing a highly dynamic environment for Web content management? The answer is a resounding *yes*. Our experience suggests not only that the business rule approach supports them quite well but also that there might not

The "Old" Issue of Scalability

Understanding the Problem

The basic problem with bridges and interfaces (data feeds) is relatively straightforward. Suppose you have a large number of different data sources and a significant number of applications that use them. Typically, these data sources and applications will have accrued one by one in largely unplanned fashion over a number of years. I say years because that is how long it *used* to take—in Web time, it can now take only months or even weeks.

In such an unplanned environment, each application typically has its own interface to each data source it uses. In the worst case, this means that if there are m number of data sources and n number of applications, you must manage $m \times n$ number of interfaces. As the following sample numbers suggest, this total can spiral out of control very quickly as the environment grows over time!

m	n	m $\times$ n
1	1	1
2	3	6
5	15	75
10	25	250
and so on	and so on	and so on

Each interface must be managed. As these sample numbers suggest, the overhead associated with simply managing the interfaces can escalate rapidly. So too can the opportunities for misinterpreting and misusing the source data. Making changes in data definition also becomes increasingly more difficult since such change must be propagated faithfully across the ever-growing number of interfaces. In a word, this approach simply does not *scale*.

Correcting the Problem

The problem of scalability is one reason why the business rule approach puts such an emphasis on integrating and sharing data. In the ideal case, this solution reduces the number of data sources to $m = 1$. Now, the growth factor is simply additive. Each time you add a new application, the number of interfaces is simply $n + 1$, rather than $m \times n$.

Unfortunately, in the real world (yes, that does include the Web), things are usually not that simple, and m cannot be reduced to the minimum $m = 1$. A common solution is to provide an intermediate staging area—a database or repository into which the data from the m sources is imported and consolidated.

For m data sources, this approach means creating m import interfaces. An export interface is still also needed for each of the n applications. (Now these n export interfaces are from the staging area rather than from the original data sources.) Consequently, the total number of interfaces to be managed is $m + n$, instead of $m \times n$. Each new data source or application means simply $m + n + 1$ interfaces to manage. As the following sample numbers indicate, this becomes more and more significant as the number of data sources grows. In other words, this is an approach that *does* scale.

m	n	m $\times$ n	m + n
1	1	1	2
2	3	6	5
5	15	75	20
10	25	250	35
and so on	and so on	and so on	and so on

The Universal Content Repository

How does this discussion apply to the Web environment? Many companies are beginning to realize that they have a problem with *content* management. Often, there are a significant number of sources for this content (m) and an ever-expanding number of Web applications (n) that use it. In Web time, the $m \times n$ factor can spiral out of control almost before you know it.

The remedy, of course, is to create an intermediate staging area, which can be called a *universal content repository*. As before, this brings the $m \times n$ interface total back to the more manageable $m + n$ case. This is simply an old solution applied to a new problem, but as they say, sometimes the more things change, the more they stay the same!

even be any viable alternative. There are many ways in which this is true, but let me single out three especially important ones.

Developing the Vocabulary

The Web environment brings to the business many new concepts and, in many cases, strange new terms to go along with them (for example, *extranets, eMarketplaces, eMarketMakers, affinity sites, commerce engines,* and so on). The business rule approach places strong emphasis on defining terms and organizing concepts up front and on doing so in a *business-driven* manner. This emphasis on vocabulary and foundation business knowledge is just the thing to make sense of the muddle—and to help you do it before any coding starts.

Building for Change

In several of our recent projects, the focus was on building highly tailored eCatalogs that target individual eChannels. Often, these eCatalogs are specific to individual customers and/or promotion efforts. The number of possible variations in composition, pricing, frequency of distribution, and so on (not to mention all the exceptions and restrictions on them, legal and otherwise) is staggering. Furthermore, these variations must be adjustable in close to real time to keep pace with ever-changing business factors.

In the Web-based commerce arena, any architecture that cannot support such real-time adaptability is a nonstarter. What is the optimal approach for making an ever-changing array of selection options accessible and relatively easy to change? This is precisely the area where business rules and business logic technology excel.

Harnessing Marketplace Forces

Although a rule-based approach is essential for dynamic content management, it is not in and of itself sufficient. With so many rules and such rapid change in them, it is almost inconceivable that they can be defined effectively by a central group, no matter how highly qualified that group might be.

Having a central group manage all the rules mimics the top-down control practices of command economies (for example, communism). That approach is inherently flawed at real-world levels of complexity. In macroeconomics, the solution is open marketplaces in which thousands (or hundreds of thousands) of individual consumer choices constantly fine-tune the balance between supply and demand.

A corresponding approach must be adopted for the rules governing use of the universal content repository, covering all the choices to be made about content selection, organization, and delivery frequency for the eCatalogs. These rules must be pushed out to all the individual consumers of the content, that is, to all the individual business users responsible for the particular eChannels.

The term we use for business-side, rule-based specification of any kind of service agreement is *eDeal*. The particular manifestation of eDeals appropriate for Web content management is *eSubscription*. Each eSubscription establishes the parameters of a finely tuned pipeline (that is, eCatalog) of content for a particular highly focused Web commerce channel. The eSubscription is set up by the business staff closest to that particular business activity—the people in the best position to determine the optimal tactics and tradeoffs for each particular case.

What about the central group responsible for managing the universal content repository under this approach? To facilitate specifying eSubscriptions, this group would probably define generalized rule templates that reduce much of the business user activity to point-and-click selection of appropriate parameters.

The most important thing to remember about the central group, however, is that it acts as neither creator (supplier) nor consumer of content. Instead, it supports the inner workings of the content marketplace. Working in much the same manner as the support staff for stock or commodity exchanges, the central group's basic role is as enabler of intrabusiness content exchange and as enforcer for the basic corporate rules of fair trade.

Reference

Ross, Ronald G. 1978. *Data Base Systems: Design, Implementation and Management.* New York: AMACOM.

CHAPTER 3

Serving Up Knowledge

The Need to Know

What Is Knowledge Management?

And What Does It Have to Do with Business Rules?

I am frequently asked whether the business rule approach bears any relationship to knowledge management. Although many in the field have failed to make the connection yet, the answer is *yes*. The following set of questions and answers reveals how the business rule approach and knowledge management are linked.

What is knowledge management about?
According to experts in the field, the central concerns are generally as follows:

- Organizing the process of capturing and leveraging enterprise knowledge in order to further business strategy
- Organizing knowledge to get the right answers the first time, *every* time
- Changing corporate culture to encourage the sharing of knowledge, by allocating power to those who share rather than to those who hoard
- Making sure that the company does not lose vital knowledge

- Enabling less experienced staff to answer questions as correctly as the most knowledgeable people in the enterprise
- Enabling people outside the company to answer questions on their own
- Answering every question well, even if the person who is asking cannot ask the question exactly right

Where have the early successes been?
The focus of attention has been on call centers and help desks, for the most part.

Where do new applications with the highest potential lie?
Self-service and Web applications offer a rich set of opportunities.

What new challenges do these applications present for designers?
The challenges for designers lie in building structured dialogs in environments where human intervention (which is expensive!) needs to be kept to a minimum and where *everything* is subject to rapid change. In short, such dialogs must be *smart*.

A *smart dialog* is characterized as follows.

1. The right question is asked at the right time.
2. Suggestions and heuristics appear automatically at the optimal points.
3. Nonviable options, alternatives, and/or conclusions are eliminated as soon as possible.
4. Opportunistic questions (for example, for cross-selling) are inserted dynamically.

How does knowledge management connect to business rules?
There are two major targets for applied knowledge management.

1. Workers *inside* the company. For these, you want to codify the knowledge of the company's best people and make it available to workers at lower levels of skill or experience. (*Lower* here generally also means lower *cost*.)
2. Customers and others *outside* the company. For these, you want to codify what middlemen know and to reduce or eliminate their involvement. This is sometimes called *disintermediation*.

In either case, you must codify the knowledge—and that means business rules.

Can business logic technology play a role in knowledge management?
There is huge opportunity for this kind of connection. The last three of the four characteristics of smart dialogs (above) could be easily rule-based. Is there any better technology to accommodate rapid change? *No!*

What is knowledge?
That is a question best left for others to answer. I do know this much, however: Business rules represent that part of enterprise knowledge you can *codify*.

How can the company prevent loss of knowledge?
As above, the answer is to codify the business rules so the knowledge is no longer *tacit*. By the way, a good layperson's definition of *tacit* knowledge is this: If you lose the person, you lose the knowledge. As discussed in the boxed item, Knowledge Walking Out the Door, this represents a far greater risk than many companies realize.

Knowledge Walking Out the Door

Many companies today seem unaware of one of the biggest risks they face—their own internal brain drain. A significant portion of the company's operational self-knowledge has disappeared already—*downsized, outsourced, reengineered,* or *early-retired* away. How many people still with the company have any real idea about how critical areas of the business actually work? Who can tell you the *real* criteria for making operational-level, day-to-day business decisions?

The answer, I often find, is only one or two key people for any given business area. Sometimes they are on the IT side, sometimes on the business side. The company's exposure in this regard can be quite significant.

If your company finds itself in that situation, what should you do? The solution is an initiative to harvest and manage the business rules of the at-risk area. This is sometimes called *knowledge retention*. Otherwise, all you might have left is the program source code—and you really do not want to have to go there to access your business rules!

Personalized, Never-Ending, On-the-Job Training

Knowledge Companions for 21st-Century Line Workers

Everyone is concerned these days about the accelerating rate of change and the urgent need to build business systems that prove more adaptable. A flip side to the issue of change, however, has received very little attention. That flip side has to do with *training*.

Remember the old story about telephone operators? Use of the telephone has grown at such a rate that if automatic switching had not been invented, it is said that by now everyone in the world would be a telephone operator. Growth in the rate of change in *business* today is just as fast. Workers are being thrown into new responsibilities and procedures at an ever-increasing rate. That means they must be trained by other workers. If this keeps up, sooner or later everyone in the world will have to become a trainer.

Clearly, that cannot happen. The only solution is to make training *automatic*—that is, built right into the business systems that support the workers' day-to-day responsibilities and procedures. Business rules can make that happen. Briefly, here is how that can be done.[1]

---

1. For more discussion, refer to Chapter 7.

The business rule approach features declarative expression of each rule. Consider the following rule: *A rush order must not include more than five items.* Suppose a worker violates this particular rule while performing some procedure. What error message should pop up on the screen?

Certainly not, as all too often happens today, some obscure system code or some message in computerese. Instead, the initial message should simply be the business rule statement itself. In the business rule approach, we like to say that the business rules *are* the error messages.

Another way to look at this is that the rule statement represents a *requirement* that is pure business logic. In the business rule approach, this kind of requirement is incorporated directly when building the system, then gets output directly to inform the worker when a violation in his or her work is detected. Think of that as a communication from a worker who knows the business logic to a worker who must follow that business logic—*without these workers ever communicating directly or possibly ever even coexisting in time or space.*

A *friendly* business rule system would go a step further. When an error is detected, the business rule system not only materializes the original business logic for the worker but can also offer a canned procedure so he or she can correct the violation immediately. (This assumes, of course, that the worker is both authorized and capable in that regard.)

For the business, this capacity means achieving *real-time compliance*, eliminating costly downstream detection and corrective action. It means that mistakes can be addressed immediately so they are not compounded as other actions are subsequently taken.

For the worker, it means being constantly (re-)exposed to the business logic on a highly selective, real-time basis. Remember, the business rule could have been changed just recently, maybe even in the last few seconds.

For these reasons, I view business rule systems as instructional knowledge companions that provide personalized, never-ending, on-the-job training for harried 21st-century line workers.

CHAPTER 4

What about IT Projects?

Where the Rubber Meets the Road

If We Had Already Started Coding . . .

Meeting Those Project Deadlines

Recently, we were talking to the chief developer at a large client organization about progress on a major reengineering effort there. The project in question targeted one of the organization's core business processes. Our concern was whether the project team members could meet a deadline some nine months out for delivering a large-scale prototype. We had just spent several intensive months developing a comprehensive business model, and they still had several months of system design left to complete.

This chief developer is very sharp—not one to commit to any answer lightly. For the longest while, he said nothing, lost in thought. Finally, eyeing the detailed business diagrams plastered on the walls all around, he said, "If we had already started coding, I would say we had no chance at all. But since we haven't started coding yet, I'd say the chances are pretty good."

I had to run that by several times in my mind before I caught his meaning. "If we had already started coding, *I would say we had no chance at all.*"

I knew he thought that the application coding itself was going to be pretty tough. It would involve using business logic technology, a worldwide distribution network, graphical user interfaces (GUIs), and some significant middleware.

He was saying that if they had to resolve all the business issues while coding, they would never pull it off in time—or probably ever. However, since the project team was tackling the tough business issues up front (including specifying the business rules), he thought they had a pretty good chance of completing the code by the target date.

In large measure, the business rule approach is simply about asking the right questions at the right times. It is about being business-driven in the project approach. How important is that? Ask lead developers who *really* know their stuff (and who are willing to give you a straight story). There is only one way to honestly meet a deadline—and that is to solve the business problem *first*.

Two Things Wrong with Traditional Business Systems Development

Yes, There Is a Better Way!

Is your company as successful as it would like to be in developing business systems? Probably not. Have you identified the reasons? Here are the two most common factors we see and what you can do about them.

Never-Ending IT Projects

Problem Statement: Why do so many projects miss their deadlines? Delivery dates are adjusted time and time again. Primary requirements are forever changing midstream, causing endless rework (sometimes called "maintenance"). Some projects seem to lurch from one gridlock to the next; others run headlong into belated showstoppers. "Always time to fix it, but never time to plan it" seems to be the norm. A distressing number of projects never deliver anything at all.

> *Is this really simply a fact of computer-age life, or does it perhaps suggest that primary requirements are not being gathered completely and accurately before development starts?*

Solution: The answer is relatively straightforward. First, you must develop a true business model. (I will say more about what *true* means in a moment.)

Then, you must faithfully follow a series of continuing checks and balances against that business model when developing your follow-on requirements.

IT-Driven Business

Problem Statement, Part 1: The capabilities of IT have advanced explosively in the past decade or two. Businesses continue to devote significant resources to take advantage of these new capabilities. And there is no end in sight.

> *How does the business decide which kinds of automation are really beneficial—and which are not? How can the business be sure it will use new technology for the maximum business benefit?*

Problem Statement, Part 2: In the early days of building business systems, the business side could essentially sit back and just let them happen. The advantages of automating were so compelling that you could do virtually no wrong. Now, for all practical purposes business and IT operate inseparably. When undertaking projects, the logical step then would be to put together seamless business/IT project teams and have them follow a business-oriented approach to developing requirements. Yet many companies are nowhere close to doing that today.

> *What will it take to ensure that projects focus on achieving maximum business benefit? Can a win-win solution be found such that project participation is also individually rewarding?*

Problem Statement, Part 3: Companies often do very little to induce, structure, or reward creative business thinking in their IT projects. Neither the business side nor the IT side is really challenged to close the gap. All too often, the business side still produces fuzzy, ill-focused "requirements," and the IT side continues doing "requirements" only a notch or two above programming.

> *How can this gap between business professionals and IT professionals in developing requirements be eliminated? How can the company bring meaningful structure to the process?*

Solution: Again, the answer is relatively straightforward. The business needs an organized approach that enables business professionals to drive the development of requirements. This approach must provide a roadmap that shows how to ask the right kinds of questions about the right things at the right times. It needs a business-driven approach.

What *Business-Driven* Really Means

Getting to the Right Mind-Set

Let's start with a given. Businesses do not exist to manage hardware/software environments; rather, hardware/software environments exist to support the business. This truth should be self-evident, but in the midst of such a fast-paced technological revolution, sometimes we lose sight of it. As a result, we often find the tail seeming to wag the dog.

Clear-headed people on both the business side and the IT side know it should not be that way. The IT projects the company decides to undertake should always be, in fact, *"of the business, for the business, and by the business."* Saying it is one thing; figuring out how to accomplish it, of course, is another.

Fortunately, the business rule approach offers the well-organized roadmap you need to put the business back in the driver's seat. Later in this chapter, I will outline the particular ways in which business rule methodology structures the requirements development process to accomplish this. First, however, we should carefully examine the relevant mind-set issues, listed below. These are equally important.

1. There should be only one kind of project. In days past, IT had its projects, and the business had its projects. These were seldom if ever woven together. Clearly this approach is outmoded in the 21st century. These days, virtually every business project involves some automation—and most IT projects have direct impacts on the business. We must therefore come to a *single* kind of project with a *unified* approach for the project team to follow.

2. The business side has the knowledge to solve business problems. Clearly IT can help develop solutions, but in large measure, IT's role should be focused on designing and implementing solutions.

3. The first two issues imply this third one. What the system shows the business side once implemented should look much like the requirements that the business side articulated during development. I do not mean that in a figurative sense—I mean it in a literal sense. Business knowledge *in*, and business knowledge *out*. As I suggested earlier, *the business rules should become the error messages.*

4. Achieving this requires that the business questions be asked first, before addressing the system and implementation issues. Although this seems like an obvious point, it often does not happen that way in practice.

5. Capturing business knowledge up front requires new participatory roles for the people on the business side. It requires deeper, more focused involvement on their part. It also requires commitment of the most valuable commodity of all—their time.

6. In return (this is important!), the people on the business side have the right to expect the most conservative use of their time possible and ready-made structures (thinking tools) to help them organize their business knowledge in optimal ways.

7. This requires a structured approach where the emphasis is on asking exactly the right questions at exactly the right times. In addition, the approach must lay out exactly the right form (type of deliverable) each kind of answer should take.

8. Finally, business questions are quite often highly complex in their own right. As with any complex problem, this means the questions and answers need to be carefully factored, that is, not jumbled together as rambling statements but specifically addressed to one particular aspect of the problem at a time.

More on What *Business-Driven* Really Means

The Business Model

When the rate of change increases to the point that the time required to assimilate change exceeds the time in which the change must be manifest, the enterprise is going to find itself in deep yogurt.

—John A. Zachman [1994]

Our solution[1] to the mind-set issues described above has been greatly influenced by the work of John Zachman and his Architecture Framework.[2] If you

---

1. *Our solution* refers to the techniques of Business Rule Solutions (BRS), LLC, in Proteus, the BRS business rule methodology.

2. For more information on John Zachman's thinking, refer to Zachman [2002] and collected articles by Zachman found in the *Business Rules Journal*, available at *http://www.BRCommunity.com*.

are familiar with that body of work, I can easily position our approach by saying it addresses rows 1 and 2 of the Framework in the exact six-abstraction (column) manner he prescribes. (Our deliverables, however, are aimed primarily at the business-process level, rather than the enterprise level.)

If you are not familiar with Zachman's work, what I just said probably sounds like Greek. Fortunately, knowledge about the Zachman Framework is not a prerequisite for using the business rule approach. I can explain our solution to the mind-set issues this way. The focus is on developing a *business model* for the scope of the project, with direct participation of the business process owners, operational-level managers, and subject matter experts.[3]

Since these people constitute the audience for the business model, the approach and techniques must be specifically tailored to their perspective. This means banishing system and technical issues. Think of a business model as a business blueprint that can be read both by business people and by software design architects.

A business model must also be carefully factored to ensure that the inherent complexity of creating business solutions can be managed. What are these factors, and how does the business rule methodology address them? Again, we follow Zachman's lead on this. He indicates that there are six basic factors (abstraction) to consider. We address each head-on as follows.

- **Motivation—the "why" factor:** We address this factor first by creating a battle plan for the intended business solution. We call this deliverable a *Policy Charter*. It outlines the appropriate ends (for example, business goals) and means (for example, tactics) for solving the business problem. This includes core business rules—make-or-break policies needed to conduct business operations in their new form successfully. I will discuss this distinctive deliverable in more detail momentarily.
- **Function—the "how" factor:** We address this factor by developing business process models[4] that sequence the flow of tasks. The result is a beginning-to-end view of the transformations necessary to achieve operational business results.

---

3. See the section Why Business Rule Methodology Is Different in Chapter 13.
4. Since process and workflow models are common in techniques for business process reengineering and business-oriented requirements development, I will not discuss them at length in this book.

- **Structure—the "what" factor:** We address this "data" factor[5] by developing the standard business vocabulary of the targeted business area. These definitions are organized into a Concepts Catalog, which is essentially a glossary of terms. The Concepts Catalog is actually just one part of the larger problem—what shared operational business knowledge will be needed to run the to-be business. That knowledge is organized into what we call a *fact model*. This important type of deliverable is discussed in more detail in Chapters 5 and 14.
- **People—the "who" factor:** We address this factor by defining organizational roles and responsibilities, and the work relationships between them. Associated work products are also identified.
- **Time—the "when" factor:** We address this factor by examining the regimens needed to organize the aging of core concepts. These regimens consist of stages or states we call *business milestones.*
- **Location—the "where" factor:** We address this factor by building a Business Connectivity Map indicating business sites and their communication/transport links from the business perspective.

In addressing each of the individual factors of the business blueprint, we consciously and deliberately seek out the relevant elements of business logic—that is, the business rules—and record them. This is another area, rule management,[6] in which our approach is business-driven.

Although the business blueprint is business-oriented, it must nonetheless provide a comprehensive and complete set of requirements that system architects can subsequently use to design the actual system. The business model can be transformed directly into a first-cut system model. For system designers this means that most, if not all, of the relevant business questions have already been answered.

Developing a good system design is often quite difficult in and of itself. The business model is crucial input, giving the system designers an important head start on their work.

---

5. In a system model, *structure* could be taken to mean *data* structure, but in a business model, we think a better description is *basic knowledge* structure.
6. For more discussion of this important area, refer to the section What Rule Management Is About in Chapter 13.

The business model is also your best guarantee that the system designers (and then the implementers after that) will be far less likely to discover show-stoppers on the business side way downstream in the development process. The later that holes in the business solution are discovered, of course, the more expensive and frustrating on all sides it becomes to correct them. Avoiding such late-developing showstoppers on the business side is really the bottom line in what it means to be *business-driven.*

The Policy Charter

A Small-Sized Big Picture

Cost overruns are manageable if the project will achieve worthwhile benefits; however, failing to satisfy business goals is always unacceptable.

　　　　　　　　—Gladys S. W. Lam [1997], Principal, Business Rule Solutions, LLC

Recently, a business project sponsor confided to us her frustration with the project team she had put together to kick off a project. Basically, her complaint boiled down to this: Despite many months of hard work, she felt like she was still missing the big picture. And if *she* was still missing it, she was pretty sure the team members were still missing it too.

The irony was that the team members *had* produced a "big" picture—a very big picture indeed! They had produced documentation covering features, workflows, data models, technical architectures, migration issues, support requirements, problem areas, "open" issues, and still more—hundreds and hundreds of pages of it. In all those pages, however, there was no answer to what the sponsor really wanted to know—the *why* of it all.

As we discussed this more, it became clear that the sponsor wanted a focused statement of what the new capabilities would mean to the business. Specifically, she wanted to know what business tactics (courses of action) and policies (core business rules) would be supported and why these would be best for meeting the business goals. In other words, the business sponsor wanted to see the underlying *motivation* laid out—not for the new system per se but for a new way of doing business.

She did not mean a business case. They had done a high-level cost/benefit analysis previously and had long since satisfied themselves on that score. The business sponsor wanted proof that the business implications had been examined and resolved before they went into actual design and development. That meant answering two fundamental business questions: one working *down* from the business goals, and the other working *up* toward those business goals.[7]

- *Working down from the business goals:* What are the most effective business tactics and policies[8] for achieving the business goals, and how would the associated risks and conflicts be resolved?
- *Working up toward the goals:* What is the business motivation for each tactic and policy, and given the business goals, why is each tactic or policy the most appropriate?

As you might already see, these are merely two sides of the same coin. They require what we call a *Policy Charter*, a key element of the business rule approach.[9] In our experience, a Policy Charter does not need to be all that large—just a small-sized big picture.

The True Business Analyst

The Go-To Guy for 21st-Century Business Systems

The key role in solution development for the 21st-century business is that of *business analyst*. Does your company have business analysts? Can you define the role they need to play? What they need to know? What they need to be able to do?[10]

A good starting definition for the role of business analyst is "business problem solver." (Read on to find out why that is not sufficient, however.) To perform the role of business problem solver, a business analyst must be a generalist. He or she must be able to grapple with a problem in any of a number

---

7. I do not mean project goals or project objectives, so to avoid confusion I will continue to say *business goal* rather than simply *goal*.

8. I mean *core business rules* here, but management tends to think in terms of setting policies (hence the name *Policy* Charter). Either term is acceptable in this context.

9. See also the section Why Business Rule Methodology Is Different in Chapter 13. For additional information, refer to Lam [1998]. For an enterprise-level approach, refer to the landmark work by the Business Rules Group [2000].

10. For an excellent look at the practical side of being an effective business analyst, refer to Seer [2002].

of dimensions, whether involving tactics and policies, infrastructure, organization, information systems—or, more likely, some mix of all the above.

To be a business problem solver, a business analyst also must be in touch with the reality of the "as is" business. Think of a business analyst as the person most likely to be able to tell you (or find out for you) how some aspect of the business *really* works—and what is wrong with it. To put that a little more strongly, if the business analyst *cannot* tell you (or find out for you), then he or she is simply not doing the job.

That is just for starters. Business analysts must also be able to visualize and develop "to be" solutions. To do that, they need the skills of a system analyst or of a business process engineer.

So which is it: system analyst or business process engineer? The correct answer is both—and neither. By *both,* I mean that a business analyst should feel comfortable with both the IT side and the business side of developing systems. Indeed, if a business analyst is *really* good, he or she might not even clearly understand the difference. After all, in the information age, what *is* the difference?

Here's what I mean by *neither.* On the one hand, a business analyst is definitely *not* a traditional IT system designer. More times than not, IT designers are really more interested in getting to the code than in rolling out a complete business solution or doing much planning.

Fortunately, many companies are beyond that point. Even so, they often still fall well short of having true business analysts (even if they use that term). For example, a business coordinator for system change requests is *not* a true business analyst. Yes, adding a field or two to a GUI in a legacy system is often no trivial matter. However, that rarely amounts to problem solving where competitive advantage or corporate survival is at stake. That is the kind of problem solving with which a *true* business analyst must contend.

On the other hand, I do not mean a high-level business process reengineering expert either. By *high-level,* I mean the type of business planner who is more comfortable with value chains and business strategies than with operational tactics and the nuts and bolts of business processes.

A true business analyst is someone who can help put together a full set of requirements, that is, a complete business model covering all aspects (factors) of the target area. The test for such a model is that you must be able to transform it (with a lot more work, of course) into a workable system design.

The assumption here, by the way, is that at least some of the design is likely to be automated.

This leads me back to the earlier point about why *business problem solver* fails to capture entirely what true business analysts are about. Certainly, they do fix business problems. Business analysts, however, must be equipped to develop solutions in terms of better infrastructure, not just in terms of direct fixes (even detailed ones) for the immediate problem at hand. *Better infrastructure* in turn implies longer, multifaceted projects. It also requires a structured approach to business analysis—that is, to the development of the comprehensive requirements necessary to create a workable "to be" world. That set of comprehensive requirements, of course, represents a business model.

The business rule approach provides the structured approach to business analysis needed in the 21st century. The business analyst then must be directly involved in capturing policies (core business rules), creating fact models, developing "to-be" workflows, and so on.

The other issue—how to support longer, multifaceted projects—requires a better understanding of basic project management tools (that is, time lines, budgets, resource allocation, and so on). This is the stuff good project managers bring to the table. Unfortunately, good project managers are also in short supply, but that is a different story for a different day.

References

Business Rules Group (Ronald G. Ross and Keri Anderson Healy, eds.). 2000. "Organizing Business Strategy: The Standard Model for Business Rule Motivation." Version 1, November 2000. Available at *http://www.BusinessRulesGroup.org.*

Lam, Gladys S. W. 1998. "Business Knowledge—Packaged in a Policy Charter." *DataToKnowledge Newsletter* (formerly *Data Base Newsletter*), May/June. Available at *http://www.BRCommunity.com.*

———. 1997. Originally from a lecture, quote reprinted with permission in *Data Base Newsletter* 25(2):5.

Seer, Kristen. 2002. "How to Develop Effective Business Analysts," Parts 1, 2, and 3. *Business Rules Journal,* May, July, and September (respectively). Available at *http://www.BRCommunity.com.*

Zachman, John A. 2002. *The Zachman Framework: A Primer for Enterprise Engineering and Manufacturing* (electronic book). Available at *http://www.zachmaninternational.com.*

———. 1994. Originally from a lecture, quote reprinted with permission in *Data Base Newsletter* 22(6):16.

Business Rule Concepts
The Mechanics of Business Systems[1]

Overview

Part II of this book explains the basic ideas of the business rule approach and explores the breakthrough innovations it offers. These culminate in Chapter 7, which presents revolutionary new ideas for organizing work in the 21st century.

To develop these ideas, I use an extensive analogy to the human body—in particular, the mechanical system of the human body. That analogy is presented in this Overview. As it will explain, the mechanical system has three fundamental components. Each of the three chapters in this part of the book examines one of these fundamental components as it relates to business systems.

The Marvelous Organism

The human body is marvelous in many respects, not the least of which is its mechanics. Roughly, support for the mechanics of the human body has three basic components, separate yet intimately interconnected, as follows.

> **Structure** is provided by the bones, which are organized and connected within the skeleton. The skeleton provides both a framework for carrying the weight of the other components as well as a semirigid scheme around which the other softer components can be organized.

---

1. Acknowledgment: I would like to thank Keri Anderson Healy, Editor of the *Business Rules Journal*, *http://www.BRCommunity.com*, for her editorial assistance and her many suggestions for clarifying and enhancing the original draft of this material.

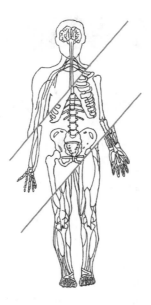

Mechanical Components
→ Structure: Skeleton
→ Power: Muscles
→ Control: Nerves

Power is provided through the muscles, which are connected to the bones. The muscles enable motion based on the framework provided by the skeleton. Since motion is what we see happening from outside the body, the muscles seem most directly responsible for the behavior we perceive.

Control is provided by the nervous system, which connects to the muscles. Nerves indirectly connect muscles to other muscles through long series of connections passing through the brain. Responses to all stimuli are coordinated through the firing of nerve impulses—no firing, no movement, and therefore no behavior.

These basic mechanical components are familiar to us all. In a moment, we will see how the mechanics of business systems can be viewed in the very same terms. As we examine the analogy, several observations about the mechanics of the human body are worth keeping in mind.

- All three components are *essential*. The human body literally cannot function without all three.
- The three components are all interconnected—that is, they are *integrated* with each other. For example, tendons connect muscle to bone. Successful behavior depends on this integration.

- Each of the three components is *specialized* for a particular role or responsibility. Each optimizes for its particular task. Mixing or combining the three components would provide a much less effective solution. Also, specialization provides for greater simplicity. Think about how much more complex bones would be if they incorporated muscles or how much more complex muscles would be if they incorporated nerves.
- The nervous system in some sense is the most important component because it provides control for the other two. The body is certainly capable of behavior without a well-organized nervous system—but not *effective, adaptive* behavior. Literally, you cannot operate at your best with only half a brain!

A New View of Business Systems

I believe that business systems should be organized in a manner similar to the mechanical system of the human body. Let's revisit the three components of that system, thinking now about the business (or some business capacity within it[2]) in place of the human body.

Structure

Structure is provided by organized—that is, *structured*—knowledge about the most basic things we can know about the business. These "basic things we can know" are often simply taken for granted—just like the human skeleton in everyday activity. They consist of core *concepts* of the business and the basic *logical connections* we make between them.

Think of these core concepts as bones and the logical connections as ligaments (that is, bone-to-bone connections).

- Just as each bone has a particular shape that is optimal for its purpose and location, so too must each core concept have a carefully crafted "shape." A concept's shape is given by its definition, which must be clear, concise, and well suited for its business purpose. Every bone or concept

---

2. By *business capacity* I mean some significant subset of the business, possibly encompassing one or more business processes and/or functional areas. To simplify matters, from this point forward in the discussion I will drop the additional *or some business capacity within it* whenever *business* appears and assume you understand I also mean any significant subset of the business.

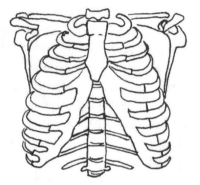

Mechanical Components
→ **Structure: Skeleton**
→ Power: Muscles
→ Control: Nerves

must also have a standard name. In the business rule approach, the standard names for concepts are called *terms*.

- Each ligament also has a particular shape that is optimal for its purpose and location. Similarly, each logical connection between concepts must have a standard "shape." In the business rule approach, these logical connections are called *facts*. Their standard shapes are given by *fact statements*, which reference the appropriate terms.

A drawing or diagram of the complete human skeleton helps us understand how all the bones fit together. To illustrate the overall structure of terms and facts, it is likewise helpful to create a drawing or diagram. Our name[3] for such a diagram is *fact model*.

A fact model provides a framework, in many ways like a skeleton, in two basic respects.

1. A fact model literally provides a standard scheme around which the other components can be organized—that is, the "basic things we can know" *in common* throughout the business.
2. A fact model carries the "weight" of the organization—that is, when eventually implemented as a database, it will carry the cumulative record of past interactions (the history).

---

3. *Our name* refers to the name that Business Rule Solutions (BRS), LLC, uses in Proteus, the BRS business rule methodology.

> **Mechanical Components**
>
> → Structure: Skeleton
> → Power: Muscles
> → Control: Nerves

Power

Power is provided by processes, which operate on the terms and facts. Whereas the fact model provides structure, the processes enable activity.

When we think about a business system, the processes are often the first things that come to mind. They represent the most visible aspect of the business system because they literally *do* what the business needs to get done (for example, take the customer's order). However, viewing a business system as merely a collection of processes makes no more sense than viewing the human body as merely a collection of muscles. Any organism is much more than that—whether human or business.

Control

Control is provided by rules, which constrain processes (the "muscles") to act only in certain ways deemed best for the business as a whole. In the human body, there are literally hundreds of muscles, which must act in concert. If they do not, the resulting behavior at best will be less than optimal. At worst, serious damage can result (for example, hyperextension of a limb) that will significantly reduce the body's overall capacity to act.

Similarly, business systems literally consist of hundreds (or thousands) of "muscles" (processes), which must act in concert. If they do not, the business

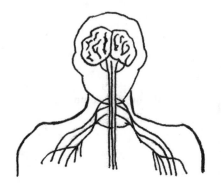

> **Mechanical Components**
> → Structure: Skeleton
> → Power: Muscles
> → Control: Nerves

will also behave in a less than optimal fashion. In some cases, serious damage can result (for example, loss of customers, squandering of resources or opportunities, and so on) that will significantly reduce the business's overall capacity to act (that is, its competitiveness and/or effectiveness).

In the human body, we take many control actions of the nervous systems for granted. For example, who thinks about the impulses sent to the heart to make it beat—unless, of course, something goes wrong? Or who in the process of saying, "Ouch!" thinks much about the jerk reflex that causes the hand to move so quickly off the hot stove? As long as all runs smoothly, we can apply our mental faculties to a higher purpose—whether for working, solving problems, or simply planning a fun lunchtime getaway.

Similarly, while things run smoothly in the business, we can take the control actions of the rules for granted and concentrate on matters requiring a higher order of intelligence. Until a rule "breaks" somehow—and that is a very important possibility, of course—we can focus on the more creative aspects of business operation and strategy.

A business is very much like a human body—a living organism. Let's revisit the observations I made earlier about the mechanics of the human body, now applying them to business systems.

- All three components—structure (terms and facts), processes, and rules—are *essential*. A business literally falls apart—disintegrates—without all three.
- The three components are obviously interrelated. For example, processes act to record information about the things represented in the fact model.

These actions, in turn, are subject to the rules. Successful business behavior depends on effective *integration*. These fundamental interrelationships must obviously be taken into account.

- Each of the three components is *specialized* for a particular role or responsibility and optimized for its particular task. Mixing or combining them would provide a less effective solution. The business rule approach therefore recognizes the importance of factoring out the rules. We[4] call this *Rule Independence.* As a fringe benefit comes a huge simplification in the processes (the "muscles" of the business system). In the business rule approach it is legitimate for the first time to talk of truly *thin* processes—a long-standing goal among many information technology (IT) professionals.

- In many ways rules are the most important component since they provide control for the other two. The business and its systems are certainly capable of behavior without a well-organized set of rules—but not *effective, adaptive* behavior. Literally, rules are what make a business more than half-smart in how it operates.

The second point above emphasizes that the three basic components of business systems must interrelate in an integrated fashion. Just how they do that represents the new vision of business systems at the heart of the business rule approach. Some of the implications of this new vision are profound.

In the human body, each of the three individual components of the mechanical system also has its own inner workings. In fact, there are individual sciences focusing almost exclusively on each particular component.

Each of the three basic components in the business rule approach must also be understood individually. Each too has its own particular "physiology." These individual "physiologies" are examined one at a time in the three chapters that follow in this part of the book.

- Chapter 5 examines structure, as embodied in the core concepts of the business and their logical connections. In particular, this chapter explains fact models and what they represent.

---

4. At certain points in the discussions that follow in this part, I mention elements of methodology or deliverables that pertain specifically to Business Rule Solutions, LLC. When I use *we* or *our* in these contexts, please note that I am referring to the Principals of Business Rule Solutions.

- Chapter 6 examines control, as embodied in rules. This chapter provides exciting new insights about the inner workings of rules.
- Chapter 7 examines power, as embodied in processes. The business rule approach offers a new view of processes, one that is radical in its simplicity. Ironically, it is in that very simplicity that the big picture of business systems emerges in the business rule approach.

> . . . cyberspace is a new form of community. Remember its motto—No Rules? But soon there were etiquette rules called Netiquette posted in every chat room. *You can't have a sense of community without rules* [emphasis added].
>
> —Judith Martin (Miss Manners)[5]

5. From "10 Questions for Judith Martin," *Time Magazine,* December 2, 2002, Vol. 160, No. 23, p. 18.

Organizing Basic Business Knowledge

*What You Need to Know
about Terms and Facts*

In the human body, structure is provided by the bones, which are organized and connected within the skeleton. The skeleton provides both a framework for carrying the weight of the other components as well as a semirigid scheme around which the other softer components can be organized.

A business system must have a corresponding structure. In the business rule approach, this structure is visualized by means of a fact model. Without any exaggeration, a good fact model is no less important to a business system than a strong and complete skeleton is to the human body.

A fact model appears to many IT professionals as more or less equivalent to a high-level data model[1] or class diagram.[2] It some ways it is, but in other, very important ways it is not. I want to highlight those differences for interested readers, so comparisons between fact models and data models appear at several points in this discussion as separate boxed items.

---

1. Sometimes also known as an *entity model* or *entity-relationship* diagram.
2. *Class diagram* is more or less the corresponding term in object orientation. I certainly understand that important distinctions can be made between a data model and a class diagram—and even that these distinctions themselves can be controversial. However, this discussion is informal. For the sake of simplicity, I will simply say *data model* from this point on and assume you understand I also mean class diagrams of a corresponding nature.

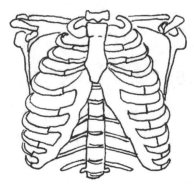

> **Mechanical Components**
> → Structure: Skeleton
> → Power: Muscles
> → Control: Nerves

To the Data Modeler: Data Models versus Fact Models

IT professionals might see a fact model as nothing more than simply a high-level data model. The distinction, however, is an important one. It revolves around the basic purpose—*who and what is the model for?*

Data Models

Many IT professionals use data models as the front-end basis for designing a database or as the data integration blueprint for building a data warehouse. No matter how the data model is developed, it ends up being used primarily as a system development tool. Once created, you are not likely to see business-side workers making continuous use of it thereafter.

Also, although many practitioners do recognize the importance of terminology in creating a good data model, data models in general tend not to be comprehensive about *business* vocabulary. Such parsimony probably arises for both organizational and technical reasons. This practice usually does not cause problems for data models since they are usually not used to support declarative specification of rules on a large scale. By *large scale*, I mean hundreds or thousands of rules.

Fact Models

In contrast with data models, to be successful, a fact model needs to become a central fixture of the operational business. The reason is simple: the fact model represents the basic vocabulary for expressing its rules. When these rules number in the hundreds or thousands, this vocabulary *must* be comprehensive.

This intense focus on business vocabulary in fact models often requires a special business-side support role for its ongoing coordination.[3] Such business-side specialists sometimes already exist in companies today, but rarely if ever do they work with data models.

Although a fact model should serve as an initial blueprint for data design, that use is not its primary purpose. Rather, the purpose of a fact model is literally to *structure basic knowledge of the business.* Creating a successful fact model[4] means capturing that business knowledge from the business-side workers and managers who possess it. This ability is central to the business rule approach. As discussed in Part I, the skill of distilling that business knowledge is essential for business analysts.

Unfortunately, many business-side workers and managers have been intimidated in the past by data models. I want to emphasize that there is no need whatsoever to view a fact model as representing anything technical.[5] It is true that a good fact model can be hard to create. If you have the relevant business knowledge, however, it should never be hard to understand. If it is, somebody is doing something wrong!

Terms and Facts

In the human body, the skeleton has two basic components: the bones and the ligaments that connect the bones. Even though the bones are larger and in a sense more basic, both components are essential.

A fact model represents the basic "skeleton" for the knowledge structure of a business system. As in the skeleton for the human body, a fact model likewise has two basic components: terms and facts. These are equivalent to

---

3. Half-jokingly, we call this role the *terminator.* Refer to Chapter 14 for additional discussion.
4. For an in-depth discussion of how to create a fact model, refer to Ross and Lam [2000].
5. I mean *technical* here in the sense of IT, not in terms of the products or services of the business. These products or services might, of course, be highly technical in their own right.

the bones and ligaments, respectively, in the human body. These terms and facts structure basic business knowledge—that is, they identify things that it is possible to know about.[6]

 Terms and facts structure basic business knowledge.

About Terms

A *term* is a basic word or word phrase in English or another natural language[7] that workers recognize and share in the business. A term carries a particular meaning for the business, which should be unambiguous given a particular context of usage.[8] Terms are always nouns or qualified nouns. Here are some examples.

customer	employee name	date
prospect	delivery date due	high-risk customer
shipment	manager	employee
order	gender	line item
invoice	status	quantity back-ordered

Our meaning of *term* comes straight from *Webster's*.[9] Note the key words "precise meaning" in this definition.

Term: *A word or expression that has a precise meaning in some uses or is peculiar to a science, art, profession, or subject.*

—Merriam-Webster's Collegiate Dictionary, Tenth Edition

---

6. Workers, of course, can know many things about the basic operations of the business. Terms and facts establish which of all those basic things the workers will *share*.

7. For convenience, I will drop the phrase *or another natural language* in the discussion from this point on, with the implicit understanding that the discussion applies to any language, not just to English.

8. We take a fact model to represent a single context of usage. This context of usage represents the scope that the fact model covers (sometimes called a *domain of discourse*). From this point forward in the discussion, I will drop *context of usage* when discussing the meaning of terms, with the implicit understanding that this qualification is nonetheless a highly significant one.

9. Refer to Chapter 16 for the meaning of *term* in formal theory.

It is important to note that the particular word or phrase selected as a term represents merely the tip of the iceberg with respect to meaning. More fundamental is the business *concept* for which the word or phrase stands. This concept *must* be defined. That is, the concept a term represents should never be taken for granted. As one practitioner put it, "The more self-evident the meaning of a term is, the more trouble you can expect." As an example, another practitioner from a medium-sized company rattled off six different (and conflicting!) definitions of *customer* from different parts of his organization.

In the business rule approach, a precise definition for each term must be given explicitly in business-oriented (that is, nontechnical[10]) fashion. All facts (and rules) that reference the term will depend on this meaning. Here is an example of a definition.

> *Customer:* An organization or individual person that has placed at least one paid order during the previous two years.

To be included in a fact model, a term should satisfy all three of the following fundamental tests.

Basic: Terms in the fact model represent the most basic things of the business—that is, terms that cannot be derived or computed from any other terms. Any term that can be derived or computed should be expressed as the subject of a rule.

Atomic: Terms in the fact model should represent things that are indivisible—that is, not composite—at least as seen from the business's point of view. Terms that have a collective sense (for example, *merchandise, personnel, inventory,* and so on) should be broken down into their atomic constituents before being represented in the fact model.

Knowable: Terms in the fact model should always represent things we can know something about, rather than something that happens. In other words, a fact model is about *knowledge*, not about the actions, processes, or procedures that produce that knowledge. A fact model, for example, might show the terms *customer* and *order*, but it would not show the action *take customer order*.

---

10. Again, I mean *technical* here in the sense of IT, not in terms of the products or services of the business. The definition of some terms can be highly technical in a business sense.

In the business rule approach, the collection of all terms and definitions is called a *Concepts Catalog*.[11] In one sense, this label is merely a dressed-up name for a glossary. Because definitions are so crucial to organizing large sets of rules, however, this glossary needs to be automated. Such support permits changes in the terms to be coordinated directly with all the rules where they appear.

 Every term requires a definition, and every definition belongs in the Concepts Catalog.

Using the Concepts Catalog is the way to avoid a "Tower of Business Babel" when building complex business systems. Here then is a fundamental (and obvious) principle of the business rule approach: We will inevitably work more effectively if we all speak the same language!

 A fact model establishes common business vocabulary.

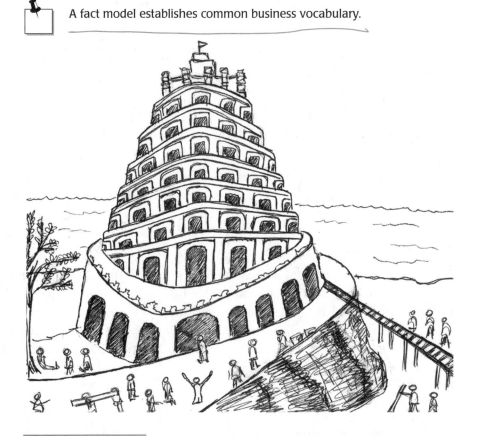

---

11. This is the term used in the current work (2002) of the Business Rules Group (*http://www.BusinessRulesGroup.com*). The Business Rules Group is using the term Concepts Model to refer to the combination of the Concepts Catalog and the associated fact model.

To the Data Modeler: Types versus Instances

The most basic terms in a fact model represent *types* of things rather than *instances* of those things. For example, a business might have 10,000 customers, but they are represented by the single term *customer*. Incidentally, since the term refers to the type rather than to instances, the term's singular form is preferred for the fact model (that is, *customer* rather than *customers*).

These prescriptions are generally the same as for data models. In data modeling, however, terms almost always represents types of things rather than instances of those things. This is not true for fact models.

Rules often reference things that data modelers would see at the instance level. As a simple example, the terms *male* and *female* might be handled in a data model using a *type code*—a special kind of attribute for distinguishing the type of instances (for example, M = male, F = female). Rules expressed at the business level, however, should reference *male* and *female*, not *M* and *F*. Therefore, *male* and *female* might be included in the fact model, whereas the tendency in data modeling probably would be not to include them.

Many such cases involve far more than just two instance-level terms. For example, an organization that inspects ships has thousands of rules that reference hundreds of individual parts of a ship. A health insurance company has thousands of rules that reference hundreds of individual health care treatments. Similarly, many organizations—perhaps even most—have thousands of rules that reference hundreds of individual instance-level terms related to their particular lines of business.

For that reason, standardization of terms at the instance level is often required in the business rule approach. Such standardization focuses on things whose instances can be predicted or prescribed in advance (for example, ship parts, health care treatments, and so on). Handling these more extensive cases requires extensions to fact models that we call *instance models*. As in the examples of ship parts and health care treatments, such instance models often (but not always) involve the product or service of the business. (Refer to Part IV for additional discussion.)

Standardizing instance-level terminology is even more of a business problem than is standardizing type-level terminology. This is something for which data modelers are often not prepared. Nonetheless, the business benefits are substantial—for starters, such standardization enables *knowledge transfer* and *knowledge automation*. These are hardly luxuries in a world where staffs are ever more volatile and where self-service is rapidly becoming the norm.

About Facts

Facts are given by simple, declarative sentences that relate appropriate terms, much as ligaments connect bones in the human skeleton. Here are some examples of fact statements.[12] Note that in each of these examples, a verb or verb phrase (italicized below) connects some of the terms listed earlier.

> Customer *places* order.
>
> Order *is included in* shipment.
>
> Employee *has a* gender.
>
> Manager *is a category of* employee.

Several observations are worth making.

1. Facts represent common or shared verbs and verb phrases of the business. In other words, a fact model extends the common business vocabulary in important ways.

    A fact model extends the common business vocabulary.

2. Every fact is always expressed using a complete sentence, generally following a strict subject-verb-object structure—for example, *Customer places order*.[13] This sentence provides a template, a structured way to talk about how the terms logically connect to each other.

    Facts structure the logical connections we want made between concepts.

3. The collection of all such sentences establishes the full and complete scope of the business system in a very important sense. Even if a worker

---

12. Since this discussion is informal, I will use the word *fact* instead of the more correct *fact statement* in the discussion that follows. The distinction is that the same fact can be given by statements in different forms and/or by statements in different languages (for example, French, Mandarin, and so on). In other words, there can be many different *fact statements* for exactly the same *fact*.

13. In formal terms, such sentences represent *predicates*. Every fact statement is a predicate. Refer to Chapter 17 for in-depth discussion. Incidentally, we do recognize unary facts.

or some automated process produces some other terms and facts, we will literally have no way to share such knowledge in a standard and consistent fashion unless the appropriate terms and facts have been included in the fact model.

 A fact model establishes basic business knowledge to be shared.

4. The sentences merely establish facts; they place no constraints on instances of these facts. For example, *Customer places order* represents a fact.[14] It is inappropriate to state the following as a fact per se: *Customer must not place more than 15 orders.* This latter statement is more than a fact—it places a *constraint* on instances of the fact. Thus this latter statement is a rule—part of the control aspect of the business system, *not* part of the structural aspect. A rule represents the nerves, not the skeleton!

 Facts recognize what it is possible to know, but given that, no other constraints.

5. Note how the facts are expressed using verbs (for example, *places*). It is important to remember that these verbs do not represent or label any action, process, or procedure per se (for example, *place order*). Any such operation represents a different aspect of the business system—the power or "muscle" aspect. Think of the fact model as providing the most appropriate way[15] to organize knowledge about the *results* of such operations. In other words, terms and facts organize what we can know as the result of actions, processes, and procedures taking place in the business.

 Fact models organize basic knowledge about the results of operations, not about how these operations actually take place.

---

14. It actually represents a fact *type*. Since this discussion is informal, however, I will avoid using the somewhat arcane term *fact type*.

15. To be precise, *the most appropriate way* means anomaly free and semantically clear. These are criteria that can actually be tested. In relational theory, normalization prescribes tests (the normal forms) for this purpose. Refer to Chapter 11 in Date [2000].

Using Graphic Fact Models

You might have noticed that even though fact models are usually rendered graphically, no diagrammatic examples have yet been presented. This is not because they are not useful. Just the opposite is true; they are *very* useful. Rather, I wanted to emphasize that a fact model is about what we can *know*. *"What we can know" can always be expressed in natural language sentences.*

A fact model also represents a kind of requirement for business system design. (For more on terms and facts as a kind of requirement, refer to the boxed item.) The sponsor(s) of a business rule project must sign off on the fact model.

We want to stress, however, that sponsors should sign off on the *sentences*—not on graphic fact models. By the way, many system development techniques that use data models have this guideline more or less *backwards!*

The principal deliverable of the fact-modeling part of a business rule project is a set of declarative sentences.

Terms and Facts as Requirements

Ask managers and workers in the business what they mean by *requirements* for developing business systems, and typically you get answers centered on functions to be performed or on the look and feel of how the system behaves through its interfaces (for example, GUIs). The answer "terms and facts" is almost never among the responses. Nonetheless, they are indeed a kind of requirement.

Terms and facts are a type of requirement.

Terms and facts are not the *only* kind of requirement in the business rule approach, of course. Without them, however, you cannot provide real meaning or coherency (sense) to all the others, especially to the rules. For that reason, terms and facts actually represent the most *fundamental* kind of requirement.

Terms and facts literally do just that—they provide *meaning*. This meaning, of course, is abstract. It might not be as obvious as what a system does or how the system looks on the outside. Just because something is less obvious, however, does not mean it is any less important. Break a bone, and see what happens to the body's behavior!

Terms and facts provide meaning and coherency to other kinds of requirements, especially rules.

Let's be very clear about this. A fact model can and should provide a first-cut blueprint for how data will be eventually organized in a database. This data design, however, is an end result—an objective toward which system developers must work. Up front, there is a lot of work to be done first. Consider another analogy.

When you pay an architect to create a blueprint, you expect a house that looks like the blueprint to eventually come out of the effort. Assuming that happens, at that point the blueprint reflects a reality—the house itself. But for the longest time (seemingly forever while you're waiting), the blueprint is nothing more than an organized attempt to determine your basic requirements. It does not really describe the house itself but what you (the owner[16]) *want* the house to be. And to be perfectly frank, deciding what you want the house to be is often the hardest part of all. That is why you hired architects to help you!

A fact model is a blueprint for basic business knowledge.

---

16. I use *owner* deliberately here. *Owner* is the term John Zachman uses in the Zachman Architecture Framework for the audience of row 2. Row 2 in the Framework focuses on the enterprise model (or business model), in contrast to a system model (row 3) or a technology model (row 4). A fact model is a fundamental part of the business model in row 2.

Zachman, incidentally, suggests the term *semantic model* for the cell in row 2 that addresses the question *what* (that is, structure or data). We believe that a fact model plus the associated Concepts Catalog fits his prescriptions for a semantic model very closely. For more information on John Zachman's thinking, refer to Zachman [2002] and collected articles by Zachman found in the *Business Rules Journal*, available at *http://www.BRCommunity.com.*

Now it might seem that writing sentences should be a lot easier than creating structured fact model diagrams. Are we letting everyone off easy? *No!* Knowledgeable workers on the business side must originate and understand the sentences; business analysts and fact modelers must help clarify and express the sentences in plain business language. This is *hard*—not because English is hard, but because determining how to express what we know about the business in an understandable, agreed-to form can be hard!

Even harder than this is getting all the sentences to fit together as if in some large jigsaw puzzle. This is where the graphic fact model diagram plays an important role.

When creating a blueprint for remodeling your house, you can quickly see when the pieces are not fitting together. The eye often spots the problems quite easily. A fact model serves a similar purpose. In working with sentences, especially a large set representing the basic knowledge of a complex business, it is often hard to spot the redundancies and overlap. Representing the sentences graphically makes this easier.

Figure 5–1 presents a simple fact model in graphic form. The facts from this fact model are listed below. This list includes several facts that are *implicit* (that is, not labeled explicitly) in the graphic fact model. These implicit facts

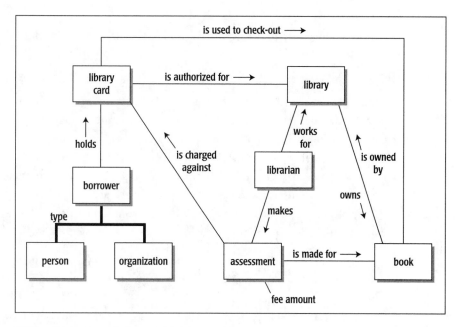

Figure 5–1 Sample fact model for a library

are discussed briefly in Fact Statements for Figure 5–1, along with some final notes on the differences between fact models and data models.

Fact Statements for Figure 5–1
Explicit

- *Library card is used to check out book.*
- *Library card is authorized for library.*
- *Library owns book. (Book is owned by library.)*
- *Librarian works for library.*
- *Librarian makes assessment.*
- *Assessment is made for book.*
- *Assessment is charged against library card.*
- *Borrower holds library card.*

Implicit

- *Person is a category of borrower.*
- *Organization is a category of borrower.*
- *Assessment has a fee amount.*

To the Data Modeler: More on Data Models versus Fact Models

"Is a Category of" Facts

Facts of the "is a category of" variety are often represented implicitly in a fact model. By *implicitly* I mean that the literal words "is a category of" are not actually shown on the model. Instead, the sample fact model in Figure 5–1 uses heavy dark lines to designate the two "is a category of" facts it includes.

Data model approaches vary in their treatment of "is a category of" facts. In some approaches, they are represented as subtypes of some business entity or data object. In others, subtypes are not recognized at all.

In any case, two important distinctions between fact models and data models should be made in this regard.

1. Because of the focus on comprehensive vocabulary in fact models, "is a category of" facts are generally used far more extensively than is subtyping in data models.
2. In fact modeling, no assumptions whatsoever are made about how an "is a category of" fact will be physically represented. In data models, in contrast, use of subtyping is often shaped (or indeed even constrained) by assumptions about the physical representation of "is a category of" facts.

"Has a" Facts

Facts of the "has a" variety are also often represented implicitly in the fact model. Again, by *implicitly* I mean that the literal words "has a" are not actually shown on the model. Instead, the sample fact model in Figure 5–1 uses a thin line for the one "has a" fact it includes (Assessment has a fee amount).

To avoid clutter, "has a" facts are sometimes omitted from the graphic fact model altogether unless they are involved in core business rules and/or computations central to the business problem. In one sense, "has a" facts represent detail that can be handled better elsewhere (for example, in a business rule repository). Indeed, they might never even be expressed as sentences. Still, it is important to recognize them as simply another kind of fact under the business rule approach.

Data models treat "has a" facts as representing attributes of some business entity or data object. Depending on the approach, such attributes might or might not be shown explicitly in the data model.

Cardinality and Optionality

Fact models do not represent certain kinds of specifications to which data modelers might be accustomed. For example, neither *cardinality* (also called *multiplicity*) nor *optionality* is ever represented for the explicit facts in a fact model.

These explicit facts roughly correspond to relationships in data models. Data-modeling techniques usually prescribe including some indication of cardinality for these relationships. For each relationship, this answers the question, "How many?" For example, can a given customer place many orders or only a single (one) order? Cardinality is important in database design; however, any type of cardinality except *many* is actually a form of rule. For example, consider the statement *An order must not be placed by more than one customer.* This statement actually represents a rule expressed for the fact *Order is placed by customer.*

The same is true about expressing the optionality of a relationship. Indicating a relationship to be mandatory (that is, not optional) is a form of rule.

The business rule approach emphasizes developing terms and facts *before* plunging deeply into the expression of any form of rules, including those pertaining to cardinality and optionality. Moreover, all rules should be stated explicitly (again, in sentences) so that their business motivations can be reviewed apart from system or data designs.

The Fact Model and Behavior

A good fact modeler seeks to ensure that each term or fact is represented in the fact model one and only one time and that it does not overlap any other term or fact. In other words, the fact model ensures that terms and facts are *unified* and *unique.* Later, this will provide a way to ensure that all rules are defined consistently and that different actions will operate in consistent fashion.

 By helping to ensure unification and uniqueness of terms and facts, the fact model ensures consistency in business behavior.

Like the skeleton in the human body, the terms and facts in a fact model should represent the *minimum* set needed to provide a suitable framework for the other components. There are no extra bones in the human body—every one has its specific purpose. Adding a bone here or there is not going to improve the body's mechanics. Anyway, bones are relatively expensive because, although essential, they represent overhead to the end result actually desired—namely, *behavior.*

Similarly, a few extra terms and facts here or there in the fact model will not help the business body operate. And they will prove expensive. A fact model helps ensure there are no extra terms and facts in the basic knowledge of the business.

 A fact model should represent a minimum set of terms and facts.

Some professionals believe that if they can get the behavior right, the structure will simply fall into place. That is not our experience at all. It's the body as a whole that matters. You can design a lot of very elegant appendages and a lot of fancy behaviors, but there had better be a well-considered skeleton to hold them all together!

References

Date, C. J. 2000. *An Introduction to Database Systems* (7th ed.). Boston, MA: Addison-Wesley.

Ross, Ronald G., and Gladys S. W. Lam. 2000. *The BRS Fact Modeling Practitioner's Guide: Developing the Business Basis for Data Models.* Houston, TX: Business Rule Solutions, LLC. Available at *http://www.BRSolutions.com.*

Zachman, John A. 2002. *The Zachman Framework: A Primer for Enterprise Engineering and Manufacturing* (electronic book). Available at *http://www.zachmaninternational.com.*

CHAPTER 6

Exercising Control

What You Need to Know about Rules

In the human body, control is provided by the nervous system, an organized collection of nerves that connect to the muscles. Responses to all stimuli are coordinated through the firing of nerve impulses—no firing, no movement, and therefore no behavior.

A business system must have similar control over behavior. In the business rule approach, this control is provided by rules.

Rules for Control

Rules are familiar to all of us in real life. We play games by rules, we live under a legal system based on a set of rules, we set rules for our children, and so on.

Yet the idea of rules in business systems is ironically foreign to most IT professionals. Say "rules" and many IT professionals think vaguely of expert systems or artificial intelligence—approaches deemed appropriate for only very specialized and/or very advanced kinds of problems. There is little recognition of how central rules actually are to the basic, day-to-day operations of the business.

Not coincidentally, many business-side workers and managers have become so well indoctrinated in *procedural* views for developing requirements that thinking in terms of rules might initially seem foreign and perhaps

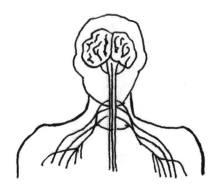

Mechanical Components
→ Structure: Skeleton
→ Power: Muscles
→ Control: Nerves

abstract. Virtually every methodology is guilty in this regard, whether for business process reengineering, system development, or software design. This is unfortunate for at least two important reasons.

1. Thinking about the control aspect of any organized activity in terms of rules is actually very natural. For example, imagine trying to explain almost any game you can think of—chess, checkers, baseball, football, tennis, and so on—without explaining the rules on which the moves in the game are based. Even if it were possible (that's doubtful!), explaining things that way would certainly not be very *effective*.
2. Business-side workers and managers have the knowledge it takes to create good rules. What *they* know makes all the difference in the world in playing the business game.

The business rule approach not only depends on good rules but also offers new insights into what they are about. Without any exaggeration, good rules are no less important to a business system than a robust, finely tuned nervous system is to the human body.

The first step in understanding the central role of rules in the business rule approach is simply to relate them to the issue of control. The boxed item, Sample Rules, presents a light sampling of typical rules,[1] each catego-

---

1. Since this discussion is informal, I will use the word *rule* instead of the more correct *rule statement* to refer to expressions of rules. The distinction is that the same rule can be given by statements in different forms and/or by statements in different languages (for example, French, Mandarin, and so on). In other words, there can be many different *rule statements* for exactly the same *rule*. (I made the equivalent distinction in Chapter 5 between *fact* and *fact statement*.) Obviously, it is desirable to use consistent conventions in creating rule statements. Such conventions are provided by RuleSpeak, as discussed in Part III.

rized according to the kind of control it addresses. Note how far-ranging these categories of control really are. *Every* aspect of operational control in a business system—or indeed in the business itself—can be addressed by rules.

 Rules provide control in the business rule approach.

Sample Rules

Restrictions
A customer must not place more than three rush orders charged to its credit account.

Heuristics
A customer with preferred status should have its orders filled immediately.

Computations
A customer's annual order volume must be computed as total sales closed during the company's fiscal year.

Inference
A customer must be considered preferred if the customer places more than five orders over $1,000.

Timing
A customer must be archived if the customer does not place any orders for 36 consecutive months.

Triggers
"Send-advance-notice" must be executed for an order when the order is shipped.

The second step in understanding rules—a crucial one—is to understand how they relate to terms and facts. In the business rule approach, rules build directly on terms and facts. Actually, a rule should simply add the sense of *must* or *must not* to terms and facts that have already been defined in the fact model and Concepts Catalog. In business problems involving hundreds or thousands of rules—not at all uncommon—there is no way to achieve consistency across such large numbers of rules without a common base of terms and facts. This important principle of the business rule approach is discussed in Part III, which explains how to express rules in appropriate fashion.

 Rules build directly on terms and facts.

The third step in understanding rules—also a crucial one—is to understand how rules relate to events. It is to that subject that we now turn.

Rules and Events

Business systems have addressed the validation and editing of data since the first computer programs for business were written many years ago. Unfortunately, the programming view of editing and validating data is a very procedural one, simply because traditional computer programs work that way. With respect to rules, however, the procedural view is a very limiting one. It definitely represents a case of "can't see the forest for the trees."

Rules in the business rule approach must be perceived and expressed *declaratively*, independent of processes and procedures. Appreciating the importance of this principle is key. It inevitably moves us away from seeing requirements for business systems as essentially a programming problem and toward viewing them as a true *business* problem. Happily, this view is also greatly simplifying. Suddenly, the forest emerges from the trees.

Understanding this fundamental principle of the business rule approach requires careful examination of the relationship between rules and events. Intuitively, we know that rules must be enforced when certain events occur. (If nothing happens, rules cannot be violated, and therefore the rules can remain dormant.) But what exactly is the connection between rules and events?

First, it is important simply to recognize that rules and events are not the same. This might seem obvious, but it is nonetheless a common source of confusion.

 Rules and events are not the same.

To understand this, we must probe into events more deeply. What is an event? There are at least two ways of looking at events, both correct.

1. **The business perspective:** For the business, an event is when something happens that requires the business to respond, even if only in a trivial way. (Usually, the response is *not* trivial.) For example, a customer might place an order. This is an event that requires a well-organized response. Often, as discussed in Chapter 7, we try to organize our response to such business events in advance—for example, with workflow models, procedures, scripts, and so on.

2. **The IT perspective:** For the business system, an event is when something happens that needs to be noted or recorded[2] because knowing about the event is potentially important to other activities, either those occurring during the same time frame or those that might happen later. In the business rule approach, of course, such recording is always based on predefined terms and facts—that is, primarily on the basis of the fact model. A business system can support the fact model in several ways (for example, as a database design, a class diagram, and so on). To simplify matters, let's just say there is some data somewhere in the business system that must be updated (created, modified, or deleted) to record the event. Otherwise, the business cannot know about the event.[3] For convenience, I will call these *update events.*

Now, how do events connect with rules? Suppose the following rule is specified for the business: *A customer must be assigned to an agent if the customer has placed an order.* Figure 6–1 shows the relevant terms and facts for this rule.

The rule itself has been expressed in a declarative manner. This means, in part, that it does not indicate any particular procedure or process to enforce it. It is simply a rule—nothing more and nothing less.

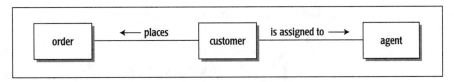

Figure 6–1 Terms and facts for the customer rule

---

2. More precisely, an *event* can be defined as any change in state. However, this discussion is informal and such an exacting definition unnecessary here.
3. Except perhaps informally, based on interpersonal or intersystem messages.

Declarative also means that the rule makes no reference to any business event or update event where it potentially could be violated and thus need to be tested. The rule does not say, for example, "*When* a customer places an order, then. . . ."

This observation is extremely important for the following reason. "*When* a customer places an order" *is not the only event when the rule could potentially be violated.* Actually, there is another event when this rule could be violated. In business terms this other event might be "*When* an agent leaves our company. . . ." The corresponding update event might be "*When* an agent is deleted. . . ."[4] This other event could pose a violation of the rule under the following circumstances: (a) The agent is assigned to a customer, and (b) that customer has placed at least one order.

In other words, the rule could potentially be violated during *two* quite distinct kinds of events. The first, "*When* a customer places an order . . .", is rather obvious. The second, "*When* an agent leaves the company . . .", might be much less so. Both events are nonetheless important because either could produce a violation of the rule.

This example is not atypical or unusual in any way.[5] In fact, it is quite commonplace. In general, *every* rule (in proper declarative form) produces[6] two or more kinds of update events when it could potentially be violated.

 Every rule produces two or more update events when it could potentially be violated.

About Violations of Rules

What happens when an event occurs that might violate a given rule? At least two things should happen, as follows.

1. No matter which event it is, at that point the rule should *fire*[7] so that the prescribed test or constraint can be applied.

---

4. The specific update event that poses a potential violation of the rule is actually the deletion of an instance for the "is assigned to" fact.

5. Rules do exist that are specific to individual update events, but these rules represent the exception, rather than the general case.

6. I mean *produces* in the sense of can be *analyzed to discover.*

7. I use the term *fire* in this discussion to mean loosely both *execute* (to evaluate the relevant condition[s]) and, if necessary, *take appropriate action.* Sometimes *fire* is used to refer only to the former.

2. Assuming the rule is about preventing errors,[8] a message should be returned to the end user (that is, the business worker) to explain why the violation occurred.

What should the error message returned to the business worker say? *The error message should contain exactly the same text as was originally given for the rule.* In the example above, this means the error message will literally read, "A customer must be assigned to an agent if the customer has placed an order."[9]

To put this more strongly, in the business rule approach the rule statement *is* the error message. As discussed in Part I, we believe that the architecture of business systems should always be viewed first and foremost as a *business* problem—not as a technical problem.[10] This treatment of error messages in the business rule approach supports that goal in a fundamental way. It also has important implications for the front-end requirements-gathering process, as discussed in the boxed item, Rules as Requirements.

 The rule statement is the error message.

Rules as Requirements

In the business rule approach, the principal error messages end users will see once the system is operational should be the very same rules that knowledgeable workers on the business side gave as requirements during the earlier design of the business system.[11] The error messages and the requirements are literally one and the same. Well-expressed rules during the requirements process mean well-expressed error messages; poorly expressed rules during the requirements process mean poorly expressed error messages.

Continued

---

8. That is, the rule does not perform an automatic computation, inference, and so on. Later in this chapter I will call rules that prevent errors *rejectors*.

9. Additional text can be provided, of course, to explain the relevance of the rule to the specific event, to suggest corrective measures, and so on.

10. In a truly *friendly* business rule system, when a rule is violated, a procedure or script can be made available to the end user to assist in taking immediate corrective action. This opportunity is discussed in Chapter 7.

11. The actual rule statements can be refined or supplemented, of course, during prototyping and/or system testing (or afterward).

Several observations about this principle are worth making. First, direct assistance in expressing the rules up front will prove extremely valuable to the workers involved. We see this as an important skill for the business analyst, a role described in Part I.

Second is the potential for closing the requirements gap between the business side and the IT side that still plagues so many companies. In traditional approaches, much is usually lost in the translation of up-front requirements to the actual running system. In the business rule approach, the business side gets back whatever it puts in. This is exactly as it should be for a business-driven approach.

 The business rule approach helps to close the requirements gap.

In summary, what does this analysis reveal about the relationship between rules and events? First, it illustrates the basic point that rules and events, while related, are not the same. Second, it illustrates that there are always potentially multiple events when any given rule could be violated. Figures 6–2 and 6–3 provide additional examples to reinforce this crucial point. In the business rule approach, rules are central—*not* events.

 In the business rule approach, rules—not events—are central.

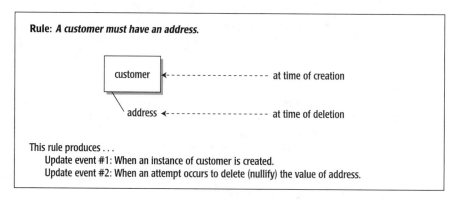

Figure 6–2   Multiple events for a simple rule

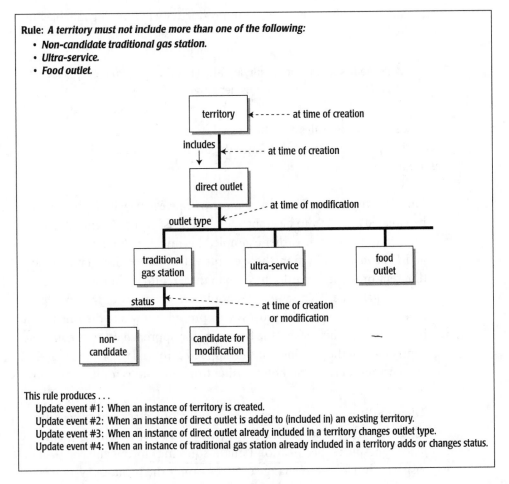

Rule: *A territory must not include more than one of the following:*
- *Non-candidate traditional gas station.*
- *Ultra-service.*
- *Food outlet.*

This rule produces . . .
  Update event #1: When an instance of territory is created.
  Update event #2: When an instance of direct outlet is added to (included in) an existing territory.
  Update event #3: When an instance of direct outlet already included in a territory changes outlet type.
  Update event #4: When an instance of traditional gas station already included in a territory adds or changes status.

Figure 6–3   Multiple events for a more complex rule

Implications of Rules Playing the Central Role

Let's examine some of the implications of this central role for rules. On the technical side, discovering and supporting update events becomes a crucial implementation concern. Fortunately, business logic technology[12] can often

---

12. By *business logic technology,* I mean *rule engines, decision management platforms, business logic servers,* and so on. Since this discussion is focused on concepts rather than technology, I will not use any of these more technical terms in this part of the book.

do this automatically—a huge boost to productivity in building reliable business software.

 Automatic support for identifying and supporting update events for rules is an important feature for business logic technology.

The emphasis on rules and their separation from events opens many new doors of opportunity for both IT and the business. Among these opportunities are the following.

Simple consistency: The two or more update events when a rule might be violated are likely to be embedded in at least two different processes or procedures. (In the earlier example, this might include *Take an order* and *Drop an agent*.) Often, these events will be embedded in many more different processes or procedures than that. Yet for all of these, there is only a *single* rule. That same rule should fire when any of the update events occur in any of the processes or procedures where the rule might be violated. By this means, the business rule approach ensures complete consistency in the "editing criteria" applied across all these procedures. It also ensures there are no holes arising from omissions for less than obvious kinds of events.

Adaptability: Separating the rule from the processes and procedures where it can be violated allows the rule itself to be specified *in one place*. One-place specification (single-sourcing) means the rule will be easier to find—and to change quickly—once the business system is implemented.[13]

Reengineering: Business processes and procedures are generally organized as responses to business events. Declarative rules, however, are specified in *eventless* fashion. They are the pure essence of the business—the Rule Book for the business game. (Refer to the boxed item, About the Rule Book, for additional discussion.) This clarity opens up altogether new horizons for reengineering business processes.

---

13. This includes prototypes in which end users test-drive new processes and procedures *before* implementation.

Rules are key to reengineering business processes.

About the Rule Book

The Rule Book[14] should not be paper-based but rather automated. That way it can play a very active role not only during the system development project but once the new business system becomes operational as well. Software tools are now available that enable direct *business-side* management of rules, opening unprecedented opportunities for the business. (Refer to Chapter 13 for more about rule management.)

Does the Rule Book complicate matters for the business? *No!* A business system is no more complicated by having independent rules than are the games of chess, baseball, and football by having their own independent rule books. I believe the value of Rule Independence speaks for itself.

Rather, the point we take is the following. Your approach for developing requirements should put the Rule Book on at least an equal footing with deliverables for developing processes and procedures (such as workflow models, use cases, scripts,[15] or other techniques). These latter deliverables are needed to produce the raw power to do work—muscles for the business to flex. A Rule Book represents a well-developed nervous system, a way to ensure your business works *smart*.

Ways in Which Rules Can Exercise Control: Functional Categories of Rules

Rules come in three basic varieties with respect to the type of control they exercise: *rejectors*, *producers*, and *projectors*. All rules fall into one of these three functional categories, which are discussed briefly below. Chapter 10 provides a more complete classification including relevant subcategories. Additional discussion appears in Part V, Appendix C.

---

14. A Rule Book is a key deliverable of Proteus, the Business Rule Solutions, LLC, business rule methodology.
15. We use the term *script* for any detailed procedure workers can follow. Scripts are discussed in Chapter 7. BRScripts are a rule-based form of specifying procedures in Proteus.

Rejectors

Many rules are naturally rejectors—that is, left to their own devices,[16] they simply reject any event that would cause a violation to occur.[17] The specific sequence of activity would occur more or less as follows.

1. An end user initiates a procedure to do some work, for example, *Take a customer order.*
2. The end user's activity produces an update event to record the results of the work, for example, *Create an instance of order.*
3. The update event causes a rule to fire, for example, *An order must have a ship-to address.*
4. The rule checks whether the end user has actually given a ship-to address with the order. Suppose the end user has *not* done so.
5. The rule causes the update event to be rejected—that is, the action fails, and the order is *not* created.[18]

This analysis reveals the following important point about rejectors. In their native form, rejectors are very narrow-minded. Either the end user plays by the rules, or the work will not be accepted. If there is any question about the quality of the work—that is, about the quality (consistency) of the data that would result from it—the work will simply be rejected (until correct). In other words, rejectors *insist* upon data quality and do so by active, real-time interventions in ongoing work.[19]

    Rejector-type rules address data quality.

---

16. Often, such rules are not left entirely to "their own devices." For example, when a rule fires and a violation is detected, a user-friendly business rule system might automatically offer a script that the user can follow to correct the violation. Such capability is discussed in Chapter 7.

17. Rejectors are constraints, but then, formally, so are projectors. It is therefore misleading to use the term *constraint* exclusively for rejectors, even though this practice is common among IT professionals, especially those involved with database technology.

18. For simplicity, I am ignoring the opportunity to invoke an appropriate script at this point to allow the user to correct the violation immediately.

19. In general, a rule cannot *directly* prevent a user from doing something wrong inside a process. A process is more or less like a black box whose semantics are unknown. However, the rule can prevent the *results* of the process from being recorded. In other words, the rule can reject the data that the process "wants" to leave behind once it finishes executing if the rule is not satisfied with the results.

This brings me to another point. The business rule approach emphasizes real-time enforcement of rules—in other words, *real-time compliance*. The objective is to coordinate ongoing activities, to ensure optimal (that is, correct) results on an as-you-go basis in doing work. Rejectors therefore play a high-profile role in the business rule approach.

 The business rule approach emphasizes real-time compliance.

Producers

A producer-type rule never rejects update events. Instead, it always accepts them and automatically calculates or derives something for the end user. In performing this computation the producer uses all relevant data, whether old or new (that is, resulting from the most recent update event). For example, in taking an order, a producer-type rule might recompute the current order total each time a new line item for the order is entered.

Producers automate computation. In other words, no programming is required to implement them. The results computed from a producer are guaranteed to be both current and correct.[20] Moreover, since producers are generally multievent like all rules, rule-based computation means there is no chance of missing less than obvious kinds of events where recomputation needs to occur.

Producers are really simply *functions* defined in a declarative manner. Producers seem much friendlier than rejectors because they do not inhibit update events but rather provide additional mileage from them. Their overall purpose is to boost end-user and programming productivity.

 Rule-based functions enhance productivity.

Projectors

A projector-type rule is the exact opposite of a rejector in a fundamental way. Specifically, a projector-type rule never rejects update events. Instead, like producers, it always accepts them and automatically takes some other action—that is, produces some other event—as a result.

---

20. That is, correct given how the rule was specified. If the rule was specified imprecisely, the results, of course, might not be as intended.

In general, a projector can be expressed as *if this, then that too*. In other words, a projector literally projects "this" to "that."[21] There are actually many kinds of automatic events that projectors can cause, but among the most important are the following.

- *Inference:* Infer new facts—that is, knowledge—from existing facts, providing automated assistance in making decisions.
- *Triggers:* Execute processes and procedures automatically.

Like producers, projectors seem much friendlier than rejectors because they do not inhibit update events but rather provide additional mileage from them.[22] Also like producers, projectors provide automatic value-adding behavior; that is, they eliminate given behavior as an end-user responsibility, providing automated assistance in performing operational work.

 Projector-type rules provide automatic value-adding behavior.

Projectors extend the overall range of rules significantly. The complete spectrum of rules is examined more closely in the boxed item.

The Spectrum of Rules

The business rule approach covers the entire spectrum of rules, from the simplest kind of validation rules to the most advanced forms of inference. The goal is a unified approach to the capture and management of all such rules.

---

21. The projection from "this" to "that" might or might not be immediate when the event occurs. This depends on the particular business logic technology and on how it is used. In the classic use of expert systems, for example, the firing of rules was often delayed—that is, not inline with actual ongoing events. More recent practice, however, has emphasized firing rules on a more immediate, inline basis. In general, this approach proves much more effective for operational business purposes.
22. This is not entirely accurate. For example, a projector can be used to switch on (that is, enable) a rejector-type rule in appropriate circumstances. The net result would be potential rejection of update events in those circumstances.

To illustrate the extremes in this spectrum of rules, consider the following situation that might occur in a baseball game. Suppose it is the bottom of the seventh inning, with two outs, two strikes on the batter, and two base runners. The score is tied. The batter is left-handed.

Rejector: A validation rule might ensure that the batter still gets only three strikes even if the pitcher is changed.

Producer: A computation rule might compute the batter's hit percentage in similar prior circumstances.

Projector: Inference rules might help choose the best relief pitcher under the given circumstances.

Logic Traces

In the latter two cases above, especially for projectors, the results might very well prove unexpected or nonintuitive. This can often happen when larger sets of inference rules are involved in automatic "reasoning" performed by business logic technology. The user (in this case, say, the pitching coach) would be entirely justified in wanting to ascertain *how* the results were produced.

Continued

To pursue this, the user must be able to audit the result,[23] preferably in real time if the situation permits. This means being able to work (or trace) backward from the result through the chain of rules that fired to produce it. The business logic technology must, of course, support this need—a capability called *logic traces.*

 Logic traces allow decision-making logic to be directly audited.

Several scenarios are possible as the user traces back through the logic. A subject matter expert might find flaws that need correcting, or he or she might have new insights about where improvements can be made. Someone less expert about the particular decision will simply learn more about the basic knowledge of the business.

This is an important way in which a business rule system is instructional. Even more than that, logic traces take business rules to the next higher level—a step closer to what in Part I were called *knowledge companions.* All this is possible because business rule systems always ensure that business logic is visible to authorized users.

 The business rule approach always supports visible logic.

Expanding the Coverage of Rules

Suggestions and Guidelines

As discussed earlier, the business rule approach emphasizes rules as a principal way to exercise control. Rules can also be used, however, to *influence* behavior rather than to control it directly. Such rules act more as guidelines or heuristics—that is, as *suggestors* [Ross 1997]—instead of hard-and-fast rules. An example illustrates such use.

Consider the sample rule discussed earlier: *A customer must be assigned to an agent if the customer has placed an order.* Let's make a simple change in the wording, switching *must* to *should*. The rule now becomes: *A customer should*

---

23. Assuming, of course, that the user is properly authorized.

be assigned to an agent if the customer has placed an order. The original rule has now been converted into a suggestor. The boxed item (The Form, Fit, and Function of Suggestors) examines important details about this transformation.

The Form, Fit, and Function of Suggestors

Form

The form of the suggestor remains exactly the same as before the transformation. The only modification is that the word *must* has been changed to the word *should.* This consistency in form represents an important aspect of the business rule approach. Put simply, if you have a way to express rules for behavior, then you already have a language for expressing guidelines for behavior. The consistency in form also again suggests the potential of the business rule approach for knowledge management.

 Suggestors are expressed in the same form as other rules.

Fit

The firing of the suggestor remains exactly as before. Specifically, a suggestor fires upon the occurrence of any of the two or more kinds of update events in which the suggestor could be "violated." Also, like any rule, the suggestor should not be embedded in the procedures that produce those events. This allows for easy change in the suggestor. Such adaptability again is the result of Rule Independence.

 Suggestors fire the same way as other rules.

Function

Apart from the word change, the enforcement level of the suggestor is the only thing that differs after the transformation. Rules, of course, take whatever action necessary for enforcement. For the given rule, normally this would mean rejecting any update event that would cause a violation. As a suggestor, no such enforcement action is taken. The update event is *not* prevented. Instead, the end user is just informed of the guideline.

Continued

A suggestor is merely a rule that fires but is not currently enforced.

As always, the rule statement should pop up on the end user's screen. For the suggestor, however, the text is not an error message but merely a guideline. It informs the worker that under the given circumstance, some particular action (update event) is, or is not, appropriate. In other words, suggestors impart business knowledge to influence how work is conducted, but they do not attempt to control the work outright.

 A suggestor imparts business knowledge to influence how work is conducted.

Handling Exceptions

When introduced to the business rule approach, the first reaction some people have is that their business has far more exceptions to rules than rules per se. They question how all these exceptions can be handled in any organized fashion. This is a valid concern.

The business rule approach offers no silver bullet to the *business* problem of having too many exceptions to rules. It does, however, offer a very simple *technical* answer. This technical answer, in turn, does have implications for business process reengineering and for streamlining business operations. I will comment briefly on that momentarily.

First, let's examine the issue of exceptions to rules from the technical point of view. Consider the following rule: *A library card must not be held by more than one borrower, unless one of the borrowers is Bill Gates.* This rule includes a clear-cut exception. The normal rule for library cards is *A library card must not be held by more than one borrower.* Loosely stated, the exception is *Don't enforce this normal rule if Bill Gates is one of the borrowers who holds the library card.*

Careful examination of this exception reveals something quite interesting. Reword the exception to delete *Don't enforce* and incorporate the more rule-like *must be disabled.* The exception now reads as follows: *The normal rule for library cards must be disabled if Bill Gates is one of the borrowers who holds the library card.* What emerges is another rule!

Specifically, what emerges is a projector. This new rule "watches" for events that could affect evaluation of the condition *if Bill Gates is one of the borrowers who holds the library card.* If the condition is found to be true, the new rule takes an action automatically in response. The particular action it takes is to disable (switch off) the original rule, so that it will no longer be enforced for that particular library card. The bottom line is that *the exception to the rule is simply another rule!*

As a technical matter, the business rule approach *always* views exceptions to rules as simply more rules. This puts exceptions to rules on the same playing field as all other rules. This recognition has important consequences on the business side too, as examined briefly in the boxed item, The Cost of Exceptions to Rules.

 Exceptions to rules are always expressed as rules.

The Cost of Exceptions to Rules

Recognizing that exceptions to rules merely represent more rules is crucial for a business reason—one that touches on requirements development, on business process reengineering, and, indeed, on the business itself. Briefly, the reason is simply this: *All rules cost something.*

 All rules cost something.

The cost of rules is not simply the direct cost of their implementation and maintenance in business systems. The real cost often lies hidden in the associated documentation, training, administration, and time—the time it takes to communicate the rules and the time it takes to change the rules. In the 21st-century business, of course, time is among the most precious of commodities. Your business does not need *more* rules—it probably needs fewer (*good*) rules!

 Having fewer (good) rules is generally better than having more rules.

Rules and Guidance in the Business Rule Approach

To conclude this discussion, let's revisit the question of how rules provide control in the business rule approach. In the human body, nerves connect to muscles, the source of power for behavior. The nerves guide and control the muscles and, by that means, the resulting behavior. However, the nerves are not actually embedded within the muscles themselves.

In a business rule system, rules are like the nerves. They connect to processes—the source of power for behavior. The rules control the processes and, by that means, the resulting behavior. However, as we have discussed, the rules should not actually be embedded within the processes.

Processes or procedures connect to rules via update events. When a process or procedure attempts to satisfy some business event, the corresponding update event will occur. This can fire one or more rules, which will determine whether the event is undertaken correctly or will produce a desired outcome. Depending on the result, appropriate action will be taken. The exact nature of the action depends on the type of rule.

Control is externalized from the processes or procedures and is established in a separate rule layer or component. This permits *direct* management of the rules, which in turn permits much closer tie-in to the business side. This idea of Rule Independence is a centerpiece of the business rule approach. The various principles underlying Rule Independence are enumerated at the end of Chapter 7, after the additional implications for processes and procedures are reviewed.

 Rule Independence is key to business-driven systems.

Looking briefly ahead to those implications, one result is simplicity. To borrow a popular IT buzzword, taking out the rules means the processes and procedures become *thin*. The direct benefits of thin processes and procedures are significant in their own right. On a far grander scale, however, we believe Rule Independence can revolutionize how work in the company is organized and conducted. That potential is examined in the next chapter.

Reference

Ross, Ronald G. 1997. *The Business Rule Book* (2nd ed.). Houston, TX: Business Rule Solutions, LLC. Available at *http://www.BRSolutions.com.*

CHAPTER 7

Doing Work

What You Need to Know about Processes

In the human body, power is provided through the muscles, which enable motion. Motion results in the behavior that we see from the outside. On the inside, however, the muscles are connected to the skeleton, which provides a framework. The muscles are also connected to the nerves, which provide control. Without these other two vital internal components, meaningful behavior would be impossible.

A business system must have similar "power." This power—the power that produces the "motion" of the system—is provided by processes.

In general, a process takes some input (often provided by an end user working through some computer screens) and transforms it into some desired output. The process operates according to an algorithm provided by its designer or programmer. Simple as that. The only problem is that in traditional approaches, the processes are *not* all that simple. In fact, they are quite complex and therefore quite difficult to change.

The business rule approach offers powerful innovations for processes. By taking the rules out of the processes, it can produce processes that are relatively simple—ones that *can* be changed as the need arises.

 The business rule approach produces processes that are easier to change.

Mechanical Components
→ Structure: Skeleton
→ Power: Muscles
→ Control: Nerves

This simplification has repercussions far beyond IT—indeed, it has far-reaching consequences for the business as a whole. In particular, it can change the very nature of *work* in the business. We like to say that rules can revolutionize work. This chapter suggests how that can happen.

 Rules can revolutionize work.

Challenges Facing Businesses Today

Before examining how the business rule approach enables this innovation, let's review some of the challenges facing 21st-century businesses, particularly as they relate to business processes.

> **Time shock**: As the rate of change accelerates, workers are constantly thrust into new roles and responsibilities. They must be guided through unfamiliar procedures as thoroughly and as efficiently as possible—but with minimum human intervention. The business pays a price, either directly or indirectly, if getting the workers up to speed is too slow (or too painful).

> **Training**: The flip side of time shock is the issue of training—*how* to get the workers up to speed. Training is an expensive and time-consuming

affair. Yet as the rate of change accelerates, more and more (re)training is required. What is the solution? Training must be built into the business systems that support workers in carrying out daily processes and procedures. We believe *business rules*—not computer-assisted training or anything like that—can help make that happen. We like to say that business rule systems are instructional. Later in this chapter, I show how this goal can be achieved.

Adaptability: In the National Football League (NFL), if a play is not working for a team, it will be gone from its play book within a couple of games (possibly along with a coach or two!), and a new play will be substituted for it. In effect, the plays are essentially throwaways—cheap enough to discard readily, with minimum disruption or cost to the team. The reason NFL plays are throwaways is that the knowledge necessary to run them is embodied elsewhere—in the scoreboard,[1] in the skills of the players, in the heads of the coaches, and most importantly, in the NFL rule book.

Similarly, businesses need to view their own procedures as throwaways—that is, cheap enough to discard and replace readily when the procedures no longer work well (that is, no longer make "yardage" for the business). Today, this generally means throwing away whole applications (or legacy systems) and replacing them with new ones, either built in-house or purchased from an outside source. Such replacement, of course, is far too expensive to do frequently. So businesses are stuck with procedures that work poorly (and only seem to get worse with time), often watching helplessly as the competition introduces better ones.

 Throwaway procedures are a must for the business to remain competitive.

What can a business do about these challenges? In the discussion that follows, I explain how business rules can fundamentally change how work is organized and managed in the business. The implications are indeed far-reaching.

---

1. The names of the variable information posted on the scoreboard are terms that represent the most basic knowledge constructs of the game of football—for example, *quarter, time, score, down,* and so on.

Putting Business Rules to Work

It is generally true that the more you know, the better you can do. If this were not the case, businesses would not spend resources on training and education. We would not spend the first decade or two of our lives in school, or bother to read, or even have libraries. There would be no dictionaries, no encyclopedias, no phone directories, and no Web.

Business rules are about *knowing*—that is, about basic business knowledge. Specifically, as explained in Chapters 5 and 6, business rules represent the terms, facts, and rules of the business. *Knowing* seems passive. So what do business rules have to do with *doing* work? This is no idle question. After all, it's doing the work that gets the product out the door and into the customers' hands.

A time-tested maxim in training is always *to build on what you know*. There are several ways in which this idea applies to developing a new approach for work (that is, the *doing*) in the business rule approach. To understand these ways better, let's restate the maxim in two parts as follows. First, always build on what you know. Second, always build on what you already know how to do. Each of these two points is examined in detail in the remainder of this chapter.

 Always build on what you know—and already know how to do.

Building on What You Know

Let's briefly review some of the basic ideas of the business rule approach so we can apply them to rethinking how work in the business should be organized.

Basing Procedures on Terms and Facts

A basic principle of the business rule approach is that terms and facts (the most basic forms of knowing) should be shared and defined independently of the doing. As discussed in Chapter 5, this objective is supported by developing a fact model and Concepts Catalog.

Procedures should always comply with these predefined terms and facts; that is, procedures should always reuse these terms and facts instead of developing their own, private versions. So the first and most basic aspect of understanding how work is organized in the business rule approach is the principle that no procedure ever defines "data" on its own (if it intends to share it). Do not underestimate how dramatically this principle in itself simplifies procedures under the business rule approach.

 Sharing common terms and facts simplifies procedures.

Basing Procedures on Rule Independence

The business rule approach shifts into high gear, of course, by recognizing that rules are also part of knowing. Like all parts of knowing, rules should not be embedded in the doing. We call this *Rule Independence.*

Only a relatively small portion of traditional applications literally support the actual steps of a procedure (that is, the doing) from a business perspective. Most of the code is devoted to editing, validations, derivations, and calculations—in other words, to supporting business rules.[2] When you take the rules out of traditional application logic, the result is a *thin process.*

I mean *thin* in the following sense: The process or procedure prescribes *only* the necessary series of steps to accomplish the desired work result. Excluded are all the rules—and all the error handling when violations of rules occur. (I will get to that crucial aspect a bit later.)

 Rule Independence results in thin processes.

Now, an initial image of work (that is, doing) in the business rule approach emerges. Work should be viewed literally as a series of steps needed to accomplish a work result.

A play in football is a good analogy. If you have ever seen a diagram of a football play in a play book, it is literally represented as a series of orchestrated steps needed to accomplish the desired result (to advance the ball). It is nothing more and nothing less. No rules—nor penalties for violating these rules—are embedded within the play. A play simply focuses on *doing.*

---

2. The code also addresses the issue of control (made largely unnecessary by rules), certain housekeeping chores (which generally also could be expressed as rules), and the detection and management of events (which can be taken over by the business logic technology).

For business systems, I can be more precise about the "plays" the business runs. In the business rule approach, we call them *scripts*.[3] "A series of steps" is a good description of what a script looks like; "a prescribed series of requests" is an even better one. Refer to the boxed item, More on Scripts in the Business Rule Approach, for additional discussion. Scripts, of course, *never* include embedded rules (nor the violation-handling activity for such rules).

 A script is a procedure consisting of a series of requests with no embedded rules.

More on Scripts in the Business Rule Approach

We like to describe a script as a prescribed series of requests. The word *series* is self-evident, but the words *prescribed* and *requests* deserve closer examination.

Prescribed means that the given series of steps *can* be followed to achieve the desired results, but not that they *must* be followed. For example, there might be one or more other series of steps that can be followed to achieve the

---

3. These are called *BRScripts* in Proteus, the business rule methodology created by Business Rule Solutions, LLC.

same results. To say *must be followed* represents a rule about sequencing,[4] and even that type of rule should not be embedded in the process or procedure.

By *requests* I mean requests for action. When the request is made to some software component, this action is taken in the form of executing some program. Such software components might include any of the following:

- Database management systems (to create, retrieve, modify, or delete data)
- GUIs or other screen objects
- Service providers, such as print routines
- Interfaces to legacy systems
- Special-purpose rule technologies

Examples of situations in which scripts could be applied include the following. Note that, as is typical, these scripts target bread-and-butter business activities. In each case, the script would provide a pattern for doing the operational-level work.

- Take a customer order.
- Evaluate a medical claim.
- Book a reservation.
- Assign a professor to a class.

 Scripts provide patterns for doing work.

Often a script is undertaken in response to something a human or organization does (for example, a customer places an order). A script can also be undertaken in response to some timing criteria (for example, time to bill customers) or some predefined condition (for example, inventory quantity on hand is below a certain threshold). In the latter two cases, appropriate criteria for initiating the scripts automatically can be expressed as rules.

---

4. *Sequencing* is not quite the right word here. Since rules are declarative, *required antecedents* is probably more precise.

Including People in Scripts

Do scripts specify requests only among software components? *No!* In many respects, the most important source or recipient of requests in scripts is a real person. After all, real people still do a significant amount of the actual work. It would be rather shortsighted to leave them out.

 Scripts involve real people too.

These people might be either *inside* the company (that is, workers) or *outside* the company (for example, customers). Although all these people might be "users" of the business system, for scripts we prefer the term *actors*. The term *user* suggests outside beneficiaries of system services, whose own work and interactions are outside scope. *Actor*, in contrast, suggests someone whose own activity or role is integral to understanding and doing the work. An actor is someone whose own work is definitely within scope.

 An actor's work is within scope.

What can human actors do to get work done? They can perform actions, of course. They can also make requests for action—requests to software components and, either directly or indirectly, to other actors.

This begins to bring the new image of work in the business rule approach into sharper focus. Work is performed as human actors and software actors interact with each other, following scripts. In the thin-process, throwaway world of scripts, the emphasis is on choreographed collaboration between actors, both human and machine.

 Business rules enable adaptable, throwaway collaborations involving people and machines.

Implications for the Business Side

Does all work have to be scripted? *No!* The boxed item, About Unscripted Work, explores that issue further.

About Unscripted Work

Not all work must be scripted in advance. In fact, in a dynamic business environment, not all events and circumstances can even be predicted, much less prescripted.[5] This fact has several important implications.

- Ad hoc database access will always be a significant factor for business systems. This is an additional reason why it is so important to define terms, facts, and rules independently of processes and procedures.
- Criteria must be identified to determine when it might not be cost-effective to script work in advance, even when some event *can* be predicted. Scripting work for low-frequency events performed by only a few actors, for example, is often not cost-effective.
- The Rule Book (in automated form, of course) can be used to guide work in a timely fashion that has not been scripted in advance. The lack of a script might occur either because the event could not be predicted or because scripting the work in advance would not be cost-effective. Having the Rule Book for such situations is a crucial advantage of the business rule approach.

Building scripts for predictable, repetitive work, however, is quite useful. Remember, because the scripts are thin, the collaborations they prescribe need not be static but, rather, can be dynamic and constantly evolving. This is exactly what 21st-century businesses need to meet the challenge of rapid change.

This approach is consistent with current thinking about how IT should be used to transform organizational structures. Deep hierarchies, with many layers of middle management, are out. Flattened hierarchies, with empowered end users and flexible patterns of collaboration, are in.

Another current business trend centers on automating the extended value chain, crossing organizational boundaries between suppliers, producers, and

---

5. It could be argued that this fact makes business systems notably different from other kinds of computing problems such as real-time systems, process control software, systems software, and so on.

customers. The real goal here is *compacting* the value chain, allowing direct, dynamic interaction between empowered actors anywhere along the way.

It is interesting to note that both of the above trends involve eliminating certain types of organizational roles. In the case of reengineering, the target has often been middle-level managers. In the case of compacted value chains, the target is *middlemen in general*, and with that focus, the goal is *disintermediation*.

All such roles served in times past not only to filter information—the responsibility commonly ascribed to them—but also to know and enforce business rules. In their absence, having a Rule Book becomes all the more critical. Otherwise, how can the business communicate its rules and ensure that the behavior of all actors remains consistent with the business goals? The importance of this principle is examined more closely in the boxed item, Eliminating the Human Actors in the Middle.

 The Rule Book retains knowledge for the business.

Eliminating the Human Actors in the Middle

As middle-level managers were eliminated in the reengineering and downsizing initiatives of the 1980s and 1990s, they essentially took knowledge about many business rules with them. Indeed, we commonly now hear the complaint that *the systems seem to be running the business.*

As a result, many companies are facing tough choices in trying to regain that lost knowledge. One approach is to attempt to mine the business rules from the legacy code (not an easy prospect!). The alternative is either reengineering the business systems from scratch or replacing them with expensive (and often painful) implementations of packaged software. An important lesson can be learned from this: Never lose your business rules!

 Never lose your business rules!

Any business initiative whose direct or indirect effect might be to eliminate human actors "in the middle" should call on business rule techniques. Following this principle is a wise—and probably *essential*—safeguard for your business in the 21st century.

Back to Training

Let's now reconsider the problem of training in the 21st-century business. At any given time, actors participating in scripted collaborations might be found at virtually any stage of time shock. Significant time shock can occur when switching to new scripts, changing roles within the same script, or even performing the very same role for the very same script as the rules change.

Sometimes, you might find the actors completely up to speed; other times, it might seem they have suddenly dropped in from another planet. Most of the time, they will probably be somewhere in between. This poses daunting problems not only for training the actors but also for building the business systems that support them.

IT professionals tend to design toward the more advanced workers, either by necessity or by choice. This tendency often leaves the novice hopelessly befuddled when trying to use the system. This is a long-standing problem in software development.

An alternative is to build an additional stripped-down version for the novice worker, heavily laden with "help." This alternative doubles development work and creates significant maintenance and upgrade problems. This solution is not really best for all the in-between users—which, for whatever reason, usually includes most of us. And, of course, the help never really seems to help at all!

The solution is more or less obvious. If software were clothing, it would be called *one-size-fits-all*. The key is an environment that *stretches* as the end user grows in capabilities.

With respect to organizing work, *one-size-fits-all* means that the same script must be usable for actors at any stage of time shock. This is no small challenge, but the business rule approach to organizing work provides an innovative solution. The key lies with remembering that *all* potential errors (that is, mistakes that end users can make in matters related to the business) are handled by rules, which are *separate* from the scripts. The rules, and the necessary activity to handle violations of them, are invoked (that is, become visible to the actor) only when mistakes are actually made. The net effect, as explained in the boxed item, One-Size-Fits-All Software Environments, is to make the environment seem very different to the novice user than to the advanced (that is, up-to-speed) user.

One-Size-Fits-All Software Environments

A novice benefits directly when work is already scripted simply because there is a ready-to-use template to follow when performing the work. Even better, this template was presumably created on the basis of best practices—the how-to knowledge of those workers who already know what works best.

The novice (or time-shocked) actor will inevitably make *lots* of mistakes when performing a script. To this actor the business rule software environment seems big. Actually, all the rule violation activity that makes the system seem so big represents inline, automatic *training*—a business investment in getting (or keeping) that actor up to speed. In other words, business rule systems are instructional by design.

 Business rule systems are instructional.

The advanced actor, in contrast, can be expected to make *few or no* errors when performing a script. For this actor, the same business rule software environment will seem small. In fact, if sufficiently knowledgeable and properly authorized, the advanced actor might elect not even to use a predefined script to do the work. Instead, the actor might elect to wing it— that is, make the appropriate requests on the fly. The rules, of course, will still catch violations if the actor makes any mistakes.

Even for the advanced actor, however, the work environment might not stay small all the time—especially if the rules themselves are in rapid flux. That possibility, of course, is a likely one for the 21st-century business. These days, *no* worker can safely assume immunity from time shock.

 No worker is ever immune to time shock.

The key to one-size-fits-all scripts, of course, is Rule Independence— that is, capturing and implementing the rules separately. Even that, however, is not enough. Something more is necessary to guide and instruct actors effectively in doing work (that is, in performing scripts). In particular, the error messages human actors get back from the system when a rule is violated should succinctly state the business rule that the error represents. Only by this means can the actor get up to speed on the business itself.[6]

As indicated in Chapter 6, in the business rule approach the rule statements *are* the error messages! As workers bump into the rules, they learn simply by reading from the Rule Book then and there.[7]

 Workers learn by reading the Rule Book inline as the need arises.

Building on What You Already Know How to Do

In real life, there are generally two ways in which we build on what we already know how to do. These two ways are discussed from the business rule perspective below. The first is relatively straightforward; the second brings business rule thinking about organizing work to its culmination. Both pertain to *reuse* of scripts when doing work.

Reuse of scripts implies reuse of software as a given. Our goal, however, is *business*-level reusability. Focusing narrowly on *software*-level reusability misses this bigger picture.

 The business rule approach focuses on business-level reusability, not just software reusability.

Normal Reuse of Scripts

The most obvious form of reusing what we already know how to do is simply invoking one procedure or script from within another. The invoked procedure or script indicates how one step is to be taken within that larger procedure or script, whose purpose is broader or more general. Here are some simple examples from real life.

This Reusable Procedure . . .	Can Be Reused In . . .
Tying your shoes	Getting dressed
Making spaghetti sauce	Cooking an Italian dinner
Driving a car	Visiting your in-laws

---

6. Rule traces are another important capability in this regard.
7. Assuming the workers are authorized, of course.

This Reusable Procedure ...	Can Be Reused In ...
Throwing a football	Running a play
Typing	Using a computer program

Such reuse of scripts is commonplace when building business systems. For example, the script *Fill out address* can be reused in many other, broader scripts, potentially including *Take customer order, Record prospect information, Create shipment, Hire employee,* and so on. This form of reuse is obvious and very important for many reasons, including the following:

- The software to support it need not be rewritten but can be reused as is, saving time in development and maintenance.
- Reuse of any kind produces consistency, which in turn generally raises productivity.
- A worker who already knows the invoked script need not learn anything new to do that part of the work. This head start is highly desirable for time-shocked workers.

Such normal reuse of scripts involves no special use of rules. The business rule approach simply adopts it as a given.

   Normal reuse of scripts whenever possible is a given.

Abnormal Reuse of Scripts

Abnormal reuse does not imply abnormal scripts (whatever that might mean). Rather, it implies that a script already used in normal circumstances also gets used under abnormal circumstances. Such abnormal reuse is the final, crucial piece in rethinking work for the 21st-century business. Real life again provides good examples.

Procedure	Normal Circumstances	Abnormal Circumstances
Climb a tree	Recreation	Escape a vicious dog
Kick a soccer ball	Play a soccer game	Kick a penalty shot
Heat an item in a microwave oven	Warm up leftovers	Melt crystallized honey
Make a telephone call	Talk to your spouse	Call 911 for emergency assistance
Write in longhand	Sign a check	Take notes when your laptop is down

To understand abnormal reuse, it is important to understand exactly when abnormal circumstances occur. In many approaches, defining where and when abnormal circumstances occur is something of a mystery. The business rule approach, in contrast, is quite precise in this regard: *Abnormal business circumstances occur when and only when a worker makes a request resulting in a violation of a rule.* By implication, if no rule is violated, the circumstances are *not* abnormal. By the way, satisfying all rules does not necessarily mean the circumstances are *desirable.* It might simply mean some rules are missing.

Rules then *by definition* indicate the threshold between normal and abnormal business circumstances. Rules and only rules (actually, just rejectors) perform this role.

 Rules always define the threshold between normal and abnormal business circumstances.

Supporting abnormal reuse of scripts is therefore straightforward. It comes about as follows:

1. The worker executes a script.
2. The worker makes a request under that script.
3. The request produces an event.
4. The event fires the appropriate rules, if any.
5. Suppose one of these rules (a rejector) detects a violation in the work.
   What happens here is the crucial piece. One more capability is required so that the reuse can occur, as follows.
6. When the rule detects a violation, the business logic technology has been directed (by the designers of the script) to invoke *another* script automatically.
7. This other script offers the capability needed for the original worker (or possibly some other worker) to correct the error that caused the violation.
8. If that work is undertaken (not a given) . . .
9. And if the work is accomplished successfully such that the violated rule is now satisfied . . .
10. Then the original work can continue under the *original* script from where it earlier left off.

The simple example below illustrates the above activity step-by-step.

Normal script: *Take customer order*

Rule: *An order must be placed by a customer.*

If the rule is violated, the script to be invoked is: *Record customer information*

Actual work activity:

1. The order entry clerk executes the *Take customer order* script.
2. The order entry clerk makes out an order but fails to indicate any customer for it.
3. The update event is attempted.
4. This fires the rule: *An order must be placed by a customer.*
5. The rule detects a violation in the order.
6. The business logic technology has been instructed to pass control to the *Record customer information* script in this circumstance.
7. The order entry clerk is offered the opportunity to perform this other script.
8. The order entry clerk elects to do so.
9. This work successfully corrects the original violation of the rule.
10. The order entry clerk resumes work under the original script (*Take customer order*) from the point it was interrupted. (For example, the next action might be to schedule the order's fulfillment.)

An important comment about this example is that the script designated to handle the abnormal circumstance (*Record customer information*) is presumably the script otherwise used in *normal* circumstances for that kind of work. It would almost certainly therefore be familiar to the order entry clerk.

This represents a general principle for designing abnormal reuse of scripts: *If at all possible, any script invoked by a rule in abnormal circumstances should be a script already used for the same kind of work under normal circumstances.* In plain English, that simply means keep it as simple for the worker as possible!

Note that the script selected for the abnormal circumstances can be modified (or even replaced) *independently* of the script for normal circumstances. The latter script also can change (or be replaced) independently of the former. And all these changes can occur independently of the rule—that is, they can be accomplished with no impact on the rule itself. In these ways, abnormal reuse achieves the full potential of business rules for organizing work in 21st-century businesses.

 Business rule systems support change at a very granular level, and are therefore highly adaptive.

None of this adaptability would have been possible, of course, if the rule had been embedded within the script itself. Here, Rule Independence yields yet another major benefit—a new kind of firewall to limit the impact of procedural changes.

 Rules offer a new kind of firewall to limit the impact of procedural changes in the business.

In short, rules *will* revolutionize work! It is therefore altogether fitting that I close Part II with the Business Rule Manifesto.

Business Rules Manifesto
The Principles of Rule Independence[8]
By Business Rules Group
http://www.BusinessRulesGroup.org

1. Rules are a first-class citizen of the requirements world.
2. Rules are essential for, and a discrete part of, business models, system models, and implementation models.
3. Rules are not process and not procedure. They should not be embedded in either of these.
4. Rules build on facts, and facts build on concepts as expressed by terms.
5. Terms express business concepts; facts make assertions about these concepts; rules constrain and support these facts.
6. Rules must be explicit. No rule is ever assumed about any concept or fact unless a rule has been specified explicitly.
7. Rules are basic to what the business knows about itself—that is, to basic business knowledge. Rules need to be nurtured, protected, and managed.

---

8. Version 1.1, November 23, 2002. Edited by Ronald G. Ross.

8. *Rules are about business practice and guidance; therefore, rules are motivated by business goals and objectives and are shaped by various influences.*

9. *Rules should be expressed declaratively for the business audience, in natural-language sentences. If something cannot be expressed, then it is not a rule.*

10. *Rules are best implemented declaratively. Rules are based on truth values.*

11. *Rules are explicit constraints on behavior and/or provide support to behavior.*

12. *Rules generally apply across processes and procedures. There should be one cohesive body of rules which should be enforced consistently across different areas of business activity.*

13. *The relationship between events and rules is generally many-to-many.*

14. *A rule statement is distinct from the enforcement level defined for it. These are separate concerns.*

15. *Rules should be defined independently of responsibility for the who, where, when, or how of enforcement.*

16. *Rules often require special or selective handling of detected violations. Such rule violation activity is activity like any other activity.*

17. Rules define the boundary between acceptable and unacceptable business activity.

18. To ensure maximum consistency and reusability, the handling of unacceptable business activity should be separable from the handling of acceptable business activity.

19. Exceptions to rules are expressed by other rules.

20. Rules always cost the business something. This cost must be balanced against business risks.

21. Rules should arise from knowledgeable business people.

22. Business people should have tools available to help them develop and manage rules.

23. In the long run, rules are more important to the business than hardware/software platforms.

24. Rules should be managed in such a way that they can be readily redeployed to new hardware/software platforms.

25. A business rule system is never really finished because it is intentionally built for continuous change.

26. Rules, and the ability to change them effectively, are key to improving business adaptability.

PART III

Best Practices
for Expressing Rules

BRS RuleSpeak

Overview

BRS RuleSpeak is a set of practical guidelines that can assist business workers and IT professionals with all of the following tasks:

- Express rules in clear, unambiguous, well-structured business English
- Clarify business logic
- Find a middle ground between (a) high-level policies and directives and (b) rule specifications at an implementation level
- Improve communication about business rules between the business side and IT
- Bridge between business analysis and system design

In one way or another, each of these goals addresses difficulties in developing *requirements*. This problem is best described in the words of an experienced practitioner:

> *Another chronic problem is the difficulty of finding a common language to assure that business clients, analysts, and developers can truly communicate. Asking clients to sign off on a project is meaningless if the proposed process logic or database structure is presented in a form that they are not trained to understand. For developers, the communication medium must allow sufficient rigor to support system design and the creation of code.*

RuleSpeak provides an innovative solution. It shows how to express rules[1] in the clearest, most unambiguous form. Many users of RuleSpeak will be in IT; however, the structured English of RuleSpeak can be understood and "spoken" by large segments of the business community too.

I have divided the discussion of RuleSpeak into the following chapters.[2] Note that information about how to capture the rules themselves is not discussed in detail here.[3]

- Chapter 8 discusses the basic dos and don'ts of expressing rules. This lighter treatment is suitable for a general audience.
- Chapter 9 reviews the basic ideas of RuleSpeak and explains what it is and what purpose it serves. Included in this chapter are usage notes to ensure the best possible expression of rules.
- Chapter 10 presents the BRS Rule Classification Scheme. This chapter, a relatively brief one, provides the scheme for organizing the actual rule sentence templates presented in Chapter 11 and for organizing decision tables as discussed in Chapter 12. It also serves as a general reference point concerning the functional categories of rules.
- Chapter 11 provides the actual RuleSpeak rule sentence templates, with many examples to illustrate. These templates, which are based on the BRS Rule Classification Scheme, cover a broad range of cases.
- Chapter 12 discusses the use of decision tables to express business logic, explaining the RuleSpeak approach through relevant examples and prescriptions.

---

1. For convenience, I will often use *rule* in the discussion that follows in this part instead of the more correct *rule statement*, except where such use might cause confusion. As discussed in Chapter 6, the distinction is that the same rule can be given by statements in different forms and/or by statements in different languages (for example, French, Mandarin, and so on.). In other words, there can be many different *rule statements* for exactly the same *rule*.

2. At certain points in the discussions that follow in this part, I mention elements of methodology or deliverables that pertain specifically to Business Rule Solutions, LLC. When I use *we* or *our* in these contexts, please note that I am referring to the Principals of Business Rule Solutions.

3. Proteus, the Business Rule Solution's business rule methodology, provides comprehensive techniques and guidance to assist with this area.

Expressing Rules

The Dos and Don'ts

Expressing and communicating rules effectively is not simply a matter of following certain conventions by rote but rather requires a certain underlying mind-set. In other words, people undertaking the task of writing rules for the business should be properly oriented. This chapter provides a series of basic guidelines for that purpose. Presented in the form of dos and don'ts, they also establish assumptions on which the other chapters in this part of the book are based. All of these guidelines, by the way, are aimed at the *business* expression of rules—not IT expression per se. This orientation is consistent with the fundamental principles of the business rule approach.

Not How, Not Where, Not Who, Not When

Proposed rule: *A group must not include both union members and nonunion members.*

Acceptable? Yes.

Discussion: Removing the specifics of *how, where, who,* and *when* produces rules in declarative form. A rule statement should include no indication about any of the following:

- *How* the rule will be enforced
- *Where* the rule will be enforced (for example, within what implementation components)

- *Who* (that is, which actor) is responsible for enforcing the rule
- *When* (that is, which events) should cause the rule to be tested

Declarative expression of rules allows the most flexible rethinking of requirements and reengineering of business processes.

Not Procedural

Proposed rule: *Check the product number in database SRU [the Sandals R Us database].*

> If the product number is equal to 422 [the part number of flip-flops]
> and the product description is equal to "plastic flip-flops,"
>> then set the new product number in database ASC
>> [The Athens Sandal Company database] equal to 1547
>> and set the product description equal to "Fun-in-the-Sun Flip-Flops"
> *else if* the product number in database ASC is equal to 423 through 495 [the part numbers of all orthopedic sandals]
>> then set the new product number equal to 1647
>> and set the product category equal to "Good for You, Too Sandals"
> *else if* . . .

—Example of "business rules" from a recent software vendor white paper

Acceptable? No.

Discussion: This "rule" is obviously not in declarative form. Use of the control word *else* (among other things) indicates that the "rule" outlines processing logic rather than business logic. This type of rambling statement for expressing rules should be carefully avoided. It does not isolate individual pieces of business logic, nor does it communicate well for the business side.

Not Inscrutable

Proposed rule: *No savings and loan holding company, directly or indirectly or through one or more transactions, shall acquire control of an uninsured institution or retain, for more than one year after other than an insured institution or holding company thereof, the date any insured institution subsidiary becomes uninsured, control of such institution.*

—From the Code of Federal Regulations

(chosen as the winner of the annual "Legaldegook" contest by the Plain Language Committee of the State Bar of Texas)

Acceptable? No.

Discussion: The most basic test for a good rule statement is that it can be readily understood by any business worker who reads it—and that it always produces the same interpretation.

Not Impossible

Proposed rule: *Regardless of anything to the contrary in this booklet, if your medical insurance terminates for any reason including death, you . . . may elect within 30 days . . . to continue such medical insurance.*

—From the booklet "Group Insurance for I-14 Employees"

(consolidated group trust of a major insurance company)

Acceptable? No.

Discussion: Rules can be impossible for many reasons, including status (as above), time constraints, direct conflicts, and so on. Obviously, rules that are impossible should be avoided.

Always Built on Terms and Facts

Proposed rule: *A customer may* place *an order only if the customer* holds *an account.*

Fact: A customer places an order.

Fact: A customer holds an account.

Terms: Customer, order, account

Acceptable? Yes.

Discussion: The business rule approach prescribes that rules always build on facts and that facts always build on terms. A rule really lies in the "must-ness" (or the "should-ness") of its expression. For the most part, everything else in the rule should represent terms and facts.

A structure to organize these underlying terms and facts is therefore an essential tool in expressing rules. As discussed in Chapter 5, this requires a fact model. The fact model serves as your reference source for standard term and fact names. This is illustrated in Figure 8–1, which shows a rule based on the same fact model that appeared in Figure 5–1.

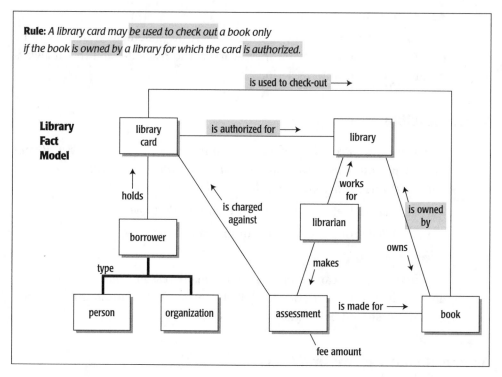

Rule: *A library card may be used to check out a book only if the book is owned by a library for which the card is authorized.*

Figure 8–1   A rule whose wording is based directly on a fact model

Standard term and fact wordings should be used faithfully in expressing rules. This practice ensures basic consistency and helps to avoid ambiguities—issues that rapidly become primary in importance as the set of rules grows larger and larger in number.

No AWOL Facts

Proposed rule: *An order must not be shipped if the outstanding balance exceeds credit authorization.*

Acceptable? Probably not.

Discussion: There seems to be AWOL[1] (hidden or missing) facts in this rule.

---

1. From the military term *AWOL*, which stands for "absent without leave."

- Outstanding balance of what? Order? Customer? Account? Shipment?
- Credit authorization of what? Order? Customer? Account? Shipment?

Ambiguities can result whenever references to relevant facts are omitted from a rule. First clarify the facts, then revise the rule. The appropriate facts for the rule above might be as follows.

Fact: *Customer* has credit authorization.

Fact: *Customer* holds account.

Fact: *Account* has outstanding balance.

An appropriate revised rule based on these facts appears below.

Revised rule: *An order must not be shipped if the outstanding balance of the customer's account exceeds the customer's credit authorization.*

No Fluff

Proposed rule: *Programmers must always work on a system.*

Acceptable? Could be better.

Revised rule: *Programmers must work on a system.*

Proposed rule: *Shipments must have a status at all times.*

Acceptable? Could be better.

Revised rule: *Shipments must have a status.*

Discussion: Words and phrases added for emphasis just add clutter. They should be avoided to keep the rule statements as succinct as possible. For example, assume a rule implies *always* or *at all times* unless explicit qualification is given.

No Plural Subjects

Proposed rule: *Programmers must work on a system.*

Acceptable? Could be better.

Revised rule: *A programmer must work on a system.*

Proposed rule: *Shipments must have a status.*

Acceptable? Could be better.

Revised rule: *A shipment must have a status.*

Discussion: Use a singular subject for all rules. This is the first of many points below about the importance of carefully identifying and expressing the *subject* for every rule. Selecting an appropriate subject is a critical step in expressing rules well.

Careful about Iffy Starts

Proposed rule: *If an employee is retired, then he must not be assigned an employment counselor.*

Acceptable? Could be better.

Revised rule: *A retired employee must not be assigned an employment counselor.*

Discussion: Always start a rule with an appropriate subject. If qualification is necessary (for example, an *if* clause), place it at the end of the rule.[2]

This guideline also applies to timing clauses. An additional example illustrates this.

Proposed rule: *By the close of registration, a student must be enrolled in at least two courses.*

Acceptable? Could be better.

Revised rule: *A student must be enrolled in at least two courses by the close of registration.*

Discussion: *Close of registration* refers to an event. An event is a *when*, which is not appropriate as the subject of a rule. This event (or more precisely, the appropriate point in time) can be included in the rule as a timing clause, as illustrated above, to indicate when enforcement of the rule should begin.

No AWOL Subjects

Proposed rule: *No less than two people in booths between 9 A.M. and 1 P.M.*

—Restaurant in Alameda, CA

Acceptable? No.

Discussion: What is the subject of the original rule? It is AWOL—missing. The implied "There may be . . ." is not a subject! Identifying the appropriate

---

2. This guideline is discussed more in Chapter 9.

subject is an important step in moving from informal expression of a rule, where the context is obvious, to more formal expression.

Revised rule: *A booth must not be occupied by a party of one between 9 A.M. and 1 P.M.*

This step often leads to additional insights about the true meaning or implications of a rule. For example, since *zero* number of people is probably an acceptable (and necessary) clarification for the original rule, the revised rule introduces the term *party*.

Careful about Actors as Subjects

Proposed rule: *A customer may make a withdrawal only if his or her account is active.*

Acceptable? Probably not.

Discussion: Only customers? What about preauthorized third parties? What about the bank itself? What about other actors?

Carefully examine any rule that indicates an actor as a subject. Does the rule really pertain only to that actor? Often, the answer is no. If not, substitute a nonactor subject; for example, in the revised rule below, *withdrawal* is substituted for *customer*. Be careful not to confuse rules, which express constraints or guidance for behavior, with workflows or procedures, which indicate what actors actually do.

Revised rule: *A withdrawal from an account may be made only if the account is active.*

No Commands

Proposed rule: *Don't ship orders if the outstanding balance of the order exceeds the customer's credit authorization.*

Acceptable? No.

Discussion: What is the subject of this rule? The implied subject is *you*. *You* represents an actor—a very vague one at that!

The command form of rules is common in communication between actors. In general, commands suffice as long as the actors share the same context. For rules, however, communication contexts can never be taken for granted.

Rules must establish their own contexts—that is, their expression should communicate universally to all actors within the scope of the business problem.

Again, the crucial step is to ask what term is the appropriate subject for the rule. This question might result in the following revision of the rule above.

Revised rule: *An order must not be shipped if the outstanding balance of the order exceeds the customer's credit authorization.*

No CRUD

Proposed rule: *Update product cost when the cost of any component changes.*

Acceptable? No.

Discussion: The implied subject of this command is again *you*. In this case, however, the command verb *update* represents a system event. Is the implied *you* the system? If not, then who?

System events should never be used as the subjects for rules. (*CRUD* stands for *create, retrieve, update, delete*—all system events.) As before, the crucial step is to ask what term is the appropriate subject for the rule. For computation rules such as the one above, a term representing the result of the computation should be indicated as the subject, as in the following revision.

Revised rule: *A product's cost must be computed as the sum of the cost of all its components.*

Another problem with referencing an event as the subject of a rule is that most rules need to be tested during *more* than one event.[3] If a particular event is referenced as the subject of a rule, the other events might be missed in interpreting or enforcing that rule. In the original rule statement above, for example, the additional events *when a component is added to a product* and *when a component is removed from a product* are probably also relevant since they too can affect a product's cost. The revised rule covers these other events as well.

Careful about Events as Subjects

Proposed rule: *When an order is created, it must have a promised shipment date.*

Acceptable? Could be better.

---

3. This topic is discussed in Chapter 6.

Discussion: *When* always indicates an event. As discussed above, rules are usually not specific to a single event. Should not an order continue to have a promised shipment date? Would it be appropriate just after an order is created to delete the promised shipment date? This rule is almost certainly not specific to the event indicated by *when*. Therefore, the reference to the event should be removed from the rule. This removal actually results in a simpler statement, as follows.

Revised rule: *An order must have a promised shipment date.*

Stating a rule in an *event-less* fashion is an important step in ensuring consistent and complete enforcement across all relevant events. The rule above is a very simple one. For most rules, the other relevant events will be less obvious—and more numerous!

Careful to Qualify

Proposed rule: *A project team member should not be rotated off the project until finished.*

Acceptable? Could be better.

Discussion: To what does the qualification *until finished* apply? The project team member is finished? The project is finished? Be careful about the placement of a qualification relative to the term it logically qualifies. Make that term explicit as needed to avoid ambiguity.

Revised rule: *A project team member should not be rotated off the project until the project is finished.*

Be especially careful about time-based qualifications. To avoid ambiguity, include an explicit reference to the event being qualified as needed. The example below further illustrates this point. An event referenced in this fashion should not, of course, be indicated as the subject of the rule.

Proposed rule: *A purchase order must be approved by at least two managers during a snowstorm.*

Acceptable? Could be better.

Revised rule: *A purchase order taken during a snowstorm must be approved by at least two managers.*

Careful to Extract Embedded Computations

Proposed rule: *The sum of all payment amounts applied to an order must be greater than or equal to the amount due for the order.*

Acceptable? Could be better.

Discussion: This rule includes both a computation and a constraint on the result of that computation. Extracting the computation is highly desirable for the following reasons.

- It enhances *clarity*.
- It allows the two resulting rules to be validated and changed *independently* of each other.
- It permits *reuse* of the computation logic by other rules. These other rules can simply reference the result of the computation by name, ensuring logical consistency across all the rules.
- It *isolates* the logic of the computation to a single rule, no matter how many times this logic is reused by other rules. This segregation facilitates change.

The computation embedded in the rule above should therefore be expressed as a separate rule. The subject of this rule should be the result of the computation. The original constraint on that result (*must be greater than or equal to*) should be expressed as a second rule. These revisions are illustrated below.

Extracted computation rule: *The amount paid for an order must be computed as the sum of all payment amounts applied to the order.*

Revised rule: *The amount paid for an order must be greater than or equal to the amount due for the order.*

Careful to Isolate Your Logic

Proposed rule: *A customer whose outstanding balance exceeds $1,000 on each of his or her last three successive invoices must not place an order for an item whose cost exceeds $500.*

Acceptable? Could be better.

Discussion: The specific conditions found in a rule can often be named. Sometimes a standard or common-use name already exists in the business. Such conditions should be broken out as separate rules and then the names of the conditions substituted for the conditions in the original rule. This has several important advantages paralleling those resulting from extracted computations.

- It leaves the original rule simpler, thus enhancing *clarity.*
- It allows the two or more resulting rules to be validated and changed *independently* of each other.
- It permits *reuse* of the condition's logic by other rules. These other rules can simply reference the name of the condition, as appropriate. The result is a higher degree of logical consistency across the rules.
- It *isolates* the logic of the condition to a single rule, no matter how many times this logic is reused by other rules. This segregation facilitates change.

The significant conditions in the rule above should be expressed as separate rules. The subjects of these rules should be the names of the conditions. The constraint from the original rule (*must not place*) should be expressed as yet another rule. These revisions are illustrated on the next page.

Extracted rule: *High-risk customer means the outstanding balance exceeds $1,000 on each of the customer's last three successive invoices.*

Extracted rule: *Big-ticket item means the item's cost exceeds $500.*

Revised rule: *A high-risk customer must not place an order for a big-ticket item.*

And No Etc.

Proposed rule: *A territory must not include any noncandidate traditional gas station if it includes any ultra-service or food outlet; must not include any ultra-service if it includes any noncandidate traditional gas station or food outlet; etc.*

Acceptable? No.

Discussion: Including *etc.* or similar indefinite words (for example, *vice versa*) in rules invites misinterpretation. Often, as illustrated below, a much simpler way can be found to express the rule.

Revised rule: *A territory must not include more than one of the following:*

- *Noncandidate traditional gas station*
- *Ultra-service*
- *Food outlet*

The Lighter Side of Rules[4]

Try This On . . .

Notice: This garment meets the general wearing apparel requirements of the Flammable Fabrics Act; however, it is flammable and should not be worn near sources of fire.

> —Tag on an item of apparel from a Massachusetts clothing outlet

User-Friendly Rule . . .

Visitor should be not ironed—cooked—washed.

> —Guest rule posted in a Vietnamese hotel

---

4. Editor's note: This material was forwarded to the author via e-mail. Original source unknown.

About Those Really Exclusive Clubs . . .
Members and non-members only.
—Sign posted at a discotheque entrance

Give Me a Break . . .
Gasoline must not be sold to anyone in a glass container.
—Sign at a Santa Fe gas station

Unhelpful Hint . . .
Exit access is that part of a means of egress that leads to an entrance to an exit.
—Government fire-prevention pamphlet for homes for the elderly

Strange Labor Rule . . .
No children allowed.
—Sign posted at the entrance to a Florida hospital's maternity ward

Beat the Heat . . .
River inhabited by crocodiles. Swimming prohibited. Survivors will be prosecuted.
—Sign posted on the Ramganga River,
Corbett National Park, Uttar Pradesh, India

Better Left Unsaid . . .
Bags should be used in case of sickness or to gather remains.
—Instruction on a Spanish airline's air sickness bag

Continued

Say Again . . .
Members of the immediate family of an authorized exchange patron who are
not otherwise authorized admission to AAFES-Eur facilities in the company of
the authorized patron except for those members of the immediate family who
reside in the country where the AAFES-Eur facilities are located.

—U.S. Air Force regulation

On Being in Two Places at Once . . .
No refreshments shall be supplied to any member after the above-named
hours, and none shall be supplied for consumption off the club premises except to a member on the premises at the time.

—Bylaw in a private social club rule book

Ask about Pants . . .
No shirt, no shoes, no service.

—Sign posted on the wall of a beach restaurant

A Definition to Remember . . .
For purposes of paragraph (3), an organization described in paragraph (2)
shall be deemed to include an organization described in section 501 (c) (4), (5)
or (6) which would be described in paragraph (2) if it were an organization described in section 501 (c) (3).

—The Internal Revenue Service

CHAPTER 9

Developing Rule Statements

The Basics of BRS RuleSpeak

About the Rule Sentence Templates

A rule sentence template is a basic sentence structure or pattern in English[1] that can be used to express a rule in a consistent, well-organized manner. Each RuleSpeak template is aimed toward a particular kind of rule based on its functional category. These categories are discussed in Chapter 10. The actual rule sentence templates are presented in Chapter 11.

   The purpose of the templates is to ensure that written rules are more readily understood. The templates also help ensure that different practitioners working on a large set of rules express the same ideas in the same way. Such consistency would not result if rules were expressed in a free-form manner.

   The templates are not technical in nature. In other words, they do not represent a formal language for implementing rules at the system level (for example, in business logic technology[2]). Rather, they are aimed toward improving communication at the *business* level.

---

1. Templates could be offered for other languages (for example, French, Mandarin, and so on); however, this discussion addresses only English.
2. By *business logic technology,* I mean *rule engines, decision management platforms, business logic servers,* and so on.

They also address a key challenge in rule management—tracing changes to rules to and from the business side.

Using the templates to express rules requires a measure of discipline. This discipline can be achieved through a modest amount of practice and through an understanding of certain fundamentals about rules discussed in this chapter. Such discipline will not constrain creative development of rules but rather will enhance it greatly.

Success Factors in Using the Templates

What is important—and what is *not* important—when you apply the Rule-Speak templates? Obviously what is *not* important is how you will actually implement the rules using a particular programming language or business logic technology. Appreciating this distinction can be difficult for those responsible for actually implementing the rules. They often tend to want to go too deep too soon. This tendency often works against analysis and management of the rules from the business perspective.

It is also important to understand the level of rules to which the templates should be applied. The templates are not aimed at the automated level of rules. They are also not aimed at the highest level of governing rules (that is, the language of laws, regulations, contracts, policies, and so on). Rather, the templates are aimed at *operating rules*. Refer to the boxed item, The Levels of Rules, for the important distinctions between these three levels of rules.

The Levels of Rules

In the broadest sense, rules fall into one of three levels with respect to the purpose and style of their expression, as described below. RuleSpeak is aimed at expressing the intermediate level, operating rules. This is the critical transformation stage between governing rules as handed down from the business side and rules suitable for implementation in technology platforms (that is, automated rules).

Governing rule: Examples of governing rules include legal statements (for example, laws, acts, statutes, and so on), formal regulations, binding agreements (for example, contractual obligations), higher-level business policies or directives, and so on. Governing rules are often aimed at guiding or constraining the business, regulating its interactions with external parties, and/or limiting its exposure to risks or threats. Governing rules often must be interpreted into one or more operating rules to be applied in an actual business process or used for system design.

Operating rule: An operating rule is a declarative statement in well-structured business English, suitable for direct application to a business process and for consideration in a system design. An operating rule should be unambiguous and stated in a manner directly relevant to the internal workings of the business. Operating rules can be derived or interpreted from governing rules or sometimes reverse-engineered from automated rules.

Automated rule: An automated rule is a specific rule of the business, stated in a form recognizable by business logic technology, a programming language, an application generator, or similar technology. An automated rule is the implementation counterpart to an operating rule.

Operating rules guide and control the business on a day-to-day basis. Often, operating rules must be interpreted from governing rules in order to clarify them, remove ambiguities, and achieve the right perspective for the business area to which they apply. The templates facilitate such interpretation by providing predictable formats of expression. This is also true, by the way, if operating rules are being harvested bottom-up from existing implementations or documentation or captured on a facilitated basis from business-side workers.

Fundamental Concepts

Understanding several fundamental ideas about rules will greatly help you express rules effectively. These fundamental ideas are briefly discussed below.

Every Rule Has a Functional Category

The functional category of a rule reflects how the rule reacts to events. These categories, which are presented in Chapter 10, are intrinsic, definitive, and nonoverlapping. For that reason, they provide a sound foundation for a comprehensive set of sentence patterns. The RuleSpeak templates presented in Chapter 11 directly reflect these categories.

Every Rule Should Have a Subject

In good English construction, every sentence has a subject. Although this subject might be implied or the sentence inverted, more often than not an explicit subject appears as the first word or phrase in the main body of the sentence. Such sentences are usually direct and, if well written, easy to follow.

RuleSpeak strongly encourages you to place an explicit subject at the very beginning of each rule statement. Such a lead-in subject is desirable for rules in every functional category. This approach promotes overall clarity and consistency.

Some rule languages—often at the level of business logic technology or programming languages—feature *If . . . then . . .* syntax. In such languages, the true subject does not appear until the *then* clause.

We find that the *If . . . then . . .* syntax proves unfriendly for many kinds of rules.[3] The best construction for computation rules, for example, is always to put the result of the computation (the subject) as the very first thing in the sentence. By this means, what the rule computes is clear from the start. The *If . . . then . . .* syntax is also often unnatural for basic kinds of validation rules.[4] For example, it is much more natural simply to say *Customer must have an address* than *If customer exists, then customer must have an address.*

Every Rule Should Use a Rule Word

Every rule can be stated by using one of the following keywords. These keywords are called the *rule words*. It is very important that every rule statement includes one.

- *Must* (or *should*), including *must not* (or *should not*)
- *Only*, often as in *only if*

Every Rejector Has a Flip Side

Every validation rule[5] has a flip side—that is, circumstances to which the rule does *not* apply. Any statement that identifies such circumstances is called a

---

3. Refer to Part V, Appendix D for more discussion.
4. I really mean *rejectors* here.
5. Again, I mean *rejector* here.

permission statement. Such a statement indicates that workers are not constrained by any rule in that situation and, therefore, are free to exercise judgement or discretion in taking relevant actions.

Permission statements should be recorded if they represent an important clarification of policy or if they represent resolution of some particularly difficult business issue. Whenever recorded, they should, of course, be stated in a fashion consistent with rules. Here is an example.

> **Rule:** *Orders on credit over $1,000 must not be accepted without a credit check.*

> **Permission statement:** *Orders on credit $1,000 or under may be accepted without a credit check.*

> **Comment:** Note how the permission statement addresses the reverse of the condition (over $1,000) included in the rule. Note also that the permission statement does not include a rule word.

Also worth noting is that a permission statement can sometimes essentially represent an exception to some other rule and therefore can actually appear to be a rule itself. For example, suppose the original rule above had omitted the qualification *over $1,000.* Then the permission statement would represent an exception and therefore should be viewed as a rule.

This is another reason it can be useful to record permission statements, especially during the early phases of rule capture when the rules are not likely to be stated so precisely. (*Precisely* here means considering all possible conditions—for example, *over $1,000.*)

Every Permission Statement Should Use a Permission Word

Just as there are special rule words for rules, there are also special permission words for permission statements, as follows.

- *May*
- *Need not*

Any permission statement can be expressed using one of these forms. Several examples follow.

> **Permission statement:** *An account may be held by a person of any age.*

> **Permission statement:** *An employee need not be a manager.*

> **Permission statement:** *A customer need not place any orders.*

Any Rule Can Be Qualified

Any rule can include a qualification (that is, a condition) indicating the circumstances under which the rule should be enforced. Such qualification should start with either the word *if* or *when*, as appropriate.[6] Here is an example.

> **Rule:** *A shipment must be insured if the shipment value is greater than $500.*

The word *if* should be used if the qualification is continuous over time. The word *when* should be used only if the rule is to be enforced at a particular point in time, as shown below.

> **Rule:** *A student's semester-fees-owed must be set to $3,065 when the student registers for a semester.*
>
> **Comment:** This rule will be enforced only at the point in time when the student registers for a semester. At any other time, the rule will not be enforced—that is, the value of the student's semester-fees-owed need not be $3,065.

An *if* clause should not be used in a rule if some term exists that refers to the condition and this term can be used as the subject of the rule. An example illustrates.

> **Rule:** *An employee must not have an employment counselor if the employee is retired.*
>
> **Revised rule:** *A retired employee must not have an employment counselor.*
>
> **Comment:** The *if* clause has been eliminated in the revised rule, which uses the qualified term *retired employee* as its subject. The resulting expression is more compact and readable.

Any Rule Can Include a Time Bracket

You can indicate a time bracket as qualification for a rule by using one of the following time words.

---

6. We prefer that the *if* or *when* be set off by a comma, to clearly indicate the start of the qualification. Here is an example: *A shipment must be insured, if the shipment value is greater than $500.* However, this is a relatively minor point, and since shorter rules generally read better without it, we do not usually insist on it.

- *Before* (date/time)
- *On or before* (date/time)
- *During* (named date/time . . . for example, summertime)
- *By* (date/time)
- *After* (date/time)

Some examples appear below.

Rule: *A student must not live off-campus before his or her junior year.*

Rule: *A student must not join clubs on or before the close of registration.*

Rule: *A student must live on-campus during summertime.*

Rule: *A student must be enrolled in at least two courses by the close of registration.*

Rule: *A student must be enrolled in at least two courses after the close of registration.*

Any Rule Can Reference a Value

For clarity, specific values included in a rule can be enclosed in single quote marks. Here is an example.

Rule: *Normal-tax-return-due-date must be set to 'April 15.'*

Comment: This rule references the value *April 15.*

Basic Usage Notes

Based on experience, we have found that certain conventions work better than others for expressing rules. The related issues are discussed below. These usage notes help explain the particular wording for rules you will see in the RuleSpeak templates in Chapter 11.

Using *Shall*

Some organizations prefer using the word *shall* in place of the word *must*. This is basically a cosmetic choice. However, we prefer the word *must* since we find it generally more appropriate for the operating-rule level.

Using *Should*

Any rule can be stated by using *should* instead of *must*. This choice reflects an assumption or decision about the enforcement level of the rule. Generally, *should* suggests the sense of "enforce or do *if possible*," whereas *must* has the sense that there is no choice about whether enforcement will occur. We generally use whichever word conveys the best sense for the rule as currently understood. Although *should* is not illustrated explicitly in the templates, its usage is always optional.

Using *May*

Unfortunately, the word *may* can be used in English in several different ways. The resulting ambiguity is particularly troublesome for expressing rules. Consider the following examples.

1. *A volunteer organization may not make a profit.*
   In everyday conversation, *may* often conveys the sense of *might*. Is the sentence above simply an observation ("A volunteer organization *might* not make a profit"), or is it a legitimate rule ("A volunteer organization *must* not make a profit")? Especially taken out of context, the sentence is ambiguous.
2. *A plane may take off only if given clearance by air traffic control.*
   The second sense of *may* is that of permission being granted or denied. Such use of *may* for expressing rules is a valid and often necessary one.
3. *A car may be started only if the car is not in gear.*
   Here *may* is probably being used incorrectly. Rather than expressing a rule that grants or denies permission (for example, to the driver), the sentence actually simply describes a fundamental characteristic or capability of a car. Since *capacity* is at issue, the word *can* should be used instead. The sentence above should therefore be rewritten as *A car can be started only if the car is not in gear.* This sentence does not express a rule.

To summarize, to express rules we never use *may* in the first or the third sense above. That is, we never use *may* to mean either *might* (that is, that something might occur or be true) or *can* (that is, that some capacity does or does not exist). The only valid use we recognize for *may* is in the second sense above—that is, where permission is being granted or denied. We deem this sense the correct one for rules.

Using *No*

The word *no* in conjunction with *must* can produce awkward rule statements. This occurs when the rule expresses an upper limit. An example illustrates.

> **Rule:** *An adjudicator must be assigned to assess no more than 15 claims.*

> **Comment:** The structure of this rule statement is unnecessarily awkward. The rule starts off with *must*, as if the adjudicator will be obligated either to have something or to do something. The *no* reverses that sense by indicating a limit (*no more than 15 claims*) that the adjudicator must not exceed. The rule can be made clearer by using *must not* rather than *must . . . no*, as the following revision illustrates.

> **Revised rule:** *An adjudicator must not be assigned to assess more than 15 claims.*

> **Comment:** The structure of this rule statement is better. The rule starts off with *must not*, which is reinforced, rather than contradicted, by the upper limit (*more than 15 claims*).

In general, the word *no* should always be avoided if possible in expressing rules. This guideline is also true where *no* is used in the sense of *zero*. Here is an example.

> **Rule:** *A team assigned to a high-security project must include no trainees.*

> **Revised rule:** *A team assigned to a high-security project must not include any trainees.*

> **Comment:** Note the use of *not . . . any* to replace *no* in the original version.

Using *Not . . . Not*

Double negatives, especially using two *nots*, often makes a rule's logic unnecessarily difficult. The *nots* can generally be eliminated by restating the rule in a more positive form, producing a version that is easier to interpret. An example illustrates.

> **Rule:** *A withdrawal from an account must not be made if the account is not active.*

Revised rule: *A withdrawal from an account may be made only if the account is active.*

Comment: Note the use of *may . . . only if* to replace the *not . . . if . . . not* phrase in the original version.

Do Double Dos Make a Not?[7]

A linguistics professor was lecturing to his class one day. "In English," he said, "a double negative forms a positive. In some languages though, such as Russian, a double negative is still a negative. However," he pointed out, "there is no language wherein a double positive can form a negative."

A voice from the back of the room piped up, "Yeah. Right."

Using *Or* and *And*

In complicated rules, mixed series of *ors* and *ands* can easily produce confusion and misinterpretation. (Strict series of only *ands* or only *ors* raise an additional question, which is discussed later in this chapter.) Embedded parentheses can be used to clarify the intended logic; however, the resulting expressions often remain difficult for business-side workers to follow.

To alleviate this difficulty, we recommend eliminating the *ors* and *ands* in favor of bulleted lists of conditions. To introduce any such list of bulleted conditions, use one of the following two phrases.

1. For *or*, use *At least one of the following is true.*
2. For *and*, use *All of the following are true.*

These phrases and lists of bulleted conditions can be nested (with appropriate indentation) as required.

Rule: *A credit check must be performed for a customer if all of the following are true:*

---

7. Editor's note: This material was forwarded to the author via e-mail. Original source unknown.

- *A credit check has not been performed for that customer in the last 6 months.*
- *The customer places an order for which any of the following is true:*
  - *The order total is more than $500.*
  - *The outstanding balance of the customer's account plus the order amount is more than $600.*
  - *The account designated for the order is not older than 30 days.*
- *A waiver has not been authorized.*

Comment: This rule has been specified without *ors* and *ands* by using lists of appropriately indented, bulleted conditions. To introduce lists of bulleted conditions, the phrases *at least one of the following is true* and *all of the following are true* have been used as appropriate.

Several related observations should be made. We recommend avoiding the words *both* and *either* for lists of only two bulleted conditions because if additional bullets are added in the future to such a list, the sense of *both* or *either* will no longer apply. Two examples illustrate this.

Rule: *An order may be accepted only if both of the following are true:*
- *A delivery address is given.*
- *The customer's credit is good.*

Comment: It is very likely that additional conditions will be added to the bulleted list of conditions specifying whether an order should be accepted. Therefore, we recommend replacing *both* with *all*, as shown below.

Revised rule: *An order may be accepted only if all of the following are true:*
- *It includes at least one item.*
- *It indicates the customer who is placing it.*

Rule: *An order may be shipped only if either of the following is true:*
- *Payment for the order has been received.*
- *The customer's credit is good.*

Comment: It is possible that some additional condition(s) (for example, *A valid credit card number is given*) will be added to the bulleted list of conditions specifying whether an order may be shipped. Therefore, we recommend replacing *either* with *at least one*, as shown on the next page.

Revised rule: *An order may be shipped only if at least one of the following is true:*

- *Payment for the order has been received.*
- *The customer's credit is good.*

More on the Lighter Side of Rules[8]

In a laundromat: Automatic washing machines. Please remove all your clothes when the light goes out.

In an office: After the tea break, staff should empty the teapot and stand upside down on the draining board.

On a church door: This is the gate of heaven. Enter ye all by this door. (This door is kept locked because of the draft. Please use side entrance.)

In a safari park: Elephants Please Stay in Your Car

On a repair shop door: We can repair anything. (Please knock hard on the door—the bell doesn't work.)

In a London loo: Toilet out of order. Please use the floor below.

On a hair dryer: Do not use while sleeping.

On a frozen TV dinner: Serving Suggestion . . . Defrost

On the bottom of a dessert box: Do not turn upside down.

In the instructions for an iron: Do not iron clothes on body.

On a children's cough medicine: Do not drive car or operate heavy machinery.

On a Korean kitchen knife: Warning. . . . Keep out of children.

On a Japanese food processor: Not to be used for the other use.

On an airline snack pack of nuts: Open packet, eat nuts.

On a Swedish chainsaw: Do not attempt to stop chain with your hands.

---

8. Editor's note: This material was forwarded to the author via e-mail. Original sources unknown.

Special Usage Notes

Using Rule Types in RuleSpeak

Rule types are names for specific kinds of rules based on the nature of the test they perform. Common examples include the following.[9]

- Mandatory
- Mutually exclusive, mutually inclusive, mutually prohibited, and so on
- Unique
- Ascending, descending
- Frozen

Use of such rule types in rule statements is optional. Whenever such a rule type is used in a rule, it has a very specific effect on the structure of the rule statement—namely, the subject and object(s) of the sentence get switched around, as illustrated below.

Rule that does not include a rule type: *An employee must have an employee-name.*

Rule that includes a rule type: *Employee-name is mandatory for an employee.*

---

9. Refer to Chapter 18 for additional discussion.

Comment: Note how the subject and object get switched around from the original version of the rule when the rule type *mandatory* is added into the sentence.

Because a rule statement can have multiple objects, the surrogate words *the following* can be used as the subject of the sentence in which a rule type appears. This indicates that a list of relevant items and conditions will subsequently appear in the rule. Several examples illustrate.

Rule: *The following are mandatory for an employee:*
- *Employee-name*
- *Employee-SSN*
- *Employee-address*
- *Employee-hire-date*
- *Employee-salary*

Rule: *The following are mutually exclusive for an order:*
- *Requested-pick-up-date-time*
- *Promised-delivery-date-time*

Rule: *The following must be frozen for a closed order:*
- *Which customer placed the order*
- *All line items of the order*
- *Order-total-amount*

Using *A, Some,* and *Each*

Use of the word *a* (or *an*) in a rule statement is imprecise with respect to quantification[10]—that is, whether *at least one* or *all* is intended. This problem can be corrected by disallowing the word *a* (or *an*) altogether, and substituting the word *some* if *at least one* is meant, and the word *each* if *all* is meant. The discussion and examples below explain.

We leave to the practitioner to decide whether this usage guideline should be followed in expressing rules. The improved clarity that results from using *some* and *each* in rules is significant. On the other hand, *a* and *an*

---

10. I use the word *quantification* deliberately here. Predicate calculus (refer to Part V) offers two quantifiers, EXISTS (the *existential quantifier*) and FORALL (the *universal quantifier*), which correspond very closely to the cases of *at least one* or *some,* and *all* or *each,* respectively, as discussed here.

are very natural in English. Disallowing them can be counterproductive, especially during start-up activity. For that reason, we elected not to eliminate them in all the examples included in this text.

Rule: *A service representative must be assigned to a high-volume customer.*

Comment: The second *a* in this rule almost certainly is not intended to indicate at least one high-volume customer but rather all high-volume customers. Therefore, substituting *each* for this *a* would be appropriate. On the other hand, the first *a* probably does not mean *all* (that is, that all service representatives must be assigned to each high-volume customer). Therefore, substituting *some* for this *a* would be appropriate. The revised rule appears next.

Revised rule: *Some service representative must be assigned to each high-volume customer.*

To test this revision, let's restate the rule with the subject and object of the sentence reversed, again using *some* and *each* as appropriate. The reversed rule is as follows.

Reversed rule: *Each high-volume customer must be represented by some service representative.*

Comment: This reversed version of the rule expresses the same intention as the rule above.

Which of the two latter versions of the rule is preferred? In general, we prefer a subject that can be qualified by *each* rather than *some*. This way the rule statement starts off with clearer intention—that is, the rule indicates up front that it applies to each and every instance of the subject of the sentence.

It should be noted, however, that there are circumstances in which this guideline cannot be followed, as the following, less restricted version of the rule illustrates.

Rule: *Some high-volume customer must be represented by some service representative.*

Comment: This rule (a bit strange) is satisfied if at least one high-volume customer (not all) is represented by at least one service representative (again, not all).

It should also be noted that *each* can appear more than once in the rule, as illustrated by the following revised version.

Revised rule: *Each high-volume customer must be represented by each service representative.*

Comment: This rule (again, a bit strange) is satisfied only if all high-volume customers (not just one) are represented by all service representatives (again, not just one).

Using Strictly ANDed and ORed Conditions

A rule can include a direct list of bulleted conditions that are strictly ANDed. By *direct* I mean that the list is not subjected to an *if* clause. By *strictly ANDed* I mean that the list contains no *ors* at the same level of logic as the *ands*. Such a rule can be broken into an appropriate number of separate rules, each addressing only one of the original conditions.[11] The resulting rules are more atomic but usually *not* better for business-side communication and validation. The following example illustrates this kind of rule.

Rule: *A claim must indicate all of the following:*
- *The active policy that covers it*
- *The claimant*
- *The health care provided*
- *The health care provider providing the health care*
- *The injury/illness*
- *The initial date of the injury/illness*

Comment: This rule has a directly ANDed list of six bulleted[12] conditions. The rule can be broken into six individual rules, as follows.[13] Nonetheless, we prefer the original consolidated version above for communication and validation.

---

11. This reduction to atomic form is permitted under an assumption in rule theory that is sometimes called the *universal and*. This assumption simply means that since all rules must be satisfied, an implicit *and* must therefore be considered to exist for all rules within scope (or more formally, within the *universe of discourse*).

12. Rather than bullets, it might be desirable to provide item identifiers (for example, a, b, c, and so on) in case exception-type rules need to be expressed that are selective with respect to individual items.

13. In formal rule theory, the implicit *ands* would appear for the *right-hand expression* of the rule. (Refer to Chapter 16.) Such rules can always be reduced to individual rules, as illustrated by this example.

Rule 1: *A claim must indicate the active policy that covers it.*

Rule 2: *A claim must indicate the claimant.*

Rule 3: *A claim must indicate the health care provided.*

Rule 4: *A claim must indicate the health care provider providing the health care.*

Rule 5: *A claim must indicate the injury/illness.*

Rule 6: *A claim must indicate the initial date of the injury/illness.*

A rule can also include a list of bulleted conditions subjected to an *if* that are strictly ORed. By *strictly ORed* I mean that the list contains no *ands* at the same level of logic as the *ors*. Such a rule can also be broken into an appropriate number of separate rules, each addressing only one of the original conditions. The resulting rules are more atomic but, again, usually *not* better for business-side communication and validation. Here is an example.

Rule: *An order must be credit-checked if any of the following is true:*
- *The order total is more than $500.*
- *The outstanding balance of the customer's account plus the order amount is more than $600.*
- *The customer's account is not older than 30 days.*
- *The customer's account is inactive.*
- *The customer is out-of-state.*

Comment: This rule has an implicitly ORed list of five bulleted conditions subjected to an *if*. The rule can be broken into the following five individual rules, as follows.[14] Nonetheless, we prefer the original consolidated version above for communication and validation.

Rule 1: *An order must be credit-checked if the order total is more than $500.*

Rule 2: *An order must be credit-checked if the outstanding balance of the customer's account plus the order amount is more than $600.*

Rule 3: *An order must be credit-checked if the customer's account is not older than 30 days.*

---

14. In formal rule theory, the implicit *ors* would appear for the *left-hand expression* of the rule. (Refer to Chapter 16.) Such rules can always be reduced to individual rules as illustrated by this example.

Rule 4: *An order must be credit-checked if the customer's account is inactive.*

Rule 5: *An order must be credit-checked if the customer is out-of-state.*

Here You Have It . . .

The subject of a sentence and the principal verb should not, as a rule, be separated by a phrase or clause that can be transferred to the beginning.

—A line in the famous writing manual *The Elements of Style*[15]

---

15. Strunk, William, Jr., and E. B. White. 1979. *The Elements of Style,* 3rd ed. New York: MacMillan, p. 29.

CHAPTER 10

Functional Categories of Rules

The BRS Rule Classification Scheme

The BRS Rule Classification Scheme reflects how rules react to events. A given rule can react in one of only three possible ways to an event—hence there are three fundamental categories of rules in the scheme.

These three categories, which are defined in Table 10–1, are *rejectors*, *producers*, and *projectors*. Because these three categories are intrinsic, definitive, and mutually exclusive, they provide a sound foundation for the comprehensive set of rule sentence templates in RuleSpeak. They also have well-defined subcategories, as the table also indicates. These subcategories provide an even richer basis for organizing the templates—as well as for gaining a better understanding of your company's rules.

Table 10–1 The BRS Rule Classification Scheme

Functional Category/ Subcategory	Common Name	Definition
1.0. Rejector	Constraint[a]	Any rule that tends to disallow (that is, reject) an event if a violation of the rule would result. Rejectors shield the business from incorrect data (or incorrect state)—that is, from information that violates business rules. For example, a rejector might be specified to prevent a customer from placing an order on credit if the customer has a poor payment history.
2.0. Producer	—	Any rule that neither rejects nor projects events but simply computes or derives a value based on some mathematical function(s).
2.1. Computation rule	—	Any producer-type rule that computes a value following standard *arithmetic* operations (for example, sum, multiply, average, and so on) specified explicitly. A computation rule provides a precise formula for how a computed term is to be calculated. For example, a computation rule might be given to compute a customers' annual order volume.
2.2. Derivation rule	—	Any producer-type rule that derives a truth value (that is, true or false) based on *logical* operations (for example, AND, OR, NOT, EQUAL TO, and so on) specified explicitly. A derivation rule provides a precise definition for a derived term— that is, a truth-valued term whose value (true or false) is always established by the specified logical operations. For example, a derivation rule might be given to indicate whether a project is at risk depending on whether the project is over budget or understaffed.
3.0. Projector	Stimulus/ response rule	Any rule that tends to take some action (other than rejection) when a relevant event occurs. A projector never rejects events (as rejectors do); rather, it *projects* them—that is, causes some new event(s) to occur as a result. Projectors generally prescribe automatic system behavior, providing a productivity boost for workers. For example, a projector might be specified to reorder stock automatically if the quantity on hand drops below a certain point.
3.1. Enabler	Toggle	A projector that toggles something on or off.
3.1.1. Inference rule	—	An enabler that infers something to be true under appropriate circumstances. For example, an inference rule might be given to indicate that a person must be considered a woman if criteria for that person's age and gender are satisfied.

a. In formal rule theory, certain kinds of projectors (especially inference rules) are also considered to be constraints, so this common name can be misleading.

3.1.2. Rule toggle	Exception-type rule	An enabler that turns another rule on or off under appropriate circumstances—that is, makes it capable or incapable of firing. For example, a rule toggle might be given to indicate that some normal operating rule is to be suspended under emergency circumstances.
3.1.3. Process toggle	—	An enabler that turns an operation, process, or procedure on or off under appropriate circumstances—that is, makes it capable or incapable of executing. For example, a process toggle might be given to indicate that a sensitive process cannot be executed while a security breach is suspected.
3.1.4. Data toggle	—	An enabler that creates or deletes instances of actual data under appropriate circumstances. For example, a data toggle might be given to indicate that a juvenile's criminal record must be erased when he or she reaches 18 years of age.
3.2. Copier	—	A projector that replicates (copies) actual values.
3.2.1. Imprint rule	—	A copier that sets the value of something that persists (for example, something in a database). For example, an imprint rule might be used to initialize the tuition owed by a student in a given semester to the base tuition for that semester when the student enrolls.
3.2.2. Presentation rule	—	A copier that establishes a value or parameter related to how data is to be presented (for example, on a screen, in a report, and so on). For example, a presentation rule might be given to indicate that an order is to be displayed on the screen in red if the order is overdue.
3.3. Executive	Trigger	A projector that causes an operation, process, or procedure to execute or a rule to fire.
3.3.1. Process trigger	—	A projector that causes an operation, process, or procedure to execute. For example, when an order is shipped, a process trigger might be given to execute a process that automatically sends the intended recipient a notification.
3.3.2. Rule trigger	—	A projector that causes a rule to fire. For example, when data about a shipment is displayed to the screen, a rule trigger might be given that fires another rule to predict the shipment's arrival date.

CHAPTER 11

Sentence Patterns for Rule Statements

The RuleSpeak Templates[1]

The BRS RuleSpeak sentence templates are presented below, with examples and comments. These templates are organized according to the functional categories defined in Chapter 10. Shorthand forms are suggested where appropriate. The entire set is summarized in Table 11–1 at the end of this chapter.

1.0. RuleSpeak Templates for Rejectors

A rejector is a rule that tends to disallow (that is, reject) an event if a violation of the rule would result.

1.1. "Must" Template

The most basic template is for rules that involve a *must* condition.

Examples:

Rule: *A shipment must have a status.*

Rule: *An order must indicate the customer that places it.*

Rule: *A purchase order taken during a snowstorm must be approved by at least two managers.*

---

1. Version 6.

1.2. "Must Not" Template

Rules expressed by using the must rule word can also involve conditions that are not permitted.

Examples:

Rule: *A freshman must not participate in any honors club.*

Rule: *A retired employee must not have an employment counselor.*

Rule: *The number of seats for a course section must not exceed 30.*

Rule: *An order must not be shipped if the outstanding balance of the customer's account exceeds the customer's credit authorization.*

Rule: *An order must not contain more than 99 line items.*

Rule: *A territory must not include more than one of the following:*

- *Noncandidate traditional gas station*
- *Ultra-service*
- *Food outlet*

1.3. "May . . . Only If" Template

Use of the word *may* rather than *must* is appropriate when the rule word *only* is used to express a rule. The *only* condition indicates the specific circumstances under which permission is granted.

Examples:

Rule: *A customer may purchase a pesticide from a supplier only if the supplier actually sells that pesticide.*

Rule: *A customer may place an order only if the customer holds an account.*

Rule: *A withdrawal from an account may be made only if the account is active.*

1.4. "May . . . Only [Preposition]" Template

Rules using the rule word *only* can be expressed without the additional word *if* when a preposition[2] immediately follows the word *only*.

---

2. Generally, these prepositions are actually included in the fact statements that underlie the rules. For example, the fact underlying the rule *A salaried employee may work only in a budgeted department* should include the preposition *in* (that is, *Employee works in department*).

Examples:

Rule: *A salaried employee may work only in a budgeted department.*

Rule: *A rush order may be approved only by a supervisor.*

Rule: *An account may be opened only on a workday.*

Rule: *A suspension may be imposed only for a serious offense.*

Rule: *A self-study award may be given only to a senior.*

Rule: *A tool properly stored may be used only with permission of the owner.*

Templates for Permission Statements

A permission statement is a statement indicating the absence of any rule under a particular set of specified conditions. Such a statement indicates workers are not constrained by any rule in that situation and therefore may exercise judgment or discretion in taking relevant actions.

A. "May" Template

A permission statement can be formed by using the permission word *may*.

Example:

Rule: *An order on credit totaling over $1,000 must not be accepted from a customer if the customer's credit has not been checked.*

Permission statement: *An order on credit totaling $1,000 or under may be accepted from a customer even if the customer's credit has not been checked.*

B. "Need Not" Template

A permission statement can be formed by using the permission word phrase *need not*.

Example:

Rule: *A customer must place at least one order.*

Permission statement: *A customer need not place any orders.*

2.0. RuleSpeak Templates for Producers

A producer is a rule that neither rejects nor projects events but simply computes or derives a value based on some mathematical function(s).

2.1. Templates for Computation Rules

A computation rule always involves one or more arithmetic operations.

Keyword phrase: *must be computed as*

Examples:

Rule: *A product's cost must be computed as the sum of the cost of all its components.*

Rule: *The amount paid for an order must be computed as the sum of all payment amounts applied to the order.*

2.1.1. Shorthand for Computation Rules

If desired, a computation rule can be expressed in shorthand form as follows.

Keyword: =

Examples:

Rule: *A product's cost must be computed as the sum of the cost of all its components.*

Shorthand version: *Product's cost = the sum of the cost of all its components.*

Rule: *The amount paid for an order must be computed as the sum of all payment amounts applied to the order.*

Shorthand version: *The amount paid for an order = the sum of all payment amounts applied to the order.*

2.2. Templates for Derivation Rules

A derivation rule always involves one or more logical (truth-valued) operations (for example, AND, OR, NOT, EQUAL TO, and so on). A derivation rule provides a precise definition for a derived term; therefore, the keyword *means* is always used for its specification.

Keyword phrase: *must be taken to mean*

Examples:

Rule: *At-risk project must be taken to mean the project is over budget or understaffed.*

Rule: *High-risk customer must be taken to mean the outstanding balance exceeds $1,000 on each of the customer's last three successive invoices.*

Rule: *Big-ticket item must be taken to mean the item's cost exceeds $500.*

Rule: *Midnight must be taken to mean the time is equal to12:00 PM.*

2.2.1. Shorthand for Derivation Rules

If desired, a derivation rule can be expressed in shorthand form as follows.

Keyword: *means*

Examples:

Rule: *At-risk project must be taken to mean the project is over budget or understaffed.*

Shorthand version: *At-risk project means the project is over budget or understaffed.*

✦ ✦ ✦

Rule: *High-risk customer must be taken to mean the outstanding balance exceeds $1,000 on each of the customer's last three successive invoices.*

Shorthand version: *High-risk customer means the outstanding balance exceeds $1,000 on each of the customer's last three successive invoices.*

✦ ✦ ✦

Rule: *Big-ticket item must be taken to mean the item's cost exceeds $500.*

Shorthand version: *Big-ticket item means the item's cost exceeds $500.*

✦   ✦   ✦

Rule: *Midnight must be taken to mean the time is equal to12:00 PM.*

Shorthand version: *Midnight means the time is equal to12:00 PM.*

3.0. RuleSpeak Templates for Projectors

A projector is a rule that tends to take some action (other than rejection) when a relevant event occurs. A projector (sometimes called a *stimulus/response rule*) never rejects events (as rejectors do); rather, it *projects* them— that is, causes some new event(s) to occur as a result.

3.1. Templates for Enablers

An enabler (also known as a toggle) is a rule that turns something on or off.

3.1.1. Template for Inference Rules

An inference rule always infers something to be true about the subject of the rule if the *if* condition is satisfied.

Keyword phrase: *must be considered*

Examples:

Rule: *A person must be considered a woman if the person is female and the person's age is 21 or over.*

Comments:

The subject of this rule is *person*.

The rule will infer something to be true about this subject (namely that a person is a woman) if the specified condition holds. In other words, the rule will toggle *woman* to true.

The specified condition is given by the *if* clause.

Rule: *The go/no-go decision must be considered no-go if the tank status is questionable.*

3.1.1.1. Shorthand for Inference Rules

If desired, an inference rule can be expressed in shorthand form as follows.

Keyword: *is*

Example 1:

Rule: *A person must be considered a woman if the person is female and the person's age is 21 or over.*

Shorthand version: *A person is a woman if the person is female and the person's age is 21 or over.*

Example 2:

Rule: *The go/no-go decision must be considered no-go if the tank status is questionable.*

Shorthand version: *The go/no-go decision is no-go if the tank status is questionable.*

3.1.2. Template for Rule Toggles

This template is the preferred form for expressing exceptions to rules at the atomic level of business logic. The subject of a rule toggle (exception-type rule) is always some other rule.

Keyword phrase: *must (not) be enforced*

Example:

Rule: *The one-borrower-per-library-card rule must not be enforced if one of the borrowers who hold the library card is Bill Gates.*

Comment: The subject of the rule, *one-borrower-per-library-card*, is the name of the rule that must not be enforced if the condition (*one of the borrowers who hold the library card is Bill Gates*) holds true. This rule can be of any kind—that is, a rejector, a producer, or a projector.

3.1.3. Template for Process Toggles

This form of toggle-type rule indicates that a process or procedure must not be executed (either by users, by rules, or by any other means) for as long as the condition(s) included in the rule, if any, hold true. The subject of such a rule is always a process or procedure.

Keyword phrase: *must be enabled/disabled*

Example:

Rule: *Send-appointment-notice must be disabled if the client's address is unknown.*

Comments:

The subject of the rule, *send-appointment-notice,* is the process to be disabled.

This process can be an operation, a method, an action, a procedure, and so on—anything that can be executed.

3.1.4. Template for Data Toggles

The subject of this kind of toggle-type rule is always some form of data.

Data toggles should be used only with great caution. The *created* form (see below) implies that data must be created from nothing. The result would therefore be arbitrary. (A copier-type rule should be used when the desired data *can* be identified—a much more likely circumstance. Refer to the discussion of copiers below.)

Keyword phrase: *must be created/deleted*

Examples:

Rule: *Lottery-winner-number must be created when lottery-date equals today's date.*

Comment: This rule essentially acts (hopefully!) as a random number generator.

Rule: *Each outstanding case issue must be deleted when the case is closed.*

Comment: This rule will cause *the outstanding issues* data to be lost (deleted) at the point in time that a case is closed.

3.2. Templates for Copiers

A copier is a projector that replicates (copies) values.

3.2.1. Template for Imprint Rules

An imprint rule is a copier that sets the value of something that persists (for example, something in a database).

Keyword phrase: *must be set to*

Examples:

Rule: *Normal-tax-return-due-date must be set to April 15.*

Rule: *Applicable-sales-tax must be set to 8.25%.*

Comment: The value 8.25% is probably referenced by many rules. Instead of embedding the value in each of these many rules—not a good idea since the value might be changed—this imprint rule introduces a variable named *applicable-sales-tax* in which the current value can be held. All other rules referencing the value should use this variable name instead. By this means, the atomic piece of business logic is isolated to a single rule.

Rule: *Applicable-sales-tax must be set to 8.25% if order-fulfillment-date = 2001.*

Comment: If the value of *applicable-sales-tax* is potentially reset each year, consider using a decision table instead of individually defined rules to set the year-by-year values. (Decision tables are discussed in Chapter 12.)

Rule: *A student's-semester-fees-owed must be set to $3,065 when the student registers for a semester.*

Comment: Use of the time word *when* indicates that *student's-semester-fees-owed* is merely being initialized to a certain value at the given point in time. Presumably, this value will be incremented subsequently—for example, if the student registers for a particular course that has lab fees.

3.2.2. Template for Presentation Rules

A presentation rule is a copier that establishes a value or parameter related to how data is to be presented (for example, on a screen, in a report, and so on).

Keyword phrase: *must be displayed*

Following *must be displayed,* say where and how.

Examples:

Rule: *An order must be displayed to the screen in red if the order is overdue.*

Rule: *Potential Suppliers must be displayed in the Potential Suppliers Report in alphabetical order.*

Rule: *A client's–favorite-stock must be displayed to the screen when the client's–favorite–stock price varies by more than 8% over the past four hours.*

Comment: This last rule is an example of an *alerter.*

3.3. Templates for Executives

An executive (commonly known as a trigger) is a rule that under appropriate circumstances causes actual executions. A *process trigger* executes an operation, process, or procedure; a *rule trigger* "executes" a rule (that is, causes it to fire).

Executives differ from process toggles and rule toggles in the following way. Toggles merely enable (or disable) the process or rule, that is, make them capable (or incapable) of executing or firing. In contrast to executives, toggles do not *directly* cause actual executions (or firings).

3.3.1. Template for Process Triggers

The subject of a process trigger is always a process. This process can be an operation, a method, an action, a procedure, and so on—anything that can be executed. The word *when* is usually appropriate for process triggers since the process's execution is usually intended for a point in time, as given by the rule's condition.

Keyword phrase: *must be executed*

Example:

Rule: *Send-advance-notice must be executed for an order when the order is shipped.*

Comment: The subject of the rule, *send-advance-notice*, is the process to be executed.

3.3.2. Template for Rule Triggers

The subject of a rule trigger is always another rule. The word *when* is usually appropriate for rule triggers since the rule's firing is usually intended for a point in time, as given by the rule's condition.

Rule triggers should be used cautiously since *point in time* generally implies some event, and rules should normally be expressed without reference to any events. Rule triggers are sometimes used to indicate a preferred *firing order* for other rules—that is, that one rule should be fired before another when both can be fired in response to the same event.[3]

Keyword phrase: *must be fired*

Example:

Rule: *The projected-shipment-date-rule must be fired when a shipment is displayed to the screen.*

Comment: The rule *projected-shipment-date-rule* must be fired (evaluated) at the specific points in time (events) that a shipment is displayed to a user.

---

3. We do not necessarily endorse this practice. Scripting the desired order of firing is probably a more appropriate choice.

Snow-Blinded by Rules[4]

A man and his wife are sitting down to their usual cups of morning coffee, listening to the weather report coming over the radio: "There will be three to five inches of snow today, and a snow emergency has been declared. You must park your cars on the odd-numbered side of the streets." The man gets up from his coffee and replies, "Jeez, O.K."

Two days later, again they are sipping their morning coffee when they hear the weather forecast: "There will be two to four inches of snow today, and a snow emergency has been declared. You must park your cars on the even-numbered side of the streets." The man gets up from his coffee and replies, "Jeez, O.K."

Three days later, again they are sitting down with their cups of coffee and listening to the weather forecast: "There will be six to eight inches of snow today, and a snow emergency has been declared. You must park your cars on the—" and then the power went out and they didn't hear the rest of the instructions.

He says to his wife, "What am I going to do now?"

She replies, "Aw, just leave the car in the garage."

---

4. Editor's note: This material was forwarded to the author via e-mail. Original source unknown.

The Basic RuleSpeak Templates at a Glance

Table 11–1 provides a quick reference for the complete set of basic sentence templates in RuleSpeak. These templates are meant to provide basic structures for rule statements given in English so they can be captured and communicated consistently. The set of templates given in the table are not intended to constitute a formal or complete language.

As always in RuleSpeak, the templates are organized by a rule's functional category. Each category has one or more special *rule keywords*, each of which is the word or short phrase that appears distinctively in a particular sentence template for that category. (These special rule keywords appear in all capital letters in the table simply for emphasis.) The simple syntactical conventions used in the table are explained in the following list.

- The symbols < > indicate the syntactical item inside is mandatory.
- The symbols [ ] indicate the syntactical item inside is optional.
- The symbol / indicates that only one syntactical item of the two or more listed need be selected.
- *Condition* always involves a logical expression (something that must always be true or false). A *condition* is always based on one or more terms and facts (or data items) and may include logical operators such as AND, OR, and NOT.
- *Fact* inside brackets refers to the rest of the fact statement after the subject. For example, the <fact> for the fact statement *Customer places order* is *"places order."* Also, in all cases where *<fact>* appears, an embedded condition is permitted. For example, *"places more than ten orders"* embeds the condition *"more than ten."*
- Use of the keyword *should* in a rule statement indicates that the rule is a suggestor (that is, a guideline, heuristic, or suggestion).

Table 11–1 The Basic RuleSpeak Templates at a Glance

Category	Informal Description/ Purpose	Rule's Subject Must Be ...	Template	Example
Rejector	A constraint for maintaining correctness (consistency) by preventing violations	Term or fact	\<Subject> MUST/should [not] \<fact> [if/while \<condition>].	*An order MUST indicate the date it was received.*
Rule keywords:		*(data item also permitted)*		*A student MUST not take more than four courses while on probation.*
MUST			\<Subject> may/should \<fact> ONLY if/while \<condition>.	*A customer may place an order ONLY if the customer holds an account.*
ONLY			\<Subject> may/should \<fact> ONLY \<preposition> \<condition>.	*A salaried employee may work ONLY in a budgeted department.*
Permission statement	A policy or clarification permitting a business practice	Term, fact, rule, or process	\<Subject> MAY \<fact/rule keyword> [if/while \<condition>].	*An order on credit totaling $1,000 or under MAY be accepted from a customer even if the customer's credit has not been checked.*
Rule keywords:		*(data item also permitted)*		
MAY			\<Subject> NEED NOT \<fact/rule keyword> [if/while \<condition>].	*A customer NEED NOT place any orders.*
NEED NOT				
Computation rule	A statement or arithmetic formula indicating how to calculate a numeric value	Computed term	\<Subject> must/should [not] BE COMPUTED as \<mathematical formula> [if/while \<condition>].	*The amount paid for an order must BE COMPUTED as the sum of all payment amounts applied to the order.*
Rule keywords:		*(data item also permitted)*	*Shorthand:*	
BE COMPUTED			\<Subject> = \<mathematical formula> [if/while \<condition>].	*The amount paid for an order = the sum of all payment amounts applied to the order.*

Rule type / keywords		Definition	Syntax	Example
Derivation rule	*Rule keywords:* BE TAKEN TO MEAN MEANS	A statement or logical expression indicating how to determine a yes/no (true/false) result. Derived term *(data item also permitted)*	<Subject> must/should [not] BE TAKEN TO MEAN <logical expression> [if/while <condition>]. *Shorthand:* <Subject> MEANS [not] <logical expression> [if/while <condition>].	*Big-ticket item must BE TAKEN TO MEAN the item's cost exceeds $500.* *Big-ticket item MEANS the item's cost exceeds $500.*
Inference rule	*Rule keywords:* BE CONSIDERED	A rule that infers a conclusion from a particular set of circumstances. Term *(data item also permitted)*	<Subject> must/should [not] BE CONSIDERED [a] <term> if/while <condition>. *Shorthand:* <Subject> is [not] [a] <term> if/while <condition>.	*A person must BE CONSIDERED a woman if the person is female and the person's age is 21 or over.* *A person is a woman if the person is female and the person's age is 21 or over.*
Rule toggle	*Rule keywords:* UNLESS EXCEPT BE ENFORCED	A rule that turns another rule on or off in a particular set of circumstances, especially for making exceptions. Rule	*Informal:* <Rule statement>, UNLESS/EXCEPT <condition>. *Formal:* <Rule name> must/should [not] BE ENFORCED if/while <condition>.	*A library card may be held by at most one borrower UNLESS one of the borrowers who hold the library card is Bill Gates.* *The one-borrower-per-library-card rule must not BE ENFORCED if one of the borrowers who hold the library card is Bill Gates.*
Process toggle	*Rule keywords:* BE ENABLED BE DISABLED	A rule that turns a process on or off in a particular set of circumstances. Process or procedure	<Subject> must/should [not] BE ENABLED/ DISABLED if/while <condition>.	*Send-appointment-notice must BE DISABLED if the client's address is unknown.*

continued

Table 11–1 *continued*

Category	Informal Description/Purpose	Rule's Subject Must Be . . .	Template	Example
Data toggle *Rule Keywords:* BE CREATED BE DELETED	A rule that deletes data (or creates it randomly) in a particular set of circumstances	Data item	<Data item> must/should [not] BE CREATED/DELETED if/while <condition>.	*Each outstanding case issue must BE DELETED when the case is closed.*
Imprint rule *Rule keywords:* BE SET	A rule that sets a stored data item to a particular value	Term or fact *(data item also permitted)*	<Term> must/should [not] BE SET to <term/value> [when/if <condition>].	*A student's-semester-fees-owed must BE SET to $3,065 when the student registers for a semester.*
Presentation rule *Rule keywords:* BE DISPLAYED	A rule that requires data to be presented in a certain manner (for example, on a screen or in a report)	Term or fact *(data item also permitted)*	<Subject> must/should [not] BE DISPLAYED [to/on/in <media>] <display manner> [if/while <condition>].	*An order must BE DISPLAYED to the screen in red if the order is overdue.*
Process trigger *Rule keywords:* BE EXECUTED	A rule that automatically executes a process or procedure in a given set of circumstances	Process or procedure	<Subject> must/should BE EXECUTED when <condition>.	*Send-advance-notice must BE EXECUTED for an order when the order is shipped.*
Rule trigger *Rule keywords:* BE FIRED	A rule that automatically fires another rule in a given set of circumstances	Rule	<Rule name> must/should BE FIRED when <condition>.	*The projected-shipment-date-rule must BE FIRED when a shipment is displayed to the screen.*

CHAPTER 12

Expressing Business Logic by Using Decision Tables

The RuleSpeak Approach[1]

In RuleSpeak, rule statements always have a subject. They also always include one or more other terms. In the context of decision tables, these other terms are known as *evaluation terms* or more generally as *decision criteria*. These decision criteria provide the basis for the *labels* of rows and columns of the decision tables.

Any specific value or value range (called a *bracket*) for an evaluation term will have a definitive effect on the rule's subject. This definitive effect is an *outcome*. The collection of all decision criteria and outcomes included in a decision table represents the decision table's *consolidated* business logic.

When Decision Tables Should Be Used

Often the need for a decision table to express consolidated business logic is recognized rather easily. In general, decision tables are useful where all of the following conditions are true.

- A significant number of rules are parallel—that is, they share the same subject,[2] have exactly the same evaluation term(s), and are equivalent (but not

---

1. Version 2.
2. This constraint does not apply to projectors.

identical) in effect. In other words, the rules[3] share a common pattern and purpose.

- Each evaluation term has a finite number of relevant values or brackets.[4]
- Given the different values of the evaluation term(s), the outcomes cannot be predicted by a single formula. (If a single formula could predict the outcomes, using a single rule or set of rules to give the unified formula is a better approach.)

Decision Tables Involving One Evaluation Term

Here is an example of a simple situation that meets all the criteria listed above.

Rule 1: *Applicable-sales-tax must be set to 6.0% if year = 1995.*

Rule 2: *Applicable-sales-tax must be set to 6.5% if year = 1996.*

Rule 3: *Applicable-sales-tax must be set to 6.5% if year = 1997.*

Rule 4: *Applicable-sales-tax must be set to 6.5% if year = 1998.*

Rule 5: *Applicable-sales-tax must be set to 6.25% if year = 1999.*[5]

Rule 6: *Applicable-sales-tax must be set to 7.0% if year = 2000.*

Rule 7: *Applicable-sales-tax must be set to 8.0% if year = 2001.*

Rule 8: *Applicable-sales-tax must be set to 8.15% if year = 2002.*

Note the following about the rules given above:

- These eight rules are exactly parallel in the sense described above.
- There is one evaluation term in each rule, *year.*
- Overall, this evaluation term has a finite number of relevant values (currently eight).
- The outcome is the value for the rules' subject, *applicable-sales-tax.*
- The outcome for each of the rules given its *year* value cannot be predicted by a formula.

---

3. Such a collection of rules is sometimes called a *decision set.*

4. To address an infinite set of values, the keyword *other* is often used to represent all values not specifically enumerated.

5. Note that the sales tax rate decreased in 1999 from the previous year. This decrease represents an apparently infrequent (and perhaps improbable!) tax cut.

The following decision table shows the consolidated business logic for the eight rules given above.

Rule: *Applicable-sales-tax must be set to the percent value in Table A for a given year.*

TABLE A

Year	Applicable Sales Tax
1995	6.0
1996	6.5
1997	6.5
1998	6.5
1999	6.25
2000	7.0
2001	8.0
2002	8.15

The original eight rules have been specified as a single table-based rule. The only evaluation term is *year*, which appears as the label at the top of the left-hand column. The relevant values of *year* appear in the left-hand column as labels for the rows. The appropriate outcomes (values of the subject, *applicable-sales-tax*) appear in the cells of the right-hand column.

Decision tables are also useful for finding missing rules—that is, for determining whether the consolidated business logic is *complete*. For example, if any cell in a decision table has no value whatsoever, then that outcome is possibly missing and should be addressed.[6] (If a majority of cells have no values, then the decision table format might not be optimal for representing the underlying business logic.) The crucial issue of completeness is discussed in greater detail later in this chapter.

Decision Tables Involving Two Evaluation Terms

The example above had a single evaluation term. The values of this evaluation term were listed as labels for the rows of the decision table. Where there

---

6. Automated rule analysis tools offer much more sophisticated capabilities. Corticon Technologies, Inc., has been a pioneer in this area.

are exactly two evaluation terms in a set of parallel rules, the values of the second evaluation term are shown as labels for the columns of the decision table. Again, the appropriate outcome for each two-way combination of values is indicated for the appropriate cell. An example using an extended version of the earlier rule illustrates such a decision table.

Rule: *Applicable-sales-tax must be set to the percent value in Table B for a given year and county.*

TABLE B

Year	County			
	Harkin	Lopes	Qwan	Quail
1995	6.95	8.2	7.35	4.0
1996	6.73	8.3	9.0	4.5
1997	6.15	8.4	9.0	5.0
1998	6.15	8.3	9.0	5.5
1999	6.15	8.4	6.75	6.0
2000	6.15	8.2	6.75	6.75
2001	5.75	8.2	6.75	7.0
2002	5.95	8.4	7.5	7.25

In this example, there are two evaluation terms: *year* (whose values appear as labels for the rows) and *county* (whose values appear as labels for the columns). The desired outcomes for the rule (the values of the subject, *applicable-sales-tax*) have been indicated as appropriate in the individual cells.

Decision Tables Involving Three or More Simple Evaluation Terms

Representing *more* than two evaluation terms using a two-dimensional media (for example, paper) is problematic.[7] If there are three or more evaluation terms, all but two (or fewer) of which are simple, the business logic can still be represented in the form used thus far. Two approaches are discussed below. Incidentally, there is more to understanding whether an evaluation

---

7. At this point, there is probably no viable substitute for an automated tool. Such tools include RuleTrack from Business Rule Solutions, LLC (*http://www.BRSolutions.com*) and Corticon Studio from Corticon Technologies, Inc. (http://www.Corticon.com).

term is "simple" than might be expected, as explained in the boxed item, A Word about "Simple" Evaluation Terms.

A Word about "Simple" Evaluation Terms

A simple evaluation term is one that has only a few values. For example, the term *gender* is simple—the possible values are just *male* and *female*. Another example is the term *is-order-overdue?* (or simply, *order-overdue*). This term has only two possible values: *yes* and *no* (or *true* and *false*).

The most important thing in this context is to recognize what "simple" does *not* imply. For example, simple values can be derived according to some logical expression (for example, "not weekend day or legal holiday") or computed according to an arithmetic expression (for example, "50% of flat rate + 1% of gross amount"). Indeed, such expressions can appear as a whole as the label for any given row or column of a decision table. (When used in this fashion, the expressions are called *decision criteria* rather than evaluation terms.)

A logical or mathematical expression can often be quite complex. An alternative to using the entire expression as a label within a decision table is to create a separate rule whose subject is an appropriate derived or computed term. This derived or computed term can then substitute for the expression in the decision table.

For example, the logical expression given above could be made into the following rule: *Workday means not weekend day or legal holiday.* Then *workday* can be used instead of *not weekend day or legal holiday* anytime this label is required for a row or column in a decision table. An added benefit is that the new term is reusable for other rules, including for labeling columns and rows in other decision tables. Since the associated logic is defined only once, it will always be applied consistently no matter how many times *workday* is used. This, of course, reflects a basic principle of the business rule approach.

Split-Row Decision Table

The first alternative for representing the business logic in such cases is to split rows and/or columns within a single array, as illustrated by the following example.

Rule: *Applicable-sales-tax must be set to the percent value in Table C for a given year, county, and commodity type.*

TABLE C

| | County | | | |
Year	Harkin	Lopes	Qwan	Quail
1995: Food	6.95	8.2	7.35	4.0
Other	9.0	9.1	7.35	9.0
1996: Food	6.73	8.3	9.0	4.5
Other	9.0	9.0	9.9	9.5
1997: Food	6.15	8.4	9.0	5.0
Other	8.55	9.5	9.9	8.0
1998: Food	6.15	8.3	9.0	5.5
Other	8.45	9.5	9.9	6.2
1999: Food	6.15	8.4	6.75	6.0
Other	8.45	9.6	8.2	7.75
2000: Food	6.15	8.2	6.75	6.75
Other	8.45	8.9	8.2	7.75
2001: Food	5.75	8.2	6.75	7.0
Other	7.75	8.2	8.3	7.0
2002: Food	5.95	8.4	7.5	7.25
Other	7.95	8.5	9.0	7.25

In this example, there are three evaluation terms: *year* (whose values appear as the outer labels for the split rows), *commodity type* (whose values appear in repeating sets as the inner labels for the split rows), and *county* (whose values appear as labels for the columns). The desired outcomes for the rule (the values of the subject, *applicable-sales-tax*) have been indicated as appropriate in the cells of the decision table. Note that there are only two values for the split-row evaluation term commodity type (*food, other*). Had there been very many more values than that, the table would quickly become quite lengthy and increasingly difficult to use.

Multiple-Array Decision Table

If the number of values or brackets is too large for a practical split-row decision table, multiple arrays[8] can be employed. In this case, there is one array

---

8. In this discussion, *array* is used in the mathematical sense—a number of elements arranged in rows and columns.

per relevant value or bracket of one (or more) of the evaluation terms. The values of each of the other two evaluation terms will appear as labels for the rows and columns in identical fashion for every array. All the cells of all the arrays represent the possible outcomes in the consolidated business logic.

Rule: *Applicable-sales-tax must be set to the percent value in Table D for a given year, county, and commodity type.*

TABLE D, ARRAY 1. FOOD

| Year | County | | | |
	Harkin	Lopes	Qwan	Quail
1995	6.95	8.2	7.35	4.0
1996	6.73	8.3	9.0	4.5
1997	6.15	8.4	9.0	5.0
1998	6.15	8.3	9.0	5.5
1999	6.15	8.4	6.75	6.0
2000	6.15	8.2	6.75	6.75
2001	5.75	8.2	6.75	7.0
2002	5.95	8.4	7.5	7.25

TABLE D, ARRAY 2. COMMODITIES OTHER THAN FOOD

| Year | County | | | |
	Harkin	Lopes	Qwan	Quail
1995	9.0	9.1	7.35	9.0
1996	9.0	9.0	9.9	9.5
1997	8.55	9.5	9.9	8.0
1998	8.45	9.5	9.9	6.2
1999	8.45	9.6	8.2	7.75
2000	8.45	8.9	8.2	7.75
2001	7.75	8.2	8.3	7.0
2002	7.95	8.5	9.0	7.25

In this revision of the previous example, there are again three evaluation terms: *year* (whose values appear as labels for the rows in each array), *commodity type* (whose values identify the separate arrays), and *county* (whose values appear as labels for the columns in each array). As before, the desired outcomes for the rule (the values of the subject, *applicable-sales-tax*) have been indicated as appropriate in the cells of the arrays.

Decision Tables Involving More Complex Sets of Decision Criteria

The most general case for decision tables involves one or more of the following:

- More than three or four simple evaluation terms
- Three or more evaluation terms that are not simple
- Some combination of these

Such decision tables can be represented using a special *header-and-body* format. The header of a decision table formatted in this fashion addresses the subject of the rule; the body presents the relevant conditions. Unfortunately, as discussed below, such decision tables are prone to anomalies, so they must be developed with care and then scrutinized closely. Here is an example.

Rule: *The delivery method for an order must be determined according to Table E.*

TABLE E

Decision Criteria	*Delivery Method for an Order*		
	Picked Up by Customer	Shipped by Normal Service	Shipped by Premium Service
Rush order	No	Yes	Yes
Order includes fragile item	No	Yes	—
Order includes specialty item	No	No	—
Order includes high-priced item	No	No	—
Order includes item involving hazardous materials	No	Yes	Yes
Category of customer	Silver	Gold	Platinum
Destination of order	—	Local	Remote

This decision table establishes the basis for determining the delivery method for an order, the subject of the rule statement. Three outcomes (possible values of the subject) have been included in the *header* of the decision table, at the top of each column. In the *body* of the decision table (the rest of the decision table below the header), seven decision criteria appear at left as labels for the rows.[9] Six of these decision criteria involve only two values (*yes, no* or *local, remote*), whereas one (category of customer) involves three (*silver, gold, platinum*). In any cell of the body of the decision table, a dash (—) indicates that that decision criteria does not matter in determining the outcome; that is, *any* value for that decision criteria will produce the same result. The choice (outcome) of delivery method for an order appropriate for the combination of decision criteria values given in any column of the body is indicated directly above it in the header.[10]

Representing the subject of the rule statement as the header in the decision table is consistent with the basic RuleSpeak guideline that the subject of a rule should always come first. For decision tables that involve more complex sets of decision criteria such as the above, we find that this approach is particularly helpful for achieving more complete and anomaly-free results.[11] The various aspects of this critical issue are explored later, after several additional notes about decision tables in header-and-body format.

- Different sets of decision criteria (that is, different columns in the body) can produce the very same outcome. (None are shown in the example above.) Appropriate formatting and/or color-coding of the header, and/ or sequencing of the columns, can make this equivalence apparent. Such multicolumn equivalence in outcome is to be expected for larger tables.
- Each such set of decision criteria (that is, each such column) in the body produces one and only one outcome in the header.
- A logical AND (rather than OR) is always assumed for the set of all decision criteria in one column of the body.

---

9. This table therefore involves seven dimensions.
10. In this header-and-body format for decision tables, the combination of values in any one column of the body is considered a *label* for the outcome just above it in the header.
11. Some approaches to formatting decision tables recommend presenting decision criteria *before* outcomes. In other words, the contents of the header for a rule in RuleSpeak format would be shown at the bottom of the decision table. This reversed form essentially puts the decision table into *If-Then* format. Often this is made explicit by literally placing the word *If* above the decision table, then splitting the decision table into two parts so the word *Then* can be placed above the second part (the outcomes). We avoid this format for decision tables for the same reasons we avoid the *If-Then* format for expressing all rules at the business perspective.

- More than one header is permitted for a decision table in header-and-body format, representing other sets of outcomes based on the same sets of decision criteria in the body. (A logical AND is again assumed.)
- A decision table in header-and-body format with only a single header is in atomic form because both the second and third bullets above are satisfied. (These two bullets represent the fundamental criteria for whether a rule is in atomic form.) A decision table with more than one header is not in atomic form because the atomic form of rules does not permit ANDed outcomes (as per the second bullet).

Multiple headers should be used cautiously for the following reason. If a value of a cell in the body is changed, the revised set of decision criteria in that column may no longer produce exactly the same set of outcomes in the headers stacked directly above the revised column. Unless properly addressed (for example, by splitting the column), flaws in the business logic will result.

Completeness

The first issue in ensuring the quality of decision tables is completeness. In this context, completeness means that all appropriate situations have been addressed—that is, that all possible combinations of values for the decision criteria involving selective outcomes have been examined.

How complete is the sample decision table above? The header shows three outcomes, and the body includes three columns of values for the decision criteria, so obviously at a minimum the decision table addresses three possible combinations of decision criteria values. Actually, the body establishes the basis for a good number more than that for the following reason.

Several cells indicate acceptance of any value—for example, either *yes* or *no*—which renders the decision criteria for that cell essentially irrelevant to determining the outcome for the given situation. For example, column 1 includes one such cell, so that column actually provides the basis for establishing the outcome for *two* combinations—one if the value for the cell were *local* and one if it were *remote*. (As explained in the boxed item, The Completeness of Sets of Values Used as Decision Criteria, this assumption is by no means a trivial one.) Column 3 includes three such cells, so that column actually establishes the basis for 2^3 or 8 outcomes. Altogether, the body of the decision table actually establishes the basis for establishing 11 outcomes $(2 + 1 + 8 = 11)$.

The Completeness of Sets of Values Used as Decision Criteria

Our analysis of the decision criteria for this sample decision table assumes that there are only two possible values for destination of order: *local* and *remote*. This assumption would need to be validated, of course, with knowledgeable business workers. Verifying that all possible values for each decision criteria in a decision table have been discovered is another critical—and very basic—issue in ensuring the completeness of consolidated business logic.

The completeness of even the simplest value sets should not be taken for granted. For example, if the value set for a particular decision criteria is simply *yes* and *no*, but then situations are discovered where neither apply, the value set is not complete (and perhaps not very well developed either!). For example, it might be assumed that the only pleas a defendant at trial could enter were *guilty* and *not guilty*. Then a defendant pleads *no contest*. At least in the defendant's view, the distinction being made is a very real and significant one. In his or her logic, neither *guilty* nor *not guilty* applies—and it certainly *does* matter.

The bottom line is that "neither applies" in a decision table should never be confused with the use of dashes for "does not matter." This is quite clear if we return to the basic RuleSpeak statements for the columns. For example, column 3 in the decision table above should be worded as follows, simply omitting any reference to the dashed items altogether.[12]

An order must be shipped by premium service if all of the following are true:
- *The order is rush.*
- *The order includes an item involving hazardous materials.*
- *The category of customer that placed the order is platinum.*
- *The destination of the order is remote.*

continued

---

12. This should serve as a reminder that decision table formats are simply convenient representation tools for decision logic involving a significant number of largely parallel rules. There is really nothing inevitable, however, about every cell a decision table contains. A cell appears in a decision table because it *might* be relevant, not because it truly is.

If the dashes were taken to mean "neither applies," the proper rule statement would be quite different. Lacking any additional information, the proper statement might be worded as follows:

An order must be shipped by premium service if all of the following are true:
- *The order is rush.*
- *Neither yes nor no can be said about whether the order includes a fragile item.*
- *Neither yes nor no can be said about whether the order includes a specialty item.*
- *Neither yes nor no can be said about whether the order includes a high-priced item.*
- *The order includes an item involving hazardous materials.*
- *The category of customer that placed the order is platinum.*
- *The destination of the order is remote.*

It is not quite clear exactly what the latter version might mean, but one thing is clear. It certainly does not mean what the former version means!

What is the total number of *possible* combinations of decision criteria values? The total possible number of value combinations for the seven decision criteria can be calculated as follows: $2^6 \times 3 = 192$. This calculation reflects the fact that six of the decision criteria have two values each (*yes* and *no* for five of them, and *local* and *remote* for the other), whereas the seventh, category of customer, has three values (*silver*, *gold*, and *platinum*).

Having determined earlier how many combinations the decision table actually does address (11), we can now determine how many it does not: $192 - 11 = 181$. *So some 181 possible combinations have not been addressed at all!* We would therefore conclude that the development of this decision table (or, more accurately, of the associated business logic) is not even close to complete.

Validity

The sample decision table above is free of obvious anomalies such as subsumptions or conflicts. These kinds of anomalies, common for decision tables involving more complex business logic, are illustrated in the decision table below.

Rule: *The delivery method for an order must be determined according Table F.*

TABLE F

Decision Criteria	*Delivery Method for an Order*				
	Picked Up by Customer	Shipped by Normal Service	Shipped by Premium Service	Shipped by Premium Service	Picked Up by Customer
Rush order	No	Yes	Yes	Yes	Yes
Order includes fragile item	No	Yes	—	—	—
Order includes specialty item	No	No	—	—	—
Order includes high-priced item	No	No	—	—	—
Order includes item involving hazardous materials	No	Yes	Yes	Yes	Yes
Category of customer	Silver	Gold	Platinum	—	—
Destination of order	—	Local	Remote	Remote	Remote

This new version is an exact replica of the previous decision table except for the two new columns added (for discussion purposes only!) on the right side. As before, a dash in any cell of the body indicates that that decision criteria is irrelevant to determining the appropriate outcome for the given combination of decision criteria values—that is, any value for that decision criteria will produce the same outcome.

Subsumation. Notice that column 4 in the new table is an exact replica of column 3 (including outcomes) except for only one difference—a dash is shown for category of customer. This dash indicates that the value platinum as shown in column 3 (or, for that matter, either of the other two values for category of customer, silver and gold) does not matter in determining the appropriate outcome, shipped by premium service, as indicated in the header. In other words, column 3—or, more precisely, the set of decision criteria values that are given there along with their associated outcome—is subsumed by column 4. Because column 3 adds no additional information for the consolidated business logic, it can be eliminated from the decision table altogether. In fact, it should be eliminated because leaving it in would open the door to specification conflicts.[13]

Conflict. Notice that column 5 in the new table is an exact replica of column 4 except for only one difference. The outcome indicated in the header for the former is picked up by customer, but the outcome indicated for the latter is shipped by premium service. Since the same customer order clearly cannot be picked up if it is shipped (or vice versa),[14] these two columns (that is, the outcomes for the given set of decision criteria values) are clearly in conflict. Such conflicts, of course, must be identified and resolved by knowledgeable business workers.

Appropriate Outcomes for Decision Tables by Functional Category of Rule

A key question for decision tables, of course, is *what goes into the cells?* The answer depends directly on the functional category (or subcategory) of the rule. The appropriate kind of outcome for each functional category is listed in Table 12–1.

---

13. The total number of combinations of decision criteria values covered by column 4 is calculated as follows: $2^3 \times 3^1 = 24$. So now (not considering column 5), the body of this decision table provides the basis for determining outcomes for 27 possible combinations of decision term values ($2 + 1 + 24 = 27$). That still leaves 165 ($192 - 27 = 165$) combinations not addressed. The consolidated business logic is still woefully incomplete!
14. That is, the outcomes are mutually exclusive.

Table 12–1   Appropriate Outcomes for Decision Tables by Functional Category of Rule

Functional Category of Rule	Informal Description/ Purpose	Appropriate Outcomes
Rejector	A constraint for maintaining correctness (consistency) by preventing violations.	An entry of *yes* or *no* (or nothing) indicating whether the rule should be enforced in the given circumstances.
Computation rule	A statement or arithmetic formula indicating how to calculate a numeric value.	The appropriate mathematical formula in the given circumstances. Alternatively, the name of another computation rule may be given.
Derivation rule	A statement or logical expression indicating how to determine a yes/no (true/false) result.	An entry of *yes* or *no* (or nothing), or an entry of *true* or *false* (or nothing), indicating the appropriate value of the derivation in the given circumstances. Alternatively, the name of another derivation rule may be given.
Inference rule	A rule that infers a conclusion from a particular set of circumstances.	An entry of *yes* or *no* (or nothing), or an entry of *true* or *false* (or nothing), indicating whether the given inference should be made in the given circumstances. The appropriate inference to be made can be shown instead.
Rule toggle	A rule that turns another rule on or off in a particular set of circumstances, especially for making exceptions.	An entry of *yes* or *no* (or nothing) indicating whether the given rule should be enabled (on) in the given circumstances. The appropriate rule that should be enabled (on) may be shown instead.
Process toggle	A rule that turns a process on or off in a particular set of circumstances.	An entry of *yes* or *no* (or nothing) indicating whether the given process or procedure should be enabled in the given circumstances. The appropriate process or procedure to be enabled may be shown instead.
Data toggle	A rule that deletes data (or creates it randomly) in a particular set of circumstances.	An entry of *yes* or *no* (or nothing) indicating whether the value(s) of the given data type should be created or deleted in the given circumstances. The appropriate value to be created may be shown instead.[a]

continued

a. The rule actually becomes an imprint rule in this case.

Table 12–1 *Continued*

Functional Category of Rule	Informal Description/ Purpose	Appropriate Outcomes
Imprint rule	A rule that sets a stored data item to a particular value.	The appropriate (set to) value to be applied in the given circumstances.
Presentation rule	A rule that requires data to be presented in a certain manner (for example, on a screen or in a report).	The appropriate graphical criteria (for example, color, sequencing criteria, and so on) in the given circumstances.
Process trigger	A rule that automatically executes a process or procedure in a given set of circumstances.	An entry of *yes* or *no* (or nothing) indicating whether the given process or procedure should be executed in the given circumstances. The appropriate process or procedure to be executed may be shown instead.
Rule trigger	A rule that automatically fires another rule in a given set of circumstances.	An entry of *yes* or *no* (or nothing) indicating whether the given rule should be fired in the given circumstances. The appropriate rule to be fired may be shown instead.

PART IV

What Is the Business Rule Approach?

Readings for IT Professionals

Overview

This part expands on the material presented in Parts I–III, with emphasis on the special features, needs, and opportunities of the business rule approach. Although this part is aimed primarily toward information technology (IT) professionals, technical details have been kept to a minimum so that a more general audience can understand the ideas presented here.

I have divided the discussion into two chapters, as follows:[1]

- Chapter 13 discusses additional ideas of the business rule approach, with emphasis on what you need to know to be successful in its application. In particular, this chapter examines the following fundamental principles.

  - Rule management: Rules can and should be managed in an organized manner.
  - The knowledge principle: What the company knows should be balanced with what it does.
  - Business-driven solutions: The business solution should be worked out completely before any system is designed—and for sure before any coding begins.

---

1. At certain points in the discussions that follow in this part, I mention elements of methodology or deliverables that pertain specifically to Business Rule Solutions, LLC. When I use *we* or *our* in these contexts, please note that I am referring to the Principals of Business Rule Solutions.

- Chapter 14 reviews fact models, with emphasis on critical success factors in their creation. It also examines how the need to support large numbers of rules shapes fact models in distinctive ways. Finally, it examines ways in which rules, in conjunction with generalized data models and database designs, can be used to support current business practices more effectively. As I explain in the chapter, this approach opens important new opportunities for building more adaptive business systems.

More Principles of the Business Rule Approach

A New View of Business Logic

Rule Management
Rules can and should be managed in an organized manner.

The Basic Principles of Rule Management

Databasing Your Rules

How many rules does your company have? A hundred? A thousand? Ten thousand? More? How easy is it to change any one of those rules? How easy is it to determine where the rule is implemented? How easy is it to find out why it was implemented in the first place?

Many companies today are starting to realize they have problems with rule management. Often, this perception did not start off that way. Initially, the perception might have fallen under some other label such as *change management, data quality, knowledge retention, communication gap,* or so on. Call it what you may, these companies are discovering that the business logic at the core of their day-to-day operations is not being managed in any consistent or coherent manner.

Databasing the Rules

The purpose of rule management is to provide the infrastructure necessary to correct that problem. Such a solution assumes, of course, that rules *can* be managed. But

179

why not? In one sense, the literal specification of rules is just data, and in general, we certainly already know how to manage data.

So the first and most basic principle in rule management is that your rules should be *databased*. In other words, you should store the rules in an automated facility or repository where they can be managed and readily accessed.

Then comes the question of what else to store besides just the rules themselves and what additional kinds of support are needed. The key lies with remembering that business rules represent *business* logic—not programming logic. The goal of rule management is to give business workers and/or business analysts the ability to manage and access their business logic directly. The focus should be on the kinds of challenges these business workers and business analysts face on a day-in-and-day-out basis.

Fundamental in this regard is vocabulary management. When rules number in the thousands—or even just in the hundreds—coordinating business terminology becomes essential. Imagine trying to understand and apply that much business logic without such coordination. In practice, rule management is not simply about coordinating rules but also about coordinating the underlying business vocabulary. It is hard to stress this point too much.

In thinking about the other needs of business workers and analysts, it turns out that many of their questions about rules are quite predictable. Frequently asked questions include those listed in Table 13–1. Although the importance of these questions is self-evident, most companies have never managed this kind of core knowledge in any coordinated or comprehensive manner.

Traceability

Another question crucial to managing rules is being able to address relationships *between* rules—that is, rule-to-rule connections. There are many ways in which rules can be interconnected, as the list presented in Table 13–2 suggests. Being able to trace these relationships easily and reliably is also crucial to rule management.

The items in this list of connections, as well as the typical questions in the earlier list, illustrate various forms of *traceability*. Comprehensive support for rule traceability is a key ingredient in successful rule management.

How can such support be achieved? *Databasing* your rules is one part of the solution. Equally important is providing appropriate access to them once stored. Predefined reports and queries provide many kinds of basic support

Table 13–1 Typical Questions Business Workers and Business Analysts Could Ask about Rules

To which areas of the business does a rule apply?

What work tasks does a rule guide?

Where is a rule implemented?

In what jurisdictions is a rule enforced?

What purpose does a rule serve?

What deliverables in a new system design need to address a rule?

When was a rule created?

When did a rule become effective?

Are there previous versions of a rule?

Is a rule still in effect, and if not, when was it discontinued?

Was a rule retired or replaced, and if so, why?

What influenced the creation or modification of a rule?

Who can answer particular kinds of questions about a rule?

Who has been involved with a rule over time, and in what way?

Where can more information about a rule be found?

in that regard. Beyond that, visualization techniques are very useful for presenting more complex or highly interrelated information.

In one way or another, I believe that every company will eventually discover the need for rule management. To support it, new techniques must be learned and new tools implemented. Fortunately, pioneering companies have already discovered what these techniques are, and good commercial tools have emerged to support them.[1] Rule management is a practical idea whose time is now!

Table 13–2 Kinds of Rule-to-Rule Connections

A rule is an exception to another rule.

A rule enables another rule.

A rule subsumes another rule.

A rule is semantically equivalent to another rule.

A rule is similar to another rule.

A rule is in conflict with another rule.

A rule supports another rule.

A rule is interpreted from another rule.

---

1. Business Rule Solutions, LLC, developed the first software tools for this area during the late 1990s. Refer to *http://www.BRSolutions.com* for current information.

The Knowledge Principle

What the company knows should be balanced with what it does.

What Is a Business Rule?

Separating the "Know" from the "Flow"

In a way, everybody knows what business rules are—they are what guide your business in running its day-to-day operations. Without business rules, you would always have to make decisions on the fly, choosing between alternatives on a case-by-case, ad hoc basis. Doing things that way would be *very* slow. It would likely produce wildly inconsistent results. I doubt it would earn very much trust from your customers.

In today's world, you cannot really operate that way—not for very long, anyway. So every organized business process has business rules. But what are they? What exactly do you use to "guide your business in running its day-to-day operations"?

In a moment, we will examine several definitions of *business rule*.[2] Before doing that, however, I should be clear about what business rules are *not*.

- **Business rules are *not* software.** Let me be a little more precise. Business rules are often *implemented* in software, but that is a different matter. In fact, application software is only one of several choices in that regard. Alternative implementation approaches include supporting them in manual procedures (not very efficient but sometimes necessary) or implementing them as rules using business logic technology[3] (a much better choice). The point is that business rules arise as an element of the *business*—as the name *business* rules suggests—not from any particular hardware/software platform that supports them.
- **Business rules are *not* process.** Roger T. Burlton[4] recently expressed the business rule message this way: "Separate the *know* from the *flow*." The implication is that the "know" part and the "flow" part are *different*.

---

2. Part V presents a formal definition of *business rule*.
3. By *business logic technology*, I mean *rule engines, decision management platforms, business logic servers*, and so on.
4. Roger Burlton has written extensively about business processes from the business perspective; see, for example, Burlton [2001].

Business rules represent the "know" part—the separate stuff that *guides* the "flow." Guidance means rules; hence the name *business rules.*

Separate the know *from the* flow.

—Roger T. Burlton

Take a look at the definitions of *business rule* listed in Table 13–3. All the definitions are valid; however, if you are interested in a historical view, the entries appear in chronological order and reflect some natural evolution over time. Several important observations are worth making about these definitions, as discussed in the related boxed item starting on page 184.

Table 13–3 Definitions of *Business Rule*

Source	Definition
"Business Rules: The Missing Link," by Daniel S. Appleton [1984][a]	". . . [A]n explicit statement of a constraint that exists within a business's ontology."[b] [p. 146]
Entity Modeling: Techniques and Application, by Ronald G. Ross [1987]	". . . [S]pecific rules (or business policies) that govern . . . behavior [of the enterprise] and distinguish it from others. . . . [T]hese rules govern changes in the status [state] of the enterprise. . . ." [p. 102]
The Business Rule Book (1st ed.), by Ronald G. Ross [1994]	". . . [A] discrete operational business policy or practice. A business rule may be considered a user requirement that is expressed in non-procedural and non-technical form (usually textual statements). . . . A business rule represents a statement about business behavior. . . ." [p. 496]
GUIDE Business Rules Project Report [1995]	". . . [A] statement that defines or constrains some aspect of the business . . . [which is] intended to assert business structure, or to control or influence the behavior of the business. [A business rule] cannot be broken down or decomposed further into more detailed business rules. . . . [I]f reduced any further, there would be loss of important information about the business." [pp. 4–5]
The Business Rule Book (2nd ed.), by Ronald G. Ross [1997]	"A term, fact (type) or rule, representing a predicate. . . ." [p. 380]

continued

a. This citation is the earliest article featuring the term business rule I have been able to find.
b. Appleton's use of *ontology* seems prescient given the growing use of this term in the industry, especially concerning rules. *Ontology* is a bit arcane, however, so I will defer explaining it until Chapter 14.

Table 13–3   *Continued*

Source	Definition
Business Rules Group (formerly GUIDE Business Rules Project), 1998[c]	"A directive that is intended to influence or guide business behavior. Such directives exist in support of business policy, which is formulated in response to risks, threats or opportunities."[d]
Capturing Business Rules, by Ronald G. Ross and Gladys S. W. Lam [2000b]	"An atomic piece of re-usable business logic, specified declaratively."[e]
Managing Reference Data in Enterprise Databases, by Malcolm Chisholm [2001]	"A single statement that takes data or information that an organization possesses and derives other data or information from it, or uses it to trigger an action." [p. 365]
Business Rules Applied: Building Better Systems Using the Business Rule Approach, by Barbara von Halle [2002]	"... [C]onditions that govern a business event so that it occurs in such a way that is acceptable to the business."[f] [p. 28]
Business Rules and Information Systems, by Tony Morgan [2002]	"Basically, a business rule is a compact statement about an aspect of the business. . . . It's a constraint, in the sense that a business rule lays down what must or must not be the case. At any particular point, it should be possible to determine that the condition implied by the constraint is true in a logical sense; if not, remedial action is needed. This interpretation, which might be described as Boolean from a software perspective, is the main reason that the term *business logic* is so commonly used."[g] [pp. 5–6]

c. From a prepublication 1998 draft of "Organizing Business Strategy: The Standard Model for Business Rule Motivation" [Business Rules Group 2000].
d. This is the definition we prefer from a business perspective.
e. This is the definition we prefer from a system perspective. We also accept the GUIDE Project definition (1995).
f. Note: von Halle adopts the GUIDE Project definition (1995). However, this excerpt is an excellent and succinct characterization of business rule.
g. Note: Morgan also adopts the GUIDE Project definition (1995). This excerpt characterizes business rule very well from a system perspective.

Observations about the Definitions of *Business Rule*

Business versus system perspective: Although all the definitions are consistent in theme, if you look closely, you will see tension between a purely business perspective (see the Business Rules Group definition from 1998) versus a system perspective (see the Ross and Lam definition from 2000). The bottom line is that *both* perspectives are correct—just different in their viewpoints.

Terms, facts, and rules: A general consensus emerged among experts in the 1990s that there are three basic categories of business rules—*terms*, *facts*, and *rules*. (This important breakthrough is credited to the GUIDE Business Rules Project and was originally reported in its 1995 paper.) Literally, in the business rule approach, the "know" part always comes in the form of a term (concept), a fact, or a rule. A business rule is *never* anything else. By the way, terms are the most basic of the three categories because facts must build on terms, and rules must build on facts. That principle produces a very powerful building-block approach for the "know" part.

Fact models: Note the term *business structure* in the 1995 GUIDE Business Rules Project definition. This term refers to basic structure for the "know" part—literally, how terms relate to one another in the form of facts. As discussed in Part II and later in this part, a fact model is the best way to express such structure.

Suggestors: The 1995 GUIDE Business Rules Project definition includes both the word *control* and the word *influence* in reference to business behavior. If you think of rules only as hard and fast constraints (asserting strict control), you miss at least half the scope of business rules. Operational-level suggestions, guidelines, heuristics, and so on (that is, *suggestors*) are *also* business rules!

Atomic form: The word *atomic* appears explicitly or implicitly in several of the definitions. This reflects an important goal for business rules—to achieve the most granular level of specification possible. Why is that so important? Because it allows for *fine-grained* change in business practices.

Reusability: Note the terms *re-usable* and *declaratively* in the Ross and Lam 2000 definition. *Declarative* specifications are what you get when you express business logic in the form of terms, facts, and rules. This approach has crucial advantages, not the least of which is that your business logic becomes reusable across both processes (the "flow") and hardware/software platforms. As such, it becomes both highly reengineerable and highly redeployable. Think of this as *business rules in a suitcase*—just the thing for a business always on the go.

Business rules really mean establishing the "know" part of your business processes as a resource in its own right. This new resource brings with it both benefit and responsibility. The benefit lies in being able to change elements of the "know" part directly, which in turn means being able to change them *faster*. (What business does not want to be able to change faster these days?)

But there is a price for that—this new resource must be managed. Therein lies the responsibility. You must now come to grips with management of that "know" part—that is, with *rule management*

A final point is this. In real life, some of the "know" part has always been separated from the "flow" part in the sense that workers carry the "know" part around in their heads. Does such *tacit* knowledge represent business rules? In the theoretical sense, *yes*, but in the sense that they can really be managed, *no*. If you need any proof of that, just think what happens when the workers retire—or go to work for the competition!

For practical purposes, business rules are that portion of the "know" part written down—that is, encoded—for ready reuse (or revision) as needed. Here then follows an additional way to describe business rules.

Business rules are literally the encoded knowledge of your business practices.

Business Rules and the "Flow"

Correcting Some Misconceptions about Business Rules

Not long ago, I received an e-mail from an IT professional. The e-mail contained serious misconceptions about business rules. These misconceptions go to the heart of the distinction between declarative versus procedural specifications (that is, "know" versus "flow"), in particular concerning *sequence*. First I reproduce the original e-mail in full, then I give my point-by-point responses.

Subject: Business Rules versus Sequence

The IT professional wrote . . .

The Ross approach to business rules . . . tends to classify business rules based on a bias toward coercing perfectly good imperative constructs into less comfortable declarative ones. Ross loses sight of the need for appropriate behavioral language in favor of a misguided attempt at a purely structural expression of a business system. For example, steps in a cake recipe might be simply . . .

1. Combine flour, water, milk, and eggs in a large bowl.
2. Mix until batter is consistent but not entirely free of lumps.

Instead, Ross would prefer . . .

- Batter is mixed.
- Flour, water, milk, and eggs are combined.
- Flour, water, milk, and eggs are ingredients.
- After mixing, ingredients become batter.
- Batter must be in a bowl.
- Batter must be consistent but must retain lumps.
- Mixing batter is performed after combining ingredients.

Ross abhors sequence. Sequence is to be asserted by means of elaborate nets of [specially typed rules]. This adds nothing to the maintainability or expressive power of a business system's definition. We already have a perfectly natural and convenient means of expressing sequence: *an ordered list*.

Point-by-Point Reply

My response . . .

>Ross abhors sequence.

>>>*Absolutely dead wrong!* Some of the most effective and pragmatic work in the business rule community has been done in the areas of workflow models (the business view of work) and procedures or scripts (the system view of work).

>>>We use rules (defined independently) to *control* the work. This is why the NFL has a rule book that is *separate* from the teams' play books. That's because today you might be running one set of plays, but tomorrow you will probably be running another. To use your analogy, today you might be making a cake, but tomorrow you might be making a pie.

> 1. Combine flour, water, milk, and eggs in a large bowl.

> 2. Mix until batter is consistent but not entirely free of lumps.

>>>This recipe represents a perfectly acceptable (albeit very simple) procedure or script. I have no problem with it. Now let's ask, what rules do we need? Potential rules to provide appropriate control might include the following . . .

- Milk must be fresh.
- Bowl must be large enough so that contents do not spill out when stirred.
- Batter may be considered "entirely free of lumps" only if there are no visible masses of congealed batter larger than 2 cm in diameter.

>>>These rules represent business knowledge that must be present when the procedure or script is performed. All work requires guidance and/or control—such guidance and control is what business rules are about. The business rule approach simply says not to embed these rules in the procedure or script directly.

>Instead, Ross would prefer:

> • Batter is mixed.

> • Flour, water, milk, and eggs are combined.

> • Flour, water, milk, and eggs are ingredients.

> • After mixing, ingredients become batter.

> • Batter must be in a bowl.

> • Batter must be consistent but must retain lumps.

> • Mixing batter is performed after combining ingredients.

>>> *No!* I want both a script to follow (your two-step recipe will do) and rules to guide me in doing the work. But most importantly, I want the script and the rules to be *separate*. So what you say I prefer above is actually the exact *opposite* of what I want—you've embedded the rules in the procedure. We do agree on one thing, however. The result is really messy!

Business Rules and the "Know"

Rules for Processes and Rules for Products/Services

Over the years, developers of expert-system applications have consistently focused on a fundamental aspect of business problems that most IT professionals fail to perceive. The reverse, however, is also true. Most developers of applications using traditional expert systems fail to perceive what IT professionals know almost intuitively. Consequently, almost all approaches to developing business systems fall woefully short in one respect or the other. Let me explain who is missing what and how the problem can be corrected.

Decision Points

Developers of expert-system applications have traditionally focused on *decision points* in the work environment. A decision point is where some critical decision (usually a complex one) must be made. Such a decision typically might have to do with one of the following kinds of tasks: classification, diagnosis, assessment, monitoring, prediction, assignment, allocation, and so on.

The rules governing such decisions are usually viewed as peculiar to and characteristic of the company's *product/service* offerings. These offerings invariably involve the company's special area(s) of expertise. Examples of such decisions include whether or not to:

- Approve an application for automobile insurance
- Pay a claim
- Buy a stock
- Declare an emergency
- Give an on-the-spot discount to a customer
- Assign a particular resource to a given request
- Diagnose a patient as having a particular disease
- Accept a reservation
- Indicate possible fraud

Such decision points, all rule-intensive, are of vital importance to the business. Capturing the relevant rule sets should therefore be a key component of a company's approach to developing its business systems.

Unfortunately, most approaches for system development used by IT professionals have never done this outright. Most such approaches are highly procedural and offer no direct support for capturing large numbers of rules in declarative form. By and large, IT professionals have not even grasped how significant this omission really is.

Work Avoidance

Turning now to developers of expert-system applications, what is typically missed in their approaches? The answer requires digging a bit deeper into two basic assumptions of traditional expert systems.

Expert-System Assumption 1. It is possible to define all relevant rules well enough for automated decision making to be effective.

There are, of course, some very difficult problems (for example, weather forecasting) where this assumption does not hold true today. In the typical business, on the other hand, a large number of important decision points in day-to-day operations come nowhere near that magnitude of complexity.

So this first assumption is basically correct for business systems. Indeed, if the business goals for a project include *disintermediation* (that is, eliminating the middleman, as in Web-based self-service applications), capturing and managing these decision-making rules is a must.

Expert-System Assumption 2.   The cost and difficulty of gathering the appropriate data is a relatively trivial issue compared with the complexity of the rules.

This is a point about *business* systems—a huge one—that developers of expert-system applications historically got wrong. In a business context it can be *extremely* costly and difficult (and inefficient) to gather all the appropriate data simply to set things up for all the decision-making rules to fire.

Let me offer a simple example. An automobile insurance company might have the following business rule: *An application for car insurance may be approved only if the applicant is at least as old as the minimum driving age.* This rule, of course, might be only one of hundreds determining whether an application should be approved. Other rules might involve creditworthiness (which could involve an extensive credit check), previous driving history (which could require requesting records from the state), and so on. In other words, there is a lot of work (time and money) involved in gathering all the data required to support all the rules.

Consequently, one of the basic goals in designing business processes is what I call *work avoidance* (no pun intended). For example, if the applicant for automobile insurance is less than the minimum driving age, why perform the credit check and acquire the driving records (and so on)? If you can determine up front in the business process that the applicant is too young, all that other data-related work can be avoided.

Simply capturing all the decision-making rules is clearly not enough for effective support of business systems. In fact, capturing the rules is only half the problem. First you need to develop the *workflow* for the business process in order to fully explore all opportunities for *work avoidance*. Rules governing the business process (such as the minimum driving age rule above) must be tested as early in the workflow as possible. Waiting to test them at some downstream decision point is simply inefficient. This early-bird testing of business process rules is a basic principle of the business rule approach.

The Workflow Imperative: Early-Bird Testing of Rules
To avoid unnecessary work, rules should be tested as early
as possible.

Business Process Rules versus Product/Service Rules

This insight sheds new light on the knowledge principle (*what the company knows should be balanced with what it does*). It comes down to these final points.

Two Kinds of Rules. To some extent, every company has both business process rules and decision-making rules (usually product/service rules). The "know" part really has two dimensions, both crucial. Examples of business process rules and product/service rules for three different organizations are given in the following boxed item.

Examples of Business Process Rules versus Product/Service Rules

Internal Revenue Service (IRS)

Business Process Rule	Product/Service Rule
Rule: *A processed tax return must indicate the IRS Center that reviewed it.*	**Rule:** *Calculated total income must be computed as tax return wages (line 1) plus tax return taxable-interest (line 2) plus tax return unemployment compensation (line 3).*

Ministry of Health

Business Process Rules	Product/Service Rules
Rule: *A claim must be assigned to an examiner if fraud is suspected.* **Rule:** *An on-site audit must be conducted for a service provider at least every five years.*	**Rule:** *A claim involving comprehensive visits or consultations by the same physician for the same patient must not be paid more than once within 180 days.* **Rule:** *A claim that requests payment for a service event that is a provision of health service type 'consultation' may be paid only if the service event results from a referral received from another service provider.*

continued

Ship Inspection Agency

Business Process Rules	Product/Service Rules
Rule: *A ship inspection work order must include at least one attendance date.*	**Rule:** *A ship area subject to corrosion must be inspected annually.*
Rule: *A ship must indicate a client who is financially responsible for inspections.*	**Rule:** *A salt water ballast tank must be inspected empty if the ship is more than five years old.*
Rule: *An inspection due for a ship must be considered suspended if the ship is laid up.*	**Rule:** *A barge must have an approved bilge system to pump from and drain all below-deck machinery spaces.*

Do the Business Process "Know" First. If a project will address both kinds of rules, workflow model(s) for the business process (and the associated business process rules) should generally be developed first. The reason is that decision-making tasks (and the associated product/service rules) are always embedded within a business process and therefore dependent on its basic sequence, specification, and vocabulary.

Do the Product/Service "Know" Too. Capturing the workflow models (the "flow") and the business process rules is by no means sufficient. To fully support the "know" part, the product/service rules must be captured in an appropriate manner too.

 Business-Driven Solutions
The business solution should be worked out completely before any system is designed—and for sure before any coding begins.

Why Business Rule Methodology Is Different

What It Means to Mean Business

Outwardly, the business rule approach produces many of the same deliverables as any other approach to building business systems—screens, processes, data, controls, and so on. In other words, the end result is almost sure to include some automated components. So why is the business rule approach any different from other system development methodologies? This section explains why.

The goal for development is to ensure a more adaptable *business*. This goal produces three imperatives.

Business Rule Systems Imperative 1: A Business Model

Application components must be seamlessly integrated into the business. Such integration requires a blueprint, a top-down business model covering the full business capacity within scope.

To say that a business rule project aims toward producing application software misses the point. The real objective is to produce a full business capacity that covers all the factors or abstractions[5] listed in Table 13–4.

Table 13–4 The Factors of a Full Business Capacity

Business Aspect	Business Component	Business Model Deliverable[a]	IT Component
Knowing	Terms and facts	Fact Model	Data
Transforming	Business processes	Business Process Models	Processes
Connecting	Business links	Business Connectivity Map	Machine links
Interacting	Roles and work products	Organizational Work Model	Human interfaces
Staging	Time frames and milestones	Business Milestones	States
Guiding	Business goals and tactics	Policy Charter	Rules

a. These are deliverables of Proteus, the business rule methodology developed by Business Rule Solutions, LLC.

---

5. Those readers familiar with John Zachman's Architecture Framework will realize that I am referring to its six columns, which address the interrogatives *what, how, where, who, when,* and *why,* respectively. For more information on Zachman's thinking, refer to Zachman [2002] and collected articles by Zachman found in the *Business Rules Journal,* available at *http://www.BRCommunity.com.*

To support this first imperative, a complete top-down business model should be developed involving key business-side workers and managers. By the way, *complete* here means the model addresses all the key business questions but *not* system or implementation questions.

With the right people and the right approach, this business model can be developed in a matter of weeks and requires relatively modest amounts of time from the business-side participants. And (this may come as a surprise), we find that these business-side participants almost always actually *enjoy* the process. I think that is simply because they find the process so relevant and valuable. To sum this point up in a word, we find they finally feel they can take *ownership*.[6]

Business Rule Systems Imperative 2: The Best Business Solution

The business needs the very best business solution possible. "Best" must be demonstrated, so a battle plan must be developed up front in which each key element of the solution is motivated from a business perspective.

A business capacity will be of little value if it addresses the wrong business goals. The key question is *why* a particular form of the business capacity is the right one for the company.

Traditional approaches for building application systems have not done a very good job of answering that key question. In the 1980s, information engineering, for example, sought to answer it by involving sponsors and key managers directly in producing deliverables. As you can imagine, this was very expensive and time-consuming. Worse, it did not even really work. Today, most projects are still managed based on cost. Money is important, of course—but it is not a substitute for knowing *why*.

The business rule approach offers a fresh approach. Briefly, the central idea is that achieving business goals[7] always involves a particular set of business risks and inherent conflicts and tradeoffs. Business tactics and core business rules are formulated to address these risks, conflicts, and tradeoffs.[8]

---

6. I use *ownership* here deliberately. *Owner* is the term John Zachman uses to describe the perspective of row 2 in his Framework, the row that has to do with developing an enterprise model (also known as a *business model*).

7. I do not mean *project* goals or *project* objectives, so to avoid confusion I will continue to say *business goal* rather than simply *goal*, as I also did in Part I.

8. For in-depth discussion, refer to Ross and Lam [2000a].

Rather than involving sponsors and key managers in data or process deliverables, the business rule approach gets those people directly focused on developing these crucial elements of the business solution. I will have more to say about the deliverable that makes this possible momentarily.

Business Rule Systems Imperative 3: High-Impact Sponsorship

Project sponsor(s) must have maximum leverage for controlling a project with a minimum investment of their time.

As mentioned above, a critical success factor for projects is to enable sponsors to manage projects by business benefit rather than primarily by cost. This is achieved by a coordinated focus on the *motivation* for the key elements of the business solution, including core business rules.

High-impact sponsorship has additional advantages, including the following.

- Sponsors can have a clear, concise, and *continuing* understanding of how the business goals are being transformed into a complete design for the desired business capacity, including (but not limited to) the automated components.
- Sponsors can detect easily and *early* in the project life cycle that the project is failing to meet the original business goals so they can take timely action as necessary.

What enables sponsors to monitor a project without lengthy participation in the development of deliverables? The answer is the *Policy Charter*.[9]

A Policy Charter outlines the business tactics proposed to meet the business goals. The business motivation for each element of these business tactics is established. This battle plan offers the sponsors a direct view of how the needs of the targeted business capacity are being addressed. It also permits the following.

- Assessment of business-side feasibility
- Examination of business risks and how they will be addressed
- Explanation of any divergence or shortfall that might have occurred in meeting the original business motivation

---

9. For more information, refer to Lam [1998]. For an enterprise-level approach, refer to the landmark work by the Business Rules Group [2000].

- Exploration of specific reengineering opportunities for the business process
- Acquisition of rapid and highly focused feedback

A page from one recent project's Policy Charter is presented in Figure 13–1. This segment (which represents about 15 percent of the entire deliverable) is presented in graphic form.[10] We find graphic presentation (as opposed to a purely textual format) enables better communication and discussion among business-side team members and sponsors.

This sample Policy Charter segment concerns a business capacity involving an insurance claim process whose reengineering featured automated handheld pads to estimate repair costs for damaged autos. The elements shown in the segment include business goals, tactics, risks, and core business rules linked in appropriate manner. Note the prominent role of core business rules in addressing business risks.

If any part of a draft Policy Charter is unacceptable, unworkable, or incomplete, sponsors can immediately take appropriate action with minimal loss of time and resources relative to the project as a whole. Such early intervention will be much less costly than during later phases of the project during which technical design, construction, and testing occur.

Our experience is that with the right people and the right approach, a Policy Charter can often be developed in a matter of days. Also, we find that sponsors almost always *enjoy* their participation in the process. We recognize this is partly because the process takes so little of their time. However, we again find it also comes down to a sense of *ownership*.

Analysis Paralysis

Preventing the Disease Behind the Symptoms

Many predators hunt based on movement. In fact, even with their keen eyesight, they cannot really see their prey unless the prey itself moves. Consequently, many hunted animals are programmed literally to *freeze with fear.* Not a bad thing to do if it saves your life!

Recently, we were asked to perform a postmortem review of a large project that had failed miserably at a major corporation. I will spare you all

---

10. Refer to *http://www.BRSolutions.com* for current information about products.

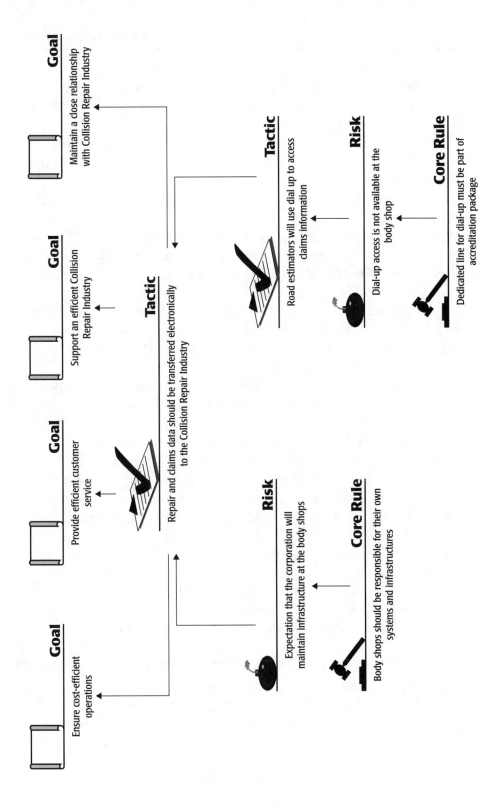

Figure 13–1 Sample Policy Charter (segment)

the unpleasant details—let's just say they started the coding phase way too early. The wounds to the business were deep, and in several ways, the company had begun to ooze red ink, its very lifeblood.

What went wrong? The diagnosis was relatively easy for us to make—no Policy Charter or other means to assess business motivation, and no true top-down business model.

They should have *frozen with fear* then and there. Instead, they jumped right on into development, loosely following a spiral "methodology" based on the mantra *analyze a little, design a little, code a little, test a little.* The company learned the hard way what that mantra means in practice—*lots of rework for lots of time!* (By the way, on other projects the company called such rework "maintenance." Sound familiar?)

Projects spiral out of control all too often. Unfortunately, there are no magic cures—just very expensive and time-consuming ones. Can the company really afford to squander its resources in this way? We think an ounce of prevention is worth a pound of cure.

Take a hard, early look at projects and learn to read the symptoms before it is too late to prevent the disease. Here are some possibilities.

- Maybe you do not really know what the business problem is. *In that case, how will you know if you are developing the right solution?*
- Maybe the business problem itself is hard. *Will thinking about it in a programming language (or in IT system models) make understanding it easier?*
- Maybe you are not getting the right answers from the right people. *Then, realistically, how good are your chances of success?*
- Maybe there are unresolved differences of opinion on the business side about what form the business solution should take. *If left to the programmers, do you think they can code their way to some satisfactory resolution?*
- Maybe future business directions are hard to predict. *Are designers and programmers in a position to make the best strategic choices?*

The next time you hear anyone say, "Watch out for analysis paralysis," take pause. Just freeze—it might save your company's life (or your own job). Somewhere close by there is probably a programmer poised to pounce on a keyboard. To stay on the safe path, think business model, Policy Charter, and business rules. Remember, every problem is first and foremost a *business* problem!

References

Appleton, Daniel S. 1984. "Business Rules: The Missing Link." *Datamation,* October 15, pp. 145–150.

Burlton, Roger T. 2001. *Business Process Management: Profiting from Success.* Indianapolis, IN: Sams Publishing.

Business Rules Group (Ronald G. Ross and Keri Anderson Healy, eds.). 2000. "Organizing Business Strategy: The Standard Model for Business Rule Motivation." Version 1, November 2000. Available at *http://www. BusinessRulesGroup.org.*

Chisholm, Malcolm. 2001. *Managing Reference Data in Enterprise Databases.* San Francisco, CA: Morgan Kaufmann.

GUIDE Business Rules Project Report. 1995. Third edition available in November 2002 as "Defining Business Rules—What Are They Really?", edited by David C. Hay and Keri Anderson Healy, Business Rules Group, July 2000, at *http:// www.BusinessRulesGroup.org.*

Lam, Gladys S. W. 1998. "Business Knowledge—Packaged in a Policy Charter." *DataToKnowledge Newsletter* (formerly *Data Base Newsletter*), May/June. Available at *http://www.BRCommunity.com.*

Morgan, Tony. 2002. *Business Rules and Information Systems.* Boston, MA: Addison-Wesley.

Ross, Ronald G. 1997. *The Business Rule Book* (2nd ed.). Houston, TX: Business Rule Solutions, LLC. Available *http://www.BRSolutions.com.*

———. 1994. *The Business Rule Book* (1st ed.). Boston, MA: Database Research Group.

———. 1987. *Entity Modeling: Techniques and Application.* Boston, MA: Database Research Group.

Ross, Ronald G., and Gladys S. W. Lam. 2000a. *The BRS Core Business Rule Practitioner's Guide: Using Business Rules in Developing Business Strategy.* Houston, TX: Business Rule Solutions, LLC. Available *http://www.BRSolutions.com.*

———. 2000b. *Capturing Business Rules.* Workbook for public seminar, presented in Boston, MA, June 19–21.

von Halle, Barbara. 2002. *Business Rules Applied: Building Better Systems Using the Business Rule Approach.* New York: Wiley Computer Publishing.

Zachman, John A. 2002. *The Zachman Framework: A Primer for Enterprise Engineering and Manufacturing* (electronic book). Available at *http://www.zachmaninternational.com.*

CHAPTER 14

More about Fact Models

Structuring the Basic Business Knowledge

Critical Success Factors for Fact Models

Organizing the Basic "Know" Part[1]

Fact models, a key deliverable in the business rule approach, were introduced in Part II. Refer to the boxed item, Again, What Is a Fact Model?, for a quick review.

Again, What Is a Fact Model?

A *fact model* structures basic knowledge about business practices from a business perspective. *Basic* means that the knowledge it represents cannot be derived or computed from any other knowledge. It that sense, a fact model is a crucial starting point for developing more advanced forms of business knowledge, including measures and rules.

In particular, a fact model focuses on assertions (called *facts*) involving core concepts of the business. In a fact model, concepts are represented by *terms*. Facts connect those terms in a manner that should reflect the real world. Both terms and facts in the fact model should be basic in the sense defined above.

---

1. This material is based on Ross and Lam [2000].

A fact model focuses on the "know" part of a business problem—that is, on how knowledge underlying business operations (the "flow") is organized. Literally, the fact model indicates what you need to *know* in order to *do* what you do.

A good fact model therefore tells you how to structure your basic thinking (or knowledge) about the business process based on a standard vocabulary. This ensures that you can communicate effectively about that knowledge with other project participants. It also allows you to exploit this standardized knowledge and vocabulary to express *other* types of requirements, especially rules—and to communicate about those effectively too.

A focus on structuring how business people can think and communicate about the business process has an important additional benefit. Inevitably, it helps bring into clear relief alternative ideas about how the business capacity itself can be best structured to satisfy business goals. When and by whom should such issues be resolved? As I have discussed, these are issues that should be resolved by *business-side* workers and managers *before* the project moves into system design or coding.

How do you know when you have done a good job on the fact model? The true test is below. By the way, *excruciating level of detail*[2] in this test means thorough business analysis—but not system design.

 Real-World Test for a High-Quality Fact Model

Once you have completed the fact model to an excruciating level of detail, you should be able to communicate with knowledgeable business workers about the basic business knowledge for the business process as if you had been in the business just as long as they have.

There should be only a single, consolidated fact model covering the entire scope of a problem domain. The goal is to unify basic business knowledge within that scope and to express each element of that basic business knowledge uniquely. This can be expressed as the following fundamental goal for fact models.

---

2. *Excruciating level of detail* is the term John Zachman [2002] uses for being very, very thorough but always staying carefully at the correct perspective for the given audience—in this case, the owners.

Fundamental Goal for Fact Models
One fact, one place, one name.

What is *not* important when you create a fact model is how you will organize any class diagram or design the database. Putting those things aside is often a challenge for IT professionals trained in those difficult disciplines.

Nonetheless, the key to success with the fact model is keeping the model focused squarely on the business perspective. All specifications (including the graphic model) should be aimed toward structuring how business people can think and communicate about the business capacity in an organized fashion. *Everything* in the fact model is about the business vocabulary needed to support such structure.

Defining Terms

Whenever possible, a native English[3] word or word phrase should be selected as the term of choice to represent a concept unless there is simply no such word in the language. Our experience is that this circumstance arises less often than might be imagined.

Moreover, instead of composing new definitions, a standard definition from *Webster's* (or another dictionary) should be selected and used for a term whenever possible. This not only saves work but also avoids arguments—it's hard to argue with standard definitions! If it is not possible to use a standard definition as is, the next choice is to extend or revise a dictionary definition as needed (carefully!). Only in the last resort should a new definition be composed from scratch.

Some approaches recommend that fundamental terms used in exactly their real-world sense (for example, *person, time,* and so on) need not be defined explicitly. This guideline can be followed with due caution, recognizing, however, that even native English words often have multiple meanings. For this reason, we prefer to make explicit the intended meaning of *all* terms, even when such meaning is simply taken verbatim from the dictionary.

If you are thinking that all this intense focus on terminology might create the need for a special skill on the project, you are right on track! Refer to the discussion in the boxed item, The Terminator.

---

3. Or whatever language is being used (for example, French, Mandarin, and so on).

The Terminator

In everyone's life, there is always *someone*—a teacher, a mother, a friend, a business colleague, whoever—who insists (maybe gently, maybe not) that things should be called by their right names. This is a person who always seems to have several words to choose from to put just the right spin on things. He or she forever has a dictionary at the ready and is never loath to use it no matter what the nature or objective of the discourse. Someone who excels at word games. Easily coins nicknames for new ideas. Knows that coining new terms is called *neology.*

Such people are the ones always called upon to do *wordsmithing* (usually not meant as a compliment). They are naturally good at turning a phrase. They think writing definitions is a really fun thing to do. As for grammar, where the rest of us see purgatory, they find poetry. They might have even been *liberal arts majors!*

Be that as it may, wordsmithing is a must-have skill for your business rule project. I mean fluency in *BusinessSpeak*, as opposed to *SystemSpeak* or *TechnoSpeak.* You need at least one team member who insists that things are always called by their right names and that proper definitions are always worked out and written down.

What you need is a *terminator.* That is what they have been called—with respect, I hope—on some of our business rule projects.[4]

Why is a terminator so fundamentally important? Remember the business rule mantra: *Rules build on facts, and facts build on terms.* Terms and their definitions are the foundation in the business rule approach. Build on a weak foundation, and your whole business logic becomes a house of cards.

The job does need a bit more dignified title than *terminator,* of course. Let me share a little dictionary research I did on this matter.

Ever heard of a *glossographer*? In case you are wondering, no, a glossographer is not someone who is good at glossing things over. I did not make up the term, either. It is a real term as well as an honorable profession (I presume).

---

4. To our knowledge, the first usage was by (and for) Karel Van Campenhout, a business-side subject matter expert who participated in a client project.

As it happens, one of the definitions of *gloss* is "a brief explanation . . . of a difficult or obscure word or expression."[5] A glossographer, then, is someone who writes down stuff like that. Unfortunately, another definition for *gloss* is "a false and often willfully misleading interpretation." That is not going to do!

What about *lexicographer*? This term means "the author or editor of a dictionary." A *lexicon* is "the vocabulary of a language, an individual speaker or group of speakers, or a subject." This sense is exactly right for what we need, but the word itself is somewhat obscure and a bit hard to say. Are there any other candidates?

The *New Oxford Dictionary of English* indicates *terminologist* to be a word in contemporary usage.[6] That label is a good one. So officially at least you should probably call your "terminator" a *terminologist*.

Relationships to Other Architectural Products in the Business Model

A fact model relates to other key deliverables in the business model for a business capacity in the following ways.

- *Concepts Catalog:* The collection of all terms and definitions for the "know" part of the business process is called a *Concepts Catalog*. Every term used for the fact model (and for any rule as well) should have a business definition in the Concepts Catalog. By the way, coordinating the Concepts Catalog is a fundamental part of rule management.
- *Policy Charter:* As described earlier, a Policy Charter is a battle plan identifying the key elements of the business solution (including core business rules). Each of these elements is implicitly based on basic knowledge that needs to be structured and standardized. Therefore, the Policy Charter is a rich source for terms (concepts) and facts that need to be included in the fact model.
- *Workflow models:* Workflow models outline the "flow" part of a business process. Performance of any given task produces knowledge (things that

---

5. This and other quoted definitions in this section come from *Merriam-Webster's Collegiate Dictionary*, 10th ed. (1999).
6. Thanks to Donald Chapin of Business Semantics, Ltd.

can be known) that should be represented by terms and facts in the fact model. Therefore, workflow models are another rich source for terms (concepts) and facts that need to be included in the fact model.

- *Rules:* A central deliverable in a business rule project is the Rule Book. Each rule will depend directly on the terms and facts developed in the fact model. Therefore, no term should appear in a rule that has not been defined in the Concepts Catalog. In addition, the fact model provides re-usable sentence patterns (the facts) for expressing the rules. As discussed in Part III, following these standard sentence patterns is essential for en-suring consistent expression and interpretation of the rules.

Again, Fact Model versus Data Model

Let's expand a bit on the distinctions made in Chapter 5 between fact models and data models.[7]

We view a fact model as part of the business model that a project should develop, whereas a data model is part of the system model it should develop. A fact model provides a business-based starting point—a blueprint—for subsequent development of a data model or database design. A good fact model can be easily transformed into a first-cut data model.

There are naturally significant differences in perspective, purpose, and success criteria between fact models and data models. In contrast to a fact model, a data model generally places emphasis on the following areas.

- *Delineating the data and its proper format to support system-level require-ments:* In a fact model, a box represents a term and the business concept for which it stands. In a data model, a box generally represents a collec-tion of attributes or fields that are structured to retain the appropriate data for storage and manipulation by applications.
- *Looking ahead toward the database environment and introducing features appropriate for database design in the given technical environment:* Exam-ples include normalization (or possibly denormalization), cardinality,

---

7. As mentioned in Part II, *class diagram* is more or less the corresponding term in object orientation. I certainly understand that important distinctions can be made between a data model and a class diagram—and even that these distinctions themselves can be con-troversial. However, this discussion is informal. For the sake of simplicity, I will simply say *data model* from this point on and assume you understand I also mean class diagrams of a corresponding nature.

associative entity types to support many-to-many relationship types, mandatory fields and relationships, and so on.

- *Addressing the complexities of time:* In general, fact models do not concern themselves with history. They simply identify what should be known about the basic business process at any given point in time. A data model, in contrast, must concern itself with the *points-over-time* aspect of data so the business (and its rules) can deal with the past (and the future). Modeling this points-over-time structure of data is one of the most important (and difficult) challenges in data modeling. I will return to this topic at the conclusion of this chapter.

None of the items above are appropriate for the fact model. Again, the primary audiences for the fact model and the data model are different. The primary audience for the fact model consists of business-side workers and managers (and business analysts), whereas the primary audience for the data model consists of system and database designers. It is very important to keep these distinctions in mind, especially since data models often use graphic conventions (boxes and box-to-box connections) that might appear similar to those used for fact models.

Getting to the Instance Level of the "Know" Part

A fact model and a data model also often have very different perspectives on the best handling of what is commonly known as *type codes*. Remember that the emphasis in fact models is on standardizing the business vocabulary and then capturing rules. The emphasis in a data model, in contrast, is often on achieving the most flexible data design possible—usually the best design for accommodating change.

The typical approach for data models therefore features special data objects or tables to handle type codes. The instances of such a data object or table represent valid type code values. This data object or table is related to any data object that is to be given one (or more) of those valid types. Creating a table for the codes in this fashion allows changes to the set of codes without impact on the database design. The data model itself, however, does not concern itself too much (if at all) with what the actual type code values might be.

Handling type codes in that manner is generally not adequate for fact models. In large measure, this is because standardized names for the *instances* of the type code are often highly relevant to product/service-type rules. Capturing and standardizing the underlying business terminology is critical.

This requires a special kind of model that focuses directly on predefining these instances. (We can stop using *type code* in the discussion at this point—it only causes confusion.) We call such models *instance models.* In all other respects, an instance model is basically like a fact model.

Consider the following examples.

- *Health care:* An instance model might be created to organize all recognized health services—for example, *Consultation, Office Visit, Hospital Admission, Surgery,* and so on.
- *Ship inspection:* An instance model might be created to organize all recognized parts of a ship—for example, *Bulkhead, Hatch Cover, Railing, Deck,* and so on.

In these examples and others like them, the business is likely to have hundreds of specialized instance-level terms and thousands of product/service rules that depend on them. Naming and categorizing these product/service terms—that is, building the appropriate instance models—is therefore crucial.

By the way, the encoding of what a company "knows" becomes so extensive at this point that the knowledge might deserve a special name. If so, that special name would probably be *ontology.* This term is defined in the related boxed item.

Definitions of Ontology[8]

1. [Philosophy] A systematic account of existence.
2. [Artificial Intelligence] (From philosophy) An explicit formal specification of how to represent the objects, concepts and other entities that are assumed to exist in some area of interest and the relationships that hold among them.
3. [Information Science] The hierarchical structuring of knowledge about things by subcategorizing them according to their essential (or at least relevant and/or cognitive) qualities. This is an extension of the previous senses of *ontology,* which has become common in discussions about the difficulty of maintaining subject indices.

---

8. From *The Free On-line Dictionary of Computing,* accessed in November 2002 at *http://www.foldoc.org/*; Denis Howe, editor.

Doing the Data Model Right for Business Rules

Using Rules to Reduce the Impact of Change

IT professionals with significant database experience generally agree that the hardest part of an operational business system to change or enhance is the database design itself. This fact is no less true for business systems developed using a business rule approach than for systems using more traditional techniques. The reason is that a database design represents *structure*. As discussed in Part II, structure is the most fundamental part of a business system—and therefore always the hardest part to change.

Change, of course, is a central fact of life for businesses today. Unfortunately, since businesses must sometimes change in fundamental ways to meet new business challenges, the potential impact for database designs can never be eliminated completely. A good data model, however, is one that reduces the need for future changes *to an absolute minimum*.

How can this objective be achieved? The answer is through rules. Rules are about control, not structure, so they can be changed or discontinued far more easily than the data model. This observation brings us to the following principle for data models in a rule-oriented environment.

 Use Rules Based on Generalized Data Models to Manage Change
Anticipate change by generalizing the data model as much as is reasonable. Then support current business practices by using rules.

The following discussion briefly suggests several ways in which this principle can be applied. One caution before continuing: The operative word in this principle is *reasonable*, which here means generalized without loss of meaning or clarity. It also means a reasonable chance exists that some change might actually occur in the future. If the chances of a future change are remote, then applying the principle in that case is *not* reasonable.

Generalizing Relationships

The idea of generalizing relationships is best illustrated by an example. Suppose Company ABC expresses the following current business practice: *Credit clerk approves order*. Its data model shows credit clerk as a subtype of employee.

Figure 14–1 illustrates how this current business practice would be directly represented in the structure of the data model.[9]

Organizational roles and their responsibilities form one of the fastest-changing aspects of most businesses. With regard to approving orders at Company ABC, the following questions would therefore be in order.

- Why are credit clerks responsible for approving orders?
- Is the role of credit clerk likely to be a stable one?
- Why not permit other types of employees to approve orders in the future?
- Is it conceivable that any employee might be permitted to do so in the future?

Because of the potential for change in the current business practice, the safe approach would be to generalize the relationship *Credit clerk approves order* to *Employee approves order*. Figure 14–2 shows the revised data model. The current business practice (that is, only credit clerks approve orders) can be handled as a rule: *An order may be approved only by a credit clerk*. This rule can be dropped or redefined in the future as circumstances warrant.

Generalizing the relationship *approves* to the supertype *employee* permits greater flexibility to accommodate future changes. A change in the current business practice (as represented by the rule) will no longer affect the database design.

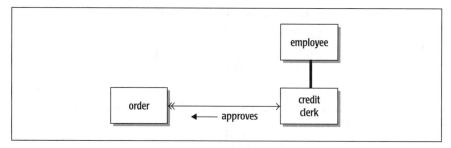

Figure 14–1   Current-practices data model (partial) for Company ABC

9. In this example and the ones that follow in this chapter, a double-headed arrow is used to represent a cardinality of *many*, and a single-headed arrow represents a cardinality of *one*. This choice of convention is unimportant with respect to the points made in the discussion.

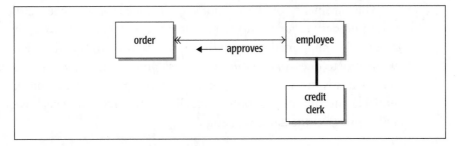

Figure 14–2   Generalized data model (partial) for Company ABC

Generalizing Cardinality

Rules offer similar flexibility in addressing the *cardinality* (also called *multiplicity*) of relationships. Again, the guideline is to design the data model for the most general case and to support current restrictions by using rules. For relationships, the most general case is a cardinality of *many* rather than a cardinality of *one*. An example illustrates.

Company XYZ currently permits an order to be shipped to only a single destination. This current business practice is reflected in Figure 14–3.

Company XYZ's customers, however, are beginning to request multidestination orders, and the database design might have to address this new requirement in the future. In anticipation of that possible change, the safe approach is to support the more general *many* case for the relationship *Order is shipped to destination.* Figure 14–4 illustrates the revised data model.

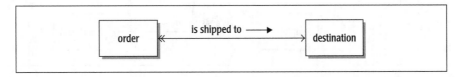

Figure 14–3   Current-practices data model (partial) for Company XYZ

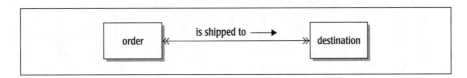

Figure 14–4   Generalized data model (partial) for Company XYZ

The cardinality of the relationship *is shipped to* has been indicated as *many* into *destination* to support the most general case. The following rule is expressed to support the current business practice limiting the relationship's cardinality to one: *An order must not be shipped to more than one destination.* Note that this rule is easily dropped (or altered) in the future, should the potential change in business policy actually occur. Such a change, however, will no longer affect the database design.

Generalizing Time

Fact models generally ignore the time dimension—that is, the past and the future—and simply express a "right now" perspective. Even for data models, ignoring time in expressing initial versions of relationships and cardinality is often expedient. Such models give point-in-time views of the business "know."

An example of a point-in-time view is the following: *An employee must not be assigned to more than one department.* This statement, of course, is actually a rule. It indicates that the appropriate cardinality for the relationship *Employee is assigned to department* is *one* into *department.* This is illustrated in Figure 14–5.

Clearly, point-in-time views are very limited. The cardinality of relationships over time is often not *one* but *many.* For example, the points-over-time view of the employee assignment relationship is probably as follows: *Over time, an employee may be assigned to many departments.* This revision clearly suggests a *many* cardinality, as Figure 14–6 illustrates.

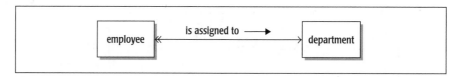

Figure 14–5   A point-in-time view of the employee assignment relationship

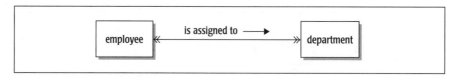

Figure 14–6   A points-over-time view of the employee assignment relationship

The actual situation for many points-over-time relationships, however, is often even more complicated. For example, the following might be true for the employee assignment relationship: *Over time, an employee may be assigned to the same department more than one time.*

The key to addressing this kind of complexity (which, by the way, is not at all unusual) is to recognize that specific kinds of events are occurring in the "flow" part of the business. These business events occur in a predictable, repetitive, and structured manner. The *result* of these events represents something we can know and therefore something that must be included in the "know" part of the system model.

In any given case, such recognition typically gives rise to a new term in the business vocabulary. In the example above, this new term might be *assignment* (of employees to departments). Up until now I have been using this term only informally.

Generalizing time in a data model means including data objects or tables to represent the results of such business events directly. The data model in Figure 14–7 illustrates this for *assignment*. It is important to remember, of course, that as included in this data model, *assignment* does not represent the actual activity but rather the knowledge that results from the activity.

Generalizing a data model by including such event-recording data objects or tables permits the expression of true points-over-time relationships. For example, it permits two or more assignments of an employee over time to be to the same department.

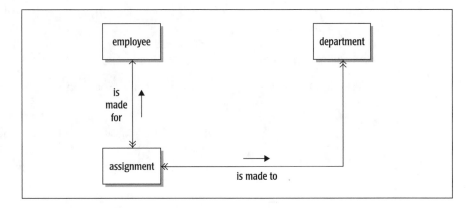

Figure 14–7 A generalized view of the employee assignment relationship

As always, current business practices should be expressed as rules. Such rules might include the following.

Rule: *An employee must not have more than one active assignment.*

Rule: *Successive assignments of an employee must not be to the same department.*

Note that either of these rules is easily dropped (or altered) in the future, should a change in the given business practice be warranted. As before, the database design is unaffected by such changes. Thus by generalizing time and expressing current business practices as rules, database designers can achieve maximum flexibility for future change.

More on the Lighter Side of Rules

Church Rules[10]

Announcement in a church bulletin for a national Prayer and Fasting Conference: "Note: The cost for attending the Fasting and Prayer conference includes meals."

"Ladies, don't forget the rummage sale. It's a chance to get rid of those things not worth keeping around the house. Don't forget your husbands."

"Don't let worry kill you off. Let the church help."

"At the evening service tonight, the sermon topic will be 'What Is Hell.' Come early and listen to our choir practice."

"Please place your donation in the envelope along with the deceased person you want remembered."

"Attend and you will hear an excellent speaker and heave a healthy lunch."

"This evening at 7 P.M. there will be a hymn sing in the park across from the Church. Bring a blanket and come prepared to sin."

"Low Self-Esteem Support Group will meet Thursday at 7 P.M. Please use the back door."

---

10. Editor's note: This material was forwarded to the author via e-mail. Original sources unknown.

"The eighth graders will be presenting Shakespeare's *Hamlet* in the Church basement Friday at 7 P.M. The Congregation is invited to attend this tragedy."

"Weight Watchers will meet at 7 P.M. at the First Presbyterian Church. Please use the large double doors at the side entrance."

"The Associate Minister unveiled the church's new tithing campaign slogan last Sunday. 'I upped my pledge. Up yours.'"

References

Ross Ronald G., and Gladys S. W. Lam. 2000. *The BRS Fact Modeling Practitioner's Guide: Developing the Business Basis for Data Models.* Houston, TX: Business Rule Solutions, LLC. Available at *http://www.BRSolutions.com.*

Zachman, John A. 2002. *The Zachman Framework: A Primer for Enterprise Engineering and Manufacturing* (electronic book). Available at *http://www.zachmaninternational.com.*

PART V

A Theory of Business Rules

A Tutorial on the Formal Basis for Business Rules and Business Rule Notation[1]

Overview

The discussion that follows provides a general tutorial on the theoretical foundation of business rules. It is aimed for those who seek a deeper, more universal understanding of business rules than is apparent in vendor software products, particular business rule methodologies, or individual business applications.

---

1. Version 8.

Acknowledgments for Part V:

Pedram Abrari and Mark J. Felder Allen, both of Corticon Technologies, Inc., provided significant contributions and continuing support in the development of this work.

My partner in Business Rule Solutions, LLC, Gladys S. W. Lam, has provided sound practical advice on numerous occasions.

Thanks are also due to Donald Chapin of Business Semantics, Ltd., and Keri Anderson Healy, Editor of the *Business Rules Journal* (http://www.BRCommunity.com), for their very helpful reviews of early drafts.

In several subsequent drafts, thanks are due to C. J. Date, who gave generously and graciously of his time and knowledge.

In addition, Michael Eulenberg, Terry Halpin of North Face Learning, Inc., Allan Kolber, and Markus Schacher of KnowGravity, Inc., provided numerous suggestions, clarifications, examples, and constructive criticisms.

To "Mary."

In this tutorial, we[2] offer specific, formal[3] answers to several of the "big questions" of the business rule approach, including the following.

- Is there a theoretical basis for business rules?
- How do the three fundamental kinds of business rules—*terms*, *facts*, and *rules*—relate to one another?
- Is there only one way to look at business rules, or are different views valid depending on one's perspective?
- What do business rules and logical deduction or inference have in common?
- How can business rules be represented in a theoretically sound manner?
- How can higher-order rules be supported?

These questions are answered using basic constructs of the[4] predicate calculus.[5] Predicate calculus is part of *formal logic*, which has a long and respected history.

The boxed item, Notes on Formal Logic and Predicate Calculus, presents some brief notes describing formal logic and predicate calculus. These notes are intended for those readers who are not familiar with these bodies of work or who need a quick refresher. Obviously, we are just scratching the surface—there is *far* more to predicate logic than these notes represent. Nonetheless, they provide sufficient background for our purposes in this tutorial.

---

2. The informal *we* used in this discussion and throughout Part V refers to the Principals of Business Rule Solutions, LLC.

3. Unless otherwise specified, I will use the word *formal* in this tutorial as in everyday usage. According to *Merriam-Webster's Collegiate Dictionary*, 10th ed. (1999, first definition), *formal* means "belonging to or constituting the form or essence of a thing." However, the theories discussed in this part (for example, the predicate calculus, relational model, and so on) are *formalizations* or *formal systems* of a special kind. (Refer to Appendix H.) Use of *formal* in those contexts (which is frequent) therefore has special status. Also, *formal logic* has a special meaning, as will be indicated.

4. There are other forms of calculus besides *predicate* calculus—for example, *propositional* calculus. The existence of multiple forms is why the definite article *the* is sometimes used in reference to *the predicate calculus* in discussions of formal logic. However, including *the* makes the text a bit unfriendly, so I will omit it from this point on in the discussion.

5. The terms *predicate logic* and *predicate calculus* are often used interchangeably in the literature. However, *predicate calculus* is a bit more accurate for our purposes in this tutorial.

Notes on Formal Logic and Predicate Calculus[6]

Logic or formal logic: ". . . [T]he science of formal principles of reasoning or correct inference" [Simpson 2000, p. 2]. "A science that deals with the principles and criteria of validity of inference and demonstration: the science of the formal principles of reasoning" [*Merriam-Webster's Collegiate Dictionary*, 1999, first definition].

Calculus: ". . . [A] general term that refers to any system of symbolic computation; in [predicate calculus], the kind of computation involved is the computation of the truth value—true or false—of certain formulas or expressions" [Date 2000, p. 772].

Predicate calculus: ". . . [A] general method or framework . . . for reasoning about any subject matter whatsoever" [Simpson, p. 2]. "The predicate calculus [also known as *first-order logic*] dates from the 1910's and 1920's.[7] It is basic for all subsequent logical research. It is a very general system of logic which accurately expresses a huge variety of assertions and modes of reasoning. . . . It is much more flexible than [Aristotelian logic]" [Simpson, p. 5].

Predicate: "Aristotelian logic begins with the familiar grammatical distinction between subject and predicate. A *subject* is typically an individual entity, for instance a man or a house or a city. It may also be a class of entities, for instance all men. A *predicate* is a property or attribute or mode of existence which a given subject may or may not possess.[8] For example, an individual man (the subject) may or may not be skillful (the predicate), and all men (the subject) may or may not be brothers (the predicate)" [Simpson, p. 3].

continued

6. For an excellent short introduction to the history and concepts of formal logic, see Simpson [2000]. For an in-depth treatment, refer to Nilsson [1998, pp. 215–358].
7. Predicate calculus, in turn, was based on a "remarkable" treatise, the Begriffsschrift ("concept script"), published in 1879 by the German philosopher Gottlob [Simpson, p. 5].
8. There are objections to this characterization of predicate. For example, C. J. Date indicates that he does not find it very helpful (private correspondence, November 11, 2001). However, I believe these difficulties probably arise from a difference in perspective, as I discuss later in the tutorial.

"... [I]n the predicate calculus [in contrast to Aristotelian logic], a subject is always an individual entity, never a class of entities. For example, an individual man can be treated as a subject, but the class of all men must betreated as a predicate.[9] ... For example, if *M* is the predicate 'to be a man' and *a* is the individual 'Socrates,' then *Ma* denotes the assertion 'Socrates is a man'" [Simpson, p. 5].

"Some predicates require more than one argument. For example, if *B* is the predicate 'bigger than,' then *Bxy* denotes the assertion '*x* is bigger than *y*'. Thus *B* requires two arguments. ... If we try to use *B* with only one argument, we obtain something like *Bx*, i.e., '*x* is bigger than'. This ... is only a meaningless combination of symbols. In analogy with English grammar, we could say that *Bxy* is like a grammatically correct sentence, while *Bx* is merely a sentence fragment. Such fragments play no role in the predicate calculus" [Simpson, p. 5].

"The essential idea of the predicate calculus is that predicates are treated as atomic (black boxes). Logical formulas are comprised of predicates and individual variables or constants, along with logical operators (e.g., AND, OR, NOT, IF ... THEN ...), and logical quantifiers[10] (i.e., the universal quantifier 'all' [or FORALL] (best read as 'for each' or 'given any') and the existential quantifier 'some' [or EXISTS] (meaning 'there exists at least one')" [Halpin 2001].

First-order predicate calculus: "We are concerned [in this tutorial] only with the *first-order* predicate calculus, which basically means that (a) there are no 'predicate variables' (i.e., variables whose permitted values are predicates), and hence that (b) predicates cannot themselves be subjected to quantification [i.e., by means of the two logical quantifiers]" [Date 2000, p. 778].

---

9. We believe the point here is simply to emphasize the sharp distinction between instance and class in predicate calculus. It is certainly possible for a class to be the subject of a predicate. C. J. Date cites the following examples: "The class of all men is finite." "The class of all men has a total biomass of less than a million tons" (private correspondence, November 11, 2001).

10. The logical quantifiers are actually shorthands useful for finite problems.

Proposition: "A proposition[11] in logic is something that evaluates to either true or false, unequivocally. For instance, 'illiam Shakespeare wrote *Pride and Prejudice*' is a proposition (a false one as it happens)" [Date 2000, p. 13].

Validity: ". . . [A] piece of formally correct reasoning is not scientifically valid unless it is based on a true and primary starting point [i.e., true and primary business rules]. . . . [A]ny decisions about what is true and primary do not pertain to logic but rather to the specific subject matter under consideration" [Simpson, p. 2].

"[Propositions presented to the system] can be checked for consistency within the world of [other propositions known to be true], but cannot be fully verified as mirroring reality in the external world. In the end, that is the responsibility of the person stating the fact" [Chapin 2001].

"*The system can't enforce* truth, *only* consistency. . . . Sadly, truth and consistency aren't the same thing! . . . **Correct** implies **consistent** (but not the other way around), and **inconsistent** implies **incorrect** (but not the other way around)" [Date 2001, original emphasis].

This part of the book shows how the fundamental ideas of business rules are directly grounded in the basic constructs of predicate calculus. The material is organized into four chapters, as follows:

- Chapter 15 presents basic ideas, including the crucial idea of perspective.
- Chapter 16 examines the formulation of rules in depth.
- Chapter 17 examines predicates and facts in depth.
- Chapter 18 provides a theoretical basis for higher-order rules.

To keep this part as readable as possible for a broad audience, including those who have never been exposed to predicate calculus, I made the deliberate decision not to introduce or use its notation. However, there is one important exception—a basic and relatively compact notation is needed to illustrate and discuss business rules.

Conventional notation for rules in formal logic is used for this purpose. This notation is extended for certain special needs, particularly for

---

11. A proposition can be viewed as a special or degenerate case of a predicate. For example, C. J. Date indicates, "A predicate has a set of arguments. A proposition is what you get if that set happens to be empty" (private correspondence, November 11, 2001).

representing facts and higher-order rules. These extensions result in a scheme called *R-Notation*.[12] This extended notation is introduced in Chapters 16 and 17 as we go along.

Higher-order rules are called *Pattern-R* rules in our approach. The typing scheme for these higher-order rules was originally developed and presented in *The Business Rule Book* [Ross 1997].[13] We believe *Pattern-R* rules hold promise for significant productivity improvements in business rule specification.

References

Chapin, Donald. 2001. Private correspondence, May 15.

Date, C. J. 2001. "Constraints and Predicates: A Brief Tutorial (Part 3)." *Business Rules Journal*, 2(12). Accessed in August 2002 at *http://www.BRCommunity.com/a2001/b065c.html*.

―――. 2000. *An Introduction to Database Systems* (7th ed.). Boston, MA: Addison-Wesley.

Date, C. J., and Hugh Darwen. 2000. *Foundation for Future Database Systems: The Third Manifesto* (2nd ed.). Boston, MA: Addison-Wesley.

Halpin, Terry. 2001. Private correspondence, July 18.

Nilsson, Nils J. 1998. *Artificial Intelligence: A New Synthesis*. San Francisco, CA: Morgan Kaufmann.

Ross, Ronald G. 1997. *The Business Rule Book* (2nd ed.). Houston, TX: Business Rule Solutions, LLC. Available at *http://www.BRSolutions.com*.

Simpson, Stephen G. 2000. "Logic and Mathematics." Available at *http://www.math.psu.edu/simpson/*.

---

12. It could be easily assumed that the *R* in *R-Notation* simply stands for *Ross*, but that is not the case. Use of the *R* in the various names that appear in this part (for example, *R-Notation* and *Pattern-R*) emerged more or less by accident during the development of this work as various contributors and reviewers communicated with me and with each other. I take the *R* to stand for *rules*, and perhaps also for *relational*. With regard to the latter, our work draws heavily from relational theory—especially the recent work of C. J. Date and Hugh Darwen [2000]. Also, both our work and relational theory are based on the same theoretical foundations—namely, predicate calculus and set theory. (Part V addresses predicate calculus directly but not set theory.)

13. This work provides numerous atomic and derived rule types, which collectively are called *Pattern-R* rule types in this part of the book.

CHAPTER 15

Three Perspectives on Business Rules

A Framework for Formal Discussion

The Three Perspectives

The business rule approach follows three major tracks, as outlined below.

1. *The business track:* Here it is an approach to creating and managing a business or business process.
2. *The system track:* Here it is an approach to developing an appropriate knowledge and/or information system to support such a business or business process. (Such a system usually involves significant automation.)
3. *The technical track:* Here it is an approach to designing a suitable implementation such a system.

There are therefore three distinct perspectives on business rules, each valid and each targeting a different audience.[1] These audiences have distinct needs and agendas, as follows.

- *The business manager's perspective:* This audience faces the challenge of creating and managing a business or business process. As seen from the other two

---

1. Followers of John Zachman will recognize these perspectives as corresponding to rows 2, 3, and 4 respectively, of his Enterprise Architecture Framework. Refer to Zachman [2002] and collected articles by Zachman found in the *Business Rules Journal*, available in November 2002 at *http://www.BRCommunity.com*.

perspectives, the business manager's perspective represents a layperson's view of system designs and IT technology. At this perspective,[2] the focus is on developing business vocabulary and business logic (that is, capturing business rules).

- *The system developer's perspective:* This audience faces the challenge of developing a sound system design. At the system developer's perspective, the focus is on rigorous specification of business rules relative to the systematic representation of information and/or knowledge. This activity involves analysis and transformation of business rules captured at the business manager's perspective.

- *The technical designer's perspective:* This audience faces the challenge of developing a suitable implementation design for the automated components of the system design. At the technical designer's perspective, the focus is on optimal implementation of business rules under the given choice(s) of IT technology.

The business rule approach is business-driven *by design*—that is, on purpose. We therefore consider the first of the above perspectives to be preeminent. If there were no business problems to solve, the second perspective and then the third perspective would not even be needed.

We believe the three major tracks of the business rule approach can be organized so that they align with one another quite closely. One additional purpose of this tutorial is to demonstrate how such alignment is achieved. Such alignment, we believe, will serve to enhance support for the business manager's perspective—which, again, we believe is preeminent.

---

2. In discussions using Zachman's Enterprise Architecture Framework, practitioners often couch statements in the following way: "at row 2," "at row 3," and so on. In this tutorial, such reference to rows might be confusing to many readers, so I have avoided it throughout. Nonetheless, I do use *at*, rather than the more proper *from*, when referencing any given perspective—for example, "*at* the business manager's perspective," "*at* the system developer's perspective," and so on. I ask for the reader's indulgence on this point.

> **Special Note about the Technical Designer's Perspective**
>
> The business manager's perspective and the system developer's perspective are intentionally independent of any specific implementation technology. At these perspectives, the discussion in this tutorial can stand on its own.
>
> The technical designer's perspective, in contrast, is technology-dependent. Any discussion at this perspective must therefore be framed in the context of a particular technology.
>
> We have elected the relational model to provide our technology context in this regard since it has had such a pervasive influence on database thinking. In particular, we find the approach of Date and Darwen [2000] to be an attractive one, and thus I comment on that approach as warranted in this tutorial.

A Word about Terms

The earlier notes about formal logic indicated the importance of distinguishing between individual things, or *instances*, and *classes*. An example of an individual thing or instance might be a particular person—for example, the person named "Mary." An example of a class of instances might be the set of all people.

Throughout this tutorial, I focus on the kinds of *terms* that can be used in formal expressions of rules, predicates, and propositions. I will give the precise definition of *term* in that context later. In general, however, the names given to either instances or classes can be terms. Where it is important to distinguish in individual cases, I will say *instance term* or *class term*.

At the system developer's perspective, this distinction in terms is relatively straightforward. A class term generally might be taken to represent what system developers see as an *entity type* or *business object*. I will refrain from using these latter terms, however, since they play no role in formal theory.

At the technical designer's perspective, the picture is more complicated. Here we are further removed from the business manager's perspective, where the terms originally arise (or *should* arise, anyway). For that reason, the issue requires closer analysis, which is given in Chapter 16 and in Appendix B.

A Word about Types

Type is unfortunately used to mean at least two quite different things in the IT world.

- Data modelers generally use the term in a way that is equivalent to *class* as described above. For example, a data modeler might speak of the employee *type.*
- Usage in the context of programming languages usually means the type (or data type) that values must have to be suitable for a variable. For example, a programmer might speak of a variable of *type* integer.

Note that the former usage is typically at the system developer's perspective, whereas the latter usage is typically at the technical designer's perspective. The conflict in the two meanings can be managed so long as any usage is carefully framed as being for one purpose or the other.

A more serious problem occurs when the former usage occurs at the technical designer's perspective. Here, the two meanings collide in troublesome ways. This problem is especially noteworthy for theoretical work whose goal is to unite databases, rules, and programming—a fundamentally important area for support of business rules. (See Appendix B for additional discussion.) That area, however, is largely beyond the scope of this tutorial.

To keep things simple, I will therefore carefully qualify any usage I make of the term *type* in this tutorial.

Special Terminology

In looking at business rules from the viewpoint of formal logic, other significant problems arise in terminology. Terms commonly used in the IT community—especially *data* and *database*—can be easily misleading in that context. For the most part, this problem stems from the simple fact that commercial products offered to date for database management have provided virtually no support for rules.

For that reason, I will generally avoid the terms *data* and *database* in this discussion in favor of ones with less baggage, as follows. The reasons for particular choices will become apparent in due course.

- *Factbase:* The store that holds persistent "data"[3] of the enterprise. The contents of the factbase are believed to be accurate and true. For this reason, the contents are called *facts.* [4]
- *Rulebase:* The store that contains the business rules for a factbase. This store roughly contains *metadata,* but with emphasis on rules and their current operational status and evaluation. These rules will have been specified in a declarative manner. (See Appendix I for discussion of what *declarative* means with respect to rules.)
- *Logicbase:* The store that contains both a factbase and its associated rulebase. The current content of the logicbase comprehensively defines *state* for the targeted area of the business—or at least those parts of it that can be automated. In other words, the logicbase should be viewed as *the* authoritative and exclusive source of information describing the cumulative effect of business operations up to the current point in time.[5]
- *Business logic server:* The runtime system software responsible for the logicbase—that is, for managing the factbase and executing the rules in the rulebase.[6] A business logic server might also be called a *rule engine, rule processing server,* or *decision management platform.* The boxed item, Rule Independence and the Business Logic Server, emphasizes the importance of business logic servers.

Several observations should be made about the terms above.

- The distinction between *factbase* and *rulebase* emphasizes that the evaluation of rules (and in particular, any information that needs to be retained *between* evaluations) should be handled separately from the persistent "data" itself. This separation ensures the highest possible degree of flexibility (tolerance of change) in the rules over time.

---

3. "Data" will always appear in quotation marks in this tutorial since whenever it is used from this point on, I actually mean *facts* (except as noted).
4. By convention, these facts are taken to be true propositions in the sense of predicate calculus.
5. Such information can, of course, include schedules for business activities that have not yet actually occurred.
6. Depending on the architecture of the business logic server, associated software facilities might include a rules compiler.

Rule Independence and the Business Logic Server

Giving a business logic server exclusive responsibility for executing the rules is highly desirable. Ultimately, the only way to ensure the integrity (that is, correctness)[7] of the logicbase is by *isolating* the rules from application processes.

Consider what might happen if the business logic server did not have exclusive responsibility for the rules: "... otherwise different users (and/or different applications) might erroneously have different notions of correctness. For example, A might believe the maximum salary is 100K while B believes it is 80K. Then A could update the [factbase] in such a way as to make it incorrect as far as B is concerned, and B might then proceed on a false assumption—*viz.*, that all salaries in the [factbase] were less than or equal to 80K" [Date 2001].

At a more technical level, suppose some outside process assigns a value of false to a variable in the logicbase while a rule "thinks" the variable should be true, or a process assigns true while a rule "thinks" it should be false. Quite simply, the business logic server will use faulty logic in reasoning.

Furthermore, the rationale for the change would be embedded in the process rather than externalized (that is, made visible) by the explicit rules. This externalization of (business) logic from processes is a fundamental goal of the business rule approach. By this means, the (business) logic is more accessible, more readily understood, and more easily changed. We call this *Rule Independence*.

- The terms *logicbase* and *business logic server* emphasize the need to view persistent "data" and rules *together* when considering business rules from the perspective of formal logic.[8] They are also meant to place emphasis on *business* logic—which of course is what business rules are all about. Unfortunately, the terms *database* and *database management system* (DBMS) do not carry that same sense, at least as commonly used in cur-

---

7. *Consistency* is actually a more precise term here. The business logic server cannot *really* know if the logicbase is correct with respect to the external real world it purports to reflect.
8. A classic work covering this area is Widom and Ceri [1996].

rent IT practice (no rules).[9] Neither do the terms *inference engine* and *expert system*, albeit for the opposite reason (no persistent "data").

- In expert systems, *expert system shell* corresponds very roughly to a business logic server. Unfortunately, *expert system shell* generally carries the following sense: ". . . short-term memory that contains specific data about the actual problem under study" [Crevier 1993, p. 156]. "Short-term memory" is clearly inconsistent with the business logic server's responsibility for managing the factbase.

- Expert systems, artificial intelligence (AI), and certain other disciplines[10] often use the term *knowledgebase*. Although *knowledgebase* can be defined in many ways (that is part of the problem!), at least for expert systems and AI it can be generally characterized as follows: "In its simplest form . . . a list of IF . . . THEN . . . rules [each of] which specifies what to do, or what conclusions to draw, under a set of well-defined circumstances" [Crevier, p. 156]. A minor concern is this emphasis on the IF . . . THEN . . . syntax. (Refer to Appendix D.) A more serious concern is that research into AI is far more ambitious—and difficult—than this "simplest form." We prefer to focus on the immediate problem of organizing and managing operational business logic—not other possible forms of knowledge. For this reason, we prefer the more cautious (and possibly more accurate) term *rulebase*.

References

Crevier, Daniel. 1993. *AI: The Tumultuous History of the Search for Artificial Intelligence.* New York: BasicBooks.

Date, C. J. 2001. Private correspondence, November 19.

———. 2000. *What Not How: The Business Rule Approach to Application Development.* Boston, MA: Addison-Wesley.

---

9. C. J. Date [2000, p. 113] writes, ". . . this is a place where the SQL vendors *really* let us down. . . . [There are] several ways in which the SQL vendors let us down, but this one is perhaps the biggest; indeed, it underlies many of the others."

10. For example, automated tools supporting enterprise architecture.

Date, C. J., and Hugh Darwen. 2000. *Foundation for Future Database Systems: The Third Manifesto* (2nd ed.). Boston, MA: Addison-Wesley.

Widom, Jennifer, and Stefano Ceri (eds). 1996. *Active Database Systems: Triggers and Rules for Advanced Database Processing.* San Francisco, CA: Morgan Kaufmann.

Zachman, John A. 2002. *The Zachman Framework: A Primer for Enterprise Engineering and Manufacturing* (electronic book). Available at *http://www.zachmaninternational.com.*

CHAPTER 16

The Theoretical Foundation of Rules

About Formal Constraints

The Formal Definition of *Rule*

At a theoretical level, rules are based directly on predicate calculus. More specifically, they are the IF-THEN connective of predicate calculus (also known as the *implication connective* or *logical implication*). The general form of the IF-THEN connective appears below. Definitions for the terms we need to explore this connective are given in the boxed item, More Notes on Terminology.

IF p THEN q

Note the following about this form.

- p and q must be Boolean expressions—that is, they must evaluate to either true or false.
- p is called the *antecedent*.
- q is called the *consequent*.
- This example can also be read as follows: "p implies q."

> **More Notes on Terminology**
>
> **Truth value:** A value of either true or false.
>
> **Boolean:** A truth value.[1]
>
> *continued*

---

1. *Boolean* as a noun is taken to mean a value of either true or false, in the same way that *integer* is usually taken to mean an integer *value*.

Truth-valued variable: A variable capable of holding a Boolean—that is, a variable of type Boolean. Truth-valued variables are also known as *Boolean variables*.

Logical operator: A nonarithmetic operation that can be performed on truth-valued variables. The three basic operators are AND, OR, and NOT. All other logical operators can be expressed in terms of these three.

Logical expression: An expression that evaluates to a truth value.[2] For example, a logical expression might be formed by using the logical connectives OR and/or AND. Logical expressions are also known as *Boolean expressions*, *truth-valued expressions*, and *conditional expressions*.

Premise: An antecedent is sometimes called a *premise*. However, the term *premise* is often used in discussion of metarules (rules about rules), which we take to be its proper (reserved) usage. An example of such a metarule is the following: (p AND q) implies p, which simply says "p is a logical consequence of (p AND q)." The premise in this example is (p AND q).

Conclusion: A consequent is sometimes called a *conclusion*. The same comment as above, however, also applies to the term *conclusion*. The conclusion in the given metarule example above is the portion of the expression after the "implies"—that is, p.

In predicate calculus, the expression IF p THEN q is *exactly* equivalent to the following logical expression, which might actually be easier to interpret correctly. (There is more here than meets the eye!)

$$OR\ ((NOT\ p),\ q)$$

The syntax is unimportant here. This expression could also be written ((NOT p) OR q).

---

2. In contrast, a *proposition* in logic is something that evaluates to either true or false, *categorically*.

This expression is precisely (and completely) the formal definition of a rule.[3] What the expression says in everyday English is simply that "Either p is not true or q is true."[4] So when can p be true? It can be true *only if* q is true. In other words, the truth of q is *required* for p to be true. If q is not true, then p *cannot* be true. Here is an example to illustrate.

p: "it is raining"

q: "streets are wet"

Rule: OR ((NOT "it is raining"), "streets are wet")

Question: When can "it is raining" be true?

Answer: Only if "streets are wet" is true.

If "streets are wet" is *not* true, then according to the rule, the expression (NOT "it is raining") must be true. The only way that (NOT "it is raining") can be true is if "it is raining" is *false*.

Several additional points should be made here.

- First, q can be true even if p is *not* true. Nothing in the expression OR ((NOT p), q) prohibits that. In other words, just because q is true does not mean that p is necessarily true. For instance, in the example above, q ("streets are wet") can be true even if p ("it is raining") is *not* true.
- It is important to remember that the expression OR ((NOT p), q) as a whole is itself also a Boolean expression—in other words, given a set of arguments (that is, specific values for p and q), the rule as a whole evaluates to either true or false. (This evaluation is in addition to the Boolean expressions p, NOT p, and q.) The complete truth table for rules and related explanations are given in Appendix A, which also explains related subtleties.
- This example illustrates that the IF . . . THEN . . . syntax is not essential for expression of the rules. The boxed item, The IF-THEN Connective versus the IF . . . THEN . . . Syntax for Rule Statements, examines the relationship between logical implication and IF-THEN syntax.

---

3. Refer to Appendix C for discussion of where computation and derivation "rules" fit.
4. The expression is also satisfied if *both* of the following are true: (a) p is not true and (b) q is true.

The IF-THEN Connective versus the IF . . . THEN . . . Syntax for Rule Statements

We use the term *rule statement* for the expression of a rule in everyday English at the business manager's perspective.[5] Such rule statements can be given using IF . . . THEN . . . syntax. An example is "*If* a person is female and of age, *then* that person is a woman."

Note carefully that the IF-THEN connective is *not* the same thing as the IF . . . THEN . . . syntax for expressing rule statements. The IF-THEN connective is simply an alternative form in predicate calculus for the logical expression OR ((NOT p), q).

Also note carefully that the IF-THEN connective *in no way mandates* use of the IF . . . THEN . . . syntax for expressing rule statements. The issue of syntax is altogether distinct. Refer to Appendix D for additional discussion.

If a given logical implication (that is, rule) is *required* to be true,[6] then that logical implication is said to be a *constraint*.[7] For example, suppose we define the earlier expression as a constraint: OR ((NOT p), q). The sense of this constraint in everyday English is: "p *must* imply q." In other words, q *must* be true when p is true.

A logical implication (that is, rule) need not necessarily be required to be true. (Here, the meaning of *rule* differs in formal theory from its everyday sense.) If we do not require it to be true, then in effect we are merely expressing some test or posing a query about the current state or *condition* of the logicbase.

---

5. Obviously, since *rule statement* as I use it here refers to the expression of a rule at the business manager's perspective, there is no correlation to *statement* as commonly used in the context of application programming languages. In the latter context, *statement* often means something imperative (that is, a command). *Rule statement*, in contrast, carries the everyday sense of *rule*—a guideline or constraint for (business) behavior.

6. This requirement might be supported in any of several ways. In one approach, the rule would temporarily evaluate to false, and the business logic server would take appropriate action (for example, returning the factbase to a previous state) to ensure that the rule evaluates to true upon subsequent reevaluation.

7. Or *integrity constraint*, which is the term used in *The Business Rule Book* [Ross 1997].

Again consider the rule OR ((NOT p), q). Defined as a test or query rather than a constraint, the sense of the expression in everyday English becomes "*Does* p imply q?" As this illustrates, we are now in effect simply asking a true-false question (that is, posing a query) that the logicbase presumably can answer.

The focus of the first three chapters of this tutorial is on the use of logical implications as constraints rather than as tests or queries. Note, however, that their use as tests or queries is important for expressing higher-order rules, as discussed later in Chapter 18. Higher-order rules typically involve complex patterns that would be difficult to express otherwise. A logical implication used as a test or query in expressing higher-order rules is called a *condition*.[8] Refer to Appendix C for discussion of constraints versus conditions.

More on Terms

In formal and informal discussions of rule theory, *term* is the word most frequently used[9] to refer to each individually named element in any given rule (for example, p, q, and so on). It is not by accident that this use correlates with the use of *term* in the business rule approach.

In expressing rules (and, indeed, for predicate calculus in general), formal theory prescribes that a term must be exactly one of the following three kinds:[10]

1. The name of an *individual thing*. The thing so named might be a particular person, place, item, concept, and so on—for example, "Mary," "Memphis," "gold," true, 5, and so on.[11]

---

8. *Condition* is the term used in *The Business Rule Book* [Ross 1997].

9. See Date [2000a, p. 778]. However, Date prefers *placeholder* or *parameter* to *term* in the context of rules (private correspondence, November 19, 2001). See also the following references: Halpin [2001, pp. 63–64] and Charniak and McDermott [1985, p. 15].

10. This restriction applies to any term used in well-formed formulas (WFFs) of predicate calculus. See Date [2000a, p. 778] and Charniak and McDermott [1985, pp. 15 and 321].

11. For discussion purposes in this part of the book, I use quotation marks to indicate alphabetic names (for example, "Mary," "gold," and so on). This convention helps distinguish them from the names of variables, which I will indicate without quotation marks (for example, XYZ, Employee, salary, and so on).

2. The name of a *variable* capable of holding a value. For example, variables defined to hold the values above might be named person, city, metal, of-age, and rank, respectively.
3. The name of a *function* capable of producing a value. Examples include ADD, SQUARE ROOT, and so on.

As this list indicates, *all* terms are names of one kind or another. There is much confusion over this point. For example, many texts simply indicate that terms can be values, variables, or functions.

Upon reflection, however, it is obvious that variables and functions cannot be terms *per se*. For example, "x" is the *name* of a variable that can hold a value—not the actual variable itself. And "+" (or ADD) is the *name* of the function that performs addition—not the actual function. For more about function names in the business rule approach, refer to the boxed item, A Note about Function-Type Terms.

In the case of terms that denote individual things, it is also obvious that the names of people, places, and items are not the *actual* people, places, or items. For example, the literal "Mary" is not the real flesh-and-blood person. The literal "Memphis" is not the actual place in Tennessee. The literal "gold" is not the real metal.

The case of terms that denote concepts or ideas, however, is more difficult. When someone says "true," is this the actual idea or simply the name of the idea? When someone says "5," is that the actual number or the name of the concept five?

The answer becomes clear when you realize that the same concept or idea can be denoted by different literals. For example, the *idea* of true can be denoted by "T" (as opposed to "F") or "on" (as opposed to "off") or "1" (as opposed to "0"). The *concept* of five can be denoted by "5" or "5.0" or "cinco" (in Spanish) or "V" (in Roman numerals). Clearly, all these literals are the names of some underlying concept or idea.[12]

 All terms are names.

---

12. C. J. Date [2000b, p. 73] refers to this underlying concept or idea as the *value*.

A Note about Function-Type Terms

As mentioned above, the names of functions are viewed by the predicate calculus as terms when included in a Boolean expression.[13] Such a function might or might not be a truth-valued function, but it must, like all functions, return a single value for any given set of arguments. Non-truth-valued functions are permitted for convenience to allow inclusion of computations (for example, add or "+", subtract or "−", or any other mathematical function).

Such non-truth-valued functions clearly represent *processes*. Since they produce values merely for evaluation within logical functions of the given rule(s), their names (for example, "add" or "+", "subtract" or "-", and so on) are generally *not* considered to be terms in the business rule approach.[14]

Terminology: Instances and Classes, Values and Variables

At the system developer's perspective, the name of an individual thing corresponds directly to an individual instance, and the name of a variable corresponds directly to a class. We mean *instance* and *class* in the straightforward sense of predicate calculus as discussed earlier. For example, "Monday" is an instance; *weekday* is a class.

A critical point is the following. At the technical designer's perspective, a variable must be capable of actually holding an instance—or, more accurately, a *value*—in some physical sense. How the variable (or class) provides this capability is a key concern. Literally, the variable or class must be some kind of container.[15] Refer to Appendix B for additional discussion.

---

13. When included in a Boolean expression in this manner, the function-type term actually refers to the function *invocation*, rather than simply to the function per se. C. J. Date argues that "exactly the same is true for names of values and names of variables—in each case, the name really stands for a certain invocation [of an appropriate kind of function]" (private correspondence, November, 19, 2001). This distinction, however, is not central to the focus of this tutorial.

14. The names of the *results* produced by such functions are a different matter. Refer to Appendix C.

15. We prefer black-box containers, but that is a different question.

At the system developer's perspective, however, we believe there is *no need whatsoever* to consider how variables provide such capability. Furthermore, we believe it is crucial to be very clear and consistent about this important difference. To minimize the possibility of confusion for that perspective, I will therefore use neither *value* and *variable* nor *instance* and *class*. Instead, I will use *instance term* (for the name of an individual thing) and *class term* (for the name of a variable) in order to stay as close as possible to the true sense of predicate calculus.

Rule Notation

In addition to terms, specifying rules also requires appropriate notation. In the following discussion, I present the notation we prefer at the system developer's perspective. Our preferences are based to a significant extent on what we find most useful for treatment of higher-order rules, which are discussed in Chapter 18.

I also explain how the notation might be read in everyday English. Such rule statements often use the IF . . . THEN . . . syntax. Note that we have certain strong reservations about the use of this syntax in capturing and expressing business rules. These reservations are discussed in Appendix D.

There are a variety of ways in which rules (logical implications) can be formally expressed; however, at the system developer's perspective[16] we prefer the following traditional symbol. This symbol is basic to R-Notation.

$$\rightarrow$$

This arrow symbol ($\rightarrow$) denotes a logical implication (rule) involving specified terms (none shown here). The arrow itself is always taken (by convention) to mean "implies." Refer to the boxed item, Creating Rules, for discussion of this symbol in the context of business logic servers.

---

16. RuleSpeak provides guidelines for specification of rules at the business manager's perspective. (Refer to Part III.) Rule specification language for the technical designer's perspective is beyond the scope of this tutorial. In any event, such language might be invisible to system developers if the notation they use in their own perspective is sufficiently rigorous—which we believe it can be.

Creating Rules

A business logic server might also view the arrow symbol ($\rightarrow$) as the name (or label) for a system *process* that might also be called CREATE RULE (or ASSERT RULE). This special process merits closer scrutiny, which requires reviewing how the execution of processes in general differs from the "execution" of rules.

A fundamental distinction between processes and rules is that *users* generally control when processes are to execute.[17] This control is accomplished by sequencing the processes or by running a program that executes the processes in the appropriate order.

A business logic server, in contrast, controls[18] when rules are to "execute" (that is, be evaluated). In other words, the business logic server causes rules to "execute" automatically when it deems changes in the state of the logicbase make that appropriate. This support is implied in saying that rules are *declarative.* (Refer to Appendix I.)

When should a given rule first "execute"? Logically at least, to ensure absolutely no chance of inconsistency in the logicbase, every rule should be first "executed" *as soon as it is presented to the system.*[19] To say this differently, the creation of a rule is itself a change in state that should cause the business logic server to reevaluate the logicbase to (re)ensure comprehensive integrity. (What happens physically might be a very different matter, of course.)

In that sense, declaring a rule must be viewed as implying the first "execution" of the rule. The logical coupling of declaring a rule and first "executing" the rule is a deeper part of what it means for rules to be *declarative* (as opposed to procedural).

Now we must add the antecedent(s) and the consequent of the rule.[20] The former is/are placed on the left-hand side of the arrow, and the latter on the right-hand side of the arrow. For the sake of simplicity, the former are

---

17. Unless some trigger—a kind of rule—has been specified.
18. Not all rule engines currently control this as thoroughly as is possible or desirable.
19. Unless some future effective date is specified that is meaningful to the business.
20. The antecedent(s) and consequent can be thought of as denoting the "input" to the invisible process underlying the rule.

therefore often called *left-hand terms*[21] (LHTs), and the latter are often called *right-hand terms*[22] (RHTs). The following example illustrates:

$$S \rightarrow U$$

The term S is on the left-hand side of the arrow and is therefore the LHT. The term U is on the right-hand side of the arrow and is therefore the RHT. This rule should be read "S implies U" or "The antecedent, S, implies the consequent, U." Expressed in IF . . . THEN . . . syntax it becomes "If S, then U." As with any rule, it could also be expressed in the form OR ((NOT S), U).

Here is another example:

$$\text{sun-above-horizon} \rightarrow \text{daytime}$$

The term sun-above-horizon is on the left-hand side of the arrow and is therefore the LHT. The term daytime is on the right-hand side of the arrow and is therefore the RHT. This rule should be read "Sun-above-horizon implies daytime" or "The antecedent, sun-above-horizon, implies the consequent, daytime." Expressed in IF . . . THEN . . . syntax it becomes "If sun-above-horizon, then daytime." As with any rule, it could also be expressed in the form OR ((NOT sun-above-horizon), daytime). What this rule "means" to the business logic server is examined in the following boxed item.

What Terms "Mean" to the Business Logic Server

When expressing a rule such as $S \rightarrow U$, it is important to remember that the business logic server does not really "understand" what the terms S (or sun-above-horizon) and U (or daytime) mean. To the system, they are simply strings of characters without intrinsic meaning. We could just as well use something like "sgjdfkkei" and "fdeoifdjfb"—as long as *we* remember what they mean.

---

21. *Anchor* is the equivalent term used in *The Business Rule Book* [Ross 1997]. *Anchor* works better for higher-order rules, which are discussed in Chapter 18.
22. *Correspondent* is the equivalent term used in *The Business Rule Book* [Ross 1997]. *Correspondent* works better for higher-order rules, which are discussed in Chapter 18.

Every rule must have at least one LHT and exactly one RHT.[23] (For more on the one-RHT issue, refer to the boxed item below.) For now, we will consider cases involving only a single LHT; the multiple LHT case is discussed later.

The Atomic Form of Rules and the One-RHT Restriction

Some experts contend that rules must be translatable to Horn clauses (named after the logician Alfred Horn), which disallow ORs among RHTs.[24] However, it should be mentioned that this is the subject of considerable research and debate, and in some approaches, rules with ORs among their RHTs are considered to be information-bearing and are exploited as such.[25] In any event, I will not directly address rules with ORs among their RHTs in this tutorial.

Any rule with ANDs among its RHTs is interpreted to represent an equivalent number of *individual* rules, each with only one RHT and all with the very same LHT(s). The former rules is not in atomic form.

By convention, if a rule is shown simply with a list of RHTs (no explicit ANDs), *implicit* ANDs among them are assumed. Although this shorthand form is generally not recommended (because such a rule is not in atomic form), the shorthand is sometimes useful for the sake of economy or emphasis.

As mentioned before, we must indicate whether we intend a rule to be a constraint or merely to ask a true-false question (that is, to be a test or query). This designation requires a *rule type indicator*. Constraints are indicated as follows:

$$S^T \rightarrow U$$

---

23. If no LHT is given or no RHT is given, the antecedent or consequent defaults to true. Then "p →" and "→ p" are both the same as "p" (C. J. Date, private correspondence, November 19, 2001).

24. For more discussion, refer to Elmasri and Navathe [1994, pp. 734–735].

25. Note that the issue of ORs among RHTs causes far more difficulty for projectors (especially inference-type rules) than for rejectors. (Refer to Appendix C for explanation of these two terms.)

A rule type indicator—the superscripted T (for true) at the left of the arrow—defines this rule to be a constraint. As before, the rule should be read "S implies U." The IF . . . THEN . . . syntax is "If S, then U."

The truth value of any LHT or the RHT can be negated, as the following example illustrates:

$$S \xrightarrow{T} NOT\ U$$

The rule type indicator again indicates that this rule is a constraint.[26] The rule should now be read "S implies *not* U." The IF . . . THEN . . . syntax is "If S, then *not* U."

Here is another example:

$$sun\text{-}above\text{-}horizon \xrightarrow{T} NOT\ nighttime$$

The rule type indicator again indicates that this rule is a constraint. The rule should now be read "Sun-above-horizon implies *not* nighttime." The IF . . . THEN . . . syntax is "If sun-above-horizon, then *not* nighttime."

If a logical implication is used as a test or query, rather than as a constraint, it is expressed as follows:

$$S \xrightarrow{?} U$$

The rule type indicator now shows a superscripted ?. This indicates that the truth value of the rule is not required to be true but rather must be determined and could in fact be false. In other words, this rule indicates a logical implication used as a test or a query rather than as a constraint. The rule should now be read as a question: "Does S imply U?" The IF . . . THEN . . . syntax is "If S, then U?"

A convenient alternative form for logical implications used as tests or queries is the following. This alternative form helps emphasize the questioning nature of such usage.

$$S \rightarrow U?$$

---

26. Remember that the truth value of a constraint can never be false—thus false (or F) is never an option for its rule type indicator, even if the rule involves negation.

This rule (logical implication) is assumed to be a test or query.[27]

A rule without a question mark or other rule type indicator is always assumed to be a constraint, rather than a test or query. For example, the following rule is assumed to be a constraint:

$$S \rightarrow U$$

In our experience with real-life business problems involving hundreds or thousands of rules, the large majority of rules do not have natural names, and no name is ever required for them. For convenience, however, rules can be given one or more names. Naming a rule is especially useful when one rule needs to refer to another—for example, in cases of rules that express exceptions. Here are two examples of naming rules:

$$R1: S \rightarrow U$$

This rule has been named *R1*. The rule (actually its truth value) can now be referenced by that name.

$$\text{Rule-for-daytime1: sun-above-horizon} \rightarrow \text{daytime}$$

This rule has been named *Rule-for-daytime1*. The rule (actually its truth value) can now be referenced by that name should the need arise, just like any other named logical expression.

As mentioned earlier, a rule is not limited to a single LHT. Any logical connective (for example, AND, OR,[28] and even logical implication itself) can be used to construct more complex expressions.[29] Any such expressions, including those formed by NOT, are called *left-hand expressions* (LHEs) for convenience. (An LHE is also permitted to consist of only a single LHT.)

---

27. C. J. Date points out, "The answer to the question is *empirical*. If you get a 'yes' you can still only say something like 'the current state of the [factbase] *is not inconsistent with the hypothesis that* S implies U.' For example, does 'being an employee' imply 'being under 50 years old'? The answer is no, but the [factbase] might currently happen to suggest that the answer is yes" (private correspondence, November 19, 2001, original emphasis).

28. Like the rule symbol, these are actually the names for (Boolean) functions, which must be supported by some (automatic) computational process. Refer to Appendix G for additional discussion with respect to higher-order rules.

29. The truth-valued comparative operators GT, GE, EQ, NE, LE, and LT can also be used, but these need not be illustrated since their use is straightforward.

Some examples are given below. All of these examples are constraints, but corresponding examples of tests or queries could also be expressed.

$$S \text{ AND } U \text{ AND } W \rightarrow Z$$

This example uses the logical operator AND twice to build a more complex LHE for the rule.[30] The rule should be read "S and U and W implies Z." It could also be written as follows: OR ((NOT (S AND U AND W)), Z). Expressed in IF . . . THEN . . . syntax it becomes "If S and U and W, then Z." The implication is that *all three* LHTs must be true in order for this rule to consider Z to be true. In other words, any one of S, U, or W alone (or any pairs thereof) being true does *not* imply Z to be true. The importance of this point will become apparent shortly.

$$\text{motor-on AND brake-off AND in-gear} \rightarrow \text{car-can-go}$$

This example uses the logical operator AND twice to build a more complex LHE for the rule. The rule should be read "Motor-on and brake-off and in-gear implies car-can-go." It could also be written as follows: OR ((NOT (motor-on AND brake-off AND in-gear)), car-can-go). Expressed in IF . . . THEN . . . syntax it becomes "If motor-on and brake-off and in-gear, then car-can-go." The implication is that *all three* LHTs must be true in order for this rule to consider car-can-go to be true. In other words, any one of motor-on, brake-off, or in-gear alone (or any pairs thereof) being true does *not* imply car-can-go to be true.

Here are two examples on using ORs.

$$S \text{ OR } U \text{ OR } W \rightarrow Z$$

This example uses the logical operator OR twice to build a more complex LHE for the rule.[31] The rule should be read "S or U or W implies Z." Expressed in IF . . . THEN . . . syntax it becomes "If S or U or W, then Z." The implication is that this rule will consider Z to be true if any *one* (or more) of the three LHTs are true.

$$\text{it-is-raining OR melting-ice OR flood-stage} \rightarrow \text{streets-are-wet}$$

---

30. We assume the precedence or priority of the AND operator is higher than that of logical implication, so the AND operator is evaluated before the logical implication.
31. We assume the precedence or priority of the OR operator is higher than that of logical implication, so the OR operator is evaluated before the logical implication.

This example uses the logical operator OR twice to build a more complex LHE for the rule. The rule should be read "It-is-raining or melting-ice or flood-stage implies streets-are-wet." Expressed in IF ... THEN ... syntax it becomes "If it-is-raining or melting-ice or flood-stage, then streets-are-wet." The implication is that this rule will consider streets-are-wet to be true if any *one* (or more) of the three LHTs are true. Refer to the related boxed item for discussion of the relationship between ORs in LHTs and atomic rule form using this multi-OR, streets-are-wet rule as an example.

The Atomic Form of Rules: ORs in LHTs

The multi-OR, streets-are-wet rule, with adjacent LHTs separated by ORs, can actually be expressed in more *atomic* form as three distinct rules, each with one of the three LHTs and all with streets-are-wet as the RHT, as follows:

R1: it-is-raining→ streets-are-wet

R2: melting-ice → streets-are-wet

R3: flood-stage → streets-are-wet

This observation raises interesting questions about when such splitting or *reduction* of rules with ORed LHTs should be undertaken. Our view is that the answer depends on the perspective at which the rule is specified. We find it is *not* desirable for rules expressed at the business manager's perspective. It is also generally not desirable for rules expressed at the system developer's perspective—at least when using higher-order rule types.

At the technical designer's perspective, reduction of rules to their most atomic form, at least internally to the rule-processing server, might be highly desirable.[32] *Or maybe not!* The answer might very well depend on the particular implementation scheme. In any event, such reduction raises questions beyond the scope of this tutorial.

 Formally, a rule is in atomic form only if both of the following are true:

- The rule has no ORs among its LHTs.
- The rule has no ANDs among its RHTs.

---

32. If a rule is reduced in this fashion, optimization might be required, recognizing common sub-expressions (C. J. Date, private correspondence, November 19, 2001).

ANDs and ORs can be mixed in the same rule. Parentheses might be necessary to ensure the proper order of evaluation, as shown in the next example.

$$(S \text{ AND } U) \text{ OR } W \rightarrow Z$$

This rule should be read "S and U (together), or W (alone), implies Z."[33]

As indicated previously, NOTs can also be used as appropriate.

$$S \text{ OR } (\text{NOT } U) \rightarrow W$$

This rule should be read "S or not U implies W."[34] This rule example bears closer examination. See anything interesting about the LHE? Refer to the boxed item, Using Rules in Specifying Other Rules.

Using Rules in Specifying Other Rules

Upon closer inspection, the NOT example (given again below) is quite interesting.

$$S \text{ OR } (\text{NOT } U) \rightarrow W$$

Note that the LHE for this rule, S OR (NOT U), can be rewritten in the form (OR (NOT U), S), which you might now recognize as the form for a logical implication (rule). Indeed, the above expression can be rewritten as follows:

$$(U \rightarrow S?) \rightarrow W$$

This revision of the former version shows a logical implication (rule) as the LHE. Note that the new logical implication (rule) is indicated as a test or query rather than as a constraint. This designation is appropriate since that logical implication is not required to be true. In other words, there is nothing *inevitably* true about the original LHE, S OR (NOT U).

---

33. This rule could be broken into two more atomic rules.
34. This rule could also be broken into two more atomic rules.

> Using logical implications as embedded tests or queries in the manner above is not particularly useful for rules expressed at such a basic level. It becomes far more useful, however, in expressing higher-order rules where the emphasis is on patterns. Indeed, this is a central idea in *The Business Rule Book* [Ross 1997].

Constraints: Rejection versus Inference

As earlier discussion explained, a constraint is simply a rule (logical implication) that must always be true. (*Always* here means, more precisely, "must always be true given instance terms for the class terms it mentions."[35]) A crucial question, however, has not yet been addressed: *What action should the business logic server take when a constraint needs to be enforced?* This circumstance happens specifically when any new state requested (by a user or application) for the logicbase is such that the LHE of a constraint would be true, but its RHE would be false.

There are two and only two choices when this circumstance occurs, as discussed below. (Refer to Appendix C for additional discussion.) See the boxed item, The Meanings of *Constraint*, for the discussion of the relationship between these two choices and the term *constraint*.

1. *Rejection:* The constraint can be instructed (by the specifier) to reject the new state—that is, to undo the results of whatever action tried to produce it. Such a constraint is called a *rejector*.

    Consider a simple rejector such as *An employee must have a name*. If any user or application attempts an action that would leave an employee without a name (as represented in the factbase), the business logic server would cause that action to be rejected (that is, to fail).

2. *Inference:* The constraint can be instructed (by the specifier) to indicate the RHE as now being true. In this case there is never any rejection of user or application actions. Instead, when the requested state of the logicbase is such that the LHE of a constraint is true but its RHE is false, the

---

35. The next chapter discusses predicates. We view a constraint to be a predicate. Like any predicate, a constraint cannot be either true or false until it is instantiated.

business logic server simply infers that the RHE has now become true. By this means, the constraint is said to enable inference or logical deduction by the business logic server.

Consider the following simple inference-type rule statement (not in RuleSpeak form to facilitate discussion): *Anyone who is female and of age should be considered a woman.* If any user or application takes an action such that the factbase indicates both *female* and *of age* are true, the business logic server will automatically *infer* that *woman* is true.[36] This example is worked out more fully later in this chapter.

The Meanings of *Constraint*

Constraint clearly has a different sense in inferencing or logical deduction than the sense typical for environments where traditional database products have been used. For the latter environments, *constraint* typically is taken to mean that any event should be rejected that would leave the database in an inconsistent state. Inferencing-type rules are also constraints, but for them, there is *no* rejection. Just the opposite: new truths are derived from existing truths.

Does this mean that there is a fundamental difference between *constraint* for inferencing or logical deduction and for database environments? The answer is *yes and no.*

At the most fundamental level, the answer is *no.* In both cases, constraints are formally rules (logical implications) that must be true. Recognizing this deep equivalence is critical since it means that both kinds spring from common theoretical roots.

At a higher level, the answer is *yes.* In business logic servers, the two kinds must exist side by side so this important distinction *must* be recognized. (Refer to Appendix C for additional discussion.)

This recognition has not been so important in the past. In practice, there has been virtually no overlap in software tools for inferencing (for example, expert systems) and software tools for managing "databases" (that is, database management systems). As this tutorial emphasizes, however, that separation *must* now end.

---

36. Actually, if the truth values of *any* two of the variables are known, the business logic server can infer the truth value of the third (C. J. Date, private correspondence, November 19, 2001).

The woman rule above shows that inference-type rules require the business logic server to make an assessment of the logicbase and possibly change the value of the rule's RHE. Often, such action logically cascades into more assessments, since one rule's RHE is often another rule's LHE. Such activity is commonly known as *inferencing* or *logical deduction.* [37]

The following simple example (using R-Notation for the rules) illustrates this. In Chapter 17, after discussing predicates and facts (which are not used below), we will revisit this same example.

Constraint statement at the business manager's perspective: *Anyone who is female and of age should be considered a woman.*

True-false question: Is Mary a woman?

Constraints:

> female AND of age → woman
>
> "Mary" → female
>
> "Mary" → of age

Female, of age, and *woman* are Boolean variables. "Mary" is a name for a real-world person. For the sake of simplicity, let's assume that any literal can be taken to imply true. Note that in essence the latter two rules are merely giving the business logic server some starting-point "data" [38] to work from. This "data" could be expressed better as facts—but that would require predicates, which have not yet been discussed! [39]

> Answer: Yes (true)

By logical deduction, *female* and *of age* are evaluated (inferred) to be true (by the business logic server). Then, in turn, *woman* is evaluated (inferred) to be true. Therefore, the answer to the question is yes—"Mary" is indeed a

---

37. In the literature of logic-based databases, a distinction is therefore made between a *deductive axiom* (something found to be true through inferencing) and a *ground axiom* (something taken to be true as a given). See Date [2000a, p. 784]. The same distinction applies in the relational model. Although the terminology is different, the concepts are the same (C. J. Date, private correspondence, November 19, 2001).

38. That is, ground axioms.

39. This system will not work when "data" about a second person, male or female, is introduced (unless the user or application discards the "Mary" "data" first). This shortcoming is one reason why treatment of facts and predicates is so fundamentally important.

woman. Refer to Appendix J for a step-by-step explanation. For discussion of support for inferencing by business logic servers, refer to the boxed item, Forward Chaining versus Backward Chaining.

Forward Chaining versus Backward Chaining

Inferencing or logical deduction as illustrated by the "Mary" example can be done in any of several ways, including the following.

- As above, starting from "Mary" and working through the other rules to see if *woman* can be reached (that is, proves true). This approach is sometimes called *forward-chaining* or *data-driven reasoning*.
- Starting from *woman* and working back through the other rules to see if they support that inference. This approach is sometimes called *backward-chaining* or *goal-driven reasoning*.[40]

The choice of which chaining technique the business logic server should employ for any particular case of inferencing should be completely hidden from all users and applications. This separation of logical expression of inference-type rules from their mechanical (that is, physical) implementation is a crucial feature for business logic servers.

We view this separation as one of two fundamental dimensions for Rule Independence. The more obvious dimension, as suggested earlier, is separation (or isolation) of rules from the *user's* procedural logic. Now we identify a second dimension—separation (or isolation) of business rules from the *implementer's* logic. (By *implementer's logic* I mean the evaluation logic of the business logic server.)

Behind the scenes (that is, invisible to users), of course, the choice of which inferencing approach is best to use for particular circumstances can be handed to system administrators who have an understanding of the characteristics of the logicbase and of the tools or algorithms available to optimize its evaluation. General heuristics are available for choosing the optimal approach in such selection.

---

40. C. J. Date [2000a, p. 775] indicates that logically this means trying to prove the contrapositive—in other words, instead of trying to prove p implies q, trying to prove that NOT q implies NOT p.

Ideally, the business logic server should have multiple algorithms at its disposal and should be sufficiently intelligent to choose the best one for any given case. In general terms, of course, this itself is a rule-oriented problem—and the business logic server should be able to use its *own* rule-processing capabilities to address it. Perhaps it could even continuously reengineer its own rules through trial and error to enhance them over time, becoming in effect a machine capable of learning from its own experience. We must, of course, view such capability as a long-term future objective.

 The second meaning of Rule Independence: The expression of business rules should be completely isolated from the implementer's logic—that is, from the evaluation logic of the business logic server, including forward chaining and backward chaining.

References

Charniak, Eugene, and Drew McDermott. 1985. *Introduction to Artificial Intelligence.* Reading, MA: Addison-Wesley.

Date, C. J. 2000a. *An Introduction to Database Systems* (7th ed.). Boston, MA: Addison-Wesley.

———. 2000b. *What Not How: The Business Rule Approach to Application Development.* Boston, MA: Addison-Wesley.

Elmasri, Ramez, and Shamkant B. Navathe. 1994. *Fundamentals of Database Systems* (2nd ed.). Redwood City, CA: Benjamin/Cummings.

Halpin, Terry. 2001. *Information Modeling and Relational Databases.* San Francisco, CA: Morgan Kaufmann.

Ross, Ronald G. 1997. *The Business Rule Book* (2nd ed.). Houston, TX: Business Rule Solutions, LLC. Available at *http://www.BRSolutions.com.*

CHAPTER 17

The Theoretical Foundation of Facts

About Predicates

Predicates and Facts

Thus far in Part V we have examined rules and terms. Let us now focus on *facts*. As evidenced by the core business rule principle *Rules build on facts, and facts build on terms*, the role of facts is fundamental. The boxed item, What Is a Fact?, takes a closer look at what facts represent.

What Is a Fact?

The everyday English definition of *fact* includes the following meanings[1]:

- A thing done
- The quality of being actual
- Something that has actual existence
- An actual occurrence
- A piece of information presented as having objective reality

---

1. From *Merriam-Webster's Collegiate Dictionary*, 10th ed. (1999).

> The use of *fact* in this tutorial does not diverge from these meanings. However, we maintain that the answer to the question "What is a fact?" depends on your perspective. We will come back to this important issue later, after reviewing relevant ideas of predicate calculus.

The central idea in predicate calculus—*predicates*—provide the formal basis for facts in the business rule approach.[2]

To understand the concept of predicates, we believe it is very important to distinguish between the three audiences discussed earlier (see Chapter 15). Corresponding to these three perspectives are three parallel interpretations of *predicate*, each correct and necessary, we believe, in its own way. Let us now examine each of these in turn.

Predicate at the Business Manager's Perspective

At the business manager's perspective, *predicate* follows the everyday definition of the word, as follows: "The part of a sentence or clause that expresses what is said of the subject and that usually consists of a verb with or without objects, complements, or adverbial modifiers."[3] Incidentally, in one way or another, this orientation toward sentences is characteristic of *predicate* at the other two perspectives as well, as we will see later. First, here is an example:

"An employee works in a department."

The subject of this sentence (a fact, or more precisely, a fact *statement*[4]) is "employee." The predicate, which asserts something about that subject, is "works in a department." This predicate also includes an object, "department." See the related boxed item for a note on subjects and objects.

---

2. The term *fact* is often used in formal and informal discussions of *predicate* in the literature of artificial intelligence and expert systems. Refer to Charniak and McDermott [1985, pp. 13, 20, 337].

3. From *Merriam-Webster's Collegiate Dictionary*, 10th ed. (1999).

4. For convenience, I will often use the word *fact* instead of the more correct *fact statement* in the discussion that follows. The distinction is that the same fact can be given by statements in different forms and/or by statements in different languages (for example, French, Mandarin, and so on). In other words, there can be many different *fact statements* for exactly the same *fact*.

An essential step in capturing business rules from businesspeople is identifying and defining all such potential subjects (and objects) within the relevant scope. Those potential subjects and objects are the *terms* at this perspective. By means of definitions and declarative statements such as the above, businesspeople are encouraged to convey how these terms (or more precisely, the underlying concepts) interrelate.

These interrelationships represent fundamental *facts* about the business. At this perspective, a fact is simply an assertion about one or more terms. It represents something that can be known about the business at the operational level, which is essential to support what the business does. See the boxed item, Another Look at Expressing Rules, for how these assertions relate to rules.

A fact is assumed true at the business manager's perspective if the businesspeople *agree* that it is true. If they disagree about an assertion being true, then for our purposes it is *not* a fact—at least until such time that the disagreement is resolved, if ever.

carefully choosing a *subject* for every rule statement.[5] (Refer to Part III for additional discussion.)

Also, the business rule approach highlights the idea that rules always build directly on facts. In RuleSpeak this means simply adding a rule word (that is, *must, only,* or *should*) to one or more fact statements. (Refer to Part III for in-depth discussion.) The rule statement above, *An employee must work in a department,* provides a trivial example. In this case, the rule word *must* is added to the fact "An employee works in a department" to form the rule.

It follows that since all facts have subjects at the business manager's perspective, all rules naturally will as well. Note that this observation runs counter to use of the IF . . . THEN . . . syntax for expressing rules at the business manager's perspective. (Refer to Appendix D for additional discussion.)

Predicate at the System Developer's Perspective

At the system developer's perspective, predicates and facts are viewed in the following way. The starting point should be some fact given at the business manager's perspective.[6] The name of the fact (that is, predicate) is created by removing the subject and all objects, if any,[7] from the fact. For an additional view of predicates, see the boxed item, Halpin on Predicates.

Let us return to the example used earlier.

"An employee works in a department."

This fact makes an assertion about the two terms "employee" and "department." The name of the fact (that is, the predicate) is formed by removing the subject ("employee") and the object ("department") as well as the article ("An"), producing simply ". . . works in. . . ."[8]

---

5. This subject actually can be a term (as in the given example), a fact, or another rule. An example of a fact as a subject is the following: *The person who manages a department must not be an employee working in that department.* The subject of this rule is the fact "Person manages department."
6. In general, it *should* be if the logicbase is developed in top-down fashion.
7. And all articles, such as *a, an, the,* and so on.
8. This approach does not preclude this same name ". . . works in . . ." from being used as the name for some other predicate. For example, in the same logicbase we might also have the fact "Employee works in shift." Obviously some means for distinguishing the predicate names at the metalevel is required.

Halpin on Predicates

Terry Halpin defines predicate as follows: "... basically a sentence with object-holes in it. To complete the sentence, the object-holes or placeholders are filled in by object-terms" [Halpin 2001, pp. 63–64]. Our view of predicate at the system developer's perspective is consistent with this definition.

For the example "... works in ...", each object-hole is represented by an ellipsis (...). The object-terms necessary to fill in the object-holes and thus complete the sentence (that is, give the full predicate), are "employee" and "department," respectively.

Again, it is important not to read too much into *object-term*. Halpin defines *object* in this usage as follows: "[a] thing of interest. An object may be either an entity or a value" [Halpin 2001, p. 714].[9] This corresponds closely to the use of *term* in the business rule approach. (Refer to Appendix E for related definitions.)

As this discussion indicates, a fact at the system developer's perspective represents an assertion about one or more terms.[10] It is important that the fact be worded as clearly and precisely as possible, not only to avoid ambiguities but also to provide an increasingly precise wording template for any rules based on that fact.

Such tight correlation between facts and rules becomes especially important as the number of rules grows and their complexity increases. Incidentally, this is an additional problem that RuleSpeak addresses.

Are all facts proper predicates? The answer is no. Predicate calculus requires every predicate to include at least one class term. If a fact does *not* include at least one class term—that is, if it includes only instance terms—then predicate calculus calls the fact a *proposition*.[11] An example might be the fact "Mary works in the payroll department."

---

9. Halpin also writes, "A term is a lexical expression—it may reference another object (if the object is an entity) or simply reference itself (if the object is a value)" (private correspondence, September 9, 2001).

10. Halpin [2001, pp. 60–92] uses the term *fact* extensively in his approach. Refer to Appendix E for his definition of *fact* and of other related terms.

11. Or, sometimes, a *degenerate predicate.*

Facts that include only instance terms are *not* prohibited in the business rule approach. Indeed, they are sometimes necessary for specifying rules at the system developer's perspective. We will return to this point later.

Predicate at the Technical Designer's Perspective

As always for the technical designer's perspective, the prescribed approach—in this case regarding predicates—depends on the choice of technology. Again, we find the approach of Date and Darwen [2000] in *Foundation for Future Database Systems: The Third Manifesto* to be an attractive one, worthy of closer examination. Refer to the boxed item, Terminology of *The Third Manifesto*, for a quick overview of their terminology. After that, let us more closely explore the essential elements of their approach that pertain to this discussion.

> ### Terminology of *The Third Manifesto*
>
> In the Date and Darwen [2000] approach, a relation as a whole should be viewed as a value. This value must be held in an appropriate variable—specifically, a named container capable of holding relation-type values. They call such a variable a *relation variable*, abbreviated in their work as *relvar*.
>
> The value (that is, relation) held in a relvar includes a heading, which provides the name and type (named, of course) of each column. (*Type* is used here in the sense of *data type* as in programming languages.) These names are the actual terms in the sense of predicate calculus. (Refer to Appendix B for additional discussion and examples.)

At the business manager's and system developer's perspectives, the relationship of *predicate* with sentences has been explicit and relatively obvious. At the technical designer's perspective, it becomes implicit and not at all obvious.

In particular, all fact names (that is, verb wordings) are removed from the system developer's version of the predicate such that the predicate now becomes entirely "objectified." This "objectification" organizes the information in a manner well suited for the automated environment.

To illustrate *predicate* effectively at this perspective, we need to expand the above example somewhat, as shown below.[12]

"An employee has an identifier, also has a name, works in a department, and earns a salary."

This fact is clearly composite (and probably incomplete). It has been written in this nonatomic form simply for clarity. Date [2000, p. 256] would call such statements informal or *external* predicates, meaning they are "understood by users, but not by the system."

If we are implementing in a relational environment, we could create the following relvar to hold these facts. Only the heading for the relvar is shown (along with the relvar name). This heading, along with any relevant constraints that might have been specified (there are none in this example[13]), is what Date calls the relvar's formal or *internal* predicate. (See the boxed item, The Golden Rule, for an important note on constraints in this context.) Date indicates that the internal predicate "is understood by both users *and* the system" [Date 2000, p. 256].

EMP

EMP# : EMP#	ENAME : NAME	DEPT# : DEPT#	SALARY : MONEY

Note the following comments.

- The name of this relvar is "EMP," an abbreviation for "employee."
- There are four attributes or columns in this relvar. (The second name in each pair of names is the domain or type on which the attribute is defined.) The names of each of these four attributes or columns can be taken as terms known to the system.
- The order of these terms (or more precisely, attribute-and-type pairs) is *not* significant. In other words, there is no inherent meaning to the order in which the columns of the relvar appear. This is a by-product of the "objectification" of the predicate.

---

12. This example is based on Date [2000, p. 66].
13. We could easily add some constraints—for example: (a) EMP.SALARY < 100K; (b) {EMP.DEPT#} subset of {DEPT.DEPT#}; (c) employee numbers unique; and so on (C. J. Date, private correspondence, November, 19, 2001).

- Presumably, there is another relvar (not shown) corresponding to "department." The values of DEPT# would refer to rows (tuples) of that other relvar.
- Collectively, the four name pairs are called the *heading* of the relvar. This heading, along with any relevant constraints that might have been specified (there are none in this example[14]), is the relvar's *internal* predicate.

The Golden Rule[15]

Although I am not illustrating constraints in this example, it is *very* important to recognize that constraints are also considered part of the relvar's predicate. This fact leads to The Golden Rule for relvars: *"No update operation must ever be allowed to leave any relvar in a state that violates its own [internal] predicate."*

Incidentally, The Golden Rule applies to all relvars—including *logical views*—a fact of significant consequence for inferencing and deduction. An example showing how logical views relate to inferencing and deduction is given later in this chapter.

Date also extends these notions to the logicbase as a whole. He defines a *database predicate* as the "logical AND of all database and relvar constraints that apply to the database in question." The extended version of The Golden Rule consequently includes this: *". . . no update operation[16] is allowed to leave the database in a state that violates its own predicate."*

Note that in the relvar's internal predicate, the verb phrases in the original fact statement (external predicate) have disappeared—that is, "employee *has an* identifier," "employee *has a* name," "employee *works in* department," and "employee *earns* salary" have all become *implicit*. They have become objectified in the sense that they are represented by terms rather than by verb phrases.

---

14. As noted before, some constraints could be easily added.

15. The discussion of The Golden Rule in this context is based on Date [2000, pp. 254–256]. Quotations in this boxed item are from p. 256 of that work.

16. *Operation* is more accurate than the term *transaction,* which appears in the original text (C. J. Date, private correspondence, November, 19, 2001). *Operation* appears in Date [2001].

Nonetheless, it is important to recognize that even though objectified in this fashion, the internal predicate's implicit sense of "sentences" is still very real. Here is what Date has to say about the above example, which is actually his own [Date 2000, p. 66, original emphasis]:

In a nutshell, therefore:

- *Types* **are the (sets of) things we can talk about;**
- *Relations* **are (sets of) things we say about the things we can talk about.**

(There is a nice analogy here that might help you appreciate and remember these important points: *Types are to relations as nouns are to sentences.*) Thus [in the relation above] the things we can talk about are employee numbers, names, department numbers, and money values, and the things we say are true utterances of the form "The employee with the specified employee number has the specified name, works in the specified department, and earns the specified salary."

By convention, the rows (tuples) in a relvar at a given time are taken to correspond to "true facts" (or, more precisely, propositions that evaluate to true at that time).[17] For example, suppose a row with the following values were found in the EMP relvar: employee number, "1065"; employee name, "P. Jones"; department, "HR"; and salary, "65,000". This row can be taken to mean that the following fact is true: "The employee with employee number '1065' has the name 'P. Jones,' works in the 'HR' department, and earns the salary '$65,000.'"

This point of view leads to a very different perception of "data" and "databases" than most people currently have, but one that aligns perfectly with the business rule approach. Date sums this point up nicely as follows.

There is another (and important) way of thinking about what data and databases really are. The word *data* derives from the Latin for "to give"; thus, data is really *given facts*, from which additional facts can be inferred" [Date, 2000, p. 13, original emphasis].[18]

---

17. It is important to remember that a row (tuple) must have satisfied the relevant internal predicate (including relevant constraints) to be included in the relvar in the first place.
18. The term *fact* is often used in discussion of *deductive* database systems. For more information, refer to Date [2000, p. 787] and Elmasri and Navathe [1994, pp. 730, 736].

The formal definition for predicate in the technical designer's view, however, is actually broader than that. Date's definition is as follows: A predicate is "a *truth-valued function*—i.e., a function that, given appropriate arguments for its parameters, returns either *true* or *false*" [Date 2000, p. 777, original emphasis].

Facts: Type versus Instance

As discussed above at each of the three perspectives, a fact always corresponds directly or indirectly to a declarative sentence in English, which asserts something about its terms. Here is an example:

"The customer Acme Supply places order a601."

This sentence makes an assertion, "places," about the terms "customer Acme Supply" and "order a601." Assuming this sentence is true, it can be considered literally to be a fact.

Certain terms in this sentence, specifically "Acme Supply" and "a601," presumably stand for or represent actual things in the real world. These names are instance terms. Certain other terms, "customer" and "order," appear to stand for or represent classes of like things to which the former things belong, respectively. These names are class terms. (Refer to the boxed item, A Note on Representing Class Terms, regarding related conventions for this discussion.)

> ### A Note on Representing Class Terms
>
> At this point, I will start using names with an initial capital letter for class terms that might be viewed as *business objects* or *entity types* at the system developer's perspective. However, I stress that this carries no innate meaning for either formal logic or machines. The convention is merely used here as a way to focus attention on the core kinds of things in the business.

Let us then rewrite the original sentence so that it mentions only instance terms or only class terms. We thereby produce two sentences, as follows:

Sentence 1: "Acme Supply places a601."

Sentence 2: "Customer places Order."

Sentence 1 contains only instance terms. Sentence 2 contains only class terms.[19]

Based on this instance versus class differentiation in terms, we can call the former sentence[20] (assuming it is true) a *fact instance*, and the latter sentence a *fact type*. Refer to the related boxed item for a note about the choice of terminology here.

- *Fact instance:* A fact instance contains only instance terms, no class terms. Sentence 1 above, "Acme Supply places a601," is a fact instance. It requires no further resolution because each of the terms (that is, "Acme Supply" and "a601") denotes an instance rather than a class.
- *Fact type:* A fact type always contains at least one class term.[21] Sentence 2, "Customer places Order," is a fact type because it contains two class terms, Customer and Order. It cannot be evaluated until appropriate instance terms are substituted for these two class terms. One such substitution for the two class terms, of course, could be "Acme Supply" and "a601," respectively. Given this substitution, or *instantiation* of the predicate, the truth of the expression now *can* be ascertained.

A Note on Terminology: *Fact Instance* and *Fact Type*

At the system developer's perspective, practitioners usually mean *fact type* when talking about "facts." At the technical designer's perspective, practitioners usually mean *fact instance* when talking about "facts." This inconsistency produces unfortunate confusion. I will avoid any ambiguity by always explicitly saying either *fact instance* or *fact type* from now on when it makes a difference in the given context.

In this book I do not offer any recommendation about what term should be used for *fact instance* at the technical designer's perspective. Date and

continued

---

19. In predicate calculus, the terms Customer and Order denote *free variables* in the context of sentence 2. Since they are not variables in the familiar sense of programming languages, C. J. Date suggests that *parameter* is a better term for them (C. J. Date, private correspondence, November, 19, 2001).
20. In predicate calculus, this would be viewed as a proposition.
21. But by definition, never a function, rule, and so on in the business rule approach.

Darwen [2000] demonstrate formally that a factbase can be constructed at an atomic level from only values, variables, and types—*instance* is extraneous. In other words, *instance* has no useful definition that is not the same as either value or variable.[22]

In this discussion I have chosen *fact type* over alternatives (for example, *fact template* or *fact pattern*) for the sake of common usage. However, as discussed earlier, I recognize that the use of *type* invites ambiguity. *Type* (as in *data type*) has a specific meaning in programming languages[23]—and what I mean by fact type does *not* conform to that definition.

Other possibilities considered but discarded for *fact type* include *relationship instance* and *relationship type*. These terms have proven much less comfortable to the business community than to IT professionals. I think *fact*, with its correct, commonsense connotation, is much better in this regard.

The complete set of all "true" fact instances that have been presented and accepted at a point in time is what we call a *factbase*. Any fact instance in such a factbase is called a *base fact*.

The distinction between *fact instance* and *base fact* should be noted carefully. These terms are not synonymous. A fact instance can be either a base fact (one given in the factbase) or a derived fact. A *derived fact* is inferred by the action of one or more inference rules from other fact instances.[24]

The equivalent distinction can be made between *base fact type* and *derived fact type*.[25] A *derived fact type* is any fact type specified as the RHE of an *inference rule*.[26]

---

22. Based on C. J. Date, private correspondence, August 24, 2001. Putting it even more strongly, Date later said, ". . . the term is *worse* than useless, because it leads to confusion" (C. J. Date, private correspondence, November, 19, 2001, original emphasis).
23. Including database theory, such as in Date and Darwen [2000].
24. For the most part, this discussion is concerned with *base facts* rather than *derived facts*. Therefore, for convenience, from this point on in the discussion I will simply say *fact* whenever I really mean *base fact*.
25. Refer to Ross [1997, pp. 108–109] for discussion of derived fact types.
26. For the most part, this discussion is concerned with *base fact types* rather than *derived fact types*. Therefore, for convenience, from this point on in the discussion I will simply say *fact type* whenever I really mean *base fact type*.

We call the complete set of base fact types that have been presented and accepted a *fact model.*[27] At the technical designer's perspective, such a fact model corresponds to a database schema or definition. In that sense, a factbase corresponds directly to what most people think of as a "database."

As this discussion indicates, the business rule approach suggests that a much more productive way to think about "data" (and "database" and "database design")—especially at the business manager's perspective—can be achieved by replacing the term *data* with the term *fact.*[28] *Facts* suggests that the database should be correct—unfortunately, *data* does not carry the same weight in that regard. We believe that integrity (that is, correctness, or at least consistency) is *the* issue in "database"—after all, *what good is the "data" if it is not correct?*[29]

The Existence Principle

Included in the notes on predicate calculus given at the beginning of Part V were the following observations.

> Some predicates require more than one argument. For example, if *B* is the predicate 'bigger than,' then *Bxy* denotes the assertion '*x* is bigger than *y*'. Thus *B* requires two arguments. . . . If we try to use *B* with only one argument, we obtain something like *Bx*, i.e., '*x* is bigger than'. This . . . is only a meaningless combination of symbols. In analogy with English grammar, we could say that *Bxy* is like a grammatically correct sentence, while *Bx* is merely a sentence fragment. Such fragments play no role in the predicate calculus [Simpson 2000, p. 5].

---

27. A fact model should address all relevant business questions, including the naming of predefined instances. As discussed in Part IV, development of such terminology often requires an extension to the fact model called an *instance model*. At the technical designer's perspective, such instances can become permissible values defined for *domains* (or types) as in Date and Darwen [2000].

28. With respect to "data models," our problem is not with *graphic* models—indeed, graphic models can be quite useful for fact modeling—but rather with the emphasis on "data."

29. As mentioned earlier, *consistent* is actually a more precise term here. The business logic server cannot really know if the logicbase is *correct* with respect to the external real world it purports to reflect. Also, note that 100 percent correctness could often be very expensive as a real-life business matter and therefore not the optimal tradeoff at the business manager's perspective. For example, consider what it would take to keep a large sales prospects address database 100 percent correct! (Example provided by Allan Kolber, private correspondence, August 24, 2001.)

We can now understand more clearly what these observations mean, again using the example above to illustrate.

Fact type: "Customer places Order."

Statement 1: "Acme Supply places a601."

Statement 1 represents a grammatically correct sentence. Instance terms for both of the class terms, Customer and Order, have been given.

Statement 2: "Best Supply Ltd. places."

Statement 2 does not represent a grammatically correct sentence. An instance term for only one of the class terms, Customer, has been given. As such, the statement is merely a "sentence fragment" and *must* be rejected.

The business rule approach depends on this basic assumption of predicate calculus. As described earlier, in the business rule approach, facts build on terms (and rules build on facts). It follows then that in giving base facts, not only must instance terms be provided for each of the class terms but that these instance terms must be valid ones as well. In other words, *these instance terms must exist in their own right.*[30] We call this the *Existence Principle*.

The Existence Principle

The following must be true about every fact: Given its fact type, each instance term for each class term must exist in its own right.

In the example given as statement 1 above, the Existence Principle requires that both "Acme Supply" and "a601" exist in their own right. If they do not, the fact instance must be rejected under the business rule approach.[31]

---

30. Remember that we are talking here only about base facts. There is a well-known example that illustrates that this observation might not be true for derived facts: "The present King of France is bald." Assume a statement in predicate calculus of the form "For all x, if x is the King of France, then x is bald." This statement evaluates to true, even though France has no King at the present time. Note, however, that the fact type "x is bald" is the RHE of the given inference rule and therefore is a derived fact.

31. What happens at the technical designer's perspective might be a different matter. For example, the technical designer might specify that for a given class term in a given fact type, an instance of the term should be created automatically when any fact is given that specifies an instance term that does not already exist. The operational effect would satisfy the Existence Principle.

The Existence Principle can be expressed more formally in the following way. A fact type always implies one or more rules (logical implications) about the terms it involves. This is illustrated in the following example:

Fact type: "Customer places Order."

Rule 1: *Customer places Order* → *Customer*

Rule 2: *Customer places Order* → *Order*

The first rule should be read "Any instance of the fact 'Customer places Order' implies that Customer exists." The second rule should be read "Any instance of the fact 'Customer places Order' implies that Order exists." For database professionals, these observations will have a familiar ring to them. Refer to the boxed item, About Referential Integrity.

About Referential Integrity

Some readers have probably recognized that this discussion pertains directly to what is traditionally called *referential integrity* in relational database design. Unfortunately, referential integrity has often been downplayed as a feature in commercial database management system (DBMS) products or not understood or used even when available.

This discussion emphasizes that such "data" integrity arises directly from the semantics of the factbase itself and is in no sense optional. Business logic servers *must* provide this fundamental and innate kind of business rule support.

For additional discussion about the issue of semantics in relational theory, including referential integrity, see Appendix F.

For the sake of emphasis, let us now combine the two rules above into a single rule with two RHTs (or, more precisely, RHEs in this case). The combined form includes a comma to indicate AND (a shorthand commonly used in this way). This combined (nonatomic) rule does not change the meaning of the original two rules in any way.

Combined rule: *Customer places Order* → *Customer, Order*

This rule indicates that every base fact for the fact type "Customer places Order" (the LHE) must include valid instance terms for each of the RHTs,

Customer and Order. In other words, a "places" base fact may exist only if *both* the Customer and the Order exist.

Included in the notes on predicate calculus given at the beginning of this tutorial was also the following observation:

> ... [I]n the predicate calculus [in contrast to Aristotelian logic], a subject is always an individual entity, never a class of entities. For example, an individual man can be treated as a subject, but the class of all men must be treated as a predicate. ... For example, if *M* is the predicate "to be a man" and *a* is the individual "Socrates," then *Ma* denotes the assertion "Socrates is a man" [Simpson 2000, p. 5].

Let us apply this restriction to the example above. We start with the following sentences:

Fact type: "Customer places Order."

Base fact: "Acme Supply places a601."

The class term Customer represents the set of all customers, including "Acme Supply." The class term Order represents the set of all orders, including "a601." According to predicate calculus (as above), both of these class terms *themselves* must also be treated as predicates. The names of these predicates could be (again as above) "to be a customer" and "to be an order," respectively. In keeping with our emphasis on sentences, however, we would prefer "Customer is" or "Customer exists," and "Order is" or "Order exists," respectively.

We can summarize as follows:

- In predicate calculus, what we think of as class terms are actually themselves predicates.
- A class term's predicate can be expressed as a sentence in the form "... is" or "... exists."
- The Existence Principle says that any instance term referenced in any base fact must also be an instantiation of its own predicate.[32]

---

32. Since it has satisfied its own predicate, by convention it can also be taken to be a "true fact."

- A final point: As above, we see that all terms, as well as all facts, are predicates.[33] In predicate calculus, *rules* are also predicates. A rule's predicate is simply one that adds the additional sense of *must* (or *only if* or *should*) to one or more underlying fact types (that is, to other predicates). Therefore, we can say that *all business rules are predicates*.

All business rules are predicates.

A Brief Introduction to R-Notation for Facts

R-Notation proves convenient for specification of facts,[34] as illustrated below. (Refer to the boxed item, About Using R-Notation for Facts, for an important clarification.) This representation is aimed at the system developer's perspective. It is especially useful in building expressions for rules having higher-order rule types, as discussed in Chapter 18.

$$\text{Fact: Customer } ^{\text{places}} \leftrightarrow \text{Order}$$

The *bi*directional arrow[35] between the two terms, along with the superscripted predicate name ("places"), indicates that this expression is a fact. The use of the bidirectional arrow is also a reminder that instantiations of the predicate (base facts) require valid instance terms for each of the specified class terms, as required by the Existence Principle.[36]

All facts with two terms are potentially reversible[37]—that is, they can be "turned around." In other words, the second term can be indicated as the subject without changing the meaning of the fact. Of course, a different form of the verb phrase, or even a different choice of verb, is usually required for the revised form to read properly.

---

33. We must allow for degenerate predicates to cover fact instances.

34. Remember that *fact* at the system developer's perspective is usually taken to mean *fact type*, so I follow that usage in this discussion.

35. We recognize that bidirectional arrows are sometimes used in formal logic to represent *if and only if* (iff). However, we do not foresee that usage as being needed by (or even familiar to) the three primary audiences addressed in Part V.

36. Some system developers like to use role names when expressing facts. We suggest that these optional role names be put in brackets, as follows:

term-A[role name-1] $^{\text{predicate name}}$ $\leftrightarrow$ [role name-2]term-B.

A classic example is the following: flight[arriving flight] $^{\text{arrives at}}$ $\leftrightarrow$ [arrival city]city.

37. In data modeling and entity-relationship approaches, "relationship (types)" are said to be inherently *bidirectional*.

About Using R-Notation for Facts

I use R-Notation for facts in this discussion primarily to assist in explaining theoretical issues, especially higher-order rules as discussed in Chapter 18. Incidentally, its use in that context clearly illustrates the powerful core principle of the business rule approach: *Rules always build on facts (and facts always build on terms)*.

When reviewing the examples that follow here and in Chapter 18, please remember that we are attempting to do in a static, tutorial mode what could be extremely powerful and effective in a point-and-click environment.

For example, "Customer places Order" could be reversed and reworded as follows: "Order is placed by Customer." Note that there is no fundamental change in meaning.

Reversed-form fact: Order $^{\text{is placed by}} \leftrightarrow$ Customer

This form of the fact is equivalent in meaning[38] to the original expression.

The following unified notation can be used to emphasize the inherent equivalence of the two versions.

Fact: Customer $^{\text{places}} \leftrightarrow ^{\text{is placed by}}$ Order

This example illustrates the optional additional inverse naming of the fact. From left to right, it reads "Customer places Order." From right to left it reads "Order is placed by Customer."

A fact, of course, can involve any number of terms, not just two. Refer to Appendix K for discussion and examples.

The examples above focused on *user-defined* facts. Several useful *predefined* or *built-in* fact types are also offered in R-Notation for facts. Refer to Appendix L for discussion.

---

38. That is, *semantically equivalent*.

R-Notation for facts can also be used to express tests or to ask questions. Such usage is often relevant when expressing higher-order rules. As before, we use the "?" symbol for this purpose.

Example: "Acme Supply"^{INST} ↔ Customer?

The inclusion of the "?" symbol indicates that this expression is a question or test. A built-in fact type INST (*is instantiation of*) is indicated. This expression can be read "Is Acme Supply an instance of Customer?"

Inferencing and Deduction Revisited: Using Predicates

To conclude this 2discussion of predicates and facts, let us revisit the example of inferencing or logical deduction given at the end of Chapter 16. In particular, I now introduce the predicate Person and also the predicate Woman, which were not used in the earlier version.

The example is given at the technical designer's perspective. It also illustrates how inferencing or logical deduction is approached by Date and Darwen [2000].

PERSON

PERSON-NAME : NAME	FEMALE : BOOLEAN	OF-AGE : BOOLEAN

The heading for the relvar named Person represents the appropriate new predicate. This predicate can be instantiated with values (that is, "data") representing "Mary." Note that for the sake of simplicity, the attributes[39] *female* and *of-age* retain type Boolean in this version of the example. Although only three attributes or columns are shown in the heading, others of course could be added.

WOMAN

WOMAN-NAME : NAME

The heading for the relvar named Woman represents the appropriate new predicate. Although only one attribute or column is shown, others (perhaps

---

39. More precisely, Date views them as *parameters* (C. J. Date, private correspondence, November 19, 2001).

from Person) could of course be added to the example. This relvar is probably a logical view, but we will get to that point in a moment.

> Constraint statement at the business manager's perspective: *A person who is female and of age must be considered a woman.*

> Constraint[40]: (Person → female AND of-age?) → Woman

This two-part expression involves (1) a test using a logical implication to determine whether a given Person is both female and of age, and (2) a constraint, to indicate that such a person must be considered a Woman. Given this kind of constraint, Date and Darwen would consider Woman to be a *logical view* in the relational sense. In their approach, a logical view is considered to be a predicate whose instantiations are derived.

> The instantiation in which we are interested is for "Mary."

> Instantiation: Person {name = "Mary", female = true, of-age = true}

PERSON

PERSON-NAME : NAME	FEMALE : BOOLEAN	OF-AGE : BOOLEAN
Mary	true	true

The appropriate row for "Mary" has been inserted into the relvar.

The business logic server then makes the logical deduction and automatically populates the logical view Woman with "Mary." [41]

---

40. For simplicity, I give this constraint in R-Notation. The actual syntax of this constraint in predicate calculus might be as follows. (Note: x is a *bound variable* in the sense of predicate calculus.)

$$\text{Person} \{ \text{person-name} = x, \text{female} = \text{true}, \text{of-age} = \text{true} \} \rightarrow$$
$$\text{Woman} \{ \text{woman-name} = x \}$$

(Courtesy of Pedram Abrari, private correspondence, August 31, 2001.)

41. Logically, the instantiation of logical view Woman is immediate. Such instantiation must also satisfy all constraints given for Woman, if any. (None are given in this example.) When *physical* population of the relvar might occur, if ever, is a different matter. For example, such population might occur only when the logical view is actually put to use in some query. "Physical materialization of views is always to be avoided if possible" (C. J. Date, private correspondence, November 19, 2001).

WOMAN

WOMAN-NAME : NAME
Mary

True-false question at the business manager's perspective: Is Mary a woman? [42]

Query: Is-Mary-a-Woman: "Mary" ^{INST} ↔ Woman?

Result: Is-Mary-a-Woman = true

This example is meant to show the logical—not necessarily physical—mechanisms of inference or logical deduction in the relational context. As this example illustrates, logical views play a crucial role. A logical view is nothing more than a predicate whose instantiations are derived through one or more rules of inference. There is considerable elegance in this approach.

Finally, as for the earlier version of this inferencing example in Chapter 16, although constraints are definitely present in this revised version, there is no sense of events being rejected to maintain integrity. As before, just the opposite is the case—these constraints ascertain *new* truths from existing ones. For additional discussion, refer to Appendix C.

References

Charniak, Eugene, and Drew McDermott. 1985. *Introduction to Artificial Intelligence*. Reading, MA: Addison-Wesley.

Date, C. J. 2001. "Constraints and Predicates: A Brief Tutorial (Part 2)." *Business Rules Journal* 2(9). Available at *http://www.BRCommunity.com/ a2001/b065b.html*.

———. 2000. *An Introduction to Database Systems* (7th ed.). Boston, MA: Addison-Wesley.

Date, C. J., and Hugh Darwen. 2000. *Foundation for Future Database Systems: The Third Manifesto* (2nd ed.). Boston, MA: Addison-Wesley.

---

42. For simplicity, I again use R-Notation here.

Elmasri, Ramez, and Shamkant B. Navathe. 1994. *Fundamentals of Database Systems* (2nd ed.). Redwood City, CA: Benjamin/Cummings.

Halpin, Terry. 2001. *Information Modeling and Relational Databases.* San Francisco, CA: Morgan Kaufmann.

Ross, Ronald G. 1997. *The Business Rule Book* (2nd ed.). Houston, TX: Business Rule Solutions, LLC. Available at *http://www.BRSolutions.com.*

Simpson, Stephen G. 2000. "Logic and Mathematics." Available at *http://www.math.psu.edu/simpson/.*

CHAPTER 18

Higher-Order Rules

Pattern-R Rule Types

The Definition of Pattern-R Rule Types

A rule (logical implication) based on a higher-order rule type has a higher level of expressive power than the rules discussed thus far. This higher level of expressive power arises because these rules incorporate not only a truth-valued function but a special "built-in" computational function, called the *yield-value function*, as well.

We call such higher-order rule types *Pattern-R rule types*. These rule types are discussed and illustrated in *The Business Rule Book* [Ross 1997].

Pattern-R rule types represent convenient shorthand expressions. Commonplace examples of Pattern-R rule types include *mandatory, mutually exclusive, unique, cyclic, frozen, timed,* and so on. Pattern-R rule types are aimed toward the system developer's perspective.

Each of these rule types represents some pattern that is found repeatedly among the rules typically specified for factbases—hence the name *Pattern-R*. There are numerous such patterns—indeed, *The Business Rule Book* identifies dozens more.

In many cases—probably most—specifying rules based on patterns will prove much more productive than doing so using the lower-level, *unpatterned* rules. We believe the potential usefulness of pattern-based rule specification is self-evident, especially for rejectors. C. J. Date comments on this point as follows.

> Recognizing frequently occurring patterns and building knowledge regarding them into "the system" effectively raises the level of abstraction. Among other things, it saves writing and simplifies thinking (like macros). A good example is "unique identification": This property *can* be expressed in a general constraint language, but the KEY shorthand is so much more convenient (not to mention the fact that it's probably capable of more efficient implementation).[1]

A Pattern-R rule type must be assembled directly from more basic components, including R-Notation rules and yield-value functions[2] of specified kinds. Such assembly, of course, is completely hidden to system developers when specifying actual Pattern-R rules. For their convenience, it is anticipated that the business logic server should offer many preassembled Pattern-R rule types.

All Pattern-R rules, by definition, are able to compute *something* apart from truth value. Sometimes this computation is for something simple, but usually it is for something more complex. Another way of saying this is that all Pattern-R rules must have some kind of computed yield value (the result of the yield-value function) *in addition to* the normal truth value. This fundamental (and powerful) feature is what distinguishes Pattern-R rules from "regular" rules [Ross 1997, pp. 3, 15–16, 35–37].

At the technology developer's perspective, a Pattern-R rule is defined formally as follows.[3]

- *Pattern-R rule:* An indivisible, two-part unit of business logic in the form of a rule (logical implication) of a known type.
- *Pattern-R rule type:* The type of a Pattern-R rule comprises both a logical function (that is, a truth-valued function) and a yield-value function

---

1. C. J. Date, private correspondence, November 19, 2001.
2. The computational function given as a yield-value function can be arbitrarily complex.
3. The correspondents(s) mentioned in the definition can also be executable operations (processes or procedures), but that takes us outside the realm of predicate calculus, so we will not discuss it here.

(which is not truth-valued). The logical function produces a set of truth values that is based on evaluating the results of the yield-value function. This yield-value function is evaluated for each specific occurrence of a reference point (called the *anchor*) and the anchor's associated correspondents. The anchor and correspondent(s) can be terms, facts, and/or other Pattern-R rules, as appropriate for the given rule.

The name of any Pattern-R rule type is the name given to its truth-valued function.[4] Thus names such as *mandatory, mutually exclusive, unique, cyclic, frozen, timed,* and so on are actually the names of truth-valued functions that have been included in the respective assemblies of these Pattern-R rule types.

Naturally, it is desirable to exploit existing operators, both logical and nonlogical, when establishing basic (that is, *atomic*) higher-order rule types. Such use of existing operators raises interesting questions, which are explored in Appendix G.

Pattern-R rules can be specified by using the same basic form as in R-Notation for rules given in Chapter 16. Since Pattern-R rules are higher-order, of course, we must also specify their types.[5] The following two examples illustrate. At the end of this chapter, we will look more closely at the assembly of the two Pattern-R rules used in these examples.

Examples of Pattern-R Rules

Example 1: The Monitor Rule[6]

Consider the following true-false question at the business manager's perspective:

Question: Does a monitor attend two or fewer patients in critical condition?

---

4. We believe this truth-valued function can be viewed as a predicate, but that is not central to the definition.

5. From this point on, I will call all untyped rules *lower-order rules.*

6. This example is adapted with permission from *The Business Rule Book* [Ross 1997, p. 64].

The Pattern-R rule for this expression (unassisted by any graphic model[7]) would be given as follows.

Given: Patient ^{is attended by} ↔ ^{attends} Monitor

           Critical-Condition-Patient ^{ISA} ↔ Patient

Then: Monitor ^{LIM, U, 2} → Critical-Condition-Patient?

Note several things about this example.

- The "givens" provide the relevant fact basis for the rule. The second fact uses the built-in fact type ISA, which means *is a category of* (or *is a subset of* or *is a subtype of*). (Refer to Appendix L for additional explanation.)
- The Pattern-R rule type for this rule is *limited*, abbreviated LIM, as indicated by the rule type indicator.
- Based on the Pattern-R rule type LIM, the rule will count (or if a constraint, *limit*) the number of fact instances for Critical-Condition-Patient (the correspondent) for any given instance of Monitor (the anchor).
- The "U" (for *upper*) and "2" are qualifiers for the rule, giving the appropriate threshold for the evaluation.
- For a given instance of Monitor, the condition (true-false question) will produce true if the number of Critical-Condition-Patients attended is two or fewer; otherwise it will produce false.

Note that this example represents a condition (as indicated by the "?") rather than a constraint. It could very easily be made into a constraint by simply removing the "?" as follows.

Constraint: Monitor ^{LIM, U, 2} → Critical-Condition-Patient

Now the rule is a constraint. The rule statement at the business manager's perspective would be as follows: *A monitor must not attend more than two patients in critical condition.*

---

7. The "given" fact types in the example—that is, "attends" and the "ISA"—would probably be implicit if specification of the rule were built in a point-and-click manner based on some model (for example, a graphic fact model or data model).

Example 2: The Union Rule[8]

Consider the following true-false question at the business manager's perspective:

Question: Does a group include only nonunion employees exclusively or union employees exclusively?

The Pattern-R rule for this expression (unassisted by any model[9]) would be given as follows:

Given: Group $^{includes} \leftrightarrow$ Employee

Non-Union-Employee $^{ISA} \leftrightarrow$ Employee

Union-Employee $^{ISA} \leftrightarrow$ Employee

Then: Group $^{ME} \rightarrow$ Non-Union-Employee, Union-Employee?

This expression conveys many things.

- The "givens" provide the relevant *fact* basis for the rule. The second and third facts use the built-in fact type ISA, which means *is a category of* (or *is a subset of* or *is a subtype of*). (Refer to Appendix L for additional explanation.)
- The Pattern-R rule type for this rule is *mutually exclusive*, abbreviated ME, as indicated by the rule type indicator.
- Based on the Pattern-R rule type ME, the rule will evaluate whether each instance of Group (the anchor) "possesses" at least one instance for each of the two correspondents, Non-Union-Employee and Union-Employee.
- For a given instance of Group, the condition (true-false question) will produce true if the Group does *not* include both Non-Union-Employees and Union-Employees; otherwise it will produce false.

---

8. This example is adapted with permission from *The Business Rule Book* [Ross 1997, p. 92]. This example is presented as a constraint in that book; however, I will treat it first as a condition in this examination.
9. As before, the "given" fact types in the example—that is, "includes" and the two "ISAs"—would probably be implicit if specification of the rule were built in a point-and-click manner based on some model (for example, a graphic fact model or data model).

Note that this example represents a condition (as indicated by the "?") rather than a constraint. It could very easily be made into a constraint by simply removing the "?" as follows:

Constraint: Group ^{ME} → Non-Union-Employee, Union-Employee

Now the rule is a constraint. The rule statement at the business manager's perspective would be as follows: *A group must not include more than one of the following:*

- *Non-Union-Employees*
- *Union-Employees*

The Assembly of Pattern-R Rule Types

As described earlier, the assembly[10] of any Pattern-R rule type involves two closely associated functions—a yield-value function and a truth-valued function.[11] Such assembly follows the general outline described below. (See the boxed item for an important note.) Each of the described functions uses normal notation for functions of the general form: $w = f(x, y \ldots)$.

Is This Assembly a Formalization of the Pattern-R Language?

To get right to the point, the answer is *no*. For a more comprehensive answer, refer to Appendix H.

Part 1: The Yield-Value Function

$$YV = yvfn_{(rule\ type)}(anchor, correspondent(s))$$

where $yvfn_{(rule\ type)}$ is the yield-value function dictated by the given Pattern-R rule type. Note the following comments on this function.

- The anchor of a Pattern-R rule corresponds *exactly* to the antecedent (that is, left-hand expression) of the rule if it were expressed in R-Notation for lower-order rules.

---

10. Again, it is important to remember that such assembly is completely hidden from users, including system developers in everyday use.

11. A *derived* Pattern-R rule type is defined on the basis of other (eventually atomic) Pattern-R rule types. So in that sense a Pattern-R rule type can have a *composite* logical function.

- The correspondent(s) of a Pattern-R rule would *generally* become the consequent (that is, the right-hand term) of the rule if it were expressed in R-Notation for lower-order rules. The parallel is not exact, however, since the correspondents must also satisfy the needs (parameters) of the rule's yield-value function.[12]
- YV is the name of a variable capable of holding the results (that is, yield values) of the yield-value function. As required for any function, this yield-value function must not produce more than one yield value for any given instance of the anchor. Refer to the related boxed item for additional discussion about the yield value.

More about the Yield Value

Yield values [Ross 1997, pp. 35–37] produced by a Pattern-R rule are held in a variable, which for convenience we call YV. This variable has a *type* (or data type) in the programming sense of that term. YV should be optionally visible to authorized users of the factbase, in which case it appears simply as a (read-only) derived attribute. The actual yield values might or might not be persistent—this choice, however, should be hidden by the business logic server from all everyday users.

Part 2: The Truth-Valued Function

$$TV = tvfn_{(rule\ type)}(YV)$$

where $tvfn_{(rule\ type)}$ is the truth-valued function as dictated by the Pattern-R rule type. Note the following comments on this function.

- The name given to the truth-valued function is the name of the Pattern-R rule type.[13]

---

12. A metarule for every Pattern-R rule is the following. For each instance of a rule's anchor (antecedent), at least one of the following must exist: yield value or at least one instance of any correspondent. This restriction ensures there is always a consequent.
13. Although not central to our arguments, we believe the *type* in Pattern-R rule *type* should also be viewed in the programming sense. *Type* in that sense requires (a) specification of a set of values and/or rules for how values of the type are formed, and (b) a set of operations whose implementations are hidden (encapsulated) appropriate to the type. For a Pattern-R rule type, this means the following, respectively: (a) a set of "atomic" rule types and a set of rules for producing derived rule types from them, and (b) yield-value function(s) that support evaluation of rules that have a given rule type.

- Truth-valued functions, of course, come in two varieties: constraints (which must produce true) and conditions[14] (which can produce either true or false). To simplify matters, a selection has not been indicated in this assembly, but it is easy to specify either variety (see Chapter 16). Recall the rule type indicators "T" and "?" used in R-Notation for rules.
- TV is the name of a Boolean variable used for the truth values produced by the truth-valued function.
- A truth-valued function *must* produce either true or false[15]—its result can never be indeterminate. If the result of the rule's yield-value function is indeterminate (that is, there is no yield value for a given instance of the rule's anchor), the truth-valued function can nonetheless produce true (for that instance) since indeterminate is the *correct* answer for the yield-value function. Refer to the boxed item, Examples of Indeterminate Results from Yield-Value Functions.

Examples of Indeterminate Results from Yield-Value Functions

The logical function of a Pattern-R rule must produce either true or false for each instance of its anchor. If the rule is a constraint, of course, it *must* produce true. What if the result of the yield-value function is indeterminate? Consider the following two sample cases:

Case 1: A Pattern-R rule requires division in its yield-value function. Suppose that for a specific instance of the anchor, this requires it to divide by zero. The rule can still produce true, since indeterminate is the *correct* answer for its yield-value function.

---

14. I really mean *higher-order conditions* since any condition used in defining higher-order rules will also have a higher-order rule type. For convenience, I will drop *higher-order* when referring to them in this discussion.

15. Note that the anchor of a condition can be another condition. In such case, the truth value of the former condition is the logical AND of the anchor's truth value *and* the result of its own truth-valued function. Informally, this simply means the test results for such conditions are cumulative, as is appropriate. Suppose this were not the case and the result of the truth-valued function of the former condition stood on its own. If the truth value of the anchor is false, the former condition—according to the rules of logical implication—would always be true (no matter what its own truth-valued function produced). That result would clearly be inappropriate.

Case 2: A Pattern-R rule requires evaluation of each value in a series of values to determine whether it is ascending in value from the previous one. Consider the first value in the series. The rule can still produce true for that value, since indeterminate is the *correct* answer for its yield-value function in that case.[16]

In the remainder of this chapter, I outline the assembly of the two Pattern-R rule types used in the earlier two examples of Pattern-R rules.

Assembly of Example 1: The Monitor Rule

In reviewing the formal assembly for the Monitor Rule given earlier, we would find the following. Part 1, the yield-value function, is addressed first.

$$\text{count-of-critical-condition-patients} =$$
$$\text{yvfn}_{(LIM)} \, (\text{Monitor, Critical-Condition-Patient})^{17}$$

where $\text{yvfn}_{(LIM)}$ counts (as dictated by Pattern-R rule type LIM) the number of Critical-Condition-Patients (producing the result as the rule's yield value, in count-of-critical-condition-patients) for each instance of the rule's anchor, Monitor.

Now the truth-valued function is addressed.

$$\text{TV} = \text{tvfn}_{(LIM)}(\text{count-of-critical-condition-patients})$$

where $\text{tvfn}_{(LIM)}$, the truth-valued function, produces true or false for each yield value (in count-of-critical-condition-patients) as dictated by the Pattern-R rule type, LIM, and the given qualification ("upper limit of 2"). The specific test in this example is as follows.

$$\text{count-of-critical-condition-patients LE 2}$$

---

16. See Ross [1997, p. 136, #545 and #547] for further examples.
17. The "given" fact types in the example—that is, "attends" and the "ISA"—are also arguments for this specification. However, these can again be assumed to be implicit if specification of the rule were based on some model (for example, a graphic fact model or data model). For that reason they are not included here.

Assembly of Example 2: The Union Rule

In reviewing the formal assembly for the Union Rule given earlier, we would find the following. Part 1, the yield-value function, is addressed first.

$$\text{count-of-correspondents-possessed} =$$
$$\text{yvfn}_{(ME)}(\text{Group, Non-Union-Employee, Union-Employee})^{18}$$

where $\text{yvfn}_{(ME)}$ determines (as dictated by Pattern-R rule type ME) the number of correspondents having at least one instance for each instance of the rule's anchor, Group. This result (which will be 0, 1, or 2 for any given instance of the anchor) will be produced as the rule's yield value in count-of-correspondents-possessed.

Now the truth-valued function is addressed.

$$\text{TV} = \text{tvfn}_{(ME)}(\text{count-of-correspondents-possessed})$$

where $\text{tvfn}_{(ME)}$, the truth-valued function, produces true or false for each yield value (that is, in count-of-correspondents-possessed) as dictated by the Pattern-R rule type, ME, and the implicit qualification ("upper limit of 1"). The specific test in this example is as follows:

$$\text{count-of-correspondents-possessed LE 1}$$

Reference

Ross, Ronald G. 1997. *The Business Rule Book* (2nd ed.). Houston, TX: Business Rule Solutions, LLC. Available at *http://www.BRSolutions.com*.

---

18. The "given" fact types in the example—that is, "includes" and the two "ISAs"—are also arguments for this specification. However, these can again be assumed to be implicit if specification of the rule were based on some model (for example, a graphic fact model or data model). For that reason they are not included here.

Part V Appendices

APPENDIX A: EVALUATING THE TRUTH VALUE OF A RULE

In predicate calculus, any rule (logical implication) can be expressed in the form IF p THEN q. This form is exactly equivalent to the logical expression OR ((NOT p), q). Table A–1 shows the truth table for evaluating such an expression.

The truth table indicates the result of evaluating a rule (this result is given in the column on the right) for each possible combination of p and q values (given in the two columns on the left). A row-by-row analysis of these results is instructive.

- *Row 1:* If p and q are both true, then the expression as a whole evaluates to true. We can say "p implies q." This result is reasonably straightforward—it conforms to use of the term *implies* in ordinary English.
- *Row 2:* Here p is true, but q is false. Consequently, the expression as a whole evaluates to false. We can say that "p does *not* imply q."[1] This result

Table A–1   Truth Table for Rules (Logical Implications)

p	q	NOT p	OR ((NOT p), q)
T	T	F	T
T	F	F	F
F	T	T	T
F	F	T	T

---

1. This statement is not the same as "p implies (NOT q)," of course.

is also reasonably straightforward—it too conforms to use of the term *implies* in ordinary English. Note that this result is *not allowed* if the rule is defined as a constraint. In other words, as a constraint, the rule would *prohibit* an evaluation to false—which in turn means that q can never be false if p is true. Informally, this probably corresponds to how most people think of a rule.

- *Rows 3 and 4:* In both these rows, p is false, yet the expression as a whole evaluates to true. This bizarre result flies in the face of common sense.[2]

  The reason, informally, is that we tend to read too much into the word *implies*. Specifically, we often associate the idea of *causation* to the IF . . . THEN . . . form. For example, we might say something like "If you will sign that petition, then I will sign it too." What that statement really means is that your action will influence or *cause* me to act or think in a certain manner. Although this usage of IF . . . THEN . . . is common in real life, it is *not* appropriate in predicate calculus. In formal logic, IF . . . THEN . . . never suggests causation or influence. Instead, it is always evaluated merely as a truth-valued expression. (For this reason, the phrases *the expression evaluates to* or *the logical expression is satisfied* are preferred over the potentially confusing *implies*.)

Charniak and McDermott [1985, p. 17] provide an excellent discussion of this issue as follows:

> Once one has accepted that the predicate calculus **if** does not express causality, it is not hard to convince oneself that the truth table must be filled out the way it is. For example, consider the [meta]rule that (**if f t**) [must be evaluated as] true. Suppose we were told that if anyone gets caught in the rain, then that person will be wet.
>
> (**if** *(anyone is caught in the rain) (that person is wet)*)
>
> One day we note that Dave is wet, but he was not caught in the rain (suppose he was sprayed with a hose). In this case we have (**if f t**). But clearly our experience with Dave does not invalidate our rule, so in this case the if-then rule must still be true. So (**if f t**) [evaluates to] true.

---

2. For additional discussion, refer to Tarski [1995, pp. 23–28] and Halpin and Girle [1981, pp. 49–52].

References

Charniak, Eugene, and Drew McDermott. 1985. *Introduction to Artificial Intelligence*. Reading, MA: Addison-Wesley.

Halpin, Terry, and Roderic Girle. 1981. Deductive Logic (2nd ed.). Brisbane, Australia: Logiqpress.

Tarski, Alfred. 1995. *Introduction to Logic and to the Methodology of Deductive Sciences* (2nd ed.). New York: Dover Publications. (Originally published in 1946 by Oxford University Press, New York.)

APPENDIX B: TERMS AT THE TECHNICAL DESIGNER'S VIEW

Variable in programming languages does not have the same connotation as *variable* in formal logic. For this reason, the question "What is a term?" cannot be answered as directly at the technical designer's perspective as at the other two perspectives.

In an automated system, a variable is basically a container capable of holding a value (possibly complex). This container must be given an identifier or name for reference purposes. This identifier or name could be meaningless (for example, "123456") which, of course, is sufficient for machines.

Technical designers often give such containers more meaningful names so the containers can be identified more readily (by the technical designers and possibly other users). For example, we might define a container *current-temperature* that holds only a single simple value (the current temperature).

Is *current-temperature* a term in the sense of predicate calculus? The answer is *no* if we mean the implementation container itself. The answer is *yes* if we remove any consideration of the implementation container and think only about the value it contains.

Now let's consider a more complex variable—in particular, a relvar as in Date and Darwen [2000]. Suppose we define a relvar called Employee. The columns of this relvar include emp-id, emp-name, SSN, emp-salary, and so on. Date and Darwen [pp. 16–17] call this set of column names the *heading* of the relvar and show that it represents the relvar's predicate.[1] (See Appendix F.) The names in this set are clearly terms in the sense of predicate calculus.

What about Employee? Is it a term?

---

1. Note that the relvar's internal predicate also includes any relevant constraints that might have been specified.

As before, the answer is *no* if we mean the implementation container itself. The answer is *yes* if we remove any consideration of the implementation container. In that case it can be argued that Employee is the *name* of the predicate and therefore does represent a term in the sense of predicate calculus.

To continue this analysis, Date and Darwen explain that each column in a relvar should be defined on some domain, which in their view is considered exactly equivalent to a type (or data type) in programming languages.[2] For example, emp-salary might be defined on the type currency-amount.

In the Date and Darwen view, however, the name of such a domain or type should *not* be viewed as a variable (container). Rather it should be viewed as a named "... **set of values**—*all possible* values of the type in question ... along with ... the valid **operators** that can legally be applied to values of that type...."[3] [Date 2000, p. 112, original emphasis]. The set of values can be given by list or by rule(s); possible (storage) representations can also be given.

In any event, such types should appear where appropriate in the heading of a relation, which makes them part of the relvar's predicate. (See Appendix F.) Because of that, the names of the types or domains are also terms in the sense of predicate calculus.

References

Date, C. J. 2000. *An Introduction to Database Systems* (7th ed.). Boston, MA: Addison-Wesley.

Date, C. J., and Hugh Darwen. 2000. *Foundation for Future Database Systems: The Third Manifesto* (2nd ed.). Boston, MA: Addison-Wesley.

---

2. Refer to Date [2000, p. 112] and Date and Darwen [2000, pp. 502–503].
3. That is, a set of operations whose algorithms are hidden (encapsulated) appropriate to the type.

APPENDIX C: THE FUNDAMENTAL KINDS OF RULES

This appendix reviews the three basic possibilities for the specification of any rule (that is, logical implication): *rejector, projector,* and *producer.* Every rule, whether lower-order or higher-order,[1] can be of one and only one of these three kinds. This appendix also examines where functions fit into this scheme.

Three Categories of Rules

The three kinds of rules are described briefly below.

- *Rejector:* A rule can be specified as a constraint that tends to[2] reject violations to maintain integrity.
- *Projector:* A rule can be specified as a constraint that tends to[3] perform inferencing or logical deduction[4] to maintain integrity. Projectors

---

1. That is, whether untyped or typed as explained in Chapter 18.
2. I say *tends to* because whether or not outright rejection occurs can also depend on the enforcement level chosen. Instead of strictly rejecting any violating event, for example, some other response might be deemed appropriate (for example, simply giving a warning or alert). Also, time may be a factor. Consider the following rejector: *A student must be enrolled in at least five courses within five days of the start of registration.* What should happen if a student is *not* enrolled in five courses by that time? Since time cannot be "rejected," some other course of action needs be indicated.
3. Here again, I say *tends to* because whether or not the actual projection occurs can also depend on the enforcement level chosen for the projector. For example, if the actual projection would result in a conflict, strict enforcement might not be indicated. However, this issue is a complex one and beyond the scope of this tutorial to address fully.
4. There are important types of higher-order projectors other than just inference-type constraints. Refer to Ross [1997, pp. 26–28]. For example, one type of higher-order projector, an *executive* (also known as a *trigger*), can be used to execute processes and procedures. This discussion does not directly consider these higher-order rule types.

essentially do just the opposite of rejectors. Projectors never reject "violating" events[5] but rather always accept them and cause new truths (or if higher-order, possibly other kinds of information) to be asserted automatically as a result. In other words, such rules can *project* an event into some new event(s) automatically.

- *Producer:* A rule (logical implication) can be specified as a test or query that can evaluate to either true or false. (For higher-order rules, as discussed in Chapter 18, such a test or query is called a *condition*.) In such case, events are never rejected or projected; only the truth value of the rule itself changes.[6] Producers are always specified only for the information they themselves produce.

These three variations are examined below in more detail using the following simple expression concerning employees. The expression has been given in IF . . . THEN . . . syntax to help make the comparison a bit more straightforward. The question mark in parentheses is a reminder that the expression can also be used as a query.

Expression: *If manager, then salaried employee(?).*

Defined as a constraint (as either a rejector or a projector), this expression could be read at the business manager's perspective as the following rule: *Each manager must be a salaried employee.*

Rejector

If the rule is defined as a rejector, the business logic server must "watch for" events producing potential violations. Such violations could occur, for example, if either of the following assertions were to be presented to the system:

- An assertion that an employee is to be a manager, but the employee is not found to be currently salaried.
- An assertion that an employee is no longer to be salaried, but the employee is found to be currently a manager.

---

5. By *violating events* I mean events that would produce changes to base facts resulting in the violation of some rule.
6. And also the rule's yield value, if a higher-order rule.

Projector

If the rule is defined as one that performs inferencing or logical deduction to ensure integrity (that is, as an inference-type projector), the business logic server must "watch for" the appropriate circumstances to do so. For example, when an assertion is made that an employee is a manager, the business logic server must automatically indicate that the employee is currently salaried (if not already so indicated). Since *salaried* has been inferred or derived according to the rule, the business logic server should disallow any direct assertion (by a user or an application) that a manager is *not* salaried (that is, that *salaried* is false).

Producer

Defined as a test or query, the expression (still actually a logical implication) could be read at the business manager's perspective as an implicit true-false question, as follows: *Are all managers salaried employees?* (With the proper qualification, it might also be read as follows: *Is any* given *manager a salaried employee?*).

Evaluating such a test or query does not involve either rejecting or projecting events. Rather, the business logic server simply needs to evaluate the current state of the factbase in order to *produce* an appropriate true-or-false answer. This true-or-false answer is given by the Boolean value of the logical implication itself.

In everyday English, *rule* is often assumed to carry the sense of *constraint*—that is, that something *must* be true or enforced. In formal logic, however, *rule* (that is, logical implication) does not necessarily carry that sense. The expression of a logical implication acts as a constraint *only* if we define it that way. Otherwise it is a merely a test or query. (Again, for higher-order rules such a test or query is called a *condition*.)

To say this another way, logical implications are like AND, OR, or NOT in that we can use them to specify tests or ask questions (pose queries) about the logicbase. This capacity to *produce* information or knowledge is important in at least two ways.

- It permits us to ask certain kinds of interesting questions. To use an example from Chapter 16, we might ask, "Does 'streets are wet' imply 'it is raining'?"
- It allows us to support higher-order constraints that are conditional, permitting expression of complex patterns—or, more accurately, patterns upon patterns—in the factbase.

Functions

Logical implications used as tests or queries are just one kind of producer. Producers in general are always simply *functions*.

Apart from logical implications used as tests or queries, a function must involve a named result to be of interest in the business rule approach.[7] Although the formula for the function is *not* a rule in the strict sense (that is, it is not a logical implication), the name of the result is a *term*—a legitimate and important kind of business rule.

For a logical (truth-valued) function, the result is a *derived term*; for any other kind of functions, the result is a *computed term*. An example for each of these respective cases follows.

Example of a producer involving a derived term:
high-risk = over-budget OR under-staffed

High-risk is a derived term based on the given formula. Its value can be either true or false (only).

Example of a producer involving a computed term:
total-amount-owed = SUM(line-item-charge) + sales-tax
+ delivery-charge

Total-amount-owed is a computed term based on the given formula. Note that the value of total-amount-owed will not be Boolean.

The formula for a function should always be specified in a declarative manner and should embody the precise definition for the associated term. These formulas or definitions should be managed carefully—as should all business rules.

Reference

Ross, Ronald G. 1997. *The Business Rule Book* (2nd ed.). Houston, TX: Business Rule Solutions, LLC. Available at *http://www.BRSolutions.com*.

---

7. The result of a logical implication used as test or query can also be named—just like the result of any other logical function. In practice, however, such names are usually not needed.

APPENDIX D: ABOUT THE
IF . . . THEN . . . SYNTAX

IF . . . THEN . . . syntax is used in Part V to explain examples wherever helpful. Contrary to what some believe, however, the IF . . . THEN . . . syntax is *not* inevitable for expressing rules at the business manager's perspective (and quite possibly at one or both of the other two perspectives as well).[1] In particular, the IF . . . THEN . . . syntax is often not convenient for expressing rejectors, which play an important role in the business rule approach.

Consider the sample expression used in Appendix C: *If manager, then salaried employee(?).* The best way to express this as a constraint is clearly as given there: *Each manager must be a salaried employee.*[2]

Emphasis on using IF . . . THEN . . . syntax in certain circles of the IT community probably arose from discussions of formal logic as applied to projector-type constraints (that is, rules aimed toward inferencing or logical deduction), most likely at the system developer's or technical designer's perspective. In any event, retrofitting the IF . . . THEN . . . syntax to the business manager's perspective is inappropriate.

---

1. For good discussions of theoretical difficulties with the IF . . . THEN . . . syntax as used in everyday English sentences, refer to Tarski [1995, pp. 23–28] and Halpin and Girle [1981, pp. 49–52].
2. The underlying expression in predicate calculus for the rule makes use of IF . . . THEN . . . ($\rightarrow$) as follows: Forall x (Manager $x \rightarrow$ SalariedEmployee x) (Terry Halpin, private correspondence, September 9, 2001).

References

Halpin, Terry, and Roderic Girle. 1981. Deductive Logic (2nd ed.). Brisbane,
   Australia: Logiqpress.

Tarski, Alfred. 1995. *Introduction to Logic and to the Methodology of Deductive
   Sciences* (2nd ed.). New York: Dover Publications. (Originally published in
   1946 by Oxford University Press, New York.)

APPENDIX E: HALPIN'S DEFINITIONS FOR *FACT* AND RELATED TERMS[1]

Fact (elementary): Assertion that an object has a property, or that one or more objects participate in a relationship, where the fact cannot be split into simpler facts with the same object types without information loss.

Object: Thing of interest. An object may be an entity or a value.

Entity: Object that is referenced by relating it to other objects (e.g., the Country that has CountryCode 'AU').[2]

Relationship: Property or association involving one or more objects.

Association: Relationship type, usually involving at least two roles.

Role: Part played by an object in a relationship.

---

1. Reprinted with permission from Halpin, Terry. 2001. *Information Modeling and Relational Databases*. San Francisco, CA: Morgan Kaufmann, glossary entries on pp. 713–715.
2. This definition is interesting. It illustrates how the system developer's perspective differs from the business manager's perspective. At the business manager's perspective, paraphrasing John Zachman, when terms are used (for example, *employee*), they are meant to refer to the "real flesh-and-blood things." At the system developer's perspective, in contrast, the focus is on building *representations* of real-world things, as Halpin's definition suggests. C. J. Date comments as follows: At the system developer's perspective, terms "denote *surrogates* or *models* or *representatives* of those real things inside the system; the system as a whole can be regarded as a 'model of reality.'" (C. J. Date, private correspondence, November 19, 2001).

APPENDIX F: SEMANTICS IN THE RELATIONAL MODEL

Consider a relvar MMQ with the following heading:

MMQ

Major_P# : P#	Minor_P# : P#	QTY : QTY

P# and the second QTY are types or domains.

Date and Darwen [2000, p. 146] indicate, "The predicate here is:

Part MAJOR_P# (a value of type P#) contains quantity QTY (a value of type QTY) of part MINOR_P# (a value of type P# again).

(Note, therefore, that the predicate is, informally, **what the relation means**.)" [emphasis theirs].

Suppose we now instantiate the predicate (insert a row into the relvar) using the following values: {P2, P4, 7}. Date and Darwen [2000, p. 146] indicate, "The proposition (or predicate instantiation) here is:

Part P2 contains quantity 7 of part P4."

What would happen if one, two, or all three of the three terms in this proposition were missing?

Quite simply, the "proposition" would not be a proposition. "A 'tuple' that contains a null is not a tuple—and a 'domain' that contains a null is not a domain, and a 'relation' that contains a null is not a relation, either" [Date 2001].

How about inserting "unknown" for a missing term—for example, for the *quantity* value if it were missing in the expression above? "The statement

'Part P1 contains an unknown quantity of part P2' *is* a proposition, but it's not an instantiation of the predicate given!—rather, it's an instantiation of the predicate 'Part Px contains an unknown quantity of Py'" [Date 2001].

One final point is this. Note that Date and Darwen [2000, p. 146] use the word "informally" above when they say, "... the predicate is, informally, **what the relation means**." This characterization is presumably because the business logic server does not understand in any real sense what the predicate *means*.

However, this is certainly *not* true at the business manager's perspective, where development of business rules must begin. The meaning is *highly* relevant for that audience (even if informal) and hence at the system developer's perspective as well.

References

Date, C. J. 2001. Private correspondence, November 19.

Date, C. J., and Hugh Darwen. 2000. *Foundation for Future Database Systems: The Third Manifesto* (2nd ed.). Boston, MA: Addison-Wesley.

APPENDIX G: BASIC OPERATORS AND HIGHER-ORDER RULE TYPES

Higher-order rule types such as *mandatory, mutually exclusive, unique, cyclic, frozen, timed,* and so on are of obvious use to logicbase designers. They can also be easily demonstrated to satisfy the two-function criteria prescribed in Chapter 18 for higher-order rule types. Many other patterns in typical factbases can as well.

Certain more commonplace or basic operators deserve special attention. As you examine these operators below, keep in mind that all Pattern-R rules *must* include a truth-valued function as one of their two functions.

OR, AND, and NOT

OR, AND, and NOT are logical functions. Given appropriate arguments for their parameters, each returns either true or false. Are they suitable candidates to serve as higher-order rule types? The answer is *no* for various reasons.

NOT. NOT is always applied to a single Boolean variable or expression. All rules, on the other hand (including higher-order rules), involve at least two terms.[1] Therefore, NOT can be used for qualification in higher-order rules, but not as a higher-order rule type per se.

AND and OR. AND and OR are unsuitable in native form for a different reason. Obviously, specification of higher-order rules does require ANDs

---

1. NOT is a *monadic* operator, whereas logical implication (like AND and OR) is *dyadic.*

and ORs of conditions. The problem, however, is broader than simple ANDs and ORs might suggest. The Business Rule Book [Ross 1997, pp. 77–104] proposes an entire family of "mutual" rule types to provide generalized support for patterns of this kind. This rule type family includes the special cases of mutually exclusive, mutually inclusive, and mutually prohibited—and a generalized *mutual* rule type supporting any specified number of conditions.

The Quantifiers of Predicate Calculus

The two logical quantifiers—EXISTS and FORALL—are fundamental to predicate calculus. EXISTS provides a test for "at least one" or "there exists at least one." FORALL provides a test for "all" (or "for each" or "given any"). These tests are likewise essential for higher-order rule types.

However, the need for testing quantities in higher-order rules is broader than simply "at least one" or "all." Relevant quantities or limits can also fall anywhere in between "one" and "all" (and often do).

The Business Rule Book [Ross 1997, pp. 47–75] proposes a family of rule types called *Instance Verifiers* that provide generalized support for patterns that involve counting instances. Incidentally, a special case in this rule family is *mandatory*, which involves testing for "at least one."

Comparative Operators

The comparative operators—for example, *greater than* (>), *equal to* (=), *less than* (<), and so on—are logical functions, which satisfies the first criterion of the definition for Pattern-R rules.[2]

---

2. Whether or not these comparative operators are predicates is not central to these arguments. Here are relevant comments on the question.

C. J. Date [2000, p. 777] indicates that these logical operators can be viewed as predicates: "…'>(x,y)'—more conveniently written 'x>y'—is a predicate with two parameters, x and y; it returns *true* if the argument corresponding to x is greater than the argument corresponding to y and *false* otherwise."

Terry Halpin [2001] indicates "These [logical operators] may be treated as dyadic predicates. In practice however, they are normally treated as scalar operators (e.g., arithmetic or character-string operators) rather than logical operators, since their terms are not logical expressions (even though their result is Boolean)."

The second criterion requires an underlying computation (the yield-value function) to support evaluation of the truth-valued function. For the comparative evaluators there would obviously have to be a "built-in" computation that the machine performs (for example, a subtraction between the values given as arguments for the parameters) to support evaluation of the truth-valued function. So even if such a yield-value function is a given, the comparative operators nonetheless qualify "as is" as (useful) Pattern-R rule types.[3]

Arithmetic Operators

Arithmetic functions, for example, SUM, SUBTRACT, AVERAGE, and so on, obviously satisfy the computational criterion for higher-order rule types. They do not natively involve a truth-valued function, but their inherent computation function could certainly be used as the basis for one. In theory then, any arithmetic function could be defined as a higher-order rule type. In practice, these might be deemed of limited practical use since (barring machine failures) such rules would never produce false.

References

Date, C. J. 2000. *An Introduction to Database Systems* (7th ed.). Boston, MA: Addison-Wesley.

Halpin, Terry. 2001. Private correspondence, September 9.

Ross, Ronald G. 1997. *The Business Rule Book* (2nd ed.). Houston, TX: Business Rule Solutions, LLC. Available at *http://www.BRSolutions.com.*

---

3. These comparative operators constitute one of the atomic Pattern-R rule type families given in Ross [1997, pp. 151–164].

APPENDIX H: FORMALIZATION OF THE PATTERN-R APPROACH

Formalization of any system requires several things, as follows [Hofstadter 1980, p. 41].[1]

- *Axioms*—that is, the givens.
- *Rules of production*—that is, the rules you must follow in creating derived results (called *theorems*) from the axioms (and/or other theorems).
- *Decision procedure*—that is, instructions indicating how to decide whether a proposed theorem is a valid one.

Does the assembly template for Pattern-R rule types satisfy these criteria? *No.* Essentially, the assembly template merely "opens up the covers" of Pattern-R rule types and shows what is inside.

Opening up the covers is not actually necessary for the atomic rule types given in *The Business Rule Book* [Ross 1997] since these are the *axioms* of the Pattern-R system. (Of course it is interesting for implementation purposes, but that is a different matter.)

It must be remembered, however, that the set of rule types in the Pattern-R system is open-ended or extensible. Opening up the covers *is* necessary in showing how *derived* rule types (the theorems) are produced. Therefore, the assembly template can be viewed as providing *rules of production* for derived rule types. Missing, however, in both this tutorial and *The Business Rule Book* is a decision procedure for deciding whether a proposed derived rule type is valid or not.[2]

---

1. Refer to Simpson [2000, p. 10] for a somewhat different view.
2. Developing such a decision procedure is the subject of current research.

Does that complete the answer to this question about formalization? *Not yet.* There is actually a second (and simpler) level at which the question must also be addressed. This level involves everyday specification of Pattern-R rules by system developers.

At this level, both atomic rule types and provably valid derived rule types constitute the axioms of the Pattern-R system. *The Business Rule Book* offers several dozen of these. The rules of production are the grammatical rules about using these rule types correctly. These rules of production are also comprehensively documented in the book. In addition, more than 500 theorems (correct examples of their application) are given and discussed. However, again missing is a decision procedure,[3] so the system cannot be said to be formal at this level either.

References

Hofstadter, Douglas R. 1980. *Godel, Escher and Bach: An Eternal Golden Braid.* New York: Vintage Books.

Ross, Ronald G. 1997. *The Business Rule Book* (2nd ed.). Houston, TX: Business Rule Solutions, LLC. Available at *http://www.BRSolutions.com.*

Simpson, Stephen G. 2000. "Logic and Mathematics." Available at *http:// www.math.psu.edu/simpson/.*

---

3. This decision procedure exists but has not been published.

APPENDIX I: WHAT DOES *DECLARATIVE* MEAN

Any logicbase generally includes many rules—in fact, often a very large number. Fundamentally, the order or sequence in which all these rules are evaluated should make no difference whatsoever to the results eventually achieved.[1]

A more accurate way to say this is the following: The *system developers* or *technical designers* who specify the rules need not be concerned with sequence. The business logic server itself will automatically determine the proper sequence (if any) for evaluating the rules based on natural dependencies among the rules themselves.

For example, suppose a rule indicates *A discount of 15 percent must be given to a customer order if the order is for a good customer and the total amount of the order is over $1,000*. Suppose there are other rules for determining whether a customer is good and for computing the total amount of the order. Clearly, these other rules must be evaluated before the discount rule can be applied (if appropriate). However, because the rules are declarative—that is, because the business logic server *itself* can determine the appropriate order of evaluation—the user can present the rules in any order and still get the same results in the end.[2]

---

1. User friendliness might be a different issue in some cases.
2. That is, after all the rules have been presented.

In other words, the final state of the logicbase should be exactly the same for *any* sequence of presentation. This outcome is very unlike the case for processes and procedures, where the importance of explicit sequence is paramount. This *sequence independence* is the fundamental reason why rules should be considered declarative rather than procedural.

 A set of rules is declaritive if their sequence of presentation to the business logic server makes no difference to the results produced for them.

APPENDIX J: THE "MARY" INFERENCING EXAMPLE STEP-BY-STEP

This discussion works through the "Mary" inferencing example presented in Chapter 16 step-by-step using the following: (a) no facts or predicates, (b) Boolean variables, and (c) forward chaining.

Each rule is also presented in the form OR ((NOT p), q) to assist the reader in the proper evaluations. It is important to remember (as always) that each rule as a whole is a Boolean expression.

R1: "Mary" → female

This expression can also be written as:

OR ((NOT "Mary"), female)

"Mary" is an instance term and must be taken as a given (that is, as true). The expression as a whole, R1, is indicated (by default) to be a constraint and therefore true. As a result, the rule-processing server sets the Boolean variable *female* to true.

R2: "Mary" → of-age

This expression can also be written as:

OR ((NOT "Mary"), of-age)

"Mary" is an instance term and must be taken as a given (that is, as true). The expression as a whole, R2, is indicated (by default) to be a constraint and therefore true. As a result, the rule-processing server sets the Boolean variable *of-age* to true.

R3: female AND of-age → woman

This expression can also be written as:

OR ((NOT female and of-age), woman)

Resulting from the earlier evaluations, female and of-age are both known to be true. The expression as a whole, R3, is indicated (by default) to be a constraint and therefore true. As a result, the rule-processing server sets the Boolean variable *woman* to true.

APPENDIX K: MORE ON R-NOTATION FOR FACTS

Facts Involving More Than Two terms

A fact can involve more than two terms, as the following example illustrates.

"Teacher advises Student in Course."

In this example, the fact, "...advises...in...", involves three terms: Teacher, Student, and Course.

This example is written in R-Notation for facts as follows. By convention, only the first term in the fact is shown on the left side of the bidirectional arrow; the remaining terms are always shown on the right side. This approach serves as a reminder that the fact represents a sentence, and a sentence can have only one subject.

Teacher $^{\text{advises}\ldots\text{in}}$ $\leftrightarrow$ Student, Course

Note that the order of terms in the fact is significant (as always for facts specified at the system developer perspective) so that the terms "fit" into it correctly.

This fact, like all facts, must obey the Existence Principle. The rule implied by the fact under the Existence Principle is given as follows:

...advises...in... $\rightarrow$ Teacher, Student, Course

Any fact, including those involving more than two terms, can often be rephrased without changing the meaning. This typically involves a change in the order of the terms. For example, "Teacher advises Student in Course" could be reordered and rephrased as follows: "Student in Course is advised by Teacher." Note that there is no fundamental change in the fact's meaning. This revised form could be expressed as follows:

Student $^{\text{in}\,\ldots\,\text{is advised by}}$ $\leftrightarrow$ Course, Teacher

The fact name for a fact involving more than two terms may be indicated on the *right* side of the bidirectional arrow, just as for facts with only two terms. Such facts must conform to the following conventions:

- Only one term is listed on the left side of the bidirectional arrow (as always).
- The fact name is given in left-to-right order (as always).
- The terms fit into the fact name in *reverse* order.

Here is an example:

Course $\leftrightarrow$ $^{\text{advises}\,\ldots\,\text{in}}$ Student, Teacher

Inserting the terms in reverse order, this fact is read "Teacher advises Student in Course."

Facts Involving a Single Term

Most facts involve two or more terms. However, it is possible for a fact to have only a single term. An example, again starting with a sentence, illustrates:

Company pays slowly.

In this example, the fact, "... pays slowly," involves only a single term, Company. This example would be written in R-Notation for facts as follows:

Company $^{\text{pays slowly}}$ $\leftrightarrow$

This R-Notation fact type shows no terms on the right side since only a single term, Company, is involved.

As before, this fact implies a rule under the Existence Principle, as follows:

pays slowly $\rightarrow$ Company

APPENDIX L: SPECIAL BUILT-IN FACT TYPES IN R-NOTATION

Several useful predefined or built-in fact types are offered in R-Notation for facts. [1]

HASA

The first built-in fact type is HASA. The HASA fact type can be used to express closely held properties of a class term. An example using R-Notation for facts illustrates.

Customer $^{HASA} \leftrightarrow$ credit limit

This fact[2] can be read, "Customer has a credit limit."[3] This fact implies a rule under the Existence Principle, as follows:

HASA $\rightarrow$ Customer, credit limit

---

1. This discussion focuses primarily above the technical designer's perspective. Many more built-in predicates could be useful at the latter perspective. Common Prolog implementations, for example, usually feature several hundred. Many of these, however, are not relevant to business rules (Markus Schacher, private correspondence, September 5, 2001).
2. This example is a fact *type* because it includes class terms (Customer and credit limit).
3. A factbase could have literally hundreds or thousands of such HASA facts. Since all of them would have the same predicate name, ". . . has a . . .", obviously some means for distinguishing them at the meta-level is required.

ISA

Another built-in fact type—a crucial one—is the ISA fact type. The ISA fact type, which means *is a category of*, can be used to express subsets or subtypes for a class term. An example using R-Notation for facts illustrates:[4]

Rush Order ^{ISA} ↔ Order

This fact type[5] can be read "Rush Order is a category of Order," or "Rush Order is a subset of Order." This fact implies a rule under the Existence Principle, as follows:

ISA → Rush Order, Order

INST

Another built-in fact type is the INST (*is instantiation of*) fact type. The INST fact type can be used to provide specific instance terms for a class term (or fact instances for a fact type). An example using R-Notation for facts illustrates. The INST fact type is especially useful in specifying *rules* that reference instance terms.[6]

"Acme Supply" ^{INST} ↔ Customer

This fact instance[7] can be read, "Acme Supply is an instance of Customer." This fact implies a rule under the Existence Principle, as follows.

INST → "Acme Supply," Customer

SEM

Another built-in fact type is the SEM fact type. This built-in fact type can be used to indicate that certain distinct fact names represent the very same fact

---

4. It is especially important here to remember that we are *not* examining these pre-defined fact types from the technical designer's perspective. How the ISA fact type should be viewed at that perspective might be quite different.
5. This example is a fact *type* because it includes variables (Rush Order and Order).
6. The INST predicate becomes *implicit* at the technical designer's perspective. Each row in a relvar, for example, is an "instantiation of" that relvar's predicate.
7. This example is a fact *instance* because it includes no class terms. "Acme Supply" is clearly not a class term. Customer is an instance term at the *meta*-level.

type—in other words, that they are *semantically equivalent*. The names might be aliases or they might be rephrased names (with reordered terms). An example of the latter using R-Notation for facts illustrates:

is placed by $\overset{\text{SEM}}{\longleftrightarrow}$ places

This fact instance[8] can be read "'is placed by' is semantically equivalent to 'places'." This fact implies a rule under the Existence Principle, as follows:

SEM $\rightarrow$ is placed by, places

---

8. This example is a fact *instance* because it includes no variables. At the *meta*-level, both "is placed by" and "places" are instance terms rather than class terms.

Glossary

abnormal reuse (work): Using for abnormal circumstances a script that is already used for normal circumstances.

action (work): An activity, transform, transaction, or process that can be requested or used within a script to achieve a particular desired result. Upon execution, an action takes "input" and transforms it into "output." An action need not necessarily be automated.

actor (work): A real-world actor or a software actor that initiates events or performs work to respond to an event.

adaptability: The ability to make fit (as for a specific new use or situation), often by modification; that is, the ability to change quickly and easily.

anchor (Pattern-R rules): The left-hand expression of a Pattern-R rule.

antecedent (formal logic): In a specific rule, the left-hand expression.

architectural product: A deliverable necessary for prescribing the architecture of a functioning business or business capacity and/or for providing specifications essential to its construction. An architectural deliverable may be used to communicate such specifications to other project participants and/or to achieve a "sign-off" during a project, but the deliverable never exists *solely* for these latter purposes.

as-is data model: A data model for a database that has already been implemented.

as-is workflow model: A workflow model for a workflow that has already been implemented—that is, one that is currently operational. An as-is workflow model generally represents how a workflow is currently organized.

aspect: Any of the factors or requirements categories involved in building or operating a business or business capacity. These aspects are based (following the Zachman Architecture Framework where they are called abstractions[1]) on the six interrogatives, as follows:

- What (data)—what the business needs to know
- How (process)—transformations the business must be able to perform
- Where (location)—locations where work occurs and how they connect
- Who (people)—actors and how they interact
- When (time)—timing and precedence criteria for coordinating work
- Why (motivation)—appropriate guidance

assumption: Something believed to be true about the capability, knowledge, motivation, or tendencies of an actor or about the characteristics of the business environment in which the business or business capacity operates (for example, "Customers don't always know their needs or understand our products"). Such an assumption can be an internal influence that shapes rules.

atomic form (rule): A state of a rule in which it cannot be broken down or reduced into more granular rules without loss of meaning (across the entire set of more granular rules) significant to the business or business capacity. Formally, a rule is in atomic form only if both of the following are true:

- The rule has no ORs among its LHTs.
- The rule has no ANDs among it RHTs.

automated rule: An element of business logic that has been implemented in automated form. An automated rule is expressed in a form (syntax) recognizable by a rule engine, programming language, application generator, or similar technology. An automated rule is often the implementation counterpart to an operating rule.

---

1. For more information on the Zachman Architecture Framework, refer to the following references:

Zachman, John A. 2002. *The Zachman Framework: A Primer for Enterprise Engineering and Manufacturing* (electronic book). Available in November 2002 at *http://www.zachmaninternational.com.*

Collected articles by John Zachman published in the *Business Rules Journal.* Available at *http://www.BRCommunity.com.*

backward chaining: An algorithm for inference that starts from a consequent and works "backwards" (that is, through left-hand expressions of all relevant inference rules) toward known facts to see if that consequent can be proven (that is, proves true). This approach is sometimes also called *goal-driven reasoning.*

base fact: A fact that cannot be produced (computed or inferred) from other facts. Base facts reside in a factbase and are fundamental to expressing and evaluating rules. Base facts are also sometimes called *ground axioms.*

base term: A term that cannot be derived or computed (that is, produced) from other terms. Base terms are fundamental to understanding the business or business capacity since all knowledge (including facts and rules) starts with them.

Boolean: A truth value. *Boolean* as a noun is taken to mean a value of either true or false, in the same way that *integer* is usually taken to mean an integer value.

Boolean expression: See *logical expression.*

Boolean variable: See *truth-valued variable.*

bracket: Any specific value or range of values for an evaluation term.

BRS RuleSpeak: A set of practical guidelines to assist business workers and professionals with expressing rules in clear, unambiguous, well-structured business English.

business: See *enterprise.*

business analysis: Applying the skills and techniques needed to create a business model.

business analyst: A business professional responsible for the creation and revision of business capacities. A business analyst contributes to the development of business models for these business capacities by developing business requirements in a structured manner.

business capacity: Some functioning part of a business, often a business process. A business capacity provides the operational ability to support the business mission and to produce results that satisfy business goals.

Business Connectivity Map: An architectural product indicating which business locations or sites need to be interconnected and also which actors are connected at which sites. The focus of the Business Connectivity

Map is on optimization of the number and locations of sites for different purposes (for example, bank branches, factories, warehouses, distribution centers, and so on), transportation and communication between sites, communication requirements between actors at their different locations, and so on.

business event: See *event (business).*

business goal: See *goal.*

business initiative: A broad change effort set in motion by senior management to move the company (and its business systems) in a certain direction based on opportunities and/or risks. A business initiative normally takes a longer period of time than a project and may in fact involve many projects.

business logic: The basic knowledge and guidance appropriate for operating a business or business capacity—that is, business rules.

business logic server: Runtime system software that operates on the basis of business rules to automate the logic of a business process—especially the specific operational tasks, decision-making tasks, and/or creative tasks it includes. The business logic server is responsible for the logicbase, that is, for managing the factbase and executing the rules in the rulebase. A business logic server might also be called a *rule engine, rule-processing server,* or *decision management platform.*

business logic technology: Technology that aims toward managing and/or executing business logic.

business milestone: A particular stage in a Business Milestones analysis. The name of a business milestone is a term that is likely to be referenced by many rules. For example, business milestones for *order* might include *received, credit-checked, filled, shipped, invoiced,* and *completed.*

Business Milestones: An architectural product depicting all the stages (business milestones) in an organized regimen for coordinating some thing or concept (for example, *order*) from a business perspective. The emphasis in Business Milestones is on organizing the management of instances at an operational level, with special focus on standardizing the relevant vocabulary (that is, stage names such as *filled (order)*) and on identifying appropriate rules to govern transitions among the stages.

business mission: See *mission.*

business model: A collection of related architectural products for the business or business capacity aimed toward capturing (that is, describing and/or prescribing) its essential workings from a purely business perspective. The business model provides a comprehensive framework for developing requirements in a business-driven manner and for ensuring the completeness of requirements.

business process: A business capability that can take raw materials (as "input") in a certain state and transform it into some value-added form (as "output"). The inputs and outputs may be tangible (for example, physical resources or products) or intangible (for example, information).

business process owner: See *owner.*

business process rule: A rule that addresses workflow involved in operating the business or business capacity.

business rule (business definition): A directive intended to influence or guide business behavior.

business rule (business system definition): An atomic piece of reusable business logic, specified declaratively.

business rule (formal definition): A concept as represented by a term, a fact, or a rule.

business system: An automated system deployed to support the operation of a business or business capacity.

business tactics: The contents of the Policy Charter. The business tactics identify relevant ends and the means to achieve those ends.

cardinality: A data model construct that refers to the number of instances of some relationship type (usually a maximum number) that any individual instance of one of the two data objects directly related in the relationship type is permitted to possess. Cardinality usually is expressed simply as "one" or as "many." Cardinality is also called *multiplicity.*

categorization scheme: A group of two or more immediate categories in an organized scheme for categorizing instances of a concept. For example, the categorization scheme *gender* includes the categories *male* and *female* for the concept *person.* Categories included in a categorization scheme generally represent variations within a single perspective and/or different potential states for the instances of the given concept. A categorization scheme should be named (for example, *gender*).

category: A variation, kind, subset, or state of some other concept. A category should be named, such name being a term (for example, *retired employee, discontinued product*, and so on).

change effort: A formal, organized undertaking (that is, business initiative, project, or change request) that has a clear line of responsibility whose purpose is to create or change some area of the business, normally involving business systems in a significant manner. A change effort should have a well-defined beginning and end, with specific objectives to accomplish. A change effort may result in the creation of rules (and/or other parts of a business model) and/or in their modification, replacement, or discontinuation.

change request: A change effort requiring only limited resources and a relatively short duration of time whose purpose is relatively narrow.

chief policy officer (CPO): The corporate role with overall responsibility for coordinating the governance process of an enterprise, including rule management. The CPO is to business logic as the chief financial officer (CFO) is to finances.

clarification policy: An assertion made in a Policy Charter providing clarification or appropriate interpretation (that is, a definition) for some term used in the business tactics.

class (predicate calculus): A set of instances.

class term (predicate calculus): The name of a class.

computation rule: Any producer (rule or function) that computes a value following standard arithmetic operations (for example, sum, multiply, average, and so on) specified explicitly. A computation rule provides a precise formula for how a computed term is to be calculated. For example, a computation rule might be given to compute *the amount paid for an order.*

computed term: A term whose values are computed and therefore for which a computation rule could be given, for example, *The amount paid for an order must be computed as the sum of all payment amounts applied to the order.*

Concepts Catalog: A glossary of agreed-to (or proposed) terms used in the business or business capacity, along with their definitions in clear business English (or another natural language). A Concepts Catalog provides the basic vocabulary for specifying facts and rules and for developing other components of a business model.

conclusion (formal logic): In generalized reasoning about rules, the right-hand expression of a rule.

condition (Pattern-R rules): A logical implication used as a test or query in expressing higher-order rules.

conditional expression: See *logical expression.*

conflict (business tactics): A set of two or more tactics and/or core business rules recognized to be mutually antagonistic or counterproductive with respect to specified end(s). A conflict in business tactics should be resolved by means of one or more core business rule(s).

conflict (rule): A set of two or more rules recognized as being in disagreement or contradiction, indicating that at least one of the rules is impossible to satisfy if one or more of the other rules are satisfied. For example, the rule *A shipment must include at least three orders* is directly in conflict with the rule *An out-of-state shipment may include only one order.*

consequent (formal logic): In a specific rule, the right-hand expression.

consistency (logical): All relevant rules being satisfied by a set of terms and facts.

consolidated business logic: The collection of all decision criteria and their outcomes for a rule expressed in the array format of a decision table.

constraint (formal logic): See *rule (formal logic).*

constraint (Pattern-R rules): A logical implication used as a rejector or projector in expressing higher-order rules.

copier (rule): A projector (rule) that replicates (copies) actual values.

core business rule: A rule that addresses a significant risk to the business or business capacity. A core business rule also usually meets one or more of the following tests: (1) It has direct impact on customer service. (2) It relates to cost-effective use of corporate resources. (3) It has direct impact on the company's competitive standing.

corporate value: A principle or belief held to be intrinsically true (for example, "Veterans deserve special consideration," "Having more competent employees pays off in the long run, even if they cost more," and so on). Such a corporate value is part of the corporate culture and can act as an internal influence in shaping rules.

correspondent (Pattern-R rules): Any right-hand term or right-hand expression of a Pattern-R rule.

CPO: See chief policy officer

creative task: A task that always involves making a significant choice between alternatives, where neither the desired form nor the desired content of the result can be predicted in advance (except perhaps in general or "meta" terms). Creative tasks are highly knowledge-intensive, with many rules required for their correct or optimal performance (for example, design marketing logo, develop classification scheme, create architecture, and so on).

data-driven reasoning. See *forward chaining.*

data model: An architectural product focusing on delineating the required data (in appropriate format) to support system-level requirements. A data model often addresses the complexities of organizing historical data. The primary audience for a data model is system designers and database administrators (DBAs). A first-cut data model can be produced from a fact model.

data toggle (rule): An enabler (rule) that creates or deletes instances of actual data under appropriate circumstances. For example, a data toggle might be given to indicate that a juvenile's criminal record must be erased upon reaching 18 years of age.

decision crtieria: Any term, value, bracket, logical expression, or mathematical expression used as a label for one or more rows or columns of a decision table.

decision-making task: A task that always involves making a significant choice between alternatives, where the desired form of the result can be predicted in advance but not the desired content. Decision-making tasks are relatively knowledge-intensive, with rules required for their correct or optimal performance (for example, adjudicate claim, approve credit, evaluate applicant, and so on).

decision management platform: A business logic server aimed at supporting decision points. See also *business logic server.*

decision point: Any point in conducting work where a decision must be made that can influence the specific course of action to be taken in a significant way. Decision points are often reflected in decision-making tasks. Decision points also may reflect an exceptional, low-frequency, and/or ad hoc point for which no workflow task is specified. The decision to be made in a decision point may involve any of the following: classification, diagnosis, assessment, monitoring, prediction, design, assignment, planning, scheduling, modeling, and so on (for example, whether to declare an emergency situation, what on-the-spot discount should be given, what appropriate route to select, and so on).

decision table (rule): An array format effective for expressing suitable collections of rules in a consolidated form (that is, as a single rule). See also *consolidated business logic.*

declarative (specifications): Any set of discrete specifications (for example, rules) that result in exactly the same state for any sequence in which they are presented to a system. An application program (that is, lines of code) written in a traditional programming language is not declarative in this sense.

definition: A statement that expresses the meaning of a term.

deliverable: A specification, model, or document produced during some phase of a project to develop some portion of a functioning business or business capacity or to communicate and/or to achieve a necessary sign-off.

derivation rule: Any producer (rule or function) that derives a truth value (that is, true or false) based on logical operations (for example, AND, OR, NOT, EQUAL TO, and so on) specified explicitly. A derivation rule provides a precise definition for a *derived term.* For example, a derivation rule might be given to indicate whether a project is at risk depending on whether the project is over budget or understaffed.

derived fact: A fact that can be produced (computed or inferred) from other facts.

derived term: A truth-valued term whose value (true or false) is always established by specified logical operations and therefore for which a derivation rule could be given. For example, *at-risk project* means the project is over budget or understaffed.

directive: See *governing rule.*

disintermediation: Eliminating middlemen between customer and producer.

domain of discourse: The subject matter of a set of business rules.

enabler (rule): A projector (rule) that toggles (switches) something on or off.

end: A business purpose that an element of business tactics (the means) can serve or address. Ends are often goals but may also be risks. A tactic or core business rule may also be an end if there is any other lower-level tactic and/or core business rule that supports it.

enforcement level: A particular level or degree of enforcement for a rule (for example, strictly enforced, suggested, and so on).

enterprise: The entire business or organization, or some relatively self-contained line of business.

enterprise model: A business model covering the entire enterprise (that is, all business capacities).

evaluation term (rule): In the context of decision tables, any of the one or more other terms in a rule statement.

event (business): An occurrence that requires the business or business capacity to respond. Significant business events require a well-organized response, which can be developed by workflow models and/or coordinated by rules. Example of an event: Customer places an order.

event (business system): Any change in state, or any occurrence that needs to be noted or recorded. An event may cause one or more rules to fire (that is, to be tested). For example, customer places an order, which results in one or more system events to create data in a database, causing related rules to fire.

event (workflow): A business event or the completion of a task.

exception (rule): A rule that indicates another rule is *not* to be enforced under specified conditions. The former rule disables (stops the enforcement of) the latter rule under those specified circumstances. For example, in the rule *A library card must not be held by more than one borrower, unless one of the borrowers who holds the library card is Bill Gates*, the portion *unless one of the borrowers who holds the library card is Bill Gates* is an exception to the base rule, *A library card must not be held by more than one borrower.* See also *rule toggle (rule).*

executive (rule): A projector (rule) that causes an operation, process, or procedure to execute or a rule to fire.

existential quantifier (predicate calculus): EXISTS.

EXISTS (predicate calculus): See *logical quantifier.*

expert system: Runtime system software based primarily on inferencing rules, aimed toward automating decision-making tasks. Expert systems are typically interactive and generally attempt to mimic human decision-making activity.

explicit knowledge: See *explicit rule.*

explicit rule: A business rule that is formally recorded and/or encoded in a form that can be readily understood by business analysts. In contrast to tacit rules, if the person/people who know and understand an explicit rule are lost to the business or business capacity, the business rule itself is nonetheless retained.

external influence (rules): An influence arising outside the business or business capacity. Such an influence might be a law or regulation (for example, regarding taxes, fraud, personnel, government), a marketplace factor (for example, competition, customer, supplier, investor), an environmental factor (for example, nature, culture, economy, technology, experience), and so on.

fact: Something that is known or that can be known about one or more concepts or ideas. Facts structure basic business knowledge. Unlike rules, facts never place any constraints per se on this knowledge nor make any computation or inference based on it. A fact is asserted in a fact statement using an appropriate term for each concept or idea.

factbase: A store that holds base facts (loosely, persistent data) of the business or business capacity. The contents of the factbase are believed to be accurate and true.

fact instance: A fact whose fact statement(s) include(s) only instance terms. For example, "Acme Supply places a601" is a fact instance of the fact type "Customer places order."

fact model: An architectural product that structures basic knowledge about the business or business capacity in declarative form from a business perspective. Such knowledge is basic in the sense that it cannot be derived or computed from any other knowledge. In particular, a fact model provides a unified, graphic representation of fact statements. A fact model is a crucial starting point for developing more advanced forms of business knowledge, including measures and rules, and can be transformed into a first-cut data model.

fact name: The name given to a fact, often taken to be the verb or verb phrase of an associated fact statement. For example, in the fact "Customer places order" the verb "places" could be taken as the fact name.

fact statement: A declarative sentence that expresses a fact (for example, "Customer places order"). Such a sentence literally represents a "statement of fact"—something that can happen (or has happened) or that can be known (or is known).

fact type: A set of facts of the same kind. A fact statement for a fact type must include at least one class term. For example, "Customer places order."

factoring (requirements): Organizing architectural products by aspect.

FORALL (predicate calculus): See *logical quantifier.*

formal logic: A system of logic (such as Aristotelian logic or symbolic logic) that abstracts forms of thought from its content to establish abstract criteria of consistency. Also, the science of formal principles of reasoning or correct inference.[2]

forward chaining: An algorithm for inference that starts from known facts and works "forward" (that is, toward right-hand expressions) of all relevant inference rules to see if a consequent can be reached (that is, proves true). This approach is sometimes also called *data-driven reasoning.*

functional category (rule): The kind of a rule (that is, rejector, producer, or projector) based on its intrinsic operation or effect—in particular, how it responds to events.

goal: An effect (that is, a business result) that the business or business capacity wants to accomplish in performing the mission (for example, to be profitable, to keep customers satisfied, and so on). Goals can be achieved only indirectly; the business or business capacity must perform the mission in order to achieve the goals. Goals provide the ultimate motivation for core business rules.

goal-driven reasoning: See *backward chaining.*

governing rule: A legal statement (for example, law, act, statute), formal regulation, clause in a binding agreement (for example, contractual obligation), higher-level business policy or directive, and so on. Governing

---

2. From Simpson, Stephen G. 2000. "Logic and Mathematics," p. 2. Available at *http://www.math.psu.edu/simpson/.*

rules guide or constrain the business, regulating its interactions with external parties and/or limiting its exposure to risks or threats. Governing rules often must be interpreted into one or more operating rules to be applied in an actual business process or used for system design.

governance process: The business process that establishes, communicates, implements, evaluates, and retires policies and business rules for the business. The governance process addresses interpretation of governing rules to operating rules, and operating rules to implemented rules, and organizes all related review and sign-off activities.

ground axiom: See *base fact.*

has a (fact): A kind of fact relating two terms, wherein one of the terms possesses the other term as a property. For example, "Employee *has a* name."

higher-order rule: See *Pattern-R rule.*

IF-THEN connective (formal logic): See *rule (formal logic).*

IF-THEN syntax: The syntax used to express rule statements in the general form IF . . . THEN. . . . For example, *If a person is female and of age, then that person is a woman.*

implication connective: See *rule (formal logic).*

imprint rule: A copier (rule) that sets the value of something that persists (for example, something in a factbase or database). For example, an imprint rule might be used to initialize the tuition owed by a student in a given semester to the base tuition for that semester when the student enrolls.

inference: The process of inferring new facts—that is, knowledge—from existing facts by means of inference rules. Also called *logical deduction.*

inference engine: A kind of runtime business logic technology that uses an algorithm to systematically determine the truth of assertions (proposed facts), given a defined set of propositions (existing facts), in order to reason systematically about a problem of interest. Inference performed by a business logic server provides automated assistance and/or automation for making decisions.

inference rule: An enabler (rule) that infers a fact to be true under appropriate circumstances. For example, an inference rule might be given to indicate that a person must be considered a woman if criteria for that person's age and gender are satisfied. When the requested state of the logicbase is such that the left-hand expression of an inference rule is true but its right-hand expression is false, the business logic server infers that the right-hand expression has now become true. Since the right-hand expression of one rule may play a role in the left-hand expression of another inference rule, this process may cascade many times—an activity called *inference* or *logical deduction.*

influence (rules): Any factor that shapes a rule.

initiating event (workflow): The first event indicated by a workflow model.

instance (predicate calculus): Any specific member of a class.

instance model: A fact model or fact model extension that focuses on instance terms, often involving a rule-intensive product/service and/or reference data of the business or business capacity.

instance of (fact): A kind of fact relating two terms (or two other facts), wherein the first term or fact is an instance of the second term or fact. This second term or fact is the type of the first term or fact. For example, "ABC Supply, Inc." (the first term) is an *instance of* "customer" (the second term, and the type of the first term).

instance term (fact models): The name given to a member of a set wherein all members are perceived in like manner (that is, as having common characteristics). For example, Canada is an instance of the set of all countries.

instance term (predicate calculus): The name of an instance.

instantiation (predicate calculus): A substitution of instance terms for each of the class terms of a predicate.

integrity (data): Correctness.

integrity constraint: See *rejector (rule).*

internal influence (rules): An influence arising from inside the business or business capacity. Such internal influences include existing infrastructure, issues (irritants), assumptions, corporate values, and so on.

is a (fact): See *is a category of (fact).*

is a category of (fact): A kind of fact relating two terms, wherein one of the terms is a category of the other term. For example, "Employee *is a category of* Person."

issue: A problem or irritant that is cause for concern (for example, "We don't always know who our customers are"). Such an issue can be an internal influence that shapes rules.

jurisdiction (rules): Any organizational body within the business or business capacity itself (for example, an organizational unit as defined by the organizational chart), external political unit (for example, confederation of nations, nation, state, province), or geographical area (for example, North America). A jurisdiction is any organizational and/or geographical area within which a rule may be enforced.

knowledge retention: A business rule initiative to capture tacit business rules from subject matter experts and/or other business workers.

label (decision tables): The decision criteria used to identify one or more particular rows or columns of a decision table.

left-hand expression (formal logic): The complete logical expression on the left side of a rule expressed in the form p → q.

left-hand term (formal logic): Any term on the left side of a rule expressed in the form p → q.

LHE: See *left-hand expression.*

LHT: See *left-hand term.*

line of business: One or more products and/or services targeted to a particular marketplace or segment thereof.

location: Any place where any actor is located, and/or an event occurs, and/or a task takes place (for example, retail site, home office, and so on).

logic: See *formal logic.*

logical deduction: See *inference.*

logical expression: An expression that evaluates to a truth value. (In contrast, a *proposition* in formal logic is something that evaluates to either true or false, categorically.) For example, a logical expression might be formed by using the logical connectives OR and/or AND. Logical expressions are also known as *Boolean expressions*, *truth-valued expressions*, and *conditional expressions.*

logical implication: See *rule (formal logic).*

logical operator: A nonarithmetic operation that can be performed on truth-valued variables. The three basic operators are AND, OR, and NOT. All other logical operators can be expressed in terms of these three.

logical quantifier (predicate calculus): Taken to mean the fundamental tests EXISTS (the existential quantifier) and FORALL (the universal quantifier).

EXISTS provides a test for "at least one" or "there exists at least one." FORALL provides a test for "all" (or "for each" or "given any").

logicbase: A store that contains both a factbase and its associated rulebase. The current content of the logicbase comprehensively defines state for the targeted business or business capacity—or at least those parts of it that can be automated. A logicbase should be viewed as the authoritative and exclusive source of information describing the cumulative effect of business operations up to the current point in time.

logic trace: Support for auditing the results produced by a business logic server at any given point of operation. A logic trace makes it possible to work (or *trace*) backward from the result through the chain of rules (often inference rules) that produced it.

means: Any device used to achieve ends. In a Policy Charter, tactics and core business rules serve as means.

metadata: Data that defines other data.

mission: What the business or business capacity does directly, on a day-to-day basis, at the operational level. The business seeks to achieve its goals by performing the mission.

multiplicity: See *cardinality.*

objective: A specific target for a change effort. Objectives should always involve quantitative measures and end times. Objectives will be used to determine whether change efforts have satisfied their purpose.

operating rule: A declarative rule statement in well-structured business English (or another natural language), suitable for direct application to a business process and for consideration in a system design. An operating rule should be unambiguous and stated in a manner directly relevant to the internal workings of the business or business capacity. Operating rules may sometimes be derived or interpreted from governing rules or reverse-engineered from automated rules.

operational task: A task that does not involve making a significant choice between alternatives, or the creation of some new alternative(s), but rather aims at achieving a well-defined outcome whose desired form and desired content can both be predicted in advance (for example, register attendee for seminar, contact claimant for more information, report travel expenses, and so on).

optionality: A data model construct that refers to whether or not an instance of some relationship type is mandatory for a specific data object involved in that relationship type. If not, the relationship type is said to be *optional* for that data object.

organizational unit: Any body that exists internally to the business or business capacity (for example, department, team, and so on).

outcome (rule): A rule's definitive effect as expressed by one cell value in the array format of a decision table.

owner: The business-side persons(s), role(s), or organizational unit(s) who has (have) authority over setting the goals of the business or business capacity.

Pattern-R rule: An indivisible, two-part unit of business logic in the form of a rule (logical implication) of a known (Pattern-R) rule type. A Pattern-R rule has a higher level of expressive power that arises from a special "built-in" computation function, called the *yield-value function*, applied to an appropriate pattern of facts. Specification of a Pattern-R rule always includes a Pattern-R rule type, which effectively invokes the yield-value function desired for the indicated pattern.

Pattern-R rule type: The category of a rule based on the type of special computation a rule must perform. Commonplace examples of Pattern-R rule types include *mandatory, mutually exclusive, unique, cyclic, frozen, timed,* and so on. The type of a Pattern-R rule comprises both a logical function (that is, a truth-valued function) and a yield-value function (which is not truth-valued). The logical function produces a set of truth values that is based on evaluating the results of the yield-value function. This yield-value function is evaluated for each specific occurrence of a reference point (called the *anchor*) and the anchor's associated correspondents. The anchor and correspondent(s), collectively forming a pattern, can be terms, facts, and/or other Pattern-R rules, as appropriate for the given rule.

permission statement: A statement indicating the absence of any rule under a particular set of specified conditions. Such a statement indicates workers are not constrained by any rule in that situation and therefore may exercise judgment or discretion in taking relevant actions. For example, *Orders on credit for $1,000 or under may be accepted without a credit check.*

permission word: In RuleSpeak, a keyword (for example, *may* and *need not*) used to indicate that a statement represents a permission statement.

policy (Policy Charter): See *core business rule.*

Policy Charter: An architectural product that establishes the motivation for the core business rules of a business capacity. A Policy Charter identifies what tactics and core business rules are appropriate for achieving goals and other ends and what business risks are associated with them. The Policy Charter establishes an overall business approach or "battle plan" for a business process or problem, providing a basis for development of appropriate workflow models and other deliverables. The contents of the Policy Charter represent the business tactics.

predicate: A property, attribute, or mode of existence that a given subject may or may not possess.

predicate calculus: A general method or framework for reasoning about any subject matter whatsoever. Predicate calculus dates from the 1910s and 1920s and is basic for all subsequent logical research. It is a very general system of formal logic that accurately expresses a huge variety of assertions and modes of reasoning. [3]

premise (formal logic): In generalized reasoning about rules, the left-hand expression of a rule.

presentation rule: A copier (rule) that establishes a value or parameter related to how data is to be presented (for example, on a screen, in a report, and so on). For example, a presentation rule might be given to indicate that an order is to be displayed to the screen in red if the order is overdue.

procedural (specifications): Any specifications that are not declarative; that is, where a different sequence of presentation to the system can result in a different final state. An application program (that is, lines of code) written in a traditional programming language is usually procedural in this sense.

process (business): See *business process.*

process (business system): A capability for taking some input and transforming it into some desired output. A process operates according to an internal algorithm provided by its designer or programmer.

---

3. From Simpson, Stephen G. 2000. "Logic and Mathematics," pp. 2, 5. Available at *http://www.math.psu.edu/simpson/.*

process toggle (rule): An enabler (rule) that turns an action, process, or procedure on or off under appropriate circumstances, that is, makes it capable or incapable of executing. For example, a process toggle might be given to indicate that a sensitive process cannot be executed while a security breach is suspected.

process trigger (rule): A projector (rule) that causes an action, process, or procedure to execute. For example, when an order is shipped, a rule might be given to execute a process that automatically sends the intended recipient a notification.

producer (rule): Any rule that neither rejects nor projects events but rather simply computes or derives a value based on some mathematical function(s). Producers are categorized as either computation rules or derivation rules.

product: Something produced by human or mechanical effort or by a natural process that is deemed relevant to some marketplace.

product/service rule: A rule that addresses configuration, coordination, and/or constitution of a product or service of the business or business capacity.

product/service terminology model: An instance model for a particular product or service of the business or business capacity.

prohibited antecedent: A business milestone that an instance must never have achieved prior to the time that the instance achieves some other business milestone. Prohibited antecedents can be defined by means of a rule that thereby governs transition in state. For example, *A cancelled order must never have been shipped, invoiced, or terminated previously.*

project: A change effort requiring many resources and steps to accomplish but whose scope and purpose are sufficiently specific, and its duration short enough, such that the change effort can be well managed.

project manager: The person responsible for managing a project.

project objective: See *objective.*

project risk: A risk faced by a project in attempting to achieve its objectives, or a potential circumstance that may impact successful project completion.

projector (rule): Any rule that tends to take some action (other than rejection) when a relevant event occurs. A projector never rejects events (as rejectors do) but rather *projects* them—that is, causes some new event(s)

to occur as a result. Projectors generally prescribe automatic system behavior, providing a productivity boost for workers. For example, a projector might be specified to reorder stock automatically if the quantity
on hand drops below a certain point.

property (fact models): A description, characterization, or quantification established by a *has a* fact. For example, employee name could be specified
as a property of employee using a *has a* fact.

proposition (formal logic): Something that evaluates to either true or false,
unequivocally. For instance, "William Shakespeare wrote *Pride and Prejudice*" is a proposition (a false one, as it happens).[4]

provisioning process: A process that provides essential business inputs (for example, product release information, customer information, and so on)
for day-to-day operational processes. A provisioning process typically
coordinates some resource of the business.

real-time compliance: The approach of applying business rules as early as
possible in business processes, preferably at the original point where data
is created, modified, or deleted, so that downstream error detection and
resolution can be avoided.

real-world actor (workflow): An actor that has some physical manifestation. A
real-world actor may include software but never is composed purely of
software. Examples of an actor include person, role, organization, device
(for example, robot, change dispenser), and so on.

reduction: The process of breaking down a rule into more granular form,
possibly atomic.

reference data: The traditional name used in information technology for data
typically produced by a provisioning process. Reference data often appears in legacy systems as codes and/or in look-up tables. Typical kinds
of reference data include product configurations, product families, customers, geographical areas, and so on.

reference source: Any existing material, normally textual, that provides the
specific basis for a rule (for example, a law, regulation) or that provides
background, context, or explanation (for example, memoranda, system

---

4. Example courtesy of Date, C. J. 2000. *An Introduction to Database Systems* (7th ed.).
Boston, MA: Addison-Wesley, p. 13.

documentation). A reference source exists in published form (printed, electronic, and so on), and with proper authorization, may be reviewed to understand a rule more fully.

rejector (rule): Any rule that tends to disallow (reject) an event if a violation of the rule would result. Rejectors shield the business from inconsistent data (undesirable state). For example, a rejector might be specified to prevent a customer from placing an order on credit if the customer has a poor payment history. Rejectors are often called *integrity constraints* by IT professionals responsible for database systems.

resource: An available means, area of infrastructure, or logically organized set of constructs that is available to the business or business capacity to accomplish its mission and to achieve its goals (for example, personnel, customers, facilities, and so on).

RHE: See *right-hand expression.*

RHT: See *right-hand term.*

right-hand expression (formal logic): The complete logical expression on the right side of a rule expressed in the form p → q.

right-hand term (formal logic): Any term on the right side of a rule expressed in the form p → q.

risk: An exposure arising in some aspect of an endeavor undertaken by a business or business capacity that may prevent achievement of some desired end(s). Such exposure may arise either from inadequate internal support or from external factors beyond the control of the business or business capacity.

risk bracket (business tactics): A specific value or range of values established on the basis of quantitative measures (for example, specific amounts of money, a specific time frame) or other criteria (for example, category of customer) wherein a certain level of risk is perceived. A risk bracket should be addressed by a selective rule—often a core business rule.

R-Notation: A scheme based on conventional notation for rules in formal logic extended for certain special needs, particularly for representing facts and higher-order (Pattern-R) rules.

rule (business rule): An atomic piece of business logic, specified declaratively, whose intent is to control, guide, or enhance behavior. A rule may be established in order to ensure that one or more business goals are achieved, to enhance productivity in performing day-to-day work, to assist the business in making decisions, and/or to regulate or guide external activities. A rule is always based on one or more facts.

rule (formal logic): A logical expression of the form OR ((NOT p), q), where p (the premise) and q (the conclusion) must be Boolean expressions. Such a rule may also be expressed as IF p THEN q or as p → q, which can be read "p implies q." For example, it-is-raining implies streets-are-wet. In specific rules such as this example, the "p" (it-is-raining) is called the *antecedent*, and the "q" (streets-are-wet) is called the *consequent*. Rules in formal logic are also known as the *IF-THEN connective, implication connective*, or *logical implication*.

rulebase: A store that contains the business rules for a factbase. This store roughly contains metadata but with emphasis on rules and their current operational status and evaluation. These rules will have been specified in a declarative manner.

Rule Book: A compilation of business rules, preferably automated, that categorizes rules, records properties of the rules, and traces relevant links. These links may be to other rules, to information about other aspects of the business, and/or to the implementation environment supporting the rules. An automated Rule Book provides the foundation for rule management.

rule engine: See *business logic server*.

Rule Independence: The principle of specifying and managing rules apart from processes, procedures, or applications such that business logic can be accessed, analyzed, and changed directly.

rule management: The use of expertise, techniques, and tools aimed toward providing business workers and/or business analysts with the ability to manage and access business logic directly.

rule mining: Reverse-engineering the program code of legacy systems to recover the embedded business rules.

rule-processing server: See *business logic server*.

rule sentence template: A basic sentence structure or pattern in RuleSpeak for expressing a rule in a consistent, well-organized rule statement.

RuleSpeak: See *BRS RuleSpeak*.

rule statement: An assertion of a rule, usually in the form of a sentence.

rule toggle (rule): An enabler (rule) that turns another rule on or off under appropriate circumstances, that is, makes the rule capable or incapable of firing. For example, a rule toggle might be given to indicate that some normal operating rule is to be suspended under emergency circumstances. Rule toggles that turn other rules off are called *exception-type rules.*

rule trigger (rule): A projector (rule) that causes a rule to fire. For example, when data about a shipment is displayed to the screen, a rule might be given that fires another rule to predict the shipment's arrival date.

rule type: The name for a specific kind of rule based on the nature of the test it performs (for example, mandatory, mutually exclusive, mutually inclusive, mutually prohibited, unique, ascending, descending, frozen, and so on). See also *Pattern-R rule type.*

rule word: In RuleSpeak, a keyword (that is, *must, should, only*) used to indicate that a statement represents a rule.

scope: The extent of business operations to be considered by a project. See also *universe of discourse.*

script (work): A procedure with no embedded rules, consisting of a prescribed series of requests for action that workers can follow to perform work.

semantic equivalence: A circumstance in which a set of two or more rule statements, each expressed differently, are recognized to have the exact same effect as each of the others. Semantic equivalence often occurs when subjects are reversed. For example, the rule *An auditor must not audit any manager in the same city* is semantically equivalent to *A manager must not be audited by any auditor in the same city.*

service: Work done for others as an occupation or a business.

session (work): One execution of a script.

sign-off document: A deliverable that requires explicit, formal approval ("sign-off") by a project sponsor, project manager, or other project person with oversight responsibility. A sign-off document is often compiled specifically for that purpose.

single-sourcing: Originating all copies from a single source.

software actor (workflow): A logical grouping of software that appears as a discrete unit. A software actor has well-defined interfaces that can be requested to perform known services. By this means, a software actor (for example, component, Web site, inference engine, legacy system, and so on) can participate intelligently in work.

sponsor: The person responsible for providing the highest-level business view for a project, including strategic business opportunities and challenges. The sponsor is responsible for clarifying the business goals and for giving ongoing approval as to whether the project is on target with respect to supporting these goals. The sponsor also controls scope.

state: The condition in which a complex system, or any part thereof, finds itself at any given point in time.

subject (predicate): A term representing a concept about which something is affirmed or denied.

subject (rule): The first term (or fact) included in a rule statement, indicating what the rule is about.

subsetting scheme: See *categorization scheme.*

subsumation: In a set of two (or more) rules, the situation where either of the following conditions hold: (a) One rule covers a set of circumstances that represents a strict subset of the set of circumstances covered by the other(s), or (b) one rule covers the exact same set of circumstances as the other rule(s) but in a less restrictive manner. In either case, the former rule is said to be *subsumed* by the latter rule(s), the implication being that the former rule is not really necessary. For example, the rule *A rush order must have a destination* is subsumed by the rule *An order must have a destination.*

subsumption: See *subsumation.*

suggestor: A rule that fires and can detect a "violation" but takes no enforcement action. A suggestor might simply send a message reporting any violation to a worker's screen, providing guidance about a preferred course of action or outcome.

suspense criteria: The interval of time that an instance is allowed to remain in some business milestone without achieving some other business milestone. Suspense criteria are often expressed by use of a rule, which indicates what to do when the given interval of time is exceeded. For example, *An expeditor must be assigned to an order that has been shipped but not invoiced for more than a week.*

tacit knowledge: See *tacit rule.*

tacit rule: A business rule that is not formally recorded and/or encoded in a form that can be readily understood by business analysts. In contrast to explicit rules, if the person/people who know and understand a tacit rule are lost to the business, then the business rule itself is effectively lost too.

tactic: A course of action the business or business capacity might adopt to support the mission, to achieve goals, or to address risks. A tactic indicates that some capability (or a particular characteristic or feature of a capability) will provide a means to achieve the desired end(s).

task: A specific type of work or value-adding activity that must be performed, normally in response to some event, as viewed from a business perspective. A task involves one or more of the following: an activity, an approach for making a decision or producing some desired result, and/ or an organized collaboration between actors. A task represents a transformation at the business level that accepts materials and/or information in one state (the "input") and aims toward producing one or more desired results and/or materials in a new state (the "output"). The performance of a task is guided by rules. Examples of tasks include receive order, adjudicate claim, and so on.

template (rule statement): See *rule sentence template.*

term (business rules): A word or expression that has a precisely limited meaning in some uses or is peculiar to a science, art, profession, trade, or special subject. Terms are used in fact statements and rule statements to refer to some concept of the business or business capacity or of the context in which the business or business capacity operates. These concepts may be about people, places, things, and so on.

term (predicate logic): A name given to one of the following: (1) An individual thing. The thing so named might be a particular person, place, item, concept, and so on, for example, Mary, Memphis, gold, true, and so on. (2) A variable capable of holding a value. For example, variables defined to hold the values above might be named person, city, metal, and of-age, respectively. (3) A function capable of producing a value.

terminator: See *terminologist.*

terminologist: A specialist in defining, coordinating, and applying terms and definitions for the business or business capacity; that is, in developing its business vocabulary.

thin process: A process or procedure that only prescribes the necessary series of steps to accomplish the desired work result and that excludes rules and all the error handling when violations of rules occur.

time shock. Disorientation and loss of productivity as workers are constantly thrust into new roles and responsibilities due to the accelerating rate of change.

time word: In RuleSpeak, a keyword (for example, *before, on or before, during, by, after*) used to indicate a temporal qualification for a rule.

to-be data model: A data model developed to support a reengineered or revised view of the business or business capacity.

to-be workflow model: A workflow model that specifies a reengineered or revised view of a workflow.

toggle (rule): See *enabler (rule).*

traceability: The ability to explore relationships between rules, especially interpretations from governing rules to operating rules to automated rules, as well as the reverse.

trigger (rule): See *executive (rule).*

truth value: A value of either true or false.

truth-valued expression: See *logical expression.*

truth-valued variable: A variable capable of holding a Boolean, that is, a variable of type Boolean. Truth-valued variables are also known as *Boolean variables.*

type code: A special kind of attribute in a data model for distinguishing the type of instances (for example, F = female, M = male).

universal AND: An assumption in rule theory that since all rules must be satisfied, an implicit AND must therefore be considered to exist for all rules within the universe of discourse.

universal quantifier (predicate calculus): FORALL.

universe of discourse: The complete set of ideas (that is, all basic knowledge) to be entertained by a business rule system, as evidenced by terms, facts, and rules (business rules). See also *scope.*

UoD: See *universe of discourse.*

update event: An event in a business system involving the creation, modification, or deletion of data.

vision: Something the business aspires to. A vision always expresses something the business would like to be or achieve.

work: The actual collaborations between actors that occur in the business in response to some event. Work always results when actors follow a workflow model or script. Business rules provide the basic knowledge (via terms and facts) and guidance (via rules) for performing work. Work changes the state of the business and therefore the state of its knowledge.

worker: Any staff member involved in managing or operating the business or business capacity.

workflow: The sequence in which work is conducted. Workflow can be prescribed by use of a workflow model or script and managed by means of a workflow engine.

workflow engine: Runtime system software that manages workflows and/or scripts.

workflow model: An architectural product that depicts a series of organized collaborations between actors involving two or more tasks in response to some initiating event. A workflow model indicates how the end results appropriate from a business perspective are to be achieved.

work product: Anything produced under an organizational relationship between actors.

work session: See *session (work).*

yield value (Pattern-R rules): The result computed by the yield-value function associated with a Pattern-R rule type for a Pattern-R rule applied to a given set of facts.

yield-value function (Pattern-R rules): The computation function associated with a Pattern-R rule type.

Bibliography

Appleton, Daniel S. 1984. "Business Rules: The Missing Link." *Datamation*, October 15, pp. 145–150.

Burlton, Roger T. 2001. *Business Process Management: Profiting from Success*. Indianapolis, IN: Sams Publishing.

Business Rules Group (Ronald G. Ross and Keri Anderson Healy, eds.). 2000. "Organizing Business Strategy: The Standard Model for Business Rule Motivation." Version 1, November 2000. Available at *http://www. BusinessRulesGroup.org*.

Charniak, Eugene, and Drew McDermott. 1985. *Introduction to Artificial Intelligence*. Reading, MA: Addison-Wesley.

Chisholm, Malcolm. 2001. *Managing Reference Data in Enterprise Databases*. San Francisco, CA: Morgan Kaufmann.

Crevier, Daniel. 1993. *AI: The Tumultuous History of the Search for Artificial Intelligence*. New York: BasicBooks.

Date, C. J. 2001. "Constraints and Predicates: A Brief Tutorial (Parts 1, 2, and 3)." *Business Rules Journal*, July, September, and December (respectively). Available in November 2002 at *http://www.BRCommunity.com/a2001/b065b.html*.

———. 2000. *An Introduction to Database Systems* (7th ed.). Boston, MA: Addison-Wesley.

———. 2000. *What Not How: The Business Rule Approach to Application Development*. Boston, MA: Addison-Wesley.

Date, C. J., and Hugh Darwen. 2000. *Foundation for Future Database Systems: The Third Manifesto* (2nd ed.). Boston, MA: Addison-Wesley.

Elmasri, Ramez, and Shamkant B. Navathe. 1994. *Fundamentals of Database Systems* (2nd ed.). Redwood City, CA: Benjamin/Cummings.

GUIDE Business Rules Project Report. 1995. Third edition available in November 2002 as "Defining Business Rules—What Are They Really?", edited by David C. Hay and Keri Anderson Healy, Business Rules Group, July 2000, at *http:// www.BusinessRulesGroup.org*.

Halpin, Terry. 2001. *Information Modeling and Relational Databases*. San Francisco, CA: Morgan Kaufmann.

Halpin, Terry, and Roderic Girle. 1981. Deductive Logic (2nd ed.). Brisbane, Australia: Logiqpress.

Hofstadter, Douglas R. 1980. *Godel, Escher and Bach: An Eternal Golden Braid*. New York: Vintage Books.

Lam, Gladys S. W. 1998. "Business Knowledge—Packaged in a Policy Charter." *DataToKnowledge Newsletter* (formerly *Data Base Newsletter*), May/June. Available at *http://www.BRCommunity.com*.

Morgan, Tony. 2002. *Business Rules and Information Systems*. Boston, MA: Addison-Wesley.

Nilsson, Nils J. 1998. *Artificial Intelligence: A New Synthesis*. San Francisco, CA: Morgan Kaufmann.

Ross, Ronald G. 1997. *The Business Rule Book* (2nd ed.). Houston, TX: Business Rule Solutions, LLC. Available at *http://www.BRSolutions.com*.

———. 1994. *The Business Rule Book* (1st ed.). Boston, MA: Database Research Group.

———. 1987. *Entity Modeling: Techniques and Application*. Boston, MA: Database Research Group.

———. 1978. *Data Base Systems: Design, Implementation and Management*. New York: AMACOM.

Ross, Ronald G., and Gladys S. W. Lam. 2000. *The BRS Core Business Rule Practitioner's Guide: Using Business Rules in Developing Business Strategy*. Houston, TX: Business Rule Solutions, LLC. Available at *http://www.BRSolutions.com*.

———. 2000. *The BRS Fact Modeling Practitioner's Guide: Developing the Business Basis for Data Models*. Houston, TX: Business Rule Solutions, LLC. Available at *http://www.BRSolutions.com*.

———. 2000. *Capturing Business Rules*. Workbook for public seminar, presented in Boston, MA, June 19–21.

Seer, Kristen. 2002. "How to Develop Effective Business Analysts," Parts 1, 2, and 3. *Business Rules Journal*, May, July, and September (respectively). Available at *http://www.BRCommunity.com*.

Simpson, Stephen G. 2000. "Logic and Mathematics." Available in November 2002 at *http://www.math.psu.edu/simpson/*.

Tarski, Alfred. 1995. *Introduction to Logic and to the Methodology of Deductive Sciences* (2nd ed.). New York: Dover Publications. (Originally published in 1946 by Oxford University Press, New York.)

von Halle, Barbara. 2002. *Business Rules Applied: Building Better Systems Using the Business Rule Approach*. New York: Wiley Computer Publishing.

Widom, Jennifer, and Stefano Ceri (eds). 1996. *Active Database Systems: Triggers and Rules for Advanced Database Procession*. San Francisco, CA: Morgan Kaufmann.

Zachman, John A. 2002. *The Zachman Framework: A Primer for Enterprise Engineering and Manufacturing* (electronic book). Available at *http://www.zachmaninternational.com*.

Index

Note: Page numbers followed by *f*, *t*, and *n* represent figures, tables, and notes, respectively.

informIT

RANDOM HOUSE
LARGE PRINT

THE
sexy
years

DISCOVER THE HORMONE CONNECTION:

THE SECRET TO FABULOUS SEX, GREAT HEALTH,

AND VITALITY, FOR WOMEN AND MEN

SUZANNE SOMERS

RANDOM HOUSE
LARGE PRINT

*The Library of Congress has established a
Cataloging-in-Publication record for this title*

0-375-43296-5

www.randomlargeprint.com

FIRST LARGE PRINT EDITION

10 9 8 7 6 5 4 3 2 1

This Large Print edition published in accord
with the standards of the N.A.V.H.

TO MY HUSBAND, ALAN

You turn me on!

ACKNOWLEDGMENTS

I feel so blessed to have such talented people around me.

Once again, my editor, Kristin Kiser, was an enormous help to me in this massive undertaking. When I would get overwhelmed, she would be there to help me through the maze. Thank you, Kristin.

My agent, Al Lowman, is the greatest agent in the literary world. No one is better at it than Al. He is there from the very beginning to the very last detail. We've done so many books together that I have lost count. I only know I wouldn't do a book without you. Thank you, Al. I love you.

My husband, Alan Hamel, takes care of everything so all I have to do is keep on writing. I am so lucky to have Alan running the show, as they say. I'm crazy in love with you, Alan.

Sandi Mendelson and Judy Hilsinger are fantastic press agents. They are nurturing and creative simultaneously. Doesn't matter how great a book you write—if the public doesn't know about it, nothing happens. When Sandi and Judy do the press on one of my books, everybody knows about it. You two are the greatest. Thank you so much.

My lawyer Marc Chamlin, thank you once again.

My lawyer Martin Hahn, thank you.

And to my fabulous team at Crown Publishing . . .

Jenny Frost, president and publisher of Crown, this is our first book together, and what a way to start. You have been enthusiastic about this idea from the very beginning. Your getting behind this project has had a tremendous positive impact. Thank you.

Steve Ross, my publisher at Crown, you are always in my corner, but for this one even a little more so. Your enthusiasm has been catching and now everyone is feeling it. I couldn't ask for more. Thank you so much.

Philip Patrick, director of marketing, you are wonderful to work with. You have done so much front work on this project that everyone you are working with can't wait to get this book. Thanks for all the advance excitement.

Tina Constable, director of publicity, you

are a hard-working professional and so talented and creative. I have enjoyed our relationship over the years. Thanks so much for all your input and enthusiasm.

Mary Schuck, jacket designer, I love this cover. Maybe the favorite of all my books. Thank you. Just beautiful.

Elina Nudelman, interior designer. I love it. Thank you.

Amy Boorstein, Camille Smith, Leta Evanthes, Ellen Rubinstein, thanks to all of you for all your input and hard work.

Sona Vogel, you did a great job copyediting this difficult manuscript. I was impressed with your abilities, and I learned new things through your corrections. Thank you.

Thanks to Caroline Somers, my daughter-in-law, for that great idea. It was just what I needed to hear at that moment. You know how much I love you.

And Marsha Yanchuck, my assistant of twenty-six years, thank you for reading and rereading each and every draft and giving me suggestions and for your expertise on grammar and punctuation. You have helped me through so many books, but this one in particular was the most tedious. Thank you. You are more than my loyal assistant—you are my family and I love you dearly.

★ ★ ★

And now to my great doctors, who gave so freely of themselves for this book. These doctors, all of whom are cutting-edge and forward-thinking, are going to change the direction of medicine. They are pioneers who are willing to stick their necks out to get the latest information out to the public, regardless of the risks. Thank you all for allowing me to offer you a platform.

Dr. Diana Schwarzbein, you are the first doctor I found to specialize in this subject, and because of you my life has changed for the better. You have been invaluable to me as a teacher and a doctor. Thank you for the constant barrage of information you continue to send me. Words cannot express my appreciation.

Dr. Eugene Shippen, you are brilliant. Finally there is a doctor to help men through this least understood passage of male menopause. Thank you for all your help and input. I am deeply indebted to you.

Dr. Michael Galitzer, you are an absolute joy to work with and so informed and educated on this subject. Already you have helped so many people I have sent to you. Thank you for giving so freely of yourself and your knowledge.

Dr. Uzzi Reiss, you are a wonderful, compassionate, and knowledgeable doctor who is helping women more than you will ever know. Thank you for your time and information. I appreciate everything you have done for me and this project.

Dr. Laura Berman, you are an absolute font of information on this subject. Thank you for your knowledge and expertise in this area. A lot of women are going to be helped by your chapter.

Dr. Jennifer Berman, thank you for giving so freely of your knowledge. I came away impressed and grateful for your input. I also learned a lot.

Dr. Robert Greene, thank you for your beautiful foreword, your cutting-edge insights, and your profound enthusiasm for this project.

And finally, my ladies: Karen, Athena, Rita, Patricia, Eve, Marta, and my sister, Maureen Gilmartin. Each of you gave of yourselves with honesty and sincerity. You allowed me to crawl inside your heads for a few pages. You are living this passage, and your candor and wisdom are thrilling. I am grateful to all of you for your honesty and insights.

Thank you to everyone who helped me with this project. I am grateful and honored to be able to bring this exciting new information to the American public, but I could not have done it without all of you.

CONTENTS

PART IV

The Male Menopause

PART V

Beating the Clock

PART VI

Living an Authentic Life

At fifty, you get
the face you deserve.
—COCO CHANEL

FOREWORD

BY ROBERT A. GREENE, MD, FACOG

I am a reproductive endocrinologist. That means that after becoming a board-certified ob-gyn, I continued my training to become a specialist in identifying and treating hormone-related problems such as those associated with infertility, menopause, developmental problems, and premenstrual syndrome. During the last decade, I have continued to perform research in this field and apply what I learn on a daily basis to the patients whom I provide care for. Developing an understanding of the way hormones affect the brain is truly the key to lifelong health and wellness.

As a reproductive endocrinologist, my primary focus is on the sex hormones: estrogen, progesterone, and testosterone. Women today are heavily influenced by the marketing of "natural" hormones. But what do we mean by "natural"? There is no unified definition of the term "natural hormones." Natural means different things to different people. To some people natural means that it comes from natural sources. To others, it means biologically identical to what the body normally produces. That's the definition that Suzanne and I have used during our discussions of this topic. The confusion about this terminology dates back to 1941 when Russell Marker first synthesized progesterone from the wild yam, *Dioscorea*. To this day, many companies sell "natural yam extracts" as alternatives to hormones. Unfortunately, they fail to inform consumers that their bodies simply do not have the ability to convert this plant extract to an active, usable hormone, like what is accomplished in a laboratory.

The sex hormones are able to work in the body through specific receptors—imagine a lock-and-key system. Any given part of the human body has to have the proper receptor, or lock, for a specific hormone to have an effect. There are at least two different types of estrogen receptors in the body. These receptors vary in concentration in different parts of the body, which means the estrogen potency varies as well according to its ability to occupy the receptors. Understanding these variations is crucial in order to stabilize hormone disturbances that occur throughout your life because, if you're a woman, your hormone levels are shifting, sometimes on a daily basis.

Individualized regimens from your doctor provide specific treatment so that each woman can maintain optimal hormonal levels and feel her best. The word *balance* is the most important goal in maintaining a state of equilibrium.

Establishing that perfect balance is challenging; it can almost seem daunting to take the time to learn the myriad functions of the abundant hormones that direct our daily activities. Many clinicians get comfortable with one or two preparations and try to fit everybody into a "one size fits all." This just doesn't work. It might satisfy about 15 percent of the people, but the remaining 85 percent struggle with unnecessary discomfort. Achieving and maintaining your unique hormonal balance is very important, and demanding nothing less from your doctor will empower you to guide your own sense of well-being.

As a doctor and an advocate for women with hormonal imbalances, I'm frustrated. I do about 120 lectures a year in different parts of the country, primarily geared toward empathetic clinicians interested in improving health care. But we are increasingly forced to spend less and less time with our patients due to insurance company dictates. We also must stay apprised of current research findings, which are frequently misinterpreted. These constraints create barriers to communication, difficult for some in the best of circumstances. Patients are frustrated. Today's women want more than a diagnosis from their doctors. It is not an uncommon complaint of women that they feel that their physician marginalizes their complaints with tired comments: "Oh, you're just imagining things," or "You just need to accept that as a natural part of aging." This is not the kind of response a male patient would typically receive, and it's time we even the playing field. We all want to feel good and we all deserve to feel good. Physicians must recognize that their patients face new challenges and will fight to be heard, and they must respond effectively to their patients' demands.

In the absence of satisfactory health care, a schism develops when women transition into the postreproductive years. Some gain weight and can't figure out why; others might find they are suddenly difficult to get along with. These are just a few of many problems that can result because of the hormonal imbalances that occur over a woman's lifetime, compromising quality of life. Many women tell me that they know their moods are unpredictable, but in most cases they don't have any control over the chemical changes causing these mood shifts. They can't sleep, they're hot, then they are cold, they are tired all day; these are also related to chemical changes in the brain. It is true suffering. The quality of life many of these women enjoyed up until this "passage" into the postreproductive years is suddenly gone. There is a sense of betrayal. I applaud Suzanne Somers' attempt to bridge this communication gap so that women may enjoy continued wellness throughout their lives.

Suzanne asked me why I thought middle-aged men often leave their middle-aged wives. I don't believe it is because middle-aged women don't look good. The reality is women look better now at middle age than they've ever looked before because they know how to take better care of themselves. I fear that some men leave their relationships because they don't understand the effects of this hormonal passage into menopause. They don't have anything in their own physiology to compare it to. Worse yet, women are often told to "tough it out," as if it would be antifeminist to insist on continued wellness. Add to all this the zeroing out of the sex drive, and after a while some men may wind up saying, "What do I need this for?" We at least owe these couples an explanation of the physiological changes associated with hormone withdrawal in order to validate the problems that they may experience. This knowledge can provide a tremendous amount of psychological relief.

My interest in hormonal fluctuations led me

to a specific research niche more than ten years ago. Since then my research has been focused on how hormones affect the brain. The adult brain, with all its wonderful and amazing qualities, simply doesn't reach its potential in the absence of normal adult hormone levels. Once you fully appreciate that fact, it is easy to understand the consequences that result if you take those same hormones away—things start to go haywire. Most of my research has been focused on all the different nuances and subtleties of why and how the hormone-brain relationship works; but the bottom line is, you don't maintain your full capabilities if your brain is no longer exposed to the hormone balance it is accustomed to. In the end, women want to make sure they have their brain working optimally, especially since they're living longer than ever before. One of the obstacles that they often face, however, is an apprehension of cancer.

A fear of breast cancer is almost rampant in our society, and my concern is that it clouds our judgment. Cancer is scary. But let's put that fear into perspective, especially in comparison to the brain. Data from various studies show us that for 1,000 women on HRT for ten years, about six additional breast cancers are diagnosed. By comparison, other studies predict that these same 1,000 women taking estrogen

would result in about 240 fewer cases of Alzheimer's disease. When you consider that 80 to
90 percent of breast cancers are curable today
and there's no cure for Alzheimer's disease, it is
easy to realize that at the very least women
should be properly informed of all potential
benefits of hormone therapy, including healthy
aging of the brain. The connection between
loss of estrogen and Alzheimer's disease is
widely accepted among brain scientists, yet the
more general medical community is long overdue in acknowledging this connection. Even
more important is for health care practitioners
to communicate this information to their patients, which will prevent women from looking to the news media for guidance in health
matters, where information is often sensation-
alized, inaccurate, and should not be generalized to all women. For instance, the Women's
Health Initiative Memory Study (WHIMS)
came out recently suggesting that estrogen increased dementia, but the average age of the
women in that study was nearly seventy-three!
The participants were also free of symptoms
like hot flashes, night sweats, and mood
changes. The age of the study participants was
not highlighted in the popular press when they
reported this finding, however. If you actually
look at the data, the percentage of women
who developed Alzheimer's disease was less if

they were on hormone therapy (50.0 percent) than if they weren't (57.1 percent). This is a clear-cut case of the irresponsible exploitation of data to scare rather than inform. Whether we blame the scientists interviewed or the reporters is irrelevant—the target audience suffers needlessly.

Regrettably, today's health care decisions are often driven by preconception and assumption. There is a presumed relationship between estrogen and breast cancer, but once upon a time the first treatments given to women with breast cancer were high-dose estrogen therapy, and a significant percentage of women who were treated responded. The belief that estrogen is a carcinogen simply is not supported by well-designed studies or biological plausibility. Did you know that in the third trimester of pregnancy, a woman's hormone output is equal to about ninety-nine years' worth of menopausal doses of hormone replacement? Yet breast cancer is fairly uncommon during the reproductive years. Recently, one of the best-designed studies of women with some of the most common gene mutations associated with breast and ovarian cancer—BRCA1 and BRCA2—found that pregnancy was actually protective against these cancers! They also found that women who started menstruating earlier were not at higher risk despite a greater lifetime exposure to hormones. Yet the same scientists involved in this study were quoted in the *New York Times* (October 24, 2003) as supporting the removal of healthy breasts and ovaries of women with these gene mutations. I have examined the findings of many research studies and it is my belief that HRT is unlikely to be a cause of cancer; it's more likely that hormone therapy promotes the growth of existing tumors. The fear of cancer is legitimate, but it warrants a rational response.

Women come to me out of frustration. Some travel five or six hours to get to my office, which is a shame, but this is an act of desperation to receive treatment options explained in rational terms. For example, one female patient of mine participating in a study on testosterone replacement recently conducted an interview for the FDA. When asked what she would do if the hormone preparation she was taking wasn't approved, she broke into tears. She said, "I can't go back to living that way. I've been given back my life; you can't tell me it might not be approved!" It was tragic to see this spontaneous display of emotion, because you know she really meant it. I hope the FDA begins listening to these answers when they ask questions of study participants.

I believe that in the next decade replacing and rebalancing hormones lost in the aging process will become the standard of care. And not just for women, but for men as well. Until recently, the male menopause (andropause) has been almost completely ignored and men have suffered because of it. Androgen deficiency is real and can be treated. Most men live out their more gradual decline of hormone production in silence, because they feel it is an admission that they are no longer "virile" or "male." The greatest loss that they experience is fatigue and lack of energy as a result of muscle wasting and changes in their brain functioning. I have been fortunate to write articles for and act as a consultant to the International Society for the Study of the Aging Male. We are beginning to understand the role of HRT to restore the male quality of life. In 2002, the Endocrine Society, which is comprised primarily of internal medicine endocrinologists, held a symposium to present guidelines on testosterone replacement for men. This was a very bold step forward in acknowledging the impact on men's quality of life. Ironically, they have not openly embraced a comparable policy for women. Keep in mind that testosterone is no less tenuously linked to prostate cancer than estrogen is to breast cancer.

As doctors we have to listen to our patients. No one can understand a person's individual needs as well as that person. There is a new focus on improving quality of life. We need to empower people, men *and* women, to recognize the symptoms of "too much or too little"—in other words, the symptoms of hormone imbalance. In this way the patient will have sufficient information to choose the appropriate treatment for long-term health and well-being based upon this growing knowledge and understanding of the hormone-brain connection.

Today's patient and provider must form a partnership. Communication in medicine still often struggles with what I call the paternalistic style of delivery of health care. Instead of telling their patients what to do, care providers must discuss today's information openly. If they do not, then demand it; you will be heard. We have a very consumer-driven market, and the paternalistic doctors, some of whom are women, need to understand that. Women seeking answers will identify those doctors who are willing to listen to them and then explain their options with full disclosure of risks and benefits. The successful health care providers of the future will encourage thoughtful dialogue through open channels of communication.

It's taken years for the medical community to catch up with people like Suzanne Somers, who along with several others have been pioneers in equating the insulin connection with weight gain. At first these theories were disregarded, but now Suzanne's method of eating is accepted as a standard and sensible way to gain control over your weight and guide you on the path to lifelong health. A healthy diet is vital, today more than ever before. In fact, more positive application of our desire to reduce the incidence of cancers should be directed toward diet. According to the American Cancer Society, more than 50 percent of cancers in the United States are linked to obesity, including breast cancer and colon cancer.

I admire the message that Suzanne gives in *The Sexy Years*. Hormone therapy, the natural bioidentical way, does require a bit more effort. But rather than being overwhelming, it's an effort that's well spent. The fact that she has shared her personal experiences with people on a variety of subjects has probably helped far more people than she will ever know. It is a beautiful way to use her celebrity status. Suzanne speaks with a more powerful voice than many of us who have spent years in laboratories and behind office walls. She serves as a vital example of what we all can strive to achieve.

The practice of medicine is headed down a new road, one of self-directed health care, assisted by the guidance of health care educators willing to apply their communication skills. In my opinion, Suzanne Somers has earned that distinction. It's becoming more important for patients to take an active role and form alliances with their providers. As a doctor, I know it is more important to make patients comfortable with the information we can provide them than to intimidate them into following our instructions. The average person must be able to individualize his or her health care requests according to personal needs and beliefs. They're doing it anyway by self-adjustment of doses, refusal to refill prescriptions, or simply discontinuation of treatment. We have the obligation to rebuild their confidence by providing knowledge and fostering communication. Menopause and andropause are life-changing events in the lives of women and men. They are the least understood medical mystery but one of paramount importance because we're all living longer now than ever before. I am committed to helping women understand their choices and guiding them through the decision-making process.

Suzanne Somers is committed to helping women and men, and this book is on point in approaching the second half of life with joy and anticipation. The inherent bliss of perfectly balanced hormones is available to all who desire it. This passage requires work and careful consideration on the part of the doctor and patient, but together each individual can find his or her exquisite quality of life. The second half of life can indeed be the best ever, if hormone balance is truly understood. My enthusiasm for this message is unwavering.

THE
sexy
years

INTRODUCTION

I love being a grown-up, yet as a woman I have been programmed to dread this passage of life—the middle years, when I would become an over-the-hill, dried-up, bitchy, menopausal, sexless, useless, discarded, once-attractive, no-longer-desirable, stringy-haired, wrinkly old lady. That's what society tells us we will become. No wonder we women have been on a constant search for that secret elixir, anything promising the fountain of youth, whether it be the newest creams, potions, plastic surgery, or dream product that will give us just a few more years before the sentence of invisibility becomes our destiny. Make no mistake: Growing up is not for sissies. Doing it well takes work. As with any worthwhile endeavor, the time we put into preparing for growth and change determines the outcome. Medicine is changing so rapidly that as individuals we must be proactive about our health in order to take advantage of the newest breakthroughs. We're not supposed to feel worn out; we're not predisposed to get the diseases associated with aging. We are supposed to be happy and healthy, and if we work at it, there's no reason we shouldn't be.

All my life I have prided myself on being a person who looks at life with a positive spin. I have refused to be a victim, whether faced with an alcoholic father, a teenage pregnancy and subsequent divorce from the father, the struggles of single motherhood with no consistent job, a tangled affair with a married man, a catapult into stardom only to be cut short by a scandalous contract negotiation, a fight to regain my career, dealing with the complexities of blending two families into one, even a battle with a life-threatening disease. Through it all I have searched for the lessons that life brings. My abusive father unwittingly taught me to fight and believe in myself, even when I felt no one else did. My son has been my greatest gift, and I believe he was sent to me to keep me alive through one of the most difficult periods in my life. An affair turned into my future husband, my lifelong partner and ultimate soul mate. The years I lived as a destitute mother have kept me grateful for all the blessings I now have in my life. When *Three's Company* ended, I was forced to look deep within myself and develop other areas of my career beyond being a television actress—as a stage actress, an author, a lecturer, and ultimately a brand name. The hard years of blending stepchildren have paid off, as we now have a unified family that is my greatest joy . . . with six grandchildren! And cancer taught me about the enormous love that surrounds me, that I can overcome any obstacle, and to enjoy the sweet moments of each and every day.

I wasn't looking for another lesson in life, but you never know when they will arrive. Here I was, merrily handling the aging process and being grateful for the wisdom I gained in exchange for the crow's-feet around my eyes. The children were grown with families of their own, and I had decided this was going to be the best phase of my life yet. I would grow old gracefully and teach those around me that we don't have to dread this time of life. Then, suddenly, the Seven Dwarfs of Menopause arrived at my door without warning: Itchy, Bitchy, Sweaty, Sleepy, Bloated, Forgetful, and All-Dried-Up. One by one they crept into my own private cottage in the woods and started to take over my life. For me, the first to arrive was Itchy. I developed this itch on my right calf that was so irritating, I wanted to scratch the skin right off my body. Then Bitchy came to my door. No longer was my PMS contained to one or two days a month—it felt like constant PMS. Then I would swing from Bitchy to weepy—for God's sake, what was wrong with me? *Ding-dong* . . . It's the middle of the night, and Sweaty has crawled into bed with me. Oh, yes, Sweaty brought embarrassing hot flashes and introduced me to night sweats where it seemed as if a faucet had been attached between my breasts. Of course Sweaty brought about Sleepy because I was tired all the time. I would wake up so many times in the night and not be able to get back to sleep. Bloated crept in slowly. My once-svelte figure got thick through the middle section, even though I was following my weight-loss program that had worked so well for so many years! I can't quite remember when Forgetful arrived, but one day my brain stopped working. I considered myself a pretty focused woman until Forgetful came and I could not keep a coherent thought in my brain. I remember doing an interview, and I couldn't remember a single question to ask! Am I getting Alzheimer's? I wondered. Last, All-Dried-Up slowly encroached upon my happy marriage. This was probably the most unpleasant of the dwarf family. Sex was no longer on the top of my list . . . or on my list at all. My husband would give me that knowing look, and I would think, "Frankly, I'd rather have a smoothie."

Yes, menopause had hit me like a ton of bricks, and I was completely unprepared. My mother certainly never talked about it. I had no training for this! Our mates are just as unprepared. At first our men may be sympathetic, but they quickly tire of the complaining, worn-out rag of a woman formerly known as the love of their life. To alleviate our symptoms, we seek answers from our doctors and get conflicting reports about hormone replacement therapy. Yes, it will take away the symptoms, but what are the risks? I don't want cancer, but I'm so depressed! Most conventional wisdom in our fix-the-symptom medical community leads women to synthetic hormones in combination with Prozac or Paxil (which is simply Prozac turned into a pink pill for women with PMD or menopausal symptoms) to help them through this passage. This is not a cure, by any means.

So why, you ask, would I call this book *The Sexy Years*? Doesn't sound so sexy yet, eh? Because I have found the elixir—the juice of youth that has sent the Seven Dwarfs of Menopause off to the coal mines never to return! I handled this crisis like every other one in my life. I was not going to let it beat me. I would not go silently into the night and let go of the woman I wanted to be for myself and for my husband. So I fought for an answer that would work for me. I dug into research on the subject and talked to as many doctors as I could. One thing I have learned is that medicine is not black and white. No one doctor has the right answer for everyone: You must gather all the information and make the decision you feel is best for you. There are hundreds of ways to make brownies . . . you must find the recipe that you think tastes the best.

Personally, I have found my answer. What was it that sent those wretched dwarfs packing? Natural bioidentical hormones. As you will read in the coming chapters, I have learned that natural bioidentical hormones are the secret to handling this passage of life (not the synthetic hormones that only slap a Band-Aid on your menopausal symptoms and have garnered so much controversy in medical studies, and certainly not black cohosh and yams). Once I got my hormones balanced by actually replacing the lost hormones, I lost Itchy. My mood leveled off and I lost Bitchy. I got control of my body temperature and Sweaty went away. With balanced hormones Sleepy disappeared and I recovered the glorious ability to sleep through the night. Day by day my body slimmed down, so I could say good-bye to Bloated. I regained my sharp thinking—farewell, Forgetful. And the look in my husband's eye was returned with a wink and lovingly reciprocated, as I happily banished All-Dried-Up.

I am a testament that it is possible to take on this passage of life and embrace it. I will tell you that you do not have to take this transition lying down. You have choices! You have options! You have solutions! In this book I share with you my journey and several stories of what other women are dealing with so that you may find your own answers. I have interviewed cutting-edge doctors who have provided further information that natural bioidentical hormones are the way to go. This book gives you a battle plan to conquer this beast and come out the other side with a victorious song of praise.

It takes commitment to approach this time of life with grace, anticipation, and a willingness to really look at the truth about yourself, not only physically but on an emotional level as well. The amount of work you are willing to put into this passage will determine your happiness quotient—but wouldn't all the work be worth it if, in the end, you knew your life would be the best it had ever been? I can't speak for any age group but my own; however, I do know each passage brings its rewards if you know what it is you want from your life. If you grieve for your once-perfect body and your twenty-year-old looks, this book will not help you. But if what you desire is confidence, extraordinary good health, happiness, peace, serenity, fulfillment, great looks, a fabulous body, lots of fun, and a sex life like you've never had before, then by all means read on.

There is only one thing you need to know before you start reading, and it is that it's up to you. No one can help you into the next passage except you, and that is the challenge and the fun. What you resist persists; what you fear is what you draw to you. If you fear growing up, if you are afraid of evolving, you are doomed to be an immature adult. There is nothing more unattractive than an immature adult. These are the people whose lives have gone off track because they are foolishly chasing their youth instead of accepting change. But life is a flow, and we must follow it wherever it leads us. The happiest people are those who can put this into a positive perspective. Everything you think you have lost is really your opportunity to gain. It's looking at the glass as half full instead of half empty.

There is no need to dread menopause. The work I have done to understand this time of my life has brought me to a place of absolute joy. I am balanced and on track, and—no kidding—this passage has become the most glorious time of my life.

As you read this book, you will see that,

across the board, it is the women of menopausal age on natural bioidentical hormones who are enjoying the greatest health and quality of life. When you get your hormones balanced and actually replace the hormones you have lost in the aging process, you will experience the bliss, vitality, sexual vigor, and excitement that I have come to experience at this age. There is no reason to suffer through this hormonal passage, and so many women are suffering. Menopause is a challenge and it takes a lot of work to manage, but once you understand how to balance your hormones, it becomes simple. You'll wonder why you did not approach menopause this way in the first place. Honest to God! This period of my life, menopause and all, is the best I have ever felt.

Come with me on this exciting journey. I want to share everything I have learned in my search for answers. This is exciting information that you can then pass on to your daughters, sisters, and women in general. And let's not forget the men in our lives. Wait until you learn about male menopause, andropause. It's a very real passage that is highly misunderstood. In this book I will explain not only women's hormonal needs, but also men's needs for the sex hormones testosterone, estrogen (yes, estrogen), progesterone, and DHEA; and this information is life-changing. We men and women are in this together, so let's help one another.

There is so much misinformation and ignorance about this time in our lives. As baby boomers we have always demanded a better quality of life. After all, we are the generation who burned our bras; we demanded equality in the workplace; we are the first generation of women who wanted to understand the complexities of our feelings and used therapy as a learning tool. So now we've reached a time in our lives when women of prior generations suffered in silence. That silence has led to ignorance and confusion about menopause. But why shouldn't we demand optimal treatments and the best information available about this transition? Let's get it on the table. Let's let go of the shame. Let's make this the best time. Let's be creative about how we present ourselves at this age. Let's look at life as though the glass is half full. Then we can truthfully pass on to the next generation (by our example) the message that this is an enviable passage.

Imagine that you can enjoy your sexuality today in a way that will make those early years of intensity, new love, and overwhelming magic seem like child's play. You know why? Because it *was* child's play! At my present age the fears, the guilt, the embarrassment, and the worry no longer factor into my sexuality, be-

cause my life is on track emotionally and hormonally. I'm feeling frisky, and I want to tell
you how and why. As I said, growing up is not
for sissies. Achieving this bliss will require an
honest look into the part you are playing in the
drama of your life. It will require you to take
an honest look at how you are managing your
health. Once you get your hormones in balance, we will look to see what behavioral patterns you have created that are preventing you
from becoming your happiest self, a process
that requires absolute truthfulness to your self
about yourself. What is it about you that you
would prefer no one ever know? This is a good
place to start. This is where healing can begin.
These are the steps toward enjoying *the sexy
years.*

PART I

THE
hormone
connection

1
CANCER

The last words I ever thought I'd hear about myself were "You have breast cancer." It was as though someone had dropped a load of lead on my head. I felt stunned. This is something that happens to other people, I thought. Not me. I figured, I am healthy, I eat right, I have exercised all my life. My sister being diagnosed with breast cancer four years earlier was just a fluke. I mean, other than her, there is no history of breast cancer in my family, I reasoned. How could this be happening?

Every year since I turned forty I have been going to the USC/ Norris Comprehensive Cancer Center and Hospital in Los Angeles. I always looked forward to seeing my doctor, Mel Silverstein, who created the concept of the breast centers in this country. He is a nice guy and has committed his life to the care of women's breasts. My husband always jokingly tells him he is the luckiest guy around because he spends his days feeling women's bosoms.

It was time for my yearly mammogram, and I had been religious about having annual checkups since I turned forty. Because I had been so diligent, I cockily assumed that I was immune to the disease. After all, keeping such a vigilant check on my breasts would ensure that even if there was a problem, we would find it before it ever had a chance to take hold. The nurse pulled and squeezed, flattened, and pressed my poor aching breasts into positions no breast was meant to endure. But it was for a good cause, and all women know that the discomfort and humiliation are worth it in the long run, because this examination is about life, health, and prevention.

"Well, I don't see anything to worry about," Dr. Silverstein announced cheerily after looking at my mammogram.

I felt relieved, even though I hadn't even considered the possibility. Now I could go on with my life for another year knowing I had beaten the statistics once again.

I went into the changing room and hurriedly put my clothes back on. I had a busy day ahead of me—meetings with the various vendors for my jewelry business, the skin care line, updates on the fitness business, costume fittings, and a band rehearsal to get ready for an upcoming date in Las Vegas the following week. I was filled with energy and vitality.

"Suzanne?" I heard Dr. Silverstein call through the changing room door.

"Yes," I answered.

"You know, you've got such cystic breasts—lumps and bumps everywhere. How about having an ultrasound for good measure?"

I opened the door, wondering why this would be necessary. "Wasn't everything okay with my mammography?" I asked.

"Sure," Dr. Silverstein said good-naturedly. "It's just that we have this new state-of-the-art ultrasound machine. I just paid half a million dollars for it; and what the heck, let's take a look for good measure."

Why not, I reasoned. I was there, and it would only take another half hour. Surely I could fit this into my busy schedule. My health was more important than anything.

I lay down on a stationary bed in the ultrasound room, feeling no alarm, since this was just for "good measure." The technician rubbed on some cold, gooey liquid (a conductive fluid) and then began a gentle movement on my breasts with a wand about the size of a curling iron. She kept rubbing back and forth for some time in one particular area on my upper right breast. Then she excused herself and said she would be back in a couple of moments. I still felt no alarm. I had been through these exams before. Often we found cysts that were filled with fluid, which were then drained with a needle. Not the most pleasant experience, but part of the routine. I wasn't worried. Even when the technician returned with the radiologist to further probe my now rather sore and overworked breast, I heard my- self telling them, "Not to worry. I always have these cysts; they're just filled with fluid."

The tone in the room turned noticeably se- rious, and I was at a loss as to why everyone seemed so intense.

"We see something here we don't like, so we're going to stick a needle into it to see what we come up with."

Frankly, I felt relieved. It's the same old thing, I thought. "I've had needles before," I told her cheerfully.

"Well, this is going to be a bit more un- comfortable than what you are used to. We are using a bigger needle, and I will try my best not to hurt you."

The doctor inserted the needle, and this was indeed different. It felt like a carving knife be- ing plunged into my flesh.

"Yeow!" I said, trying to stifle the fact that this hurt like hell.

"You're going to feel a little pop, like a cap gun going off inside of you," she told me. "This way we can gather a piece of tissue for biopsy. Okay, ready?" she asked.

Pop! Wow! It hurt . . . a lot! It felt more like a real gun going off in my breast. Then I felt the needle ripping through my breast while the doctor pulled with all her strength to get the needle out.

"Oh, my God!" I blurted out. "That is painful."

"I know; I'm sorry," she said. "Unfortunately, we are going to have to do this several more times."

Several insertions later we were finished.

The pain was unbelievable. My breasts felt like punching bags. Okay, at least now we've done it, and I can get on with my day, I thought. As I dressed, I decided to tell Dr. Silverstein that he should have prepared me for the pain a little better. In fact, after all the pulling and probing, I wasn't feeling very cheery; and in thinking about it, I felt a little angry that Dr. Silverstein had downplayed the hurt quotient. Carefully I pulled on my jacket, which was no easy feat because of the pain in my breast, and then opened the door of the changing room. Standing in the hallway just outside were Dr. Silverstein, the radiologist, and the nurse, all with serious looks on their faces.

Dr. Silverstein took my hand sensitively and said, "We hope you will be okay."

"What?" I asked, bewildered.

"It doesn't look good," Dr. Silverstein said.

"What do you mean?" I asked. I could feel my heart pounding.

"Of course, we're waiting for the pathology report to come back in a few hours," Dr. Silverstein explained, "but from what I can see, I think we should make plans for surgery."

I experienced the next hours as though I were under water. I heard and saw everything, but it was filtered, distant. I was in shock. So many decisions had to be made. They had found a malignant tumor, 2.4 centimeters in size. It was lodged deep in my chest and had not been detected. The doctors thought it had been growing for approximately ten years. How could the mammogram have missed something so large? I kept asking myself.

Cancer is lonely. The decisions to be made are too serious and too monumental to be passed on to anyone. These were decisions I had to make. It was unfair of me even to ask Alan, my husband, what he thought I should do. Luckily, we had caught it soon enough so it didn't look as though they would have to perform a mastectomy. They would remove the tumor and some lymph nodes from under my arm. If the margins were clean, they would not have to remove the breast. I never thought that I would have my own cancer doctor; but now I had an oncologist, Dr. Waisman. I liked him. He was wise, sensitive, and smart.

I was still in a daze. Only this morning I had been getting ready to go to Las Vegas in a week with my show, and now it all seemed insignificant and unimportant. Alan and I sat in the waiting room, not knowing how to feel. I kept thinking, One day life is perfect; the next day it's as if all the balls have been thrown into the air, and you have no idea where they will land. I'd never given dying any thought. It's what happens somewhere down the line a long time from now. For the first time in my life, I was faced with the possibility of my own mortality.

We drove home in a stunned silence. Alan and I walked on the beach for a long time. Our arms were wrapped around each other, giving support. We were in this together. I couldn't think. I was being asked by so many what I wanted to do, but I couldn't give them any answers. I didn't know.

The following morning I awakened from what seemed to be a nightmare, and suddenly I knew I had to take charge. It was my body, and I *wanted* to be in charge. I called my endocrinologist and dear friend, Dr. Diana Schwarzbein, to fill her in on my condition. This was war. I began a visualization of my tumor. Inside the tumor I saw this cowardly, creepy person hiding. Every time I saw him even try to step out of the encapsulated tumor, I would yell in my mind with all the venom I could muster, *Don't even try to leave this tumor, or I'll fucking kill you.* Then I visualized the cowardly little cancer cells shrink with fear and step back inside the tumor. I know it sounds weird, but at that moment I didn't know how to keep the cancer at bay, and this was the only way I could feel that I had any control over it.

Next, I started making phone calls. My agent, Al Lowman, said, "You should talk to Selma Schimmel."

"Who's that?" I asked.

"She's one of my authors who has written a lot about breast cancer."

Selma told me about Dr. Avrum Bluming, who was doing research with women and breast cancer and hormone replacement therapy (HRT), albeit with synthetic hormones. I did not want to give up my hormones. As you will find out in the next few chapters I have expended a great deal of effort getting my chemicals balanced and learning about natural hormones; now, upon diagnosis, I was being told that hormones had to be stopped because of my breast cancer. I knew what that meant relative to the quality of my life, and I was not about to go back to feeling the way I had before I got my hormones balanced.

I started to gather doctors. Dr. Waisman came highly recommended, but I wanted other opinions. I told Dr. Waisman about Dr. Bluming, and he said that not only did he know him, but he was working with him on a study of the connection between women with breast cancer and hormone replacement therapy. Okay, this is good, I thought.

I was on the phone constantly. Cancer is like a job. The treatments are inexact. There is the "common course" of treatment, but so far everything I was being told about the common course was not appealing to me. I knew of too many people who were on the chemotherapy merry-go-round. Chemo seems to make people in treatment more ill; and frankly, it scared me to death. I was afraid of what it would do to the good cells; and I can't say that I wasn't more than a little afraid of the harshness of the treatment. First there's the hair loss and then the sickly color the complexion takes on; then there's the damage done to the parts of the body that until this time were functioning properly. The idea of ingesting potent chemicals was abhorrent and frightening to me. I am against putting chemicals into the body unless absolutely necessary, and I wanted to be sure that this was the only option before I took on something so radical.

Then it was suggested that after surgery I would take the drug tamoxifen for the next five years as a preventative. The only problem I found in doing my research was that this drug would probably make me depressed for much of the duration, plus there was a 40 percent increased risk of heart attack, stroke, and pulmonary embolism. All this for only a 10 percent greater chance that the cancer would not recur? Didn't sound like very good odds to me. I felt weary. So much information to gather, so much authority to weigh. It would be easier to just sit back and let all of "them" handle it for me. That is what I would have done in my younger years. I would have assumed that they knew better. I would have followed the common course. But things were different now. I was a grown-up, and the privilege that comes with having lived this long is the realization that no one knows better than I what I want to do with my body. I have worked too hard all my life to undo the damage of my childhood, to get out from under the grip of having been raised by an abusive alcoholic, to make something of my life, to raise a child on my own, to endure the pain of blending families, to see my career knocked out from under me in a war of egos, only to come out the loser in the whole deal. I could not have known that those earlier ordeals would give me the strength to fight this giant war now raging inside my body.

The big revelation that comes with maturity is that life is a series of highs and lows, and it's during the low points of life that you have breakthroughs. Through the negatives we are given the opportunities to have that "aha" moment where we figure out what we don't want in our lives. I didn't want to live my life as a victim; I didn't want to use the excuse that I coulda or shoulda or woulda had a great life, but I had some bad luck. It has always been the "bad luck" or the negatives in my life that have taught me and shaped me, and I wasn't going to lose this time around. Cancer was going to be my blessing. I was going to learn and grow and *survive* my way.

Surgery, frankly, is the easy part. I knew I needed to get this tumor out of me. I wanted that, and so did my doctors. It's a painful surgery because a lot of the prep is done while you are awake without the benefit of painkillers—like the wires they insert in and around your breast to create a sort of "cradle" for the tumor so the surgeon knows the exact perimeters of the diseased area.

When you have breast cancer, they know up front that it is malignant, confirmed through the biopsy and subsequent pathology. What you don't know is how far it's gone. If cancer cells are found in the lymph nodes, your chances of survival decrease. Because of this, there's definitely a lot of anxiety surrounding the surgery. I couldn't get over the déjà vu aspect of these happenings. One of the poems I wrote for my first book of poetry, *Touch Me,* in 1973, was called "For the Moment." It had to do with enjoying the moment, for you never know what tomorrow might bring.

My diagnosis and the way it had suddenly consumed my life had happened in a matter of days. Just last weekend I was fine and strong and healthy, and today I was being wheeled into unknown territory, having no idea of the outcome. I was doing my best. So far I had refused to give up my natural bioidentical hormones. As a result of intense research, it is my belief that it is an environment of balanced hormones that prevents disease, so why would I want to give up the very thing that could help me win this war? My surgeon and cancer doctors were distressed over my decision. None of them had ever known of anyone who had done this. But belief is a potent motivator. I envisioned the hormones standing like sentries, shoulder to shoulder, forming a protective circle around each of my precious organs. To me they were the front line. I needed their

help. That was my first tactic. The other decisions regarding chemotherapy, radiation, and
the follow-up drugs would be made when I
was post-op and had more time to gather my
thoughts. But first I had to get the cancer out
of me.

I remember the cocktail. Oh my, the drug
they give you to put you out for surgery is a
real thrill. I had Valium and then Demerol.
Once that stuff hits your veins, you haven't a
care in the world. As I drifted off into space, I
can recall the worried faces of my husband,
Alan, and my stepdaughter, Leslie, standing
over me, their hands holding mine. I told them
I loved them, and the next thing I knew it was
three hours later and someone handed me a
telephone receiver. It was Barry Manilow.

"Are you okay?" he asked, clearly concerned.

"You were so wonderful on your special last
night," I told him. "I loved how you sang the
closing song a cappella. It was so courageous
and moving."

"I can't believe you," he said, stunned.
"You're just being wheeled out of surgery, and
you're telling me about my television special."

I started mumbling incoherently, and Barry
said, "Let me talk to Alan so I can find out
how you are."

That's when I heard Alan telling Barry that

they felt they got it all and there was no cancer in the lymph nodes. In my drugged state I could feel the tension leave my body, and I fell into a deep, peaceful sleep until the next day.

My children took care of me. My daughter-in-law, Caroline, made delicious turkey soup for my recovery. This was the worst possible disease I could have gotten for Caroline. She lost her mother to breast cancer when she was a little girl, then her stepmother to ovarian cancer; and then her surrogate mother, her aunt, died of breast cancer. I have always assured her that I would be with her for her entire life, that I was her designated earth mother and would always be there for her. Even with my diagnosis I knew I was going to keep that promise.

My grandchildren filled my large king-size bed with their giggles; yet somehow they knew something was up. Camelia, my four-year-old, whispered into my ear, "I'm sorry you have an oowie on your booby, Zannie." They all wanted to see what it looked like.

Alan stayed in bed with me the whole time I was recovering. He's like that. He brought soup and damp, cool towels and woke me when it was time for my medication.

Bruce, my son, was traumatized. I kept reassuring him I was going to be okay. We had been through so much together in our lives, and the idea of his mother being sick was hard for him to handle.

My stepson, Stephen, and his wife, Olivia, came with the children. I felt so blessed. After all the work of bringing the two families together, Alan's children from his first marriage and my son, Bruce, I knew at this moment that we had succeeded. I could see it in their faces. This was the first blessing of cancer.

Now the decisions had to be made. Two of my doctors wanted me to start chemotherapy. Dr. Waisman felt that surgery, radiation, follow-up drugs, and discontinuing hormones would be sufficient. I had found the tumor early. I now realize that is the difference between living and dying. If this tumor had been allowed to grow inside of me for another year until my next mammogram, I would most certainly have had to undergo a mastectomy and harsh chemotherapy. Because of early detection, my margins were clean; in other words, the surgeon found no evidence that the cancer had spread. This was the best-case scenario of a bad situation. The bad news was that my type of cancer had a high return rate. What I chose as aftercare was extremely important. I was struck over and over by the fact that my wonderful breast surgeon, Dr. Silverstein, had saved my life by encouraging me to have an additional check on the ultrasound. This is the

beauty of living in a highly advanced technological age. Technology is about thinking pro-
gressively, always moving forward. This was
significant to me, because as I began to gather
information, I was leaning more toward thinking my preventative choices were going to differ from those of my doctors in some areas.

One week after surgery, I had my first post-
operative exam. Both my doctors were pleased
with the healing of the wound. It was the first
time I had actually seen what had been done.
Dr. Silverstein was able to save my breast by
filling the huge gap that had been created
when removing such a large tumor with the fat
from the underside of my breast. Even though
this breast was now slightly smaller than the
other one, my doctor had done an excellent
job of making it look beautiful. It was full and
shaped well, and the scar was stitched to perfection.

"We have to talk about your options," Dr.
Silverstein said. "We've gone over it with you,
and we feel that chemotherapy would ensure
your recovery; and radiation is a must. Also,
you have to stop taking your hormones and
start taking daily doses of tamoxifen."

"As you can imagine," I told them, "I have
done nothing but think about this all week.
I've spoken to my other two doctors and gath-
ered information from them. These are big de-

cisions, and I know time is of the essence; but I can't jump into treatment until I feel I've explored all the avenues. At the moment, I don't want to take chemotherapy—I'm afraid of what it will do to my *good* cells—and this aftercare drug you've recommended sounds terrible to me. I mean, is this the best they have to offer women? The next five years are important ones to me. I'm still young, and I want to enjoy what's left of my youth. I don't want to feel depressed and nauseated all the time. I want my hair. I don't want to be or look sick. These treatments will affect the quality of my life without a promise of success, and it most certainly will affect my ability to work."

The doctors were kind, sensitive, and respectful. We talked for a long, long time. "It's all up to you, Suzanne," Dr. Waisman said. "We will work with you and support you with whatever treatment you choose."

Now all I had to do was decide.

I must have called Dr. Diana Schwarzbein every couple of hours over the next few weeks. She helped me with research on every option. She sent me the latest studies, just as she had been doing for the last several years for my Somersize weight loss program. Giving up hormones was the biggest decision.

"I don't want to stop taking them," I told Diana over and over.

I talked to another doctor and told him the same thing. He said, "I have to recommend that you stop taking hormones, and I have to recommend that you take chemotherapy, radiation, and tamoxifen. There is a new drug called Herceptin, but it's not right for your kind of cancer." Then he leaned in to me and said, "I *have* to recommend that you do these things."

I looked at him for a while, thinking, and then asked, "Are you telling me to read between the lines?" The look on his face said yes.

I suddenly realized what he was saying. Legally, because we live in such a litigious society, he had to recommend the "common course." But he was trying to tell me to follow my instincts.

"Tell me something," I said. "If I were in my thirties and my body was making a full complement of hormones and I had this same cancer, would you remove my ovaries?"

"Of course not," he replied.

"Then why would you ask me to stop taking my natural bioidentical hormones, which are replacing the ones I have lost in the aging process?" I asked.

He paused a long time and then said thoughtfully, "We don't know."

The air between us was still for a moment. It was true: there were no studies to tell doctors in this country anything to the contrary, and I realized my doctor was being responsible. But in pursuing the logic of my thoughts, I realized he was also giving me precious information.

"Thank you," I said gratefully. I had my answer. Women are deprived of their hormones when they have cancer because it is thought to be safer, legally, to take them off hormones *in case* hormones feed tumors. Also, I knew most doctors thought of "hormones" as the synthetic type, which are really not hormones at all. Synthetic "hormones" create hormonal imbalance (which I will explain later in the book), and hormonal imbalance leaves you open to disease. I was taking natural hormones, and my system was in balance. Now I was on to something.

I called Diana Schwarzbein. "Isn't it an environment of balanced hormones that prevents disease?"

"Absolutely," she said, and went on to explain. That's why young people do not get the diseases of aging, because aging is loss of hormones. It's like watering a plant. With water the plant flourishes if it is in the right environment for itself. If you stop watering the plant, it will continue to grow; but over time it will stop looking so good, and eventually the plant will keel over and die. The same thing happens

to humans. As we lose our hormones in the
aging process, we continue to look and feel
good, much like the plant; but eventually,
without our hormones, which provide nourishment to our organs, we start to have problems. A disease here, a medical problem there;
and eventually we die because we are no
longer being nurtured, nourished, and fertil-
ized by our hormones. It is then that our bodies give out on us.

In my youth I would have followed the
doctor's orders. As a grown-up I had the abilities to gather information and decipher. And
now I knew what I wanted to do.

I called Diana. "I've made my decision," I
told her. "I'm going to continue to take my
hormones, I am not going to take chemotherapy, I *am* going to have six weeks of radiation,
and I am not going to take tamoxifen."

She paused for a while and then said, "You
know, I've tried to walk in your shoes for the
last few weeks; and although I would not and
could not tell you what to do, I thought about
what I would do in your situation. I know I
would absolutely be making the same decisions
as you. I believe your thinking is not only on
track, but cutting-edge."

I cannot tell you the relief I felt at hearing
her say that. I was dealing with my life, a life
that I have worked hard at correcting and fix-

ing so that I could be my best and healthiest self. I didn't want to blow it. I didn't want to make decisions about my life that could possibly shorten it or harm me. Diana is one of the people I admire and respect deeply. I knew she would not say anything to me that she did not mean. Now I felt secure in the treatment schedule I had prescribed for myself.

I'm out of estrogen and I have a gun.

2

HORMONES

Getting cancer reinforced the importance of being proactive about my health. I knew I needed to work extra hard to keep my body in balance as I aged by continuing my regimen of natural bioidentical hormones. I became very involved in learning about hormones when I started to experience the symptoms of menopause a few years ago. If you're in or approaching middle age, you know exactly what I'm talking about. Our skin begins to change (enter Itchy); we lose vaginal lubrication (here comes All-Dried-Up); we start getting aches and pains that don't go away; we are hot, then cold (Sweaty is really fun); and we can't sleep, which puts us in an unbearable mood over time because we are exhausted. In addition, as we lose our hormones in the aging process, we leave ourselves open to a variety of diseases of aging, and then the Big Unmentionable—many of us lose our sex drive.

Menopause (or, as I call it, men-on-pause) is traumatic. I always wondered why men leave their wives of long standing at middle age. It's not because their wives are getting older or that they don't look good anymore; they leave because women become impossible to live with during this passage. Plus, a lot of women have *no* interest in sex. I experienced this phenomenon. Honestly, it was like losing an old friend. I felt a sadness and a sense of betrayal, because women of prior generations never prepared me for this loss. Why hasn't this been discussed? I wondered. Am I the only woman to ever have this experience? I think this subject has been in the closet so long that women have chosen to endure it silently. It's like admitting that the reason Bitchy is here today is that you have PMS. No one likes to admit that because it connotes weakness, that we are out of control. And pity the poor man who suggests that you might be unreasonable today because of your period. This could be construed as grounds for war.

For over thirty years, the sexual part of the relationship between my husband and me has always been thrilling. It has been where we connect intimately, where we have experienced an indescribable closeness, trust, passion, and sexual adventure. It has been where we solve our problems; where we allow each other to be exactly what we are feeling at that particular moment. Suddenly, in our thirty-first year together, with no warning, I felt dead inside. I didn't understand it. Where I once was always in the mood, now I felt nothing. I did it, but I felt nothing. My friskiness was gone, my sense of adventure left me. I had no energy. I felt like crying all the time. I didn't want to get out of bed in the morning. I couldn't remember anything. I was afraid I had early-onset Alzheimer's disease because I couldn't hold a thought. Itchy appeared and my skin itched horribly and I found it impossible to sleep for more than fifteen minutes at a time; and then Sweaty appeared and I would awaken soaking wet from hot flashes. What a life, huh? What had happened?

I didn't completely understand at the time, but what was happening to me is common to most women as we get older. I had zeroed out hormonally. I was no longer making my full complement of hormones. Because of that, I had no life-restoring nutrients feeding me metabolically. My organs were shutting down from lack of nutrients. These are strictly lay terms; but for you and me, it's easier to understand with this terminology. We are our hormones. Without them we die. In fact, aging is the loss of hormones. From the middle to late thirties (and it differs by a few years from person to person), we make a full complement of hormones. Then we hit perimenopause, and our hormones begin to fluctuate as they start to diminish, until they get close to zeroing out in menopause. Women lose 90 percent of their hormones over a two-year period, once we begin to go into menopause. No wonder we feel crazy!

This is a difficult passage of life. All the balance of your life gets jumbled. Suddenly your husband doesn't understand you anymore. He says things like "What's wrong with you?" Your insides are screaming, *I don't know, I don't know.* On top of it, here comes the weight gain; every day your favorite pants are getting tighter and tighter. You feel dumpy and you start to notice what great shape all the other women are in. You remember when you looked like that. What has changed? You are eating the same as before, maybe even less. You've stopped with the desserts; you're trying to exercise, but you're so tired from not sleeping; and the hot flashes—those embarrassing hot flashes—wake you up continuously all through the night. You feel ugly and fat, and now you have no desire for sex. Is it because you are so tired? That's what you keep telling him, because he's starting to get irritated that "you're never in the mood anymore." Secretly you're wondering also, *Why* don't I want to have sex? You do it because you don't want him to be angry with you all the time, but you can't *feel* anything. *Nothing!* All there is is a sensation that something is inside you, but it might as well be the probe the gynecologist inserts, because the sensation is about the same; and it isn't a sexual feeling.

I felt this. I was *dead* inside. It was sad and lonely, humiliating, confusing, and isolating. I didn't want to talk to my husband about it because I was afraid he would find the whole thing such a turnoff.

I remember Howard Stern asking me on his radio show one morning, "Are you in menopause?" He asked in such a way that he made it sound disgusting. I felt the shame women talk about regarding the subject. I answered, sounding equally disgusted, "Of course not," hoping my astonishment at the question would ward off his suspicions. Howard was not unique. Most men find menopause icky. If they are with us during this passage, it reminds them that they, along with us, are aging; and if they are young, like Howard, they know only what they have heard—that women turn into lunatics during this passage and it's best to avoid them at all costs. Several times in my life I have heard men referring to an older woman as a "dried-up old menopausal bitch." So we're supposed to be looking forward to this passage?

Why must we do penance for coming to this age? It seems unfair to me that the payoff for a woman who has spent much of her life happily devoted to raising her children and being a good wife is to turn into such a monumental bitch that no one in the family wants to have anything to do with her. What kind of payoff is that?

In the research for my first Somersize book, *Eat Great, Lose Weight,* I knew the key to understanding weight loss was an understanding of the hormone insulin. I also knew that if one hormone in the system is off, then the entire system is out of whack. I knew that hormones were behind the symptoms that I and all other women experience when we hit middle age, but it was clear to me, from watching what was happening to women I knew and from my research, that for the most part the medical community didn't have a clue how to deal with hormones and menopause.

The most logical source of information for women about their health is their gynecologist. Unfortunately, few gynecologists are versed in natural bioidentical hormone replacement. In fact, if they haven't specialized, they don't know much about the hormonal system at all. Most gynecologists and doctors other than endocrinologists who have chosen to specialize in the hormonal system, have had four hours of study devoted to learning about this crucial internal system. So many gynecologists go with the accepted program—they find that once a woman is put on a synthetic pharmaceutical (drug) hormone, like Prempro (the combination of Premarin and Provera), or Premarin alone, she stops complaining about the uncomfortable symptoms. If she continues to complain, Prozac, Paxil, or some other form of antidepressant is prescribed. Again, she stops complaining and lives in a lethargic, medicated state that sometimes continues for the rest of her life. The tragedy of this lack of understanding is that women taking synthetic hormones are not *replacing* lost hormones. Women are simply suppressing their symptoms while their bodies are breaking down internally from a lack of nutrients being supplied to organs.

I just didn't want to take the standard course of action of synthetic hormone replacement therapy for my menopause, and I went from doctor to doctor to try to come up with a plan that would work for me. "Well, it's just a lot of guessing," my first gynecologist said. "Let's try putting you on black cohosh [a useless herb in my opinion, relative to menopause] because you don't want the synthetic hormones. Frankly, though," she said, "I don't know why you don't want to take Premarin or Provera, the synthetic hormones, because they are so much easier and there's no guesswork."

"I don't want to ingest chemicals," I told her over and over. I got no relief from this doctor, so I tried another one.

"Well, look at it this way," said the next doctor; "in days of old, women didn't live much past their childbearing years, around age forty. I mean, after all, ha, ha, ha, when you stop being able to bear children, what good are you?" He was kidding, of course, but in my state, I didn't find it very humorous.

I went on to yet another doctor, one who came highly recommended. He asked, "Why do you want to take natural hormones?"

I said, "Because I want to replace the hormones I've lost in the aging process, not simply take away the symptoms."

At that, he patted me on the head and said, "The drug companies know best, dear."

I thought, You old fool. I know that wasn't very kind of me, but come on. Often doctors are influenced in various ways by the drug companies; and because of that, many of them have forgotten that the studies they read are funded by the pharmaceutical companies that actually make the drug. So of course it all sounds wonderful! All I knew was that as I looked around, most of the women who were taking synthetic hormones were getting fat. In my own research, I already knew that hormonal imbalance is the reason one gets fat. I know that insulin is the fat-storing hormone and that insulin resistance is a result of hormonal imbalance. It was all connected. I had to find a way to not only balance my hormones by eating the Somersize way, but also to replace the hormones that I had lost. Then I would be on track.

Don't think I disregard traditional Western medicine. I am the first one in line for Western medicine when it is warranted. I would not have wanted to go through my cancer without my wonderful doctors; but I believe that in today's world it is vitally important to be proactive about your health. No one can rely upon their individual doctor to have all the answers. What I object to is doctors working outside their areas of expertise. If they don't know anything about hormones, they should say so.

The statistics are clear—we're living longer than ever before. In days of old, women died around age forty, at the end of their childbearing years. Life had many hardships then and there were few medical advances, so people died much younger than they do today. But now many of us are going to live to be in our late nineties or even our hundreds. If this is so, then we have to figure out how we are going to live a quality life for the time remaining to us. If menopause as currently experienced is any indication of what is to come, it's going to be a society of some pretty unhappy women and the people who live with them.

Enter Dr. Schwarzbein! I had heard about this woman in Santa Barbara who specialized in thyroid imbalances, diabetes, and menopause. Could it be? A doctor who gets it? Probably, I thought, she's an old bag with the usual treatments for this time of life. I was not prepared for the young, vivacious, beautiful woman who greeted me at the door. Things were about to change. Finally I was sitting before someone who understood the hormonal system. Dr. Schwarzbein told me what I inherently knew but had no basis or abilities to verify.

"Because we are living longer, we have to treat the second half of life differently," she told me.

Yes! I thought. We talked for three hours and forged what has become one of my most important relationships. Over the years she has been one of my greatest teachers. As Dr. Schwarzbein explained to me, because we are

living longer, it is necessary to replace the hormones that have been lost in the aging process
with natural bioidentical hormones that repli-
cate exactly the hormones we make in our
own bodies; synthetic hormones remove some
of the symptoms but do very little to replace
those hormones that have been lost in the aging process. Dr. Schwarzbein says that real hormones—estradiol, progesterone, testosterone,
and levothyroxine, which is the thyroid hormone—are identical to those found in the human body. Synthetic hormones are drugs like
Premarin, which are conjugated estrogens;
Provera, which is medroxyprogesterone acetate; and methyltestosterone. These are
chemicals not found in the human body.
Armour thyroid contains real hormones but
does not contain the correct composition.

So what does this mean? Instead of a doctor prescribing for me a synthetic "one pill
fits all" type of regimen, my hormones are
tracked through blood tests to see exactly
where my levels are; and because of this, an
endocrinologist can prescribe combinations
of the real bioidentical hormones to replace
what has been lost. (Don't worry, I'll explain more about all of this in the next few
chapters.)

This was a revelation to me, and I was ready

to get with the program and have Dr. Schwarzbein replace all my lost hormones. Who wouldn't want this? But it wasn't as simple as that. I said to Dr. Schwarzbein, "If you know what I'm missing hormonally, why don't you give me an exact dosage for my levels?"

"I can't do that," she explained. "It took a long time for you to lose these hormones, and we have to replace them gradually or else you'll feel crazy. Hormones are not to be played around with. Too much is as bad as too little. We will eventually build your levels to the perfect balance for you, but it has to be done gradually."

Each of us is made up of a completely different chemical composite from the next person. What I require is going to be different from what you require, even if our blood work shows that you and I have the exact same hormonal levels. I may require more estrogen to feel good or more or less progesterone to feel good than you might. In the next chapter, I'll talk more about how you can work with your doctor to come up with a program that works just for you. Believe it or not, one of the more exciting aspects of treating hormonal decline is working in concert with your doctor. It is up to you, the patient, to know when your body is feeling at optimum or if new blood work is required to find out if your levels have changed. When hormones are imbalanced you will not be able to operate at peak performance for your age and lifestyle.

The good news was that I started to feel relief immediately. I began to sleep better, the hot flashes subsided, and slowly my sex drive returned. My thinking also got better, and the horrible itch on my legs went away. I was still battling a little weight gain; but, luckily, I had been eating on my Somersize plan for so long that my weight was being controlled through that.

"When your hormones get in full balance," my doctor explained, "the weight gain will disappear because you already have great eating habits."

When you get your hormones balanced by taking bioidentical hormones and eating right and exercising, you will achieve your ideal body composition. We don't have to be pear shaped or apple shaped in middle age, and this alone would make natural bioidentical hormones preferable. Synthetic (drug) hormones cannot offer this to a woman. Add to that other health benefits such as more youthful skin, more energy, sharper thinking, no memory loss, fewer mood swings, less depression, less anxiety, greater muscle definition, enhanced sexuality, sleeping through the night, elimination of hot flashes, and the advantages of staving off the diseases thought to automatically accompany growing older, and it is clear that this magic "cocktail," tailored just for you, is the answer.

I was beginning to see the light. It all made such sense to me. If I were a diabetic, my doctor would not prescribe the same amount of insulin for me that he did for every other patient. Every diabetic patient needs an individualized insulin "cocktail," and this is calculated through blood work to determine exactly how much insulin is needed to balance that person's glycemic index.

The same goes for menopause. Every woman is different. Hormone levels are determined by many factors. Happiness, depression, stress, and a high-stress lifestyle are all factors determining every woman's hormone levels. I have a particularly high-stress lifestyle. I always have to "go on," whether it's for a television show, my nightclub act, or a lecture, running my businesses, or getting interviewed; and all these activities are stressful and produce a level of false adrenaline. False adrenaline levels block hormone production. Therefore, at times I have to have blood work done more often to determine if during this period I need to add or take away either estradiol or progesterone. It is this constant tracking due to my high-stress lifestyle that allows me to enjoy the bliss that comes with balanced hormones. In the next few chapters I'll explain just what I mean by "constant tracking" and how I monitor my hormone levels with my doctor to stay at my peak.

It has been four years now, and I am feeling like a thirty-year-old. My hormones are perfectly balanced. I now realize that this is the secret elixir we have all been looking for. Balanced hormones are the true "fountain of youth." People are always saying to me, "You look great," and I can see them studying my face. It's simply that I have replaced the hormones I have lost, and my body, mind, and spirit are now working at optimum. It is our hormones that give us our youth, so when they are balanced, one of the positive by-products is a more youthful appearance. Since I began HRT I feel happy almost all the time. I feel a sense of balance and the serenity that comes with that. I don't feel stressed; I feel calm; I don't sweat the small stuff. I can handle a lot of things at the same time without feeling crazy because my thinking is so clear and sharp. Best of all, my sex drive is back with a vengeance. I'm in the mood for love. It's so great at this age, after thirty-five years of marriage, to look at my husband and feel all "wiggly" inside. And is he ever happy! Our kids are grown up and have started their own lives, and we have this great relationship, plus the freedom to "date" each other again just as when we first fell in love.

My life has been totally changed by taking bioidentical hormones. Do you know any woman who says synthetic hormones make them feel great? Do you know one woman on synthetic hormones who isn't complaining about her weight gain or bone loss? Doesn't it make sense to replace the hormones we are losing with exact replicas of those we make ourselves? There is no drug that can possibly be better than what we make inside our own bodies.

I hope this chapter has intrigued you. I've managed to turn my life around through HRT, and you can, too. In the next two chapters I will explain more about how hormones actually work in our bodies, what bioidentical hormones are, and how you can find the right doctor and figure out what you need to do to get with the program. This will not be an easy journey. There are very few doctors who understand real bioidentical hormone replacement. But if you are willing to do the work, the rewards will be worth it. I will walk you through my own program and give you a set of questions you can ask your own doctor. I'm not a doctor and don't pretend to be one, but I'm a passionate layperson. The next chapters will be a good introduction to the wonderful world of bioidentical HRT.

Perks of being over forty: You can live without sex, but not without glasses.

HOW IT WORKS

Now that you understand my passion for taking natural hormones, let's get down to business and talk about exactly what these hormones are and how they work in our bodies. Trust me, this information is fascinating and will help you better understand how your body works, so that you are able to take care of it to the best of your ability.

Let's first talk about what hormones really are and where they come from. Dr. Uzzi Reiss, a Beverly Hills gynecologist well versed in natural hormones, explained to me: "Hormones are secreted by glands, such as the adrenals, ovaries, and thyroid, that are governed by higher centers of the brain. Hormones travel throughout your bloodstream in a communication network that links the higher centers of your brain to the DNA command posts operating in the several hundred trillion cells of your adult body. On the outer and inner membranes of the cells are receptor sites that function like locks on a door. In order to get in and tell the DNA what to do, you need the right key, and hormones are the keys. They travel to specific target cells, unlock the receptor sites, and deliver their biochemical message for processing. They turn on or turn off specific cellular functions and measure cellular activity throughout the system." Clearly, hormones make things happen in the body. They are responsible for getting our cells to do the things they are supposed to do.

There are two classifications of hormones in the human body: major hormones and minor hormones. The major hormones have the greater role in determining what happens within your cells, and the minor hormones have the lesser role, but both major and minor hormones play a role in keeping you alive.

The major hormones are the first to be secreted in response to our constantly changing nutrition, lifestyle, and environmental signals. The major and the minor hormones communicate with each other, but the major hormones have the greater influence.

According to Dr. Schwarzbein, "The three major hormones are adrenaline, cortisol, and insulin. These hormones are crucial for life-sustaining functions such as regulating heartbeat and blood pressure and also maintaining the pH balance between blood acidity and alkalinity. So if you are missing any one of the major hormones, you will get sick quickly and not live very long. These hormones keep you alive, so there is no question as to their importance to your health and well-being." If these major hormones are low or missing, there is no controversy about whether or not to replace them. You would never deny a diabetic regular shots of insulin.

But there is a lot of controversy about replacing the minor hormones, such as estradiol,

MINOR HORMONES

ESTROGEN: Produced in the ovaries, body fat, and other parts of the body. Occurs in the body in three compounds—estradiol, estrone, and estriol. Estrogen stimulates growth in breasts, ovaries, and the uterus so the body will create eggs. Can also protect heart and brain function and promote bone strength.

PROGESTERONE: Produced primarily in the ovaries. With estrogen, progesterone prepares the lining of the uterus.

TESTOSTERONE: An androgen; produced in the ovaries and the adrenal gland. Provides sex drive.

DHEA: Made by the adrenal glands, converted into testosterone.

progesterone, testosterone, dehydroepiandrosterone (DHEA), and HGH (human
growth hormone). Should you replace them
or not? If any of the minor hormones fall too
low, you will have many complaints, including
fatigue, mood changes, and weight gain, but
these aren't necessarily life-threatening problems. Your heart keeps beating, your blood is
reasonably balanced, and your blood pressue is
still within normal parameters. You are alive,
but you just don't feel as well as you could if
you balanced your minor hormones by replacing the ones you have lost. In *The Schwarzbein
Principle II,* Dr. Schwarzbein writes, "The loss
of a minor hormone will shorten your life
span. However, because the loss of any one of
the minor hormones does not cause immediate
death, it is harder to understand their roles in
sustaining health and promoting longevity."

In short her book says: "With the loss of a
major hormone, you absolutely know that
something is medically wrong with you, and if
the major hormone is not replaced, you will
die rather quickly. With the loss of a minor
hormone, you will not feel well, but you are
likely to attribute your health to normal aging
and not seek medical attention. You will eventually die from the loss of a minor hormone,
but when you die ten to fifty years later, who

is to know that the minor-hormone loss contributed to your death?"

You know what Dr. Schwarzbein is talking about here by saying "normal aging"—we have all seen our mothers and their friends get older and suffer the effects of aging. We think it's normal to feel lousy when we get older—it's just something that happens when we age, right? But now that you see how important hormones are to our physiology, you can understand how vital it is to keep them balanced so we can live longer and be healthy. Because very few people understand the importance of hormones, we look for quick fixes when we start to encounter the wild fluctuations of our hormones in perimenopause and the loss of hormones in menopause. When we can't take the bad moods anymore, the irritability, the sleeplessness, and the hot flashes, we beg our doctors to take care of our symptoms, thinking that by doing this, we are taking care of the problem. Before the Women's Health Initiative (WHI) released their study in 2002 saying that HRT increased the risk of breast cancer, heart attacks, and blood clots—thus scaring many women off HRT—women thought they were finding a measure of relief in the common course of HRT, which traditionally meant prescribing Prempro, a combination of Premarin (an estrogen substitute made from pregnant mares' urine) and Provera (a progesterone substitute). But at what cost? As I explained earlier, these synthetic hormones do not in any way replace the hormones that are being lost in the body, because they are not identical to what is made in our bodies.

Drugs like Prempro do take away some of the symptoms, so there is relief and, therefore, a belief that all is well again. But then comes the weight gain—the menopausal body, as I call it. You can see the change in yourself and in your friends. Women become thicker, fuller, everywhere, with bigger arms, neck, bosom, waist, hips, legs, and butt. Where is that cute shape you once had? The clothes you once loved now fit you as though they belong to your daughter. It's hard to get dressed; nothing fits anymore. For the first time you find yourself shopping in a different department—bigger shirts, sweaters, jackets that cover the new fullness. It's depressing. You start dieting for the first time in your life. Now you are eating less, but the weight keeps coming on. Your body is not experiencing the most annoying and disturbing menopausal symptoms now, because the synthetic hormones have alleviated them, so you do not realize that your body has regrouped into survival mode to help you be-

YOUNG WOMEN BEWARE— YOU CAN LOSE YOUR HORMONES, TOO

Hormonal loss does not affect just menopausal women and men as they age. Younger women can also experience the loss of their hormones. Today's young woman is the new "superwoman." She does it all: has a successful business, runs the house, is the perfect mother, shows up for school events, makes cupcakes for the class, works out, gives exemplary dinner parties, sits up at night with her sick child, and so on. But stress blunts hormonal production, so this high-stress lifestyle starts to take its toll. Soon she is not looking or feeling well, her temper is out of control, she loses or gains weight, her libido shuts down, and she takes to weeping. She tries to put on an outward appearance that all is well, but it's not.

Though she may be years from menopause, the effects of stress on a young woman's body can be remarkably similar to what a woman in menopause is going through, because these young women are losing their hormones. Even younger women can benefit by temporarily replacing lost hormones due to a high-stress lifestyle and bad dietary habits. During these high-stress times a cutting-edge endocrinologist or gynecologist who understands and specializes can help by tracking hormone levels in a woman's blood work and replacing the hormones that are either high or low. Taking hormones will help you to better manage your stressful life and get things under control. It's vital to do this—stress and hormone loss will quickly age your body.

cause it realizes that without hormones everything metabolically is starting to shut down.

Without hormones your bones also start to lose their density. So the body helps out by fattening you up to protect you in case of a fall. If you have a lot of extra padding, you might not break one of those now brittle bones. Menopausal women are the first to experience this loss, but make no mistake about it, your husbands will also experience this same phenomenon. We will talk more about this in part 4.

I will go into more details in chapter 4 about the medical benefits of replacing hormones. This isn't only about fighting weight gain and getting rid of hot flashes, it's also about increasing the quality and length of your life. You can't replace your declining hormone levels with synthetic hormones, *only* with bioidentical hormones. So what are these bioidentical hormones, anyway, and exactly how does a doctor figure out what a woman needs to take?

Dr. Schwarzbein has some very good advice for those who want to replace synthetic HRT with bioidentical HRT. You can read about this in her own words in the Q&A I have done with her (see chapter 5), but, in brief, she recommends you follow these four rules:

1. *Don't take a hormone that's not low or missing.*
2. *Take only bioidentical hormones.*
3. *Mimic normal physiology as much as possible.*
4. *Track the hormone levels and their effects.*

The success of this program begins with a visit to your doctor. Your doctor will monitor through blood work the hormones that need to be replaced. The goal is to try to re-create the hormonal balance experienced in your thirties (which is why I recommend that younger women get their hormone levels checked so they will know when they get older what these levels looked like in their prime). For me, it's all about trying to mimic the natural hormones I have lost, which means as I go through menopause I am low in DHEA, estradiol, and progesterone. HRT with bioidentical hormones allows us to re-place our body's estrogen (called estradiol), progesterone, and testosterone (if needed) with substances that are synthesized in a lab from extracts of yam and soybeans. These hormones are not available in health food stores or from naturalists or herbalists. The bioidentical hor-mones are by prescription only, but they are not drugs. They are prescribed by your doctor

SYNTHETIC VS. BIOIDENTICAL HORMONES

ESTROGEN

SYNTHETIC: Premarin and other conjugated estrogens (though Premarin has dominated the market in the United States). These are derived from the urine of pregnant mares and are sometimes called "natural," but they are not natural to our bodies.

BIOIDENTICAL: Estradiol, estrone, estriol. These are synthesized in a lab from plant extracts such as soybeans and yams. Though they are created in a laboratory, they are designed molecularly to be the same as the hormones in our bodies.

PROGESTERONE

SYNTHETIC: Provera, Amen (medroxyprogesterone acetate); also norethindrone, norgestrel, and norgestimate. Prempro is a combination of Premarin and Provera.

BIOIDENTICAL: USP progesterone (Pro-Gest, Prometrium, Crinone). Extracted from a variety of wild yam, designed to be molecularly the same as the hormones in our bodies.

TESTOSTERONE

SYNTHETIC: Methyltestosterone. You can also get a combination of estradiol and synthetic testosterone called Estratest, or Premarin plus synthetic testosterone. You can get testosterone in drops, gel, patch, or cream.

BIOIDENTICAL: Dehydroepiandrosterone, or DHEA, an adrenal precursor for testosterone.

Plant-based herbs for menopausal symptoms are also available, including black cohosh and lignans for estrogen effect and chasteberry and wild yam for progesterone effect, but I got no relief from these substances.

———— ———— ———— ———— ———— ———— ———— ————

so you can get the *exact* dosage *you* require. These bioidentical hormones exactly mimic the effects of the estradiol and progesterone that our own bodies create. You can argue that yams and soybeans are no more natural to our bodies than the pregnant mares' urine found in Premarin, an estrogen substitute, but Premarin is not synthesized to mimic exactly what our own bodies do.

Now you know, through initial blood work, which hormones need replacing. Your doctor's prescription will indicate what amounts of which hormone you need and whether you will be taking capsules, liquid, gel, or cream (different doctors prefer different ways to prescribe these hormones, based upon your needs and your ability to absorb). You can't just go to the pharmacy and buy one pill—remember, this is not a "one pill fits all" kind of therapy. You can get your dosages at compounding pharmacies, which will make preparations for you based upon your individual needs. If you don't have a compounding pharmacy in your area, I have included a list of them at the back of the book. Is this more difficult than the "one pill fits all" theory behind synthetic HRT? Absolutely, but I hope you are seeing how important it is to replace the hormones you are losing in your body with exact replicas of what has been lost, and the only way you can do that is by filling a prescription written just for you.

The goal of HRT is finding out how to mimic our physiology through the use of bioidentical hormones—it is a challenge to match the normal production and secretion of the hormone that needs to be replaced. We secrete different amounts of hormones all day long at different times of the day. If we are in a calm period, without stress, happy with our lives and relationships, maintaining a balanced HRT is rather easy. Your trip to the doctor and the results of your blood work indicate which hormones are low. Replace them in those amounts and life gets back on track. But if your life is filled with everyday stresses, compounded by deadlines and pressure, you will blunt your hormone production and your levels will change. Then it's time to call your doctor and describe the stresses you are going through. Your doctor might suggest that you

COSTS

You may be wondering about the expense involved in using natural hormones. As a general rule, natural hormones cost around $65 a month. The first visit to your doctor costs anywhere between $100 and $300, depending upon the doctor. Usually, that is the most comprehensive and expensive appointment. After that you can do most everything else through a phone appointment with your doctor, the cost of which will vary from doctor to doctor.

Tracking your blood levels varies from person to person. With my high-stress lifestyle and the fact that I have had cancer, I usually have my blood work done every three to six months. If your lifestyle is calmer than mine, it might be as simple as having your blood work done once a year. The cost varies from lab to lab, but it is usually around $100, and it is generally covered by insurance.

Different doctors approach natural hormones in different ways. Dr. Schwarzbein, who is my personal doctor, gives natural hormones in a way that mimics normal physiology, which means I have a monthly period. My doctor administers my hormones to me in capsule form. If I have a symptom or symptoms, depending upon their severity, she prescribes a new dosage. If my symptoms are very severe, she will ask me to have blood drawn so she can see exactly where my levels are at the moment.

Dr. Uzzi Reiss administers natural hormones in liquid, gel, or cream form. When his patient is experiencing symptoms, he asks her to call him and explain the symptoms; and then he says to take more of this gel or less of that cream and check back with him to tell him whether or not the dosage works. With this technique you would probably be having blood drawn less often and, therefore, it would be less expensive.

——— ——— ——— ——— ——— ——— ——— ——— ——— ———

"wait it out" to see if everything returns to normal—or, if that doesn't seem likely, tell you that it's time to take another blood test to see if you need to increase or decrease your levels.

This is difficult because it takes time. Most women opt for the drug hormones because there is no additional blood work and no levels to check. The "drug hormone" has only one job, and that is to take away your symptoms, but the tragedy is that nothing is being replaced. The lost hormones are gone for good. The life-sustaining nutrients supplied by your hormones are absent, and silently you begin to shut down metabolically. Aging and all that comes with it—aches, pains, weight loss or gain, disease, memory loss, and loss of mobility, agility, and libido—begin to set in.

In addition to mimicking our body's natural physiology by taking bioidentical hormones in dosages that replace exactly what our body is missing, *how* we take these hormones is important. Some doctors prescribe what is called continuous combined hormone therapy. Combined hormone therapy is taking low levels of estrogen and high levels of progesterone on a daily basis, so that your body does not get a period. Dr. Schwarzbein says, "The purpose of combined therapy was to give a woman the advantage of HRT after menopause without the uncomfortable withdrawal period. Women were actually told they had a choice, which I now know is wrong. The thinking was, take HRT and have a monthly period, or take HRT and have no uterine bleeding. Who wouldn't want the benefits of not having a period?"

Appealing as it sounds, not having a period is actually harmful, because taking hormones this way does not mimic physiology—in other words, it does not mimic the way your body used to make them. In fact, instead of decreasing the risks of certain diseases that are known to be helped by estradiol, taking HRT the wrong way increases the risk. For example, women who take combined therapy are at greater risk for heart attacks, strokes, and breast cancer. The only way to mimic the normal menstrual cycle is to take HRT and have monthly withdrawal bleeding. Taking combined therapy mimics your body's hormone balance during pregnancy, when you don't have a period (higher levels of progesterone than estradiol on a continuous basis). Postmenopausal women should not be mimicking pregnancy, since the risks associated

WATER RETENTION AND PROGESTIN

At menopausal age many women complain about water retention. Guess what? It's not a normal part of the aging process. Water retention, with very few exceptions, is caused by either too much estrogen or too little progesterone. It comes back to that same old thing: an imbalance of hormones creates imbalances in the way your body works.

Progesterone is a beautiful natural diuretic. It prevents the water retention that can be caused by estrogen. This is why combined hormone therapy is questionable. It creates imbalances. You don't have to bother with a period, but your ankles are swelling, your legs ache, your stomach is bloating, and your clothes and shoes are uncomfortable. In fact, combined therapy *increases* the risk for heart attacks, strokes, and breast cancer. The only way to mimic the normal menstrual cycle is to take HRT and have a monthly period.

Combined hormone therapy mimics your body's hormone balance during pregnancy (higher levels of progesterone than estradiol on a continuous basis). If you remember when you were pregnant, you will recall the swollen ankles and the bloated feeling you had. That is why you need to have your levels checked if you are experiencing swollen ankles. If your hormones are in balance, you'll have no fluid buildup. When I was going through radiation for my breast cancer, my hormones were being blown out by the radiation even though I was continuing to take my natural hormones. During the entire six weeks of intense radiation, and for almost a two-year period following, I was experiencing severe water retention. My ankles (which are skinny by nature) would swell up to an unrecognizable size. It took almost two years after radiation to get everything back in balance, and during this time I was reminded what it was like before I had found balance.

A new generation of progesterone substitutes, called progestins and progestogens, are being touted as the latest "natural" release from the nasty symptoms of menopause. But here's the scoop on these drugs: They cause the body to retain more fluid. The manufacturers of these products are aware that baby boomers and an increasing market of women in perimenopause and menopause are looking for a "fix" to get them through this uncomfortable life passage. But none of these products are the same as what your body makes; they have few of the protective benefits of natural progesterone and a lot of side effects and abnormal reactions.

Many qualified doctors are doing a great service to women in touting the benefits of natural progesterone and the dangers of progestins, but many physicians don't know the difference between progesterone and progestins. They haven't been trained to think about options. Some doctors don't even know that natural progesterone exists. It is your job to find out about them and to find a doctor in your area who is well versed. If your doctor is not aware of the benefits of natural hormones, perhaps you can ask him or her to read up so that the two of you can work together.

with pregnancy (heart attack, stroke, type 2 diabetes, and breast cancer) increase exponentially with age.

Combined therapy (not having a period) can elevate levels of adrenaline, cortisol, and insulin. The longer a woman takes HRT this way, the greater her chances of burning out her adrenal glands, becoming insulin resistant, or making preexisting insulin resistance worse. If a woman's adrenal glands burn out, she increases her risk for depression, allergies, and headaches. If she becomes insulin resistant, she will increase her risk for breast cancer, blood clots, strokes, and heart attacks.

The Women's Health Initiative study from 2002 concluded after 5.2 years of follow-up that women taking Prempro (continuous combined therapy with no period) were getting more heart attacks, blood clots, strokes, and breast cancer than women who were not taking anything. The study concluded that the risks of continuous combined therapy exceeded the benefits. Even with this news, many doctors are not warning their patients of the risks of taking HRT this way. Some even downplay the results, but taking HRT incorrectly is harmful! Dr. Schwarzbein warns, "For those who think that this study, which was done with Prempro, applies to synthetic HRT only, you are wrong. Bioidentical hormones given in a continuous combined way will be harmful because even though they are 'real' hormones, 'combined' HRT does not mimic normal physiology." Some doctors who don't understand prescribe combined natural hormone replacement so the woman does not have a period. In doing so, they are putting their patients at risk. Continuous combined natural HRT is harmful even though the hormones are natural, because daily low doses of estradiol and daily high doses of progesterone will cause the same increased risk of disease as with synthetic hormones. Adrenaline, cortisol, and insulin levels will rise higher than normal, and taking the hormones in a combined way, which does not mimic how our bodies work naturally, will increase a woman's risk for disease.★

You can gather from this information that I do not believe in continuous combined therapy. I am a firm believer in re-creating the body's natural functions. I understand that it is necessary to keep a steady stream of hormones coursing through my system continuously, throughout the day; so I take my hormones, estradiol and progesterone, at approximately the same time each morning and the same time

---

★ For a complete reprint of the Women's Health Initiative study, go to www.suzannesomers.com.

MY PERSONAL HRT PLAN

1. Check hormone levels with doctor through blood work.
2. Buy hormones based upon prescription at compounding pharmacy.
3. Take estradiol twice a day, every day of the month.
4. Take progesterone tenth through eighteenth day of the month.
5. Have regular checkups and additional blood work if needed to reevaluate hormone levels.

each night. That way I am getting closest to mimicking what my body would be doing naturally if it were still producing a full complement of hormones. I have my blood tested regularly, more often if I am experiencing a severe workload and stress. I talk with my doctor after she gets the results. We discuss any symptoms I might have and the possible reasons for them. If my blood work warrants, we increase or decrease my estradiol or progesterone.

I also take them in a cycling manner instead of taking combined continuous therapy. I take my estradiol every day of the month, but on the tenth through the eighteenth days I add the prescribed amount of progesterone. At the end of this cycle, I get a period. (Don't worry, when you are in menopause you cannot get pregnant because you no longer have eggs.) Later in this book I will talk with a few women who are in their fifties, sixties, seventies, and eighties so you can hear from them if having a period for their entire lives is worth the trade-off. I suspect it will be. You may have noticed references to another hormone, testosterone, in this chapter. In addition to estradiol and progesterone, I take testosterone, which I will talk about in chapter 9. As you know, your body works better when *all* your hormones are balanced, and you don't want to forget about this important one.

So now you understand that the hormones of the body are interconnected and one hormone imbalance leads to an imbalance of all hormones. It is very important to replace a hormone if it is low or missing and cannot be made by your body. When the body is in balance hormonally, the quality of your life will improve in every way. It truly is the "secret elixir" and the "fountain of youth." Who doesn't want that?

Perks of aging: Your secrets
are safe with your friends because they
can't remember them either.

FINDING THE RIGHT DOCTOR

What is the difference between young people and older people? It's vitality. Vitality is strength, vigor, excitement, curiosity, stamina, energy, a feeling of being "on the ball"! Vitality is something you radiate, it's something from within—a natural zest for life.

We don't entirely lose our vitality as we age, but in our middle years we become aware that we no longer have the kind of energy we once had. "Let the young people handle it, they have all the energy," we moan. Do you want to feel the way you did when you were young? You know the answer—get your hormones balanced!

It is my belief that in the near future the medical community will understand what we passionate laypersons and cutting-edge doctors already know: We need to balance our lost hormones by replacing them with natural bioidentical hormones that mimic what our bodies created when we were in our prime.

And why not? If the medical community is so intent upon keeping us alive until we are ninety to one hundred years old, then let's make sure those last twenty or twenty-five "extra years" are quality ones. By eating right, exercising, thinking good thoughts, avoiding chemicals, moderating alcohol intake, and eliminating smoking, you are on track. Add balanced hormones to this scenario, and wow! These last "extra years" could be your best.

What most people don't understand is that recent reports offering negative statistics about hormone replacement therapy are based upon research conducted on synthetic (drug) hormones. Most of the studies that extol the benefits of synthetic hormones are funded by the drug companies that make them. Natural hormones are not patentable, so the drug companies are not interested in them—there's no profit margin. Don't be angry, it's just business. But it's up to you to be proactive. If you want a better quality of life, it's up to you to find out all you can about options.

As I've said, when we are young our bodies produce a full complement of hormones. They keep us young and supple, agile, lubricated, sexual. Because we are living longer than ever before, the new thinking is to *replace* the hormones lost in the aging process. This *cannot* be done with the synthetic hormones put out by the drug companies; drug hormones can eliminate most of the physical symptoms of hormone loss, but they do *not replace hormones* lost in the aging process. Only natural bioidentical hormones can do that, because they are made from plant extracts and exactly mimic the hormones we make naturally in our bodies.

It is extremely difficult to find a doctor to concur with this way of thinking. Most doctors (good ones) are influenced by drug companies. They are given those free samples we all love to get when we go to the doctor's office, and then the literature and studies that are fed to doctors from the drug companies become "fact," when in many cases they have little to do with what will really heal us. Drugs in general do not heal; they abate and remove pain. Let me say again, I would not like to live in a world without pharmaceuticals. I simply feel that drugs should always be our last resort.

As I mentioned earlier, I went from doctor to doctor to get to the bottom of this "mysterious passage." I was frustrated by the answers I was getting. It wasn't until I found an endocrinologist who specialized in bioidentical HRT that I finally got some satisfaction. Frankly, "satisfaction" is not a strong enough word; "bliss" would be more apt.

As I also mentioned earlier, in medical

school our doctors get approximately four hours of training in the study of hormones. How can a doctor, even a gynecologist, be an "expert" with so little training? That is why I prefer to get my information from someone who has made the study of menopause, and andropause (male menopause), his or her specialty. Generally this is the domain of endocrinologists, but there are gynecologists and other doctors who have continued their studies and their interest in the phenomenon of natural bioidentical hormones. Finding this blissful balance is the best thing I have done for myself at this passage. I want to be involved with doctors who are forward thinking and well versed in the hormonal system. This is no time for guessing. It is too important to my well-being. I love my life, and I want to get the most out of it.

It can be very hard to find someone to help you. Finding the right doctor is difficult. Your gynecologist may not be the right person for you at this time. Menopause and hormones should be his or her specialty if you are being treated for a possible hormonal deficiency as you approach middle age. If it is not your gynecologist's specialty, then you have to find a doctor who "gets it." A gynecologist who is not well versed in the hormonal system, who is trying to treat you for menopause with synthetic hormones or claims to know about natural hormones and then gives you a prescription without requiring a blood test, is not going to be able to help you; it would be like asking your dermatologist to perform open heart surgery. It's not enough to simply know where the heart is located—the doctor must know everything about the heart and how it works. If your doctor claims to be a hormone specialist, ask about his or her credentials. This is too important—you have to ask questions.

Balancing your hormones takes knowledge, and the only professionals I am aware of who have the information to do this are endocrinologists and doctors who have made the study of natural bioidentical hormones their specialty. Even endocrinologists need to be asked if they are well versed in natural bioidentical hormones, because not all of them are up on the latest advances. Maybe when they were in school the information was not available yet, or maybe they never kept up with the latest advances. So it is up to you to scour your community to find the right professional. If you have to travel to another city to find a competent endocrinologist or specialist, believe me, it's worth the trip. Just make sure you're seeing

WHAT YOU NEED TO KNOW
WHEN YOU GO TO THE DOCTOR

1. Ask to get your baseline hormone levels checked in a lab (you need to have estradiol, progesterone, and follicle-stimulating hormone [FSH] checked).

2. Tell your doctor you want to be prescribed bioidentical estradiol and progesterone.

3. Ask your doctor to recommend a good compounding pharmacy that will combine the proper amounts of estradiol and progesterone based upon the doctor's prescription (go to the Resources in the back of the book if you don't have a compounding pharmacy in your area).

4. When you get your preparations, you will probably take your estradiol twice a day, about twelve hours apart, and one progesterone pill for fourteen days of each month—the easiest way to do this is days one to fourteen. Cycling this way mimics your body's natural production of hormones. Your dosages should be monitored by a physician, but you will most likely start with about .5 mg of estradiol twice a day, with 100 mg of progesterone a day.

5. You will get your period around the time you stop taking progesterone. If you bleed early, you may be taking either too much progesterone or not enough estradiol and you need your blood levels checked again.

a qualified M.D. and not an herbalist or a naturalist. You want a studied professional to treat you during this tricky passage. This is about the quality of your life. There is no reason to suffer. But without the right advice and program, you will, indeed, suffer through this passage and your health will gradually go downhill.

I prefer a female endocrinologist only because this is a female syndrome and I feel that a woman might have a better understanding than a male doctor; but again, there are always exceptions. Dr. Uzzi Reiss, a gynecologist, has made natural hormones his specialty, and he is kind, caring, understanding, and sensitive about women's health and this passage in particular. It is difficult for anyone to grasp the effects physically, psychologically, and emotionally of losing 90 percent of your hormones over a two-year period, but some male physicians are able to do so.

It's a simple fact that one cannot have a satisfactory life if one doesn't have satisfactory hormones. Hormones are the body's very own all-natural antiaging pill. And what a pill! Women who are afraid or confused about hormones will unfortunately experience the negative consequences of not taking them. How about rotting bones, dried-up vaginal tissue, droopy breasts, skin with no elasticity, a double chance of Alzheimer's disease, and double or triple the likelihood that sooner or later a heart attack will finish the story? That's just part of it.

Dr. Eugene Shippen, another of our country's leading endocrinologists, says, "There are astonishing advantages of hormone replacement in women. Nothing in medicine has been studied so intensively for so many years and through so many patient trials and investigations as estrogen replacement therapy. Nothing generates more controversy, phobic reactions, and confusion. Yet surprisingly, it would be hard to find a treatment in which an amazing long-term success rate is combined with so few side effects. The advantages of giving estrogen so far outweigh the risks that rational opposition to postmenopausal hormone replacement in women is very difficult to sustain. The therapy's ability to offer women aging modification, disease prevention, and improved quality of life is so remarkable and has been replicated so repeatedly in medical studies that it's sometimes hard to know what all the controversy is about."

As women, we get around forty years of life, from puberty to menopause, in which to enjoy the health-promoting benefits of estrogen. During this time we experience the life-giving benefits that come from making a full complement of hormones. When we are young, we are our healthiest. Heart attacks and strokes barely exist when we are premenopausal. Arthritis is rare; our immune systems are outstanding. It is not until after menopause that things start to go wrong. The acceleration toward poor health that then occurs in so many women's bodies is not coincidental in the slightest. It is hormonal to the core. Postmenopausally, without our hormones, we women lose the major programmer of our health.

Over the age of fifty-five, approximately 48 percent of all women die of cardiovascular disease, principally heart attacks and strokes. Twenty-four percent of us die from some form of cancer, 1.5 percent of which is breast cancer. Hormone replacement (real hormone replacement) is found in most studies to reduce the rate of death from cardiovascular disease by 30 to 40 percent, a drop in total mortality of approximately 14 to 19 percent. Meanwhile, worst-case projections show an increase in breast cancer of 10 percent, which would represent a total mortality increase of .15 percent. The cost-benefit ratio turns out to be almost fantastically skewed in favor of hormone replacement. The choice remains a very individual one for us, but based upon personal risk factors, the meaning of these statistics seems clear.

I'll say it once again (and again and again and
again): Balancing hormones is our best bet to
fight the diseases of aging. Upon middle age
(the menopausal passage), we begin to get our
first reports of high blood pressure, plaque in
our arteries, diabetes, weight gain, and personality changes. Balanced hormones are our
best defense against disease. It is not normal
to get sick as we age. But without balanced
hormones, our organs are not getting the
proper nutrients and begin slowly to break
down. It is commonly thought that middle age
brings sickness. In general it does because there
is so little understanding of hormone replacement.

I cannot tell you how great I feel when my
hormones are in balance. I spend the time it
takes to achieve this balance, despite my super-
busy schedule, because it is my belief that an
environment of balanced hormones prevents
disease. I believe this so firmly that I am relying
on balanced hormones as a means to fight my
breast cancer. I believe this is my edge over this
disease. This is my personal belief, and I am not
recommending that you do as I do. I simply
state my opinion as a means of conveying to
you how strongly I believe in HRT.

But I am not alone. Studies show that the
total improvement in life expectancy when
women remain on natural bioidentical estro-

gen replacement is more than significant. In 1966, a study was conducted by Dr. Bruce Ettinger, who followed five hundred women who belonged to the Kaiser Permanente health system in California. Two hundred and thirty-two of these women were on bioidentical estrogen replacement for an average of seventeen years, compared with 222 women who had been on estrogen for an average of less than one year during the same period. It was discovered that the death rate from all causes was lower by 44 percent in the women on estrogen for seventeen years. Remember, I am talking about natural bioidentical hormones, not drug hormones. But it begs one question: Why is the death rate so much lower for women on estrogen?

Did you know that men have significantly larger arteries than women, and because of this, it is easier for women's arteries to become blocked? Did you know that heart disease is the biggest single killer of women as well as men? Dr. Shippen says: "According to the current evidence, if not for hormones, women would be significantly more at risk for heart attacks and strokes than men. Men get heart attacks sooner, even though testosterone gives them protection; but it does not compare with the protection that hormones give to women. Once postmenopausal women lose their hormonal protection, in less than fifteen years they begin to have heart attacks as fast as men. Yet in women who replace estrogen, this change does not occur."

The *New England Journal of Medicine* conducted a study on five thousand women who were taking estrogen. It concluded, based upon improvements in their risk factors, that they would experience a 42 percent reduction in their rate of heart disease. British researchers, analyzing their own data, came up with a figure of 50 percent. According to Dr. Shippen, women who take real hormones that are balanced have:

higher levels of good HDL cholesterol.

lower levels of bad LDL cholesterol.

lower levels of fibrinogen.

lower levels of plasminogen activator inhibitor-1 (PAI-1).

lower levels of homocysteine.

lower levels of insulin.

lower levels of glucose.

lower levels of lipoprotein (a).

increases in blood flow to all parts of the body, including the brain, heart, muscles, skin, and bones.

THE SEXY YEARS 95

Now what does this mean to you and me? Well . . . here's the science: HDL cholesterol, the "good" cholesterol, transports LDL out of the tissues and back to the liver for excretion.

LDL cholesterol, the "bad" cholesterol, triggers the activity of large cells that engulf bacteria and unwanted debris, including particles of LDL. The engorged cells then become foam cells, and these trigger changes in the walls of the artery leading to plaque formation.

Fibrinogen is a natural clot-forming substance in the bloodstream. High levels of fibrinogen make it more likely that a blockage in a major artery will result in a heart attack.

Plasminogen activator inhibitor-1 (PAI-1) decreases the body's ability to inhibit the formation of blood clots. It increases the likelihood that complete blockage of an artery will precipitate a heart attack.

Homocysteine derives from methionine, an essential amino acid that is found in fairly high levels in the American diet. Estrogen helps to lower homocysteine levels and has significant lifesaving effects.

Insulin and glucose are significantly lowered by taking estrogen.

Lipoprotein is a type of cholesterol that is a particularly high risk for heart attack. It turns out that estrogen is one of the few substances that can effectively lower it.

It is misleading to women of menopausal age to have the medical community continue to put out flawed negative reports on HRT. Women are terribly confused, and no wonder why. The reports that create such alarm and cause such a media frenzy are done on "drug hormones," which contain very little in the way of hormones at all, but are simply "symptom suppressors." So certainly women taking drug hormones are having heart attacks, heart disease, high blood pressure, diabetes, strokes, Alzheimer's, and a host of other diseases. If drug hormones are simply taking away the uncomfortable symptoms of menopause, but not replacing the hormones lost in the aging process, a woman would be left open to a whole host of diseases because she has no protection. As I said before, it is an environment of balanced hormones that prevents disease.

Hormones are your protection—real hormones such as estradiol, progesterone, and testosterone are identical to the hormones found in the human body. Drugs like conjugated estrogens (Premarin), medroxyprogesterone acetate (Provera), and methyltestosterone are chemicals not found in the human body. In other words, they can't do the job properly. They will lull you into a false sense of well-being. Because you are not experiencing the miserable symptoms of menopause, you'll think all is okay again, but the organs and systems of the body are breaking down and there is nothing to build them back up. Before you know it, disease sets in.

Signs of menopause: You have to write
Post-it notes with your kids' names on them.

5

DR. DIANA SCHWARZBEIN:
MENOPAUSE

For any of you who have read any of my books on Somersizing, you know the important role Dr. Schwarzbein plays in my life. She is an awesome doctor, cutting-edge, and the first doctor I met who truly understands menopause and its ramifications. As an endocrinologist, her specialty is the chemical makeup of the body. As I struggled to find a doctor who really understood what my body was going through in menopause (before I found the wonderful doctors I have interviewed for this book), it was Dr. Schwarzbein who was finally able to help me find relief. She understands the importance of replacing the hormones lost in the aging process with natural hormones that are exact replicas (bioidentical) of the ones we make in our own bodies. Because of Dr. Schwarzbein, I am enjoying my menopause more than any other passage so far. Here is our conversation.

SS: First of all, I appreciate your giving me time to do this. I know how swamped you are at the office.

Every woman is looking for answers during this confusing passage, and you have made menopause a specialty. So let me first ask you: Because menopause is confusing not only to women but also to most doctors, how did you figure it out?

DS: Most of what I know about hormone replacement therapy in menopause I did not learn in medical school, or in medical training. It was when I was in private practice. I had four years of medical school, three years of internal medicine, then two years of endocrinology, but in nine years of training no one said, This is menopause, this is what you need to be doing.

SS: What made you pay attention?

DS: I started treating diabetic patients back in 1991, and I was noticing that a subset of my diabetic patients who happened to be menopausal women, who were following the exact same diet and exercise program as all the other diabetic patients, were not responding with the same good results. In other words, their sugars were not budging. It was startling. They were eating the same way, doing the same kinds of exercises, but their blood sugars were staying at 300, whereas the men and the premenopausal women had blood sugar levels that were coming down.

SS: What were you missing?

DS: It started to dawn on me that maybe the sex hormones were playing a role in their problem. But initially I made a lot of mistakes.

SS: For instance?

DS: If someone said to you, you can have all the benefits of hormone replacement therapy with or without a period, everyone would probably say, "Oh, without a period, please."

SS: Very understandable. I mean, who wants to have a period if they don't have to?

DS: I agree, and at that point I bought into the current standard of care that believed you could have the benefits of hormones without a period. But I found that when you give hormones that way [continuously combining an estrogen with a progestin on a daily basis], you make the patient more insulin resistant.

SS: But isn't a woman her healthiest when she is pregnant, because her body is making estrogen and progesterone simultaneously?

DS: Actually, no. Pregnancy is not the healthiest state for a woman to be in. In fact, pregnancy is one of the times when you are more insulin resistant. If you are pregnant back to back and you have many children, I guarantee you're going to end up with type 2 diabetes or another form of insulin resistance such as obesity, abnormal cholesterol levels, and/or high blood pressure. Also, we now realize that pregnant women have a higher risk of breast cancer.

SS: Why is that?

DS: I am not sure that anybody really knows, but I'm going to say I think it's because of insulin resistance. Because high insulin levels have been linked to breast cancer. For instance, women with type 2 diabetes have one of the highest risks of developing breast cancer. So do women with metabolic syndrome [an insulin-resistant problem].

SS: Okay, but why would pregnancy make you insulin resistant?

DS: It's complex, but to simplify, physiologically you have many hormonal changes in pregnancy that block the action of insulin. One of them is the high progesterone levels.

SS: But people always think of pregnancy as a high estrogen state.

DS: Actually, pregnancy produces high estrogen levels but much *higher* daily progesterone levels, and the progesterone blocks the action of estrogen every day. The result of this is a low estrogen effect in the body.

SS: So let's get back to how you started treating your diabetic menopausal patients.

DS: I started treating women with diabetes in 1991, and I prescribed Prempro to those who were in menopause. Luckily, I noticed right away that their blood sugar control worsened. This was a group of patients who were not improving despite how hard they were working at eating well and exercising. In fact, some of them were getting worse. That's when I realized Prempro was the problem. Then I switched these women to estradiol and progesterone, thinking the bioidentical hormones would be the answer. However, I still prescribed them in a continuous combined way (no periods), and their blood sugars remained elevated.

Then I thought about the four rules that I use for the replacement of any missing hormone:

1. *Don't take a hormone that's not low or missing.*
2. *Take only bioidentical hormones.*
3. *Mimic normal physiology as much as possible.*
4. *Track the hormone levels and their effects.*

Starting with rule number one—in menopause you are low in estradiol and progesterone. Rule number two, give back the same hormone in its bioidentical form. I realized that Premarin was being substituted for estradiol, and Provera was being substituted for progesterone, and this was not the right thing to do. So I prescribed bioidentical estradiol for estradiol and bioidentical progesterone for progesterone.

Then, because of rule number three, I realized that continuous combined therapy was not the way the body made these hormones. To mimic normal physiology as much as possible, these hormones would have to be taken in a cyclical manner, and then women would have to have withdrawal menses [monthly period] again.

Then, rule number four, I followed my patients by tracking their hormone levels through blood work and the effects of these bioidentical hormones.

When I followed my four rules of hormone replacement that I used in treating all types of hormone deficiencies, the blood sugars of the women with diabetes improved and their hormone levels came back into balance. Finally, these women felt well again.

I realized the mistake I was making [ten years ago] treating menopausal women with type 2 diabetes was in giving them continuous combined HRT. Remember, as diabetics they were already insulin resistant, and they became more insulin resistant on continuous combined HRT. Unfortunately, many doctors today still don't understand the link between continuous combined therapy and insulin resistance and are still making the same mistake today that I did all those years ago.

In my opinion, the harm of continuous combined therapy was confirmed in July 2002, when the first results of the Women's Health Initiative was published. There were three groups of women in this study:

1. *The observational group. These women were in menopause but were given only a placebo. They were "observed" to check for heart disease, breast cancer, stroke, blood clots, type 2 diabetes, and so forth.*

2. *Two treatment groups: subdivided by whether the woman had a uterus or did not because of a hysterectomy.*

If the woman had a uterus, she was given Prempro, a synthetic drug hormone comprising an estrogen, Premarin, and a progestin, Provera. Progestins block the effect of estrogen, so the women on Prempro did not get a period. In other words, if you take an estrogen and then block the action of it with a progestin, you end up with a low estrogen effect in the body. Hence, no bleeding.

If she didn't have a uterus, she was given Premarin alone. [Premarin is a drug that contains many different estrogens, most of which are not found or made in the human body.]

Taking Premarin alone would lead to a higher estrogen effect in the body.

SS: Interesting. And when you have a low estrogen effect because of continuous combined HRT [no period], are you subject to disease?

DS: That's what the WHI study showed. It was going to be an eight-plus-year study. They wanted to compare the outcome of the treatment groups with those of the observational group.

But at 5.2 years, the Prempro study was stopped early.

SS: Why?

DS: They started noticing that the women on Prempro [continuous combined therapy— no period] were having more heart attacks, more strokes, more blood clots, and more breast cancer than the group taking the placebo.

SS: What about the women who were taking Premarin?

DS: They haven't found the same kind of increased risk for disease with Premarin alone; therefore, that part of the WHI study is still ongoing. It is slated to be finished and reported in 2005 after eight years plus.

Last year when the news broke out about Prempro, the initial reaction was to get all women off all HRT, and to this day that is what most physicians are recommending.

SS: Why was the Women's Health Initiative done in the first place?

DS: The idea was to do a long-term prospective study on the possible benefits versus risks of the most commonly used HRT. They studied Premarin and Prempro because these are the most commonly prescribed therapies.

SS: So, when a woman takes these drug hormones, is she getting any good out of it at all, or would she be better off not taking anything?

DS: The WHI concluded that Prempro is worse than not taking anything, and I agree with the conclusion.

SS: That's a pretty strong statement.

DS: Yes, but that's what the study concluded.

As far as Premarin goes, I do not like it because it is not a bioidentical estrogen. However, it hasn't been shown to be more harmful than not taking anything at all. But this part of the study is still ongoing. It's important to know that Premarin has not yet been shown to be of much benefit, either. When it first came on the market, it was only supposed to be used in the short term to treat hot flashes, but then its use got extended (without any studies, I might add) to long-term hormone replacement therapy for menopause. As far as I am concerned, one of the uses of HRT after menopause should be for protection against heart disease. Premarin does not protect against heart disease.

SS: Well, all I know is I am feeling so wonderful that I am going to take bioidentical [natural] hormones for life, or as long as I choose to do so.

DS: And I believe it is safe for you to take bioidentical hormones for the rest of your life as long as we keep monitoring the effects of these hormones and we keep adjusting the amount to match your ever-changing lifestyle.

SS: Now what about Prempro or Premarin? Would a gynecologist put a woman on these drugs for life?

DS: I know many women who have been on these drugs for too long. There are two paralleling concepts going on: One is don't substitute a drug for a hormone; they do not do the same thing in the body. Two, do not think that you are going to come up with a better way to give these drugs than to match the physiology that already exists, as in natural bioidentical hormones.

I learned from my own studies and my treatment of menopausal women that you can approach menopause in two ways: symptomatic relief therapy on bioidentical HRT following the four rules mentioned earlier. Most gynecologists have been approaching it from the symptomatic side. They feel that as long as a woman is not having hot flashes, she is being treated properly. That is not true.

Furthermore, in my experience most gynecologists treat the uterus as the most important organ in the human body. As such, they feel their role is to keep harm from coming to your uterus. The medical literature in gynecology is filled with studies on the amount of progestin needed to protect the uterus from developing cancer. In trying to save the uterus and prescribing continuous combined therapy, gynecologists have increased the risk of breast cancer, heart attacks, and strokes in once-healthy women! Unfortunately, by messing with Mother Nature and giving drug hormones without restoring menstrual bleeding, we have done more harm than good.

SS: Okay, here we are again at having a period.

DS: You have to have a period, because this mimics normal! The normal state is not pregnancy! Prempro mimics pregnancy, so continuous combined therapy is *not* normal. Having a monthly period is normal. At one point gynecologists understood this concept. Prior to the last ten to fifteen years, most doctors did prescribe Premarin and Provera in a cycling way. That was the standard of care for quite some time.

SS: Then what happened?

DS: Primarily, women weren't feeling good on Premarin and Provera. They were complaining of bloating and irritability and on top of it were getting their period again! Then many women stopped taking HRT because they felt so poorly on it. Instead of treating women with bioidentical hormones, gynecologists tried different ways to give Provera to protect against uterine cancer and came up with continuous combined therapy without thinking about or studying the long-term consequences.

SS: Quite a dilemma. So if rule number three is to mimic normal physiology as much as possible, that would mean having a period, but is having a period *all your life* normal?

DS: Medically we are altering natural phenomena everywhere. There is nothing natural about immunizations, or open heart surgery, or hip replacement surgery. We have to decide as a society whether we are all going to honor aging or not. If we are, then I would say don't give hormone replacement therapy. But if as a society we choose to alter natural phenomena medically, we have to be consistent. Taking

HRT after menopause is not natural, but neither is performing open heart surgery.

SS: Let's talk more about rule number four—tracking.

DS: Tracking means monitoring the effect of the hormone a woman is taking. It is done through assessing hormone levels, assessing how the woman feels on hormones, when and how much bleeding she has on a monthly basis, assessing bones and cholesterol, and evaluating her uterine lining with yearly ultrasounds. It also entails following specific issues pertinent to the woman's personal health history such as blood pressure, insulin, and blood sugar levels.

Menopause is a serious condition. In other words, I don't just prescribe hormones and say, "Have a nice life, call me if you get a hot flash." Menopause needs to be followed just like any other hormone replacement therapy. Dosages of hormones may need to be continuously adjusted around a woman's aging and her changing lifestyle.

SS: What about self-medicating, as in today my breasts are a little more tender, I think I'll take a little more estrogen cream?

DS: I don't feel very comfortable with women self-medicating around symptoms. For instance, let's take breast tenderness . . . it could be from too little estrogen or too much estrogen. So how would a woman know what to do?

I'll tell you something else about estrogen: It can act like an antidepressant, and women can end up taking too much of it if left to determine how much they should be on in relation to how they feel. Then you get into the complications of high hormone effect in the system.

And then there is progesterone. Women cannot tell if they're taking too much progesterone because it is a stimulant and can initially make one feel better. It isn't until later that they can start feeling depressed or gain weight from too much progesterone, and by then they may not realize it's the progesterone because of how long it took before the symptoms occurred.

SS: Oh, so that is why you don't like women to self-adjust their hormones.

DS: Right, you have to be very careful. You do not want too much or too little. It has to be just right, and the only way to do that is through tracking.

SS: Should women and men go only to an endocrinologist who specializes in bioidentical HRT to get their sex hormones balanced?

DS: As an endocrinologist, I have chosen to specialize in sex hormones. But not every endocrinologist has the same training. I wish I could say, "Go to your local endocrinologist and everything will be okay." Unfortunately each person must find the right endocrinologist or doctor for him- or herself. It will require interviewing the doctor to see if he or she has made sex hormones a specialty.

SS: When you do get your hormones in balance (as you have helped me balance mine), life is blissful. It's worth a trip or a drive to another city to get on track. After all, it is a three-hour drive for me to see you, but you are worth it.

DS: Well, thank you. Now that you and I have worked together for all these years, you know that hormone replacement therapy can be complex.

SS: And this is where the concept of synthetic pharmaceutical hormones is screwy to me. How *can* one pill fit all?

DS: Exactly. Even though we all share the same physiology, we don't all share the same metabolism rate of different hormones. I mean, you and I have completely different body types. Let's look in the mirror at ourselves: Who has more estrogen . . . you or me?

SS: Old friendly me. Curvy body . . . you get to have a long, lean body and slim hips (I hate you, by the way). But I get your point. Every "body" has different needs.

DS: It's also genetics. It's about ratios among different hormones.

SS: Right now the ratio, the match, you have prescribed for me feels good. I'm feeling fantastic.

DS: Great. But it's sometimes a very difficult thing to find the perfect match for women. It takes patience and focus.

SS: How difficult?

DS: Well, it depends on their lifestyle and what is going on.

SS: So if a woman lived by a river and didn't work and didn't have a telephone or a television set and wasn't constantly thinking, Oh, my God, I have to juggle a million things . . .

DS: It would be easier to find a match for that woman. She could probably get away with much less estrogen, because estrogen is the multitasking hormone. But if this same woman smoked, it would make the body rid itself of the estradiol faster.

Another example is you, Suzanne, when you were going through that period where you were so stressed. Your hormone needs kept going up, so I had to keep changing your doses, yet your hormone levels stayed the same, because you were using it up so much. And then abruptly your stress stopped and the dose of your hormones was too much for you. All of a sudden you had a high estrogen effect.

SS: Right, and that was excessive bleeding . . .

DS: Yes, you called me and I decreased your doses and things got on track and in balance again.

SS: What's interesting to me as the patient who has been doing this for several years is that I have become very sensitive to when the doses are not correct. I find this an incredible way to work with you as my doctor. We are doing this in concert together, and it helps me to feel that I am in control of my health and my body.

DS: Yes, and as you recall when we first started working together, I was very clear about the fact that this is a pain in the butt. A "one pill fits all" would be a lot easier, but the rewards of doing it this way, from a health standpoint, a quality-of-life standpoint, and a longevity standpoint, are indisputable.

And it's not just about the hormones. It's about eating well and stress management, and tapering off sugar and other chemicals, and doing the right kinds of exercise. All hormones talk to one another. So you can't take estradiol and progesterone and expect to find balance if your insulin and adrenaline levels are going crazy from poor nutrition and lifestyle habits. Every hormone has to be in balance with the other hormones.

SS: That makes a lot of sense. A woman has to have better habits after menopause to keep her hormones in balance to help keep her prescribed hormones in balance, too. How do you feel about gynecologists giving antidepressants to quell menopausal symptoms?

DS: I think it's a tragedy. We are one of the first generations of women to fully experience this passage. We have much higher stress levels and more anxiety in our lives than ever before, and we are seeing menopause at earlier ages. And all this accelerated aging is due to bad lifestyle and dietary habits! Giving a woman an antidepressant to deal with the suffering of menopause does nothing to replace the hormones she has lost in the aging process. Antidepressants take away the vibration of living and create a host of other problems. Menopause is natural, but dying is natural also! Today we have ways of dealing effectively with menopause or delaying death; why wouldn't we want to take correct advantage of that? Antidepressants are not the answer.

SS: So what is the answer?

DS: Remember this concept . . . she who keeps her hormone levels highest the longest wins. That's the race, dear!

It's got to start with good nutrition. People don't realize that if they want to be busy and run around like a crazy person, and they don't eat well, then they will literally eat themselves!

If a woman of childbearing age wants to make a baby but is under any type of stress, she can end up dealing with infertility. Eggs are dispensable. This is not the time to make a baby, because she needs to use whatever she would use to make an egg for energy instead to fight off the stress.

We have advanced medically so that women no longer need to die prematurely from childbirth or from infectious diseases as they did before we had antibiotics. Women also used to die in perimenopause from infections before proper medicine was available, because we are more susceptible to infections during this phase. Women are their healthiest and strongest during their childbearing years, when they are making a full complement of hormones. The loss of hormones makes you weak.

SS: So the theory is that if I keep my hormones balanced and I continue to eat right, I can expect to stay strong and most likely avoid the diseases of aging?

DS: Right, and we now know that it's not just about menopause. It's about nutrition and stress management and sleep and exercise, and hormone replacement, if needed.

SS: Are we baby boomers the guinea pigs?

DS: I think the women who have been given the chemicals are the bigger guinea pigs. Come on, giving drugs to replace a hormone? These chemicals will cause you to lose the hormones that protect you from heart disease, namely estradiol. Real hormones provide protection from heart disease if given in bioidentical form [exact replicas of the hormones we make in our own bodies]. This was confirmed by the Howard Hodis study at the University of Southern California. He showed that estradiol—not Premarin, not synthetic hormones, not drugs, but the bioidentical estradiol found in human ovaries—will protect a woman against heart disease.

SS: Okay, Dr. Schwarzbein, we're sold, but where am I going to send women to find this kind of excellence and understanding relative to this passage? Women are barraged with bad medical advice and are highly influenced by the drug companies, so where do they go, and what should they ask their own doctor? For instance, the woman says, "I am in menopause, I am having hot flashes, I am irritable, and I am bloating."

DS: First thing to ask your doctor is to get baseline hormone levels through lab work. You want to have your estradiol, progesterone, and follicle-stimulating-hormone levels tested. If you are in menopause, you proceed to rule two.

Tell your doctor that you want to be prescribed bioidentical estradiol and progesterone. You can get the best form of these hormones from a good compounding pharmacy. Next, ask your doctor if he or she knows or works with a good compounding pharmacy. If not, or if you don't have one in your area, have them check the reference guide you have provided in the back of this book. However, some doctors won't know how to use the compounding pharmacy, so ask them to prescribe an estradiol preparation such as Estrace or Gynodiol found in the local pharmacies. There is also a non-compounded form of bioidentical progesterone known as Prometrium.

SS: How would someone know how much to take?

DS: You always want to take the lowest dose and taper up slowly.

SS: And see how you feel?

DS: Yes, and take the estradiol hormone twice a day. Estradiol is in and out of the body very quickly, so you really need to take smaller amounts more frequently to achieve the best balance. Take it twice a day about twelve hours apart, because you want to mimic a steady stream, as if your own body is still making it. The progesterone may be taken once a day or sometimes twice a day if needed.

SS: Okay, they have their estradiol and progesterone preparations. Now what?

DS: They will need to take them in a cycling manner. Take the estradiol every day of the month twice a day and add in one pill of progesterone for fourteen days out of each month. The easiest way to do this is on calendar days one through fourteen of every month.

SS: What dosage should they take?

DS: Start with about 0.5 mg of estradiol twice a day and with 100 mg of progesterone a day, and then track symptoms and levels to determine if a higher or lower dose is needed.

SS: What happens after the fourteenth day of progesterone? Is that when a woman should expect to have her period?

DS: Yes, they are supposed to be having a regular menstrual flow around the end of the progesterone or just after it is finished. . . . If they break through early [bleeding], then they are taking either too much progesterone or not enough estradiol.

SS: How will they know?

DS: They will need to have their blood levels checked to see which one it is.

Now, we are not taking into account that some people would like to be on progesterone

50 mg twice a day, not 100 mg once a day. Unfortunately, we don't have a 50 mg at every drugstore. We only have 100 mg. You have to try to work with it. But if you are able to work with a compounding pharmacy, they will be able to work it out to fit your needs more specifically.

SS: This will be a big help to women who are frustrated and do not live in an area that has an informed endocrinologist or gynecologist. As women, we have to be proactive about our health and our hormonal needs, because there is so much misinformation and lack of understanding about this passage. That is the point of this book, to empower women and men (and believe me, they also lose their hormones) to find quality health care and information about hormones for themselves.

DS: We are in a crisis as far as menopause is concerned. Doctors are going to have to learn something new, because we can't keep allowing women to suffer and become ill due to the lack of understanding that exists.

SS: So what is the future? I agree with you that menopause is a crisis at this time with this lack of understanding among women and doctors, but another generation is coming up right after us, and everyone is still in a state of confusion and frustration. Women my age are suffering, their marriages are falling apart, the divorce rate is going up, men are remarrying young girls to get the fun back in their lives, so what is going to happen? What are your hopes?

DS: Menopausal women have to demand answers. We also have to get them over their fear of breast cancer and of estrogen. One of my hopes is that the right information gets out. Women have to know that the risk of breast cancer is much less than the risk of dying from not taking hormones, or the risk of getting a heart attack or a debilitating stroke.

Let me state that insulin is a much bigger hormone relative to breast cancer than estrogen will ever be, because insulin is a major growth hormone. Insulin is a major growth hormone and estradiol is a minor growth hormone. Breast cancer is not caused because you took estradiol. Breast cancer comes from damage to DNA from the environment and damage caused by unhealthy lifestyle and dietary habits.

SS: Like . . .

DS: Stress, smoking, too much caffeine, high daily doses of progestins, lots of artificial sugar, anything that you put in your body that shouldn't be there. If you damage an area of the DNA that promotes a tumor, then that tumor is going to start to grow. Estradiol is a growth factor for normal breast tissue. So if you have normal breast tissue, but now the DNA of that normal breast tissue gets damaged, estradiol is still going to make it grow, but it didn't cause the damage.

In fact, I am going to stick my neck out and say that when we finally get around to studying bioidentical estradiol, it is going to be shown to be protective against cancers because it is an antioxidant in the human body.

Again, though, it is not about too much or too little of a hormone. The balance has to be just right.

SS: Thank you so much.

Signs of menopause: You sell your
home heating system at a yard sale.

6

MARTA: A FORTY-FIVE-YEAR-OLD EXPERIENCE

Marta is a successful television producer of megahit sitcoms, a mother of three, busy from morning until night, and she has one foot in the menopausal door. But she has not hit the wall yet; she has symptoms that come and go, and her life is extremely stressful just trying to keep it all together. She has recently begun to dabble in natural hormones, and here is what she had to say about it. . . .

SS: Obviously, menopause is right around the corner for you. You are forty-five, and this is one condition no one escapes, so how are you feeling?

MK: I'm not sure how I am feeling, but I go to Dr. Uzzi Reiss and he is amazing. He is a women's health advocate. He told me I am an estrogen type, meaning that my body makes a lot of estrogen. Normally, he said, a doctor might look at my estrogen levels and say, "You are not perimenopausal," but Dr. Reiss said that the dip in my estrogen levels is so enormous, even though I still make a lot of it, that I need to replace what I am losing. I like him because he takes you as an individual.

SS: So are you feeling better being on replacement?

MK: My problem is I have such a thing about medication of any kind, including homeopathic and holistic, that I react to doing anything daily.

SS: So Dr. Reiss is giving you hormones because your ratios are off, but you don't always take them. How long does it take before your symptoms start to reappear?

MK: Basically, I don't even notice it until the week before my period, and then I find myself crying because my coffee is too cold, or why am I yelling because I have lost my keys? It's then I look at my calendar and realize, Oh, that's what this is.

SS: Does Dr. Reiss admonish you for not taking them?

MK: Yes, he does. I think there is a little part of me that says, "My body is supposed to go through this." I have actually been working with this woman who sees menopause as an opportunity. She thinks that it is a chance in our lives to embrace the maternal. Not just as mothers, but to look at ourselves as women and totally accept what that means, and that it is a moment in time when you are changing; that it is a step forward into the rest of your life. For me right now with my TV show, *Friends,* ending, it is almost overwhelming.

SS: So there are a couple of things going on.

MK: Yes, and psychologically a part of me may be avoiding the next step. Deep down maybe I think that if I am no longer going to be a fertile woman anymore, some sort of punishment must be involved with this passage. There is a week each month where I should be locked in a closet until it is over.

SS: Those are awful weeks. But replacing lost hormones with natural bioidentical ones helps keep your brain sharp.

MK: Well, that is encouraging because I am a writer, and I am finding that sometimes I have lost words. Suddenly I can't think of the word for sock.

I had my third child at forty-three, and it was a very difficult pregnancy. I was extremely hormonal, which was a different experience. With my other children during pregnancy, I never felt better, or more sexual, or more feminine.

SS: What did your doctor say to you?

MK: He said, "Two hundred and fifty years ago you were supposed to be dead at forty-three." And that really struck me how fortunate I am not only to be alive, but also to be having a baby. This made it difficult for me, but

I dealt with it with a better sense of humor. The other thing I notice with my new hormonal imbalance is that my eating has changed.

SS: In what way?

MK: I crave the foods that are worst for me. Like chocolates, sugar, carbohydrates. Also, a year ago I became a vegetarian. On the one hand it has been great, but on the other hand it has been very difficult. I eat fish, but no white or red meat. Well, you can't eat fish three times a day, and cheese doesn't work for me, and dairy makes me sleepy, tired, and sluggish; but when I was on a low-carb, high-protein diet, I felt great and had no cravings at all.

SS: What other changes have you noticed?

MK: I get my period every three weeks now. My doctor said it's kind of like the last hurrah. So probably it will all stop in the next couple of years.

My mom went through menopause when she was fifty, and she acted horribly. I remember her celebrating when she stopped getting her period, and then it was all downhill. So that is the model I have. Maybe that is part of why I am resisting hormones.

SS: I think when the time comes you will not be resistant. The relief is so welcome because you get to feel like your old self again. Normal.

MK: As we are talking I am thinking to myself, Why am I putting myself through this? I have to get back on a schedule with my doctor and take these hormones, because when I think back to when I was taking them regularly, I realize I had tools.

I am having a hard time sleeping. I get about four or five hours a night.

SS: Do you think this is because of hormones or stress?

MK: Not necessarily stress. I've just thought this is what happens as we get older; but when I think about it, my husband sleeps.

My doctor said that if I am having a hard time sleeping to take a couple of extra drops of progesterone and twenty minutes later I will feel relaxed and able to fall asleep. So when I think back on when I was doing that, I realize that was one of the greatest gifts he ever gave me.

SS: So there's your answer.

MK: Yes, this is very good motivation for me to go back to what had worked for me last summer. I guess I got off course.

SS: Do you think that all the negative reports you hear in the media have frightened you away?

MK: That may be part of the problem, that my body is supposed to do this and why am I interfering.

My grandmother aged so magnificently. She was the cutest thing in the whole world with the most beautiful, soft wrinkles. I always wanted to touch her face. She was ninety-three when she died. My mother was much younger when she died.

SS: Did your mother work?

MK: Yes, she worked and she lost my father when she was much younger, plus she was a teenager during the Depression, so she had to work to support her family.

SS: On top of that, she probably had no understanding of menopause, so she suffered through it. But that still doesn't make menopausal women easier to live with.

MK: I know, I feel sorry for my husband.

SS: Yes, but you and I are the lucky ones because we are going through this at an age where younger doctors are saying, "Hey, wait a minute, what we've been doing has not been working; women are not having a good quality of life, plus they are getting diseases: heart disease, stroke, diabetes, plus there is the weight gain."

MK: Yes, but we are also living when pharmaceutical companies have an enormous amount of power, and I find that really frightening.

My doctor, who is cutting-edge, gave me a whole bag of homeopathic medicine before I went into the hospital to have my baby with a C-section. He said, "I can't give you this in the hospital, but I want you to take this twenty-four hours before surgery, and this is what I want you to take as soon as the surgery is over. This is what I want you to put on your skin." Then he said, "As soon as you start feeling postpartum, I want you to come in and I will give you progesterone on the spot." He said, "You are not going to believe how good you are going to feel." And he was right . . . it was as if someone had come in and lifted the dark clouds.

SS: That is the power of hormones and taking natural medicine.

MK: Well, Dr. Reiss is very empowering. His way not only appeals to my common sense, it actually excites me to think about stepping forward proudly, embracing the changes rather than fighting them off, and resolving that I am going through menopause and I don't have to suffer because of the quality care I am getting from my doctor and his understanding of natural hormones.

SS: Do you feel any of the shame that is associated with going through menopause?

MK: It's awful. On the one hand I joke about it, but I feel so undesirable and I can't help but think, how could my husband desire this? Some days I feel like a dried-up old lady.

So there is an enormous amount of shame and negativity. But my husband is really trying to be understanding, and I love him for that.

I remember someone saying to me that I had the world at my feet: the big job, a great husband, wonderful children. What is the cost? And I thought. The cost is me, personally. I don't take care of myself because I am so busy taking care of everyone and everything else. Between the work, the kids, making the lunches at night, it's exhausting, because I don't want to give anything up. But I am paying the price personally. So my reluctance to take on menopause and deal with it may be an extension of that.

SS: Do you think you're not worth it on a subliminal level?

MK: Probably . . . always thinking of everyone else.

SS: So finding balance seems to be the key. The key to replacing lost hormones, along with a host of other things, is that it keeps your brain functioning as though you are in your prime. That's very important because now it is coupled with wisdom and perspective. I would think as a writer that would be vitally important to you.

MK: I have never connected that with hormone loss. That alone does make it appealing. I love the new medicine, my doctor gave me a twenty-four-hour urine test, where you collect it hour by hour. He was able to see everything going on in my system—antioxidants, free radicals, health of my heart; he even figured that I didn't have enough salt in my diet.

SS: Yes, this is the new medicine.

MK: I have always shied away from chemicals and synthetics, and somehow hormones were caught up in that. But this new way, with natural bioidentical hormones, is appealing. It helps me to understand that not only would I benefit from replacement, but that I deserve to have quality cutting-edge information and treatment. This helps me into this next passage with new enthusiasm. Thank you.

SS: Good luck, and thank you.

Perks of aging: "I no longer have patience
for people who don't like me."

—My friend Susie Weinthal, age 69

7

DR. UZZI REISS, M.D., OB/GYN: NATURAL HORMONE BALANCE

Dr. Reiss sees six thousand women a year, most of whom come to him suffering from hormonal imbalance. They need help, and he gives them relief. Dr. Reiss is a passionate and fascinating doctor who has demystified the confusing issues surrounding this time of life. He is unique in that as a gynecologist he has researched and learned about the complexities of the hormonal system, which generally is not the specialty of gynecologists. He has been giving women natural hormones for over twenty years. His approach is learned and refreshing because he has stepped outside of the pharmaceutical common course of synthetic hormones, and as a result, women are flocking to him. He recognizes the need for women to understand their hormonal lives. The important phrase here is "natural bioidentical hormones"; Dr. Reiss is a proponent of them, and thousands of women love what he has done for them.

SS: Thank you for speaking with me, Dr. Reiss, I've heard a lot about you.

UR: All good, I hope.

SS: Absolutely. I want to talk about natural hormones. I'm in my middle fifties, and as a woman, I have been programmed all my life to think that this is the beginning of the end and that it's all downhill from here. But I have to say this passage for me is the best I have ever felt, the healthiest I have ever been, the happiest I've ever experienced, and the most fulfilled. Couple all of this with the beginnings of wisdom and perspective, and life is good. I believe the reason I am enjoying such superb quality of life is that I take natural bioidentical hormones and they are balanced.

UR: I agree, replacing bioidentical hormones gives back your quality of life. As a physician, it is my job to understand the side effects, the benefits, and how you can individualize hormone therapy for each particular person. I think the key to all of it is individualization, because women are so different. If we take a thousand women who are twenty years old who say they feel great and are mentally clear, with good energy, perfect weight, great memory, great sex drive, and clear skin, and then you measure their hormones, and for example let's say these women are in the third day of their cycle—you will see thousands of different variations. The goal is for women to achieve the perfect combination for them-selves.

SS: Help me to understand . . . how do you determine how much estrogen and how much progesterone?

UR: First I need to find the expression of the hormone inside the cell. We really don't have a direct tool to look inside the cell, so I use a blood test as an indirect tool to tell me if the levels are too high or too low.

Let me tell you how I work. There are three types of women. One is Twiggy.

SS: Twiggy? Skinny, tall, little breasts . . .

UR: Right. Tall, thin, barely any breasts, and barely any muscle. Twiggy never had acne, and you would have to take a microscope to see hair on her body. The Twiggy type is typ-ically very low in both estrogen and testos-terone and generally has relatively good human growth hormones because she is tall.

Now let's take someone else who is five feet one, D–size breasts, has no hair over her body, is not very athletic, and does not have strong muscles; this woman has extremely high estro-gen, and low testosterone.

SS: This is the curvy body?

UR: Right, this woman has about six- to sevenfold more estrogen than Twiggy. Estrogen has indeed built her breasts and has given her a happy mentality. I don't want to generalize, but women of this type are happier and less complex, and it seems that their approach to sexuality is much simpler.

Then we have the intermediate group, what I call the athlete. If you notice, most women athletes have small breasts. Not because they have low estrogen, but because they have high testosterone. You can't be an athlete and have low testosterone, nor can you be a dancer and have low testosterone, because you wouldn't have the spatial coordination and balance that testosterone gives you. Also (and I'm generalizing) athletes have nice muscles.

You see, hormone is a language, and each hormone has its own language. Hormones do specific things that they have been doing for the last billion years of evolution. A hormone is not only a number, it's also an expression of specific mentality, specific attitudes.

Let's take a simple example: A lady comes to me and says that lately she is bleeding less during her period, her vagina is dry, and her breasts are droopy. The only thing it can be is that she is making less estrogen. Estrogen builds up the lining in the uterus. When there is less estrogen, there is less lining and thus less of a period. When I give her estrogen, it fills the breast, so now the breasts are less droopy. Estrogen gives women vaginal lubrication, so when I give her estrogen the vagina becomes less dry.

We know that women have fluctuations in their estrogen during their normal cycle. A woman tends to have lower estrogen before her period than the week after because her body wants to prepare the lining of the uterus for implantation, so it shoots up the estrogen levels. If a woman comes to me and says she has been feeling good, but in the last two years she feels good only the week after she finishes her period, then I have my answer. This is the week the body makes more estrogen.

SS: So what do you do for her at this point?

UR: I start to ask specific questions. Estrogen is vitally important because it gives women their great mind; estrogen makes women happy. We have to think of what women were supposed to do fifty thousand years ago. Women's bodies are adjusted not to the life we have today, but to life fifty thousand years ago. At that time women were the center and had all the power. They were responsible for feeding everyone and keeping everyone together and happy. Women with normal estrogen are happy and outgoing, they want to teach, they want to give, they also need a lot of good deep sleep—they don't have much time left in each day because they are so busy giving of themselves.

SS: And balanced estrogen ensures a good night's sleep.

UR: Correct. That's why when a woman starts losing estrogen she has interrupted sleep.

SS: Are estrogen-dominant women happier in general than a testosterone woman?

UR: In a certain way, yes. For example, have you met a lot of models?

SS: Yes.

UR: They are tall, thin, and usually sort of subtly depressed. I ask these same women how they were feeling when they were pregnant and they usually say it was the happiest they ever felt.

This goes back to the patient's individual hormonal history, which I factor in when I design a hormonal treatment plan for that woman. I treat women with hormones from age fourteen to the age of ninety. Hormone therapy is considered the domain of menopausal women, but it applies to every age. Many women never reach their hormonal balance, which is sad because it is so easy to feel great when you find balance.

I see so many women every year. When a woman comes to see me before her period (when her estrogen is low), she usually dresses more conservatively (this is especially so with menopausal women—they dress darker and are less body conscious). The week after she is finished with her period she is happy, dresses more colorfully, is more body conscious, and cares more about her body.

When a woman comes to my office and tells me she doesn't feel right in her body anymore, I think about her with the history of hormones in mind. I usually know what is wrong before she tells me by her body shape, size, and the way she describes how she is feeling. Usually her estrogen is low. I have done this for twenty years, and I know I can't be right all the time, but the majority of the time it is the correct assessment.

Now, here is another situation where hormones are dynamic. If after you finish writing this book I send you and your husband to Tahiti for a month, and all you do is light exercise, and rest on the beach all day long, your estrogen requirements will go down by 30 percent. Last time I took my wife to Hawaii her estrogen dropped 30 to 40 percent. On the other hand, if you decide to train for a marathon, your body will consume more estrogen and you will have to increase it. That's why a "one pill fits all" as in synthetic so-called hormones can't work. Every day your hormone requirements change. When a woman is stressed, she decreases a substance in her body called cyclic AMP. It is a messenger that goes from the brain of the cell to the outskirts of the cell to get the information the hormones give to it. This messenger barely works when you are stressed.

SS: So it is up to the woman to evaluate her stress levels to know when she needs to call her doctor and get reevaluated.

UR: Most of the time I teach women how to increase and decrease the amount of hormones they use based upon how they feel and their stress levels. A few of these cases are more complex because of the degree of the problem and the fact that patients respond differently to the hormone treatment. These women require constant guidance in the initial stages of their treatment. For instance, I have a patient who came to me after having had a hysterectomy nine months ago. She has been constantly suicidal because her hormones have been so out of balance. But now, after three weeks of treating her with various doses of hormones, she is nearly a normal person.

SS: Wow! That's incredible. I know so many women who have had hysterectomies who are miserable and at times suicidal. What did you do for her?

UR: Basically, I kept adjusting and tracking the doses of estrogen and progesterone.

I think it's very important to understand that we are living in an era with the biggest assault on womanhood in history. Everyday stress takes away a woman's estrogen, and with it her sensuality, her sexuality, her smartness, her beauty, her serenity, her sleep, her memory, her passion, and her sensitivity. The stress of today's life is assaulting her estrogen, but women have become frightened of hormones because reports come out that say they are going to kill you or give you cancer.

SS: Well, what are they supposed to think when so many negative reports are put out by the media?

UR: Yes, and this information is flawed. These reports, which are always about synthetic hormones and not natural bioidentical hormones, are constantly being thrust in women's faces. These flawed studies are frightening women away from estrogen. Every day I see women who are nearly falling apart because their estrogen has been taken away from them either because their body has stopped making it or they have read these reports and stopped taking it on their own.

They have no choice but to turn to the alternatives: a sleeping pill to sleep, antianxiety pills to relax, antidepressant pills to take away their depression, Ritalin to make their memory a little better . . . And what you get is a pharmaceutical product that loses humanity.

SS: So many of the women I have talked with regarding this subject repeat the same thing: "I feel dead inside."

UR: Yes, this form of treatment takes the soul out of them. It takes away what I call the vibration of living.

Recently there was another study by the Women's Health Initiative done on Provera, a chemicalized progesterone. Provera is known to be destructive to the heart. It can close the coronary arteries, enhance the growth of arterial plaque, and make it unstable so there will be more heart attacks. There is existing literature on this drug. It is known to leech calcium from bone, and it is also known to aggressively increase breast cancer; what they haven't told you yet is that Provera is totally destructive to the brain, because Provera is like MSG. A bad MSG. Now that you know what this drug does, you understand why the study that used this drug resulted in such a bad outcome. It is not favorable to the brain. It overuses the brain, then crushes the cells.

The second drug used in this study was Premarin, an extract from the urine of pregnant mares (female horses). In other words, this is a substance that nature never intended for the bodies of human females. If we said that estrogen was the base of your mind, your mood, and your memory, then I ask you: is there anything similar between a woman and a pregnant mare? Here we have two billion years of general evolution and two million years of human evolution, and we are giving women two pharmaceutically designed hormones totally different from the hormones a woman makes in her own body.

SS: Why doesn't the medical community understand this? Why are we not giving women hormones that are an exact replica?

UR: Because natural bioidentical hormones cannot be patented. No one wants to spend money on studies of a hormone that can be copied by other companies. Instead, synthetic hormones can be patented and advertised, and no one can copy them.

Here is an example: Let's say papaya is expensive and the sellers need to put DDT in it so it will preserve itself and have a longer shelf life and also more people will be able to afford it. Then a report comes out that papaya with DDT is shown to increase breast cancer. What would be your journalistic conclusion? That papaya increases breast cancer? No. DDT increases breast cancer!

What most people don't realize is that the scientific technology for creating bioidentical hormones [hormones identical to those in our bodies] has been around for fifty years. But instead they decided to use Premarin because horses have huge bladders, and they can feed them hay, which is really inexpensive, keep them in small stalls, catheterize their bladders, and give them tranquilizers to keep them calm, so they can easily make tons of estrogen. So it's about business. But the estrogen from horses' urine is not an exact replica of what we make in our bodies. Only bioidentical HRT, synthesized in a lab, made from plant extracts, exactly replicates what our own bodies make.

The study on Premarin began fifty years ago. They started giving natural hormones to women who were menopausal. Without a doubt, thousands of studies on women from different places around the world showed the following: 50 percent decrease in Alzheimer's disease, 50 percent decrease in heart attacks, 50 percent decrease in bone loss, 50 percent decrease in blindness, and now we know 50 percent decrease in colon cancer.

With Premarin they give estrogen alone, but in the physiology of the body, estrogen always goes with progesterone. Normal physiology is required amounts of estrogen every day of the month, and progesterone on days one through fourteen. If estrogen goes up, then progesterone goes up; if estrogen goes down, then progesterone goes down. But in giving estrogen alone, women started to develop mild forms of uterine cancer. There was no balance and this is the connection that made all this mania about estrogen and uterine cancer. In addition, because Premarin is like a foreign substance to the human body, the body reacts by increasing the inflammation process. If this reaction is sustained for five to fifteen years because the foreign substance is continuously introduced to the body, it will increase the incidence of heart disease and Alzheimer's, thereby negating the original benefit.

SS: Meaning that our bodies make estrogen and progesterone and that to eliminate one of these important hormones creates imbalance, and imbalance—

UR: Creates disease. Because it was not estrogen that caused the cancer, it was the lack of progesterone. For instance, if I removed your eyes and then asked you to drive a car, you would have an accident because I took away your vision. It's the same thing. The two hormones work in concert with each other.

Now when pharmaceutical companies realized that the two hormones were important, they had to find a way to patent them. So they decided to change them pharmaceutically, and that is how synthetic hormones became the common treatment.

The way I work is, I teach women how to have control over the natural hormones they take. The modern woman is a new experiment; she is the woman who is pregnant only one or two times in her life, and she is working outside the home. These women are not healthier; they have more disease. At the beginning of the century, there was no endometriosis, there were not a lot of fibroids and not a lot of the diseases we have today.

SS: Don't you think this might be environmental?

UR: Definitely. Our unhealthful environment makes us more prone to illness and also "confuses" the natural function of our hormones. Processed foods and the materials they are packaged in are full of artificial hormones that compete with and therefore confuse women's natural hormonal balance. This, plus the enormous tasks placed on the shoulders of women in our society, makes it nearly impossible for modern women to achieve many things that are dearest to them.

I have a sentence I often say: Pregnancy is not the beginning of the extension of the family, it is the beginning of the extinction of the family.

SS: What do you mean?

UR: It's because women focus all their attention on their children and stop thinking about themselves and their relationship with their husbands. I advise every woman before she does anything when she gets up in the morning, to think about what she is going to do for herself today and what she is going to do for her partner to make their relationship grow and get better. So many women tell me that they are unable to have sex with their husbands because of the kids. By the time she puts the kids to bed, she usually falls asleep with them, then wakes up at two in the morning and her husband is already asleep, then the kids come into the bed in the morning. Women today need to reprioritize their lives.

SS: Maybe they use this as an excuse to avoid sex, and maybe that's because they are off hormonally, perhaps low testosterone.

UR: Low testosterone is not always the case. For instance, a woman athlete has high testosterone all her life. The problem is that when you take away a woman's estrogen she can't do anything with her testosterone. Testosterone by itself just makes her aggressive. When a woman is going through menopause, or is just before her period, her estrogen starts to go down: Once the estrogen goes down, the testosterone goes way up. So she goes from being serene, loving, open, and sexual to being moody, depressed, and uninterested in going outside and enjoying herself. Instead she gets mean, bitchy, upset, and short-tempered.

I saw a woman on TV who wrote a book about menopause, and I heard her say that menopause has healing power . . . she said, "I felt strong and I finally had the guts to throw him out." I say no, you lost your estrogen. Estrogen is the hormone that gives women that wonderful balance between strength, clear thinking, and patience. It makes them wise and tolerant. On the other hand, when estrogen levels sink during menopause, a woman's body releases more testosterone, which causes women to be aggressive but without that soft, clear-thinking, patient component to balance the aggression. This is the reason that many women are perceived as overly emotional during menopause. But it doesn't have to be this way. There must always be a balance between estrogen and testosterone levels.

SS: What about women who are estrogen dominant? Is that a good thing?

UR: Actually, very few women are estrogen dominant. Those who are dominant are happy and clear, but they usually have a tremendous amount of water retention, bloating, and breast tenderness and extremely heavy periods, because estrogen builds a lot of lining. In reality this woman is not estrogen dominant, she simply lacks progesterone. In menopause, when this woman starts losing her estrogen, she will get depressed and foggy, will not sleep well, and will tend to turn inward.

SS: What are the health ramifications of a woman who is estrogen dominant?

UR: She may have a slightly higher incidence of endometriosis, fibroids, and cystic breasts. But it is not from estrogen, it is from lack of progesterone. Once I give these women progesterone, I often find that now their estrogen is blocked, and it is here I discover that they are also estrogen deficient. Then I have to add a little more estrogen to find balance.

SS: Every woman's needs are different.

UR: Yes, and it takes time to find the right balance for each woman. We were all created perfect. The great thing about bioidentical hormones is that we can always find a match for your individual optimal requirements. The beauty of bioidentical hormones is that they talk to you: if you give too much, you have side effects; the same goes for testosterone, DHEA, HGH, thyroid, and the adrenal hormones. All of them are a beautiful orchestra, and it is possible to teach every woman to find balance by herself. They learn when to take a little more and when to take a little less.

SS: And when is that?

UR: It depends. At any age, hormones in the body are fluctuating. So let's take estrogen (and every woman should check with her doctor before doing this): You wake up in the morning and your thinking is a little foggy or uninspired, and you don't feel motivated, then you would take a little more of the estrogen cream. If, however, you wake up in the morning and you are a little uptight, and your breasts are tender, take minimally less. Very few women come to me and say they don't get it. The amazing thing is that we are now in an era of multiple hormonal deficiencies. It is not just estrogen; it can be thyroid or adrenal. (We could talk forever about the adrenal glands.) When a woman comes in the first time, I can't be sure which hormone deficiency is dominant, so I start her on the hormones I feel are the most needed, based upon her history and the results of her blood tests. But with time, some of the hormonal deficiencies that I believed were dominant reveal themselves to be *reactions* to the deficiencies of other hormones. From this point on, the course of treatment will focus on the "true" deficiencies.

SS: Which do you start with, progesterone or estrogen?

UR: It depends upon the situation. Recently I saw through blood work that a patient of mine was in menopause. She complained of breast tenderness and water retention. I could see through lab work that she still had some estrogen, but not the optimal amount; but she has it all the time, so we call it unopposed. This woman had certain signs of too much estrogen, but general signs of not enough—for instance, her vagina is dry, her mind is foggy, and she cannot sleep. With someone like this, I first prescribe progesterone. Progesterone is a very complex hormone, because only very young women respond to it in the way the textbooks say. Ninety-five percent of the time when you give progesterone to a young woman, she responds to it, she relaxes and calms down. But up to 50 percent of women in menopause who haven't been exposed to progesterone for a few years can react to it as if it were a toxic drug, because it drops the estrogen levels. They feel depressed, or it gives them panic attacks.

Balancing hormones is a work of art, but you can teach women how to do it. I know this because I get letters from my female patients all over the country who have taught themselves. The biggest problem I run into is that every compounding pharmacy is different, and when I write hormone prescriptions (Rx) in one pharmacy, but in another pharmacy it has another quantity, that makes it more difficult.

SS: Why isn't there any standardization?

UR: Because bioidentical hormones are not profitable, so no one is interested in funding the studies.

SS: Well, how does one know which one is a good compounding pharmacy?

UR: If a woman has a favorite pharmacy, or she comes to me from out of town and there is only one in her vicinity, I tell her that the amount I am giving her generally works, but if she is not getting the desired relief, I suggest she get her hormones from a compounding pharmacy that I work with through mail order, where I know she will get better absorption.★

SS: Yes, but isn't there the danger, especially with hormones, of thinking, If a little is good, then a lot will be much better?

UR: Well, if that were the case, why would diabetics (even children) be allowed to control themselves with insulin? We know that if you let people control themselves, the control is ten times better than having a doctor from remote deciding every month what they can use.

I tell women how to use their hormones, I prescribe the initial dose, then two to three months into the program they come back to my office so I can track their levels. Then I adjust and explain how to control the dose by paying attention to how they are feeling.

★ See the Resources for a list of compounding pharmacies.

SS: What about taking natural hormones when you have breast cancer?

UR: Do you know that one of the oldest descriptions of reasons for breast cancer is lack of DHEA? This is one of the theories that has stood the test of time. Several studies have associated higher levels of DHEA in the body with a lowered incidence of cancer.

SS: But what about those of us who took birth control pills in the 1960s and 1970s? Do you think there is any connection between birth control pills and breast cancer? I am asking only because there is such a high incidence of breast cancer with women of my age group.

UR: You are talking about the most aggressively strong estrogen ever created. When you take estrogen that is that strong, your brain stops making your own estrogen. This is the essence of how it works. When you use natural estrogen, your brain continues to produce it because your body is still fluctuating. Yet they did a study of women on birth control pills and found there was no increase of breast cancer in this group.

SS: What do you think about that?

UR: I think this is another piece of information indicating a Twiggy type: I cannot say that she will never get breast cancer and that someone with large breasts will, even though the estrogen differences between the two women is around sixfold, and in pregnancy it is about tenfold.

We do not know exactly why women get breast cancer, but it doesn't seem to appear that one of the reasons is birth control pills. The literature is mounted with data, but there is never clear scientific evidence that estrogen increases breast cancer. It appears to me that it is the lack of progesterone, or a lack of balance between the two.

Recently, the Nurses' Health Study II, conducted at the Harvard School of Public Health, published its findings regarding folic acid and breast cancer. The study compared women with the lowest folic acid levels to women with the highest folic acid levels. Women with the highest folic acid levels had 89 percent less chance of breast cancer than women with low folic acid levels. Now "they" say folic acid "may make a difference," but we already know this about folic acid. The scientific reason is that folic acid inhibits the production of 4-hydroxyestrone, an aggressive type of estrogen that can mutate DNA and start the cancer process. In other words, folic acid helps in the prevention of breast cancer.

The women I see are not forced to come to me; they come from all over the world wanting cutting-edge information. They want to combine everything—mind, nutrients, and hormones—and work toward building a protective modality toward everything in their bodies.

SS: It's clear that there are changes in the wind, but it is very hard for women to find a doctor like you. Many gynecologists are prescribing hormones, and it is not their specialty. I am finding in my research that a standard approach for many gynecologists is to give a complaining menopausal woman antidepressants like Paxil or Prozac.

UR: Yes, and that will destroy their sex lives totally. The antidepressant takes away their anxiety resulting from lack of hormones, so they think they feel better and forget that they have a sex drive deficiency. They just feel flat, or as I say, they lose their vibration of living.

You see, women are superior to men from a health aspect: they live longer and survive longer. But for every man who takes an antidepressant, twenty women are taking it; for every man who takes antianxiety medication, twenty women are taking it; for every man who takes a sleeping pill, twenty women are taking it.

SS: Why is that?

UR: It is estrogen . . . too much or too little.

That's why finding balance is so important. The problem with doctors giving hormones is that for the most part they don't give hormones, they give drugs. Pharmaceutical companies take hormones and change them, and these changes form side effects.

Bioidentical hormones give such great benefits; you have the wisdom of aging, but balanced hormones allow you to run and fly with it.

I look at many people who are aging who have not addressed their hormonal selves, and they have turned monotonic; their behavior is old, uninspired, they don't want any challenges, they want everything to be repetitious, and they are more cynical. Hormones are the essence of living as long as we don't try to change them. We are not to play God with nature, and we must respect the physiological process. Hormone replacement is a tool to stay in the game.

SS: What is your hope for the future?

UR: That women will have the choices to decide what they want to do hormonally, then learn how to individualize them, and use them continuously to be able to run, grow, dream, hope, learn, and challenge themselves. Yes, women are confused, but confusion is good when they hear an orchestra of different opinions; if women hear just one opinion, that is depressing, like a black cloud or a tunnel without an end or light. I think the light is coming and more women are hearing about it.

SS: Thank you so much.

these really ARE THE sexy years!

Signs of menopause: You're on so much
estrogen that you take your Brownie troop
on a field trip to Chippendale's.

8
SEX

It seems unfair that finally we've reached a time in our lives when we have the time for sex but not the inclination. All those years when our heads were so cluttered with lists and the needs of the children: the dance lessons, the soccer practice, Little League games, cupcakes for the class on school birthdays, the parent–teacher meetings . . . then there were the business activities and the dinner parties, getting it right and all that that entails. Sex was always something that your husband was just going to have to wait for, because how can you be thinking about quality orgasms when you have so much to do and so little time? Wasn't getting into bed at night the first time in the day when you were able to think for yourself about what needed to be done, and now *he* wants to have sex? Did you do it because he needed it, with a "let's just get it over with" attitude so he could go to sleep so you could *finally have some time for yourself?*

Okay, you've done your job now. You've done it well. The kids have kids of their own. There are no more lessons or sports activities, the business dinners are not so important anymore. You have more time to spend with your husband. It's great, you can get dressed up, go out, enjoy stimulating, mature conversation, have a great dinner that someone else prepares, have a few drinks, go home, and make wild and crazy love. Is that what is happening? If not, let me tell you, it can and should be. This is the greatest time of your life. But here's the problem: If you are "not in the mood," or if there just isn't any desire, it's because you have zeroed out hormonally. That means testosterone, too. Yes, we women have testosterone. When we stop making this hormone along with estrogen and progesterone, it's like the gas in your car running out. Without the gas, the car won't go; it doesn't matter if you push it, jump-start it, or roll it down a hill, it needs gas to operate. That's how it works with us.

Now you may feel, So what, I don't care if I have sex anymore. . . . Believe me, it's only because you have forgotten how great it can be. It also might be that your partner has been less than charismatic in the romance department. It does take two. Or it might be that you have been having gratuitous sex for so long and acting like nothing more than a receptacle all these years so that you could "get it over with." Whatever bad habits have been established, you have the power and the information to change these habits—you just need the will to do so.

The first thing you have to do is deal with your hormones. You know how important it is to do so from reading the last chapters. Have your blood work tracked to see what your levels are relative to progesterone, estrogen, DHEA, and testosterone, especially the free testosterone levels. Free testosterone determines your sexual vigor (more about testosterone and free testosterone in the next chapter). Now here's the tricky part. Very few doctors understand what to do with these levels. If there isn't a good endocrinologist in your area whose specialty is natural bioidentical hormones, insist that your doctor lead you to the right professional. This might take some work, but it is so worth it. You need to figure out which hormones you are lacking, because when you are able to replenish the ones you are missing and get your hormonal system in balance, you will notice a dramatic change in how you feel about sex. You will actually want it! I promise you when you get this figured out, you're going to be thinking of ways to drag your guy into the bedroom.

Balancing your hormones will not only

make you want and enjoy sex more, it will also help keep your marriage intact. Have you noticed how many men leave their wives at middle age? Why is that? You're looking good, you're in good shape, the two of you are best friends. Why would he ever leave you? Remember, men also experience loss of hormones. Their testosterone levels are diminishing at the same time you are losing yours. Shouldn't that put you on an equal path? The answer is no. Never underestimate a man's need to be virile. Your husband's midlife is just as disconcerting to him as yours is to you. He is losing his ability to have an erection anytime he wants. Before, all he had to do was think about it, and bingo! There it is in all its mighty glory . . . erect and tall, ready for action. But now, maybe it doesn't last as long, and it's not as mighty as it once was, and sometimes it doesn't want to salute at all. You aren't the only one who should be getting your hormones checked out. It's also time for him to get to the endocrinologist and have his DHEA and testosterone levels checked. That's all it takes for him—the endocrinologist can prescribe a dosage of hormones tailored exactly to what he requires once he's checked his levels.

I'll tell you more about men and andropause (male menopause) and what they are going through in part 4, where you can find out exactly what your husband is experiencing as he gets older, physically, mentally, and sexually, and how balancing his hormones can take care of these challenges. What he has lost in the aging process can be restored that easily, although most men are too embarrassed to try to find out what is wrong. It's not their fault; it's just how our society has approached raising men. We have been telling our sons "not to cry" and "act like a man," telling them what men do and don't do, leaning on them to handle all those things that are not in our realm. So our men have assumed the mantle because that is what is expected of them.

Suddenly at middle age, they're not going to be able to reveal lack of vitality or something as vulnerable as sexual dysfunction. But I tell you again—we are going to live almost twice as long as our grandparents, and we have to deal with the second half differently. The scary part is that most men (did you hear me), *most men,* think the problem is you, that you don't turn him on anymore. And let's face it, you probably haven't been a real pistol in that area. So what do they do? To prove that they still have "lead in their pencils," they go out and find themselves the new, improved, younger version of you. That's why you see so many old guys with young wives and new babies. It is terribly sad for the families left behind. The children you raised together feel rejected, that they're no longer the "real" family, that the new babies in their father's lives are the preferred ones. It's a syndrome that is happening all around us, and it's avoidable if you can understand the part you are playing in this scenario.

Relationships require "work" that never stops as long as you are together. You must understand that all those nights when you "weren't in the mood," or went through the motions without putting any effort into the act, spelled the beginning of the end. Time after time of having thoughtless sex, of feelingless, emotionless sex, adds up. At some point both of you stop trying. Then it is reduced to an occasional "wham bam, thank you, ma'am." At some point he's going to look elsewhere, even if he doesn't want to. There will be some new "babe" in the office who sees him as her ticket to life. After all, your husband has spent a lifetime building his business or perfecting his job so that he's now well paid and respected. Young girls find that very attractive. Many young girls don't want to go through the rough times with a guy their age. They'd like to start at the point of success. They want to move into a big house without all the trials and tribulations. They also might be looking for someone more mature. Frankly, who could blame them?

I tell you, get your hormones together and then get to work. This is for you. Stop just "lying there." Get involved. Lose weight, buy some great underwear; plan some weekends at your favorite places. Pick out places conducive to lying around having great sex. Do the things to him that you know he loves, and then do them *really well*. He will love it. *Love it!* All men love to be taken care of sexually. Don't fake that you are enjoying yourself—get into it and you'll find that you will love it, too. After all, this is your man; this is the guy you've chosen to spend your life with; this is the father of your children. He's been with you through all of it. Think about those things while you are pleasing him. You will start to feel such deep love for him that giving him this pleasure will become something you both look forward to doing. If you feel awkward and don't know if you are using the right technique, and many of us don't, rent a video or watch those kinds of movies on cable. You can learn from watching them. Once you become comfortable and look forward to this being a regular part of sex for the two of you, be sure to have him show you exactly what he wants.

The wrong technique can be a turnoff.

Every man is different. Relearn what your guy likes. You used to know how to excite him, and believe me, you will get very turned on when you know you are in control because you are giving him the most intense pleasure. When he is so aroused you can feel that he is ready to explode, it is very exciting for you. It is this intensity that makes you want to do it again and again. When sex becomes like this, no one and nothing can come between the two of you.

Believe me, a man who is getting great sex at home, and I mean horny, involved sex, is not going to be attracted to anyone outside of you. No middle-aged man walks around saying, "Boy, would I love to have a few new babies in my life. Yes, sir, I really want to get back into diapers, nursery school, baby-sitters, PTA, and teacher conferences." The reason these middle-aged men are having babies is that it's part of the deal of getting all this new and horny sex. Don't allow your relationship to digress anywhere near to this state. Take charge of your life now. Surprise him. Maybe the first time it will be awkward, but tell him why you are interested in changing your sex life. Try to really talk about the fact that this part of your life has been ignored, but that you want to change things. The discomfort will dissipate quickly.

Tell him you love him and that it's his time now. Tell him that you're sorry you've spent so many years making him last in line in the family. Tell him that you want a different kind of marriage now. This is a new passage. Make sex dates. You can go out for a nice dinner at your favorite romantic restaurant, come home, fill the bathtub, and get in with him. Have fun, laugh, wash his back, and ask him to wash yours. It will work. But don't be discouraged if he doesn't respond the way you want him to the first, second, or third time. This will be new to him, and you have trained him all these years that sex was last on your list of favorite activities. Then make love to him as though today were the last day you would ever be together in your lives. Imagine that. If you knew this was the last time, how would you act?

Now, I say this: If you don't want to do this, if it's too much effort, if the idea of it is totally unappealing, then you have to examine what you really want. If it's not worth it to put this much effort into rejuvenating your relationship, then maybe this relationship is not what you want.

On the other hand, if this is where you want to go in your relationship—if what you want is to love and be loved, to feel secure and trusting, to have an easy communication, respect, openness, and great sex—then "give it a go," as they say in England.

Keep in mind that part of the deal in pleasing your partner in ways he's never or rarely experienced is that you are part of the equation. This isn't all about him. You have to tell him what it is sexually that you've wanted in your relationship together. Anyone who has gone to certain religious schools (I attended Catholic) was groomed in a way that led to a lot of sexual hang-ups. The word was that sex and physical intimacy were to be saved for marriage only, so all the natural thoughts you had about sex in your teen years were accompanied by enormous guilt. It was a sin even to think of it, let alone "do it." My religious upbringing required that you confess your "sins" every Saturday, and that would entail the humiliating aspect of explaining your "impure thoughts," or worse, confessing that you allowed a body part to be touched. It doesn't take long before every "impure thought" makes you sick with guilt and you will do just about anything to talk yourself out of finding any kind of enjoyment in any sexual act. Then voilà, you get married and you're supposed to be some kind of little sex pistol in bed. I was afraid even to open my eyes. I became pregnant in my teen years, having had sex only one time. It wasn't really even sex as I have come to know it. It doesn't matter, because the greatest joy and achievement of my life was bringing my son, Bruce, into this world. But my point is, how do you go from one extreme to another without having some residual hang-ups?

So now what's in it for you? We're talking sexually. What do you want? First of all, when your head is focused and "there," it doesn't matter what the two of you do together as long as you are both enjoying yourself. But your involvement has to be real. If you have been faking enjoyment all these years, you can no longer do so. What's the point? The object at this age is to realize that anything the two of you want to do together is good and beautiful. You have chosen to spend your entire lives together. You know how to please him outside of the usual positions; you know how to add the element of surprise and extra pleasure. But what about you? The missionary position can be great, but has he learned about pleasing you outside of the usual things you have been doing all these years?

Most women are too embarrassed to teach their mates exactly what to do. He has to be shown. Our bodies are mysteries to men in so many ways. There are caverns and folds, layer upon layer of erotic possibilities. Most women don't want to be "traffic cops," so they feel reluctant to tell their partner where to go and what to do; but good sex requires that you physically show him what you like. Once he knows what you love, sex will be unbelievably exciting to both of you. A man can't ever understand our bodies in the way we do. They have a different physical makeup, and as we need them to teach us, without embarrassment, what feels good to their bodies, we also need to teach them how to touch us, where to touch us, and with what intensity.

It takes time and willingness for both of you to learn what works for you. The good news is that this is one place where men have all the patience in the world. They want us to have great orgasms. It is much more intense and enjoyable for men when we are as turned on as they are—or even more so! He can't rely upon knowledge from other women he has been with because we all have different likes and dislikes. But don't rely solely upon him doing all the work. Looking and watching each other during sex also adds to the erotic quality of the experience. It is uncomfortable at first if you have been used to keeping your eyes closed (as I did in my early years), but it is one of those things that makes sex "hornier." If talking to your mate about sex is too awkward, try going to a sex therapist.

Why not do these things? We're talking

about getting the most out of life and enjoying the freedom and maturity that are the inherent gifts of coming to this age. What are you waiting for? You've earned the right to have all the pleasure your body can experience. You've already been the good mother, the perfect housewife, and gone to the top in your career. There is nothing left to prove. From this point on, anything you accomplish is something you do for yourself, not for outside approval. Everyone around you is already impressed with you as a person. You've done it well. But this is for you. Have you ever noticed that some women have a certain confidence about them, as if they have validation from within? These are the women who have already figured this out. They aren't worried that their husbands or partners will stray because they know they are both getting everything they want at home. It's beyond sex; it's comfort, security, love, laughter, intelligent conversation, shared ideas, family, grandchildren, great meals, and beautiful homes. Put all of this together and the two of you will be having such a great time as a couple that each of you becomes all the other needs. Anything and anyone from the outside is simply frosting.

This is all yours to live and own, but it requires a commitment and a willingness to shift your thinking. You've got to commit to this the same way you would commit to a weight loss program. I always ask my "Somersizers" to make a "shift in your thinking," meaning that it is time to understand that your old patterns of behavior are no longer serving you well. In other words, they're not working, and the only thing you can do to reverse the situation and put it back on track is decide to change. Change requires commitment. "Today I will begin the rest of my life anew." It's truly as simple as that. Decide that you want to change and then do whatever work is necessary to make it happen.

You are in complete and total charge of your life and happiness, and that includes your sexual happiness. Now that you know how important hormones are and what role they play in sexuality, you have no excuse for not getting your blood work done to find out what hormones are depleted. If you don't make it happen, then you have to accept your unhappiness as something you have created. To put the blame on another is useless and futile. You have to take responsibility for your sexual fulfillment. If you start every sentence with "He always . . ." or "He never . . ." or "He won't . . . ," then you are looking for excuses to fail. Who wins in that scenario? Believe me, and as my friend Barry always says: "The only person who knows what you want out of life is you, and no one will be sorrier than you if you don't get it. You've got to choose to fight for what you want, no matter how difficult or insurmountable it appears to be." So go out and get your hormones evaluated. Talk to your husband about your sexual needs. Work on being fun and flirty with him. Fight for your happiness. It's a noble fight. Wouldn't the world be a wonderful place if everyone in it were happy? Idealistic? Yes, but why not? It's up to each and every one of us to make our lives the best they can be. There is no better time and no better age than right now. You finally have all the tools. You have the wisdom. You have perspective. Now go get it!

Old is when . . . your partner says,
"Let's go upstairs and make love," and you
answer, "Pick one, I can't do both."

9
TESTOSTERONE:
SEX IN A CAPSULE

Recently the media has been focusing on the decreased sex drive in women. Without professing any understanding of the role balanced hormones play in our sex drive, the television reports are telling those of us of a certain age to get testosterone cream from our gynecologists. Without hesitation our doctors are prescribing this magic potion. Hooray! Finally, a solution! But hold on, not so fast. Doesn't it sound too good to be true? Could it really be that easy? It's not quite that simple, though testosterone cream does indeed stir things up and make you feel kind of "wiggly" down there.

How can applying testosterone as a cream or taking it in pill form help restore a flagging libido? As you know, testosterone is the hormone that affects sexual desire, and there must be a balanced ratio in our bodies among amounts of estrogen, progesterone, and testosterone. Testosterone is considered mostly the male hormone because it is responsible for masculine characteristics like facial hair and a deep voice, but it is also present in much smaller amounts in women. Like estrogen, testosterone is produced by the ovaries and adrenal glands and declines gradually throughout a woman's life. Testosterone is so central to a woman's sexual function that no lover and no amount of sexual stimulation can make up for its absence. Low testosterone in women creates widely varying symptoms. Some women never notice the difference, while others are devastated by a sudden or gradual decline in libido, especially those who have had a hysterectomy and both ovaries removed. Testosterone levels decline by about a third in perimenopausal women who have had both ovaries removed. Many doctors are reluctant to prescribe testosterone because it has masculinizing side effects like increased facial hair and a deepening of the voice. It can also cause weight gain and acne. More serious side effects associated with higher doses include an increase in cholesterol levels and the risk of liver and heart disease. That is why, if you feel taking testosterone will help your sex drive, it is essential that you be under the care of a good endocrinologist (or a doctor who has made natural bioidentical hormone replacement his or her specialty) who will give you only the amount your body needs through blood testing.

Before a doctor prescribes testosterone, he or she should test your blood levels for two values: total testosterone and free testosterone.

The normal range of total testosterone in a premenopausal woman is typically between 10 and 55 ng/dL.

A postmenopausal woman's normal levels are 7 to 40 ng/dL.

A woman with little muscle and body hair might have a level of 20 to 40 ng/dL.

A more muscular and hairy woman will probably have levels of 75 to 100 ng/dL.

The availability of testosterone in the body is governed directly by the presence of the sex hormone–binding globulin (SHBG). It is also governed indirectly by estrogen. A naturally high estrogen level, or estrogen replacement, translates to an increase in SHBG. That means more testosterone is bound up and the actual level of available (free) testosterone is reduced. For this reason, it is important to have your free testosterone levels checked as well. Every woman is different. Indicators say that .06

ng/dL of free testosterone is right in the mid-dle range and more than adequate for a nor-mal, healthy sex drive. But I have no sex drive at all if my free testosterone levels reach .06. You need to be attuned to your body's needs. Even though my levels register in the normal range, my body requires more. It is up to me to inform my doctor how I am feeling so that she can make adjustments.

Dr. Uzzi Reiss says that a good indicator for a starting dose of testosterone is the amount of body hair and musculature. He says to start low if you have comparatively little hair and muscle development, or if you have more than average hair and more ample muscle de-velopment but a testosterone level over 40 ng/dL. Have your doctor increase your dosage gradually. There is a direct dosage rela-tionship to benefits and side effects. The more you take, the more the potential benefits; but the more you take, the more potential side ef-fects also. Your body will tell you within two to six weeks if you are taking the right amount.

Too much testosterone can have an effect on your personality. People might think you have become aggressive and pushy. Pay atten-tion to your moods—if you are acting more aggressive than normal, maybe you are taking too much testosterone. Watch your body, too—if your skin becomes unnaturally oily, if you begin to have acne, if you start to grow too much facial hair or lose hair on your head, then you may be taking too much testosterone. Remember, too much or too little of any hormone creates imbalance and wreaks havoc with your system. You will not get hornier if you take too much testosterone—you will feel as wiggly as you did in your prime only when you are in complete balance. Balance is what we are after.

Testosterone comes in gel, cream, drops, inserted pellets, and capsule form. Some women experience adequate day-long benefits after taking testosterone once in the morning. Others may need it twice a day. My doctor usually starts me on 2.5 mg drops twice a day when my levels go down. Testosterone pellets can be inserted in the buttocks for a slow, steady time release, lasting four to six months, if you don't want to take pills.

Testosterone cream is available from compounding pharmacies (see Resources, pages 347–348). It is applied in a small amount to the clitoris and the inner labia to help improve sensation. It also helps build up thin atrophic genital tissue. The cream is highly effective in increasing sensation during sexual stimulation.

It's great for jump-starting things. You usually have to use it for a few days to a couple of weeks to get the feelings started. It's especially useful if your head has been full of all the things you need to get done, when the lists won't go away even though you try not to think about them. This cream puts you in the mood for love, and it really works. In addition, it's a wonderful lubricant, if that is an issue. As we get older and our hormones get out of balance, most of us experience some degree of dryness in the vaginal area. Testosterone cream helps greatly. Don't forget and think this testosterone is a magic cream, like whatever you put on your face at night to fight wrinkles. Your vaginal area will be moist again and your sex drive will return because you are balancing your hormones. The cream only jump-starts things. You need to be working on a larger plan to balance your hormones—testosterone is only part of the bigger picture discussed in the first part of the book.

Understand that it takes some time to achieve balanced hormones. After all, it took many years for your body to gradually lose its ability to make a full complement of hormones, so it will take a while to build these hormones back up to a full complement.

During this time, testosterone cream is a god-send. Even after you have achieved hormonal balance, testosterone cream is something you may use occasionally when stress is a factor in your life. Nothing kills your sex drive like stress. Stress blocks hormonal production; so even if you are on hormone replacement therapy, stress can knock your levels out of whack until your doctor readjusts your dosage to compensate or until things in your life calm down. Your blood work will be a good indicator, but the way you feel is your best indicator after you have started replacement. You are not bugging your doctor if you call to ask about reactions to any new dosage. Your doctor can help you only if you work with him or her.

So keep a bottle of testosterone cream around, but understand that the need to use it is indicative of a larger issue. Something else is at work here. Use the cream to get you through this period, but don't come to depend upon it. One reason, of course, is that your hormones are out of balance—otherwise, you wouldn't need the cream—and the second reason is that using testosterone cream regularly will make you fat! Hormonal imbalance leads to weight gain. If you are using testosterone but your other hormones are not in balance, weight gain will follow. Notice the women who are regular users. Think about it—a lot of them are overweight. Why? For one thing, when your hormones are out of balance, you can become insulin resistant. This means that your cells, which comprise protein, fat, and carbohydrates, are loaded with all the sugar (from carbohydrates and foods that the body accepts as sugar) that your cells can hold. At that point, *any* sugars you ingest will be stored as fat. The most important element to remember is that testosterone, which is a hormone, needs to work in *balance* with the rest of your hormonal system. If you are giving yourself unnecessary daily doses of the cream because you think it will make you even hornier (which it won't), you will end up with increased levels of testosterone, which will put your other hormones out of balance. Hormonal *imbalance* creates weight gain because an imbalance of hormones makes you insulin resistant. So use the cream when necessary, but don't rely upon it or you will have trouble down the road.

It is your job to be attuned to your body's needs. Remember, no one will ever care as much as you do about getting it right. This is all about your quality of life. But when you have it right, everyone in your sphere will benefit. You are then able to be your "best self" in every way. You will exude happiness, security, and an overall sense of well-being. It is infectious. People will want to be around you so that some of what you've got will rub off. And you know what? It will.

ADRENAL BURNOUT

If you find that you are taking testosterone supplements and your sex drive is still not revived, then it is time to have your adrenals checked. There is a new saliva test that will accurately report not only your minor hormone levels, which include testosterone, but also your major hormone levels, which include adrenal, cortisol, and insulin levels.

Often when the body is under extreme stress, the adrenal and cortisol levels dip or, worst case, flat-line. As you have read in previous chapters, the adrenals are your major hormones along with cortisol and insulin. Without your major hormones you will not live very long. If your adrenals are low or flat-lined it will blunt not only your estradiol and progesterone levels but also your testosterone levels. No matter how much testosterone you are taking, it will not have an effect as long as your adrenals are blown out. This is a dangerous situation for your body. The symptoms of burnt-out adrenals are difficulty in sleeping, headaches, allergies, dizziness, and lack of a sex drive. If this resonates with you and your are taking testosterone supplements and still have a low libido, most likely you have decimated your major hormones. Ask your doctor about taking the saliva test, because it will indicate whether you have blown out your adrenals.

Signs of menopause: You change your
underwear after every sneeze.

———

10

DR. LAURA BERMAN:
FEMALE SEX THERAPIST

I know they write songs about "doin' a-what comes naturally," but sometimes there are reasons other than instincts that interfere with a woman's abilities to have a healthy, enjoyable sex life. Dr. Laura Berman is a pioneer in helping women with sexual problems and their individual sexuality. I found talking with her not only revelatory but fascinating. She removes all discomfort and embarrassment from such a personal subject and allows us to explore those parts of our sex life that could be improved or maximized. Dr. Laura Berman has opened the Berman Center in Chicago to address the needs of those who desire counseling and help regarding the sexual part of their lives. She has also written a book with her sister, Dr. Jennifer Berman (see chapter 12), called For Women Only.

SS: Are women getting the optimum pleasure from their sexual relationship with either their spouse or their partner?

LB: We're working on it. In the beginning,

so many women came to me and repeated over and over that they did not feel sexy or in the mood. In my practice I started to see patterns after talking to hundreds of women about their sex lives and about what went wrong. One of the things we started to see early on is that women—more often after their second child, but sometimes even after their third child— were experiencing low libido; and certainly there are a lot of social and psychological reasons why they would have low libido.

New mothers with a second child had to adjust to having a new member of the family. Taking care of the twenty-four-hour need machines that babies are, coupled with exhaustion, meant that they were not making sex their priority. Not that they didn't want it, but they were just too tired. But then, even after all of that had passed and they had plenty of child care and plenty of support, they still weren't feeling desire and felt flat sexually— they had no fantasies, no thoughts, no motivation. When we tested their testosterone levels, we found that they were extremely low. These were otherwise young, healthy women. We couldn't know if their testosterone was always low, but we did note that after the second child there was a change. I don't know if it is ovarian failure or some sort of evolutionary strategy—perhaps after having a couple of children we are supposed to focus on the offspring we have before we start making others—but we do know that a risk factor in giving birth can be resultant low testosterone.

SS: What is the most common complaint?

LB: The most common complaint is stress and depression. Women don't realize that our bodies are under chronic stress because we tend to put our own needs and our own emotional and physical feelings at the bottom of the totem pole. We have to get everything done first. So a lot of the time we don't even notice that we are having the physical symptoms of stress, or we can't do anything about the situation that is creating the stress. Women are working too hard, or balancing too much, or are in a horrible situation, but the majority of women will tell you that they experience stress on a daily basis and can't really get a reprieve from it.

SS: So does this chronic stress affect their hormone production? Is that why they have low testosterone?

LB: Yes, and the best explanation I have been given is that we used to think that everybody under stress experienced the "fight or flight" syndrome. What they found from a study at UCLA is that women do not go into fight or flight; we go into what we call the "tend and befriend" phenomenon—we want to turn inward, we want to nurture, we want to focus on our friends and family. We want to cuddle, but we don't want to have sex. Now if you think about it from an evolutionary perspective, they talk about the fight-or-flight response in terms of the caveman who is fighting off the saber-toothed tiger. With "tend and befriend," the women would go into the back of the cave and protect their children while the man fought off the tiger.

SS: What happens when you have chronic stress?

LB: There is a rise in oxytocin levels, which is our chemical of attachment. It is what we release from our breast-feeding. As our oxytocin levels go up, it creates a chain reaction that decreases the amount of free testosterone we have in our bodies.

SS: So that stress indirectly affects our testosterone production as well.

LB: Yes, but when you are thinking about younger women, the reason for a sexual dropoff is more often related to childbirth or chronic stress and depression than anything else. Of course, there are all the other emotional and relationship reasons, the most obvious being that your relationship is stressful, or your relationship isn't what you thought it would be, or your partner has gotten lazy, or you have gotten lazy, or you are too busy with the kids and work and everything else, and sleep is better than sex. All of those excuses are very real, but what I think creates a cascade of low desire is that women lose themselves, very often starting in their thirties, and become outwardly focused. One of the great things about aging is that when our kids leave home, we can really start to define and refind ourselves, and we can reach a sense of centeredness that we don't have when we are younger. Most young women start focusing so much attention on their family, managing their home, managing their kids' forty different after-school activities, cleaning the house, and all the things that they have to do that they lose sight of themselves in the process. In losing sight of ourselves—assuming there aren't other physiological factors—we tend to lose sight of our sensuality, our sexuality, and our energy, and we don't really take care of ourselves. We've been hung on by our kids all day long, we are stressed out, we see our partner at the end of the day, or we have been working all day and struggling to make ends meet, come home, and the last thing we feel like doing is having sex. It feels like another chore.

SS: That's interesting, because I interviewed a group of young working mothers, middle to late thirties, and they did refer to sex as "the dirty little chore."

LB: Yes, that is what they see it as, another chore they have to do. And their partners pick up on that. I try to counsel women and couples that they need to understand that it becomes a self-fulfilling negative cycle. As women lose interest in sex, for very real reasons—they are overworked and overtired, or there may be a hormonal or another physiological reason—they forget that for men the number one vehicle by which they achieve a sense of intimacy and connection to their partner is through being sexual. What happens when men are not getting sex is that they just inadvertently feel less close to their partner and less intimate. Therefore, they act in a less intimate and less connected way, even unconsciously. They are not doing it on purpose, but they don't think about doing the little things that mean so much to the woman.

SS: And then I suppose she becomes resentful or angry that he is not as close to her.

LB: Right; and when he complains about not having sex, she says, "All you care about is sex, and now you are not going to be romantic with me unless I have sex with you." Then she blames him for thinking only about sex when in reality the reason he is thinking about sex is not only because he wants to be sexual, and because he has the desire, but because he also wants to be close to her.

SS: Then what happens?

LB: He feels less close to her, he is less connected, he is less intimate; and because women are in large part inspired to be sexual because they feel close to their partners, she then shuts down even more sexually, and it becomes a vicious circle.

SS: I am exhausted listening to the cycle. As you were explaining I wanted to say, "*Stop! Don't you see what's happening?*"

LB: Sex feels like the dirty little chore for two reasons: one, because the woman is exhausted and it starts to feel like one more thing she has to do; and two, because she doesn't have the emotional and romantic context in her relationship to experience it as something pleasurable and loving and connecting. I don't think it starts out as a dirty little chore; I think it becomes a dirty little chore when the relationship begins to break down.

SS: Do you think that this is all part of the superwoman's desire to be perfect in everything she does? That she has lost sight of what is important?

LB: Yes. The quintessential modern woman has a career, a family, a beautiful home, and all of the material possessions she wants. In her spare time she gives back to the community and joins committee forums or alliances or whatever it is that she is interested in doing.

SS: So where in the world is she? Where is her center? Where is her identity?

LB: Everything she is doing is outwardly focused either on how she is perceived by others or on giving back to the community or to her family. Even exercise and nutrition for herself are more often about wanting to maintain a certain appearance than on enhancing herself, loving her body, or caring for her body. It is an outward focus, not an inward one.

SS: In speaking with women, I discovered that children are now sleeping in their parents' bed way too long; they are ages three, four, five, six, and older and still in their parents' bed.

LB: Yes, that is a big issue. Where there is a will there is a way to get the child out of that bed, unless it is a family who has a serious intellectual or emotional commitment to the family bed and believes that children should sleep with their parents as they grow up. But in families who are miserable, suffering with the child still in their bed, I look at that couple and wonder what purpose this child is serving. Usually one or both of them are relieved that the child is still in the bed and use the fact that the child is there as a way to avoid intimacy and sexual connection.

SS: But what about putting locks on the doors and having rules?

LB: They say they worry they are not going to hear their child, or they worry there will be an emergency, or they worry that an older kid might try to get into the room and see that it is locked and, God forbid, know what they're doing. They don't understand that the biggest gift they can give to their children is being open about the fact that Mommy and Daddy have an intimate relationship that is separate from the kids, and that they deserve privacy, and that their privacy needs to be respected.

SS: Where do you see this group down the road?

LB: Well, I think these women run a risk. It can go in two directions. More often than not, as a woman starts to reach forty and fifty she goes through a life crisis. Maybe her husband is cheating on her. Or maybe it is a child getting sick, or the child leaving for college, or a friend getting sick. Sometimes it is the woman herself getting sick. But something happens that will be a reality check to her—most often it is going through perimenopause. She will start to reorient herself and begin to turn inward a bit more and start to take care of her emotional self and her soul. But the problem is that these women run the risk of losing their partners, because as they start to go into this next passage, if the relationship has already started to disintegrate, they run the risk not only of the marriage falling apart, but also of the husband being more vulnerable to opportunities for infidelity, even if he is not seeking them out.

SS: So because he is starved for that emotional and sexual connection, he is much more vulnerable to other women.

LB: Yes, and these women want to give the connection to him.

SS: So let's go to the next group of women, who are my age, in their middle fifties, and in menopause. So many I have talked with are experiencing a lack of sexual feeling and no clitoral feeling, as though they are dead from the waist down. How much of this are you seeing?

LB: A lot of women come in complaining about this, and part of the problem is testosterone.

SS: Are you talking free testosterone?

LB: Free testosterone and testosterone in general. We have found that there are androgen receptors and genital sensation. When women have low testosterone, one of the signs, of course, is low libido, but it goes hand in hand with low genital sensation, low energy, and a low general sense of well-being. So we did sensory testing and found that women with low testosterone also had sensory impairment when we did sensory testing on their genitals.

SS: What causes the impairment?

LB: We don't know. We think it is because there are androgen receptors in the genital tissue, but we don't know what role they play. Is it for sensation, or does testosterone play a role in the nerve receptors so that nerve receptors without testosterone become atrophied? Because even when you replace testosterone, the sensation doesn't always improve as much as you would like; so is it because the nerve receptors have atrophied too long and they can't be resurged or revitalized?

SS: Can they?

LB: We only have our own anecdotal clinical experiences, but we have found that for women with low genital sensation and low testosterone, replacing their testosterone sometimes improves their sensation. Topical testosterone on the genital area or some other blood enhancers also seem to improve the sensation. The theory is that the increased blood flow pushes the nerve receptors closer to the surface of the skin, which makes them feel sensation better. So that is where Viagra and some of the other vasodilators have a role.

SS: Is there one perfect hormonal cocktail for every woman?

LB: No, every woman is different, so every woman has to find her perfect balance with the help of her doctor. It requires that the patient and the doctor work together as never before. What is likely is that as women go into menopause, with the help of their doctor they will devise the appropriate hormonal cocktail, which will hopefully include testosterone. Then, as needed, they can augment that with other medications, whether it be Viagra, one of the new incarnations of Viagra that are coming on the market, or some of the other arousal-enhancing agents that are out there.

SS: But Viagra does not put you in the mood, does it?

LB: No, but it improves genital sensation for women. You always have to be careful with hormones. Too much is not good, nor is too little. Testosterone gel or cream does get minimally absorbed into the system.

SS: But there are signs from using too much—facial hair, pimples, oily skin?

LB: Yes, so you will know if you're using too much. But testosterone creams and gels are also good for genital pain. We alternate with estrogen cream and testosterone cream because testosterone helps to toughen up the tissue as well as increase the sensation. There are other things to help also, like AndroGel.

SS: Can you give a list of what's available? Women are so reluctant to talk about this, but I know they are going to love reading about it.

LB: A good place to go is my Web site,

www.BermanCenter.com. AndroGel is approved right now for men. It is a gel that is applied on a nonhairy part of their body. We use AndroGel as a last resort, if the woman is not responding well to oral testosterone or testosterone cream. But this medication is not dosed for women. It's not easy for us to use yet and is only available as an off-label prescription.

SS: Why are there no sexual medications for women?

LB: Until several years ago, women were not allowed to be included in any clinical trials.

SS: Why—are our genitals not as important?

LB: It's just the way it has been, but things are changing. Women are involved with the drug companies, so I believe in the next three to five years we are going to see a whole array of options that will enhance sexuality for women.

SS: Well, I hope so. Before I started to write this book, I always wondered why middle-aged men leave their middle-aged wives. It's not that they don't look great. I believe that as we go through the drastic changes of hormone loss, we behave badly because our chemicals are out of whack. We can't sleep, we're hot and then cold, we're tired all the time, we have strange itches, we break out in embarrassing sweats, we're bitchy, and we lose our sex drive.

So after a while a man is going to say, "Who needs this?" and go out and find the new, improved, younger version of you.

LB: Right, but it's not so much of "Who needs this?" as something more subtle. Even with the nicest guys, their sense of self-esteem, their virility, their sense of masculinity, and their sense of attractiveness are all deeply tied to the women they love. So when they feel rejected, over time they just get more and more resentful. The majority of times when men have an affair, it has very little to do with the sex.

When a man is not having sex with his loved partner, it's because he is not feeling intimately connected with her, or appreciated, or loved, or attractive, or wanted, or desirable, or powerful, or any of those things he needs to feel good about himself. So if his self-esteem starts to dwindle, and then when he is at work or with his friends an attractive woman starts treating him as someone who is attractive and virile and powerful and whatever else, a part of him starts to wake back up.

SS: If the last resort for women is AndroGel, is it possible to bring a woman back to sexual life, or once you lose it is it gone forever?

LB: No, it is not gone. We have huge successes. The best success comes from a combined approach of medical treatment and talk therapy.

SS: Like what?

LB: Imagine a scenario where I'm talking to a perimenopausal or menopausal woman, and for medical reasons she has lost interest in sex, and the negative cycle we have been talking about exists. This condition affects the woman's self-esteem also. It affects the way she feels about herself, her body, her partner, and her relationship. Maybe there has been a rift that has been building in the relationship. So talk therapy helps the couple even if it is just getting over the awkwardness of trying to reconnect sexually. Between medication and talk therapy I would say that we have an 80 percent success rate helping women who come to us complaining of low or no desire.

SS: Tell me about your clinic.

LB: I am starting a new clinic in Chicago, offering not only medical treatment, but therapy as well, which means evaluating the couple's psychosexual history so that we get a sense of the relationship and anything that could be contributing to the problem now and in the past.

SS: Do you see them as a couple?

LB: We see the woman first individually. We spend around forty-five minutes with her, then we see them as a couple for another twenty-five minutes. They can come back for more couple sessions if necessary; but meeting them together helps us see what is going on with the couple, especially the man. This kind of therapy helps get both partners on the same page, and it helps alleviate some of the self-blame and mutual blame that they are putting on each other. This center is not only going to have ongoing individual and couples therapy as needed, but we will also have group couples, educational seminars, and physical therapy, so that when women have pain or atrophy in their genitals, we will be able to offer physical therapy to help them. We are also giving Pilates and yoga classes for strengthening pelvic floor strength. Pelvic floor strength is central to women's sexual function and starts to decline as we have children and then continues to decline. But pelvic strength is central not only to the woman's pleasure, but to her partner's as well.

Yoga and Pilates also give women an opportunity, as I was talking about earlier, to reconnect with their bodies.

SS: Well, I hate to be commercial, but that is a great use for the ThighMaster. One of its big benefits is its ability to strengthen the pelvic muscles.

LB: You know, you're right. I think I will start giving them out at the clinic.

SS: Let me ask you, aren't people embarrassed to go to a sex therapist?

LB: Well, it is a huge step for a couple to admit that they need therapy, but you would be surprised how many men call and want to make appointments for their wives. And men are so relieved that there is help available, and that we are not going to be telling them that it is all in their heads. We say to them, "Let's find out what is going on, let's look at the whole woman and see all the factors that could be contributing to her problem: the medical factors, hormonal as well as blood flow, and anything else that might be contributing from her surgical history, her past history, or any medications that she is on." We also look at her earlier sexual development, any trauma history she may have had, the messages she got about sex when she was growing up, how she feels about her body, how she feels about herself, how she is able to advocate for her sexual needs, whether she understands her body and how it works, what is happening in the relationship, what the level of communication and intimacy is, what the level of romance is, and what the level of affection is, because that is the thing that starts to go when the sex goes—they are not affectionate with each other anymore, and there are hurt feelings that need to be dealt with. You see, we can pump a woman full of all the hormones she needs, but if she is not feeling safe with her partner or connected to her partner, she is not going to be successful in her sex life.

SS: I have to say, I never knew that a sex therapist existed until I read your book.

LB: I've been working very hard to educate physicians, in particular gynecologists, because they seem to be the ones who hear a woman say as she is walking out the door, "Oh, by the way, I haven't wanted to have sex for over a year." So part of my work is collaborating with the doctors to effectively deal with women with their physical issues as well. The perfect balance is to have a sex therapist and a medical practicioner who specializes in this, and that's not easy to find.

SS: Where do we go if this is what we are looking for?

LB: There's my sister's clinic at UCLA, Dr. Jennifer Berman. There's the clinic I am opening in Chicago, and here and there, there are some doctors who have sex therapists working with them. Not many, but they do exist.

SS: As I keep telling my readers, this passage takes handling. It is really up to each woman to find the help she needs even if it means she has to drive long distances or fly somewhere. It's crucial to her well-being, her longevity, and her happiness. If a woman isn't willing to find the care she needs for herself, then she is going to end up taking an antidepressant to deal with her sexual dysfunction.

LB: Right, and then with the antidepressant her sexuality isn't helped, but she doesn't care. Then the antidepressant makes her sexual dysfunction worse. I don't understand it—there have been studies that verify antidepressants do not help with PMS and menopausal symptoms.

SS: Yes, and it seems like prescribing a Band-Aid to me.

LB: Yes, it is a Band-Aid. When someone is suicidal or unable to function, then there's a role for antidepressants. But the problem is that the primary prescribers of antidepressants are now primary care physicians. They're not doing any extensive evaluation or providing ongoing therapy to get to the core of why the woman's depressed. They're just putting a Band-Aid on it. When women have sexual problems where there may be very real emotional or physical causes, I say okay, but antidepressants are not always the answer.

SS: What needs to change relative to medical training?

LB: There is very little education about how to talk to patients about sex and about sexual medicine in general.

SS: Yet what makes the world go round?

LB: I know, it's very, very sad. Doctors don't

get the education; plus our society is litigious, and because of this many doctors have told me that they are afraid to even ask a woman about her sexual function because she may think he is sexually harassing her, or she may think it's inappropriate.

SS: Are you able to work with other doctors regarding this?

LB: I have to find ways for them to indirectly open the doors so the patient can bring it up. But the other problem is managed care. A doctor has fifteen minutes to conduct the entire visit, so how can you open up that Pandora's box? Because even if it's a physical problem, and it's causing her tremendous distress, and it's the first and only time she has the courage to bring up that her husband is disconnected from her, and she's upset, and now she's crying—doctors don't want to open that up when they have twenty patients waiting.

SS: So what's the remedy?

LB: We have this course called "Women's Sexual Health, State of the Art Series." This year we had about three hundred people, mostly health care professionals, and our goal was to educate them about sexual medicine and how to get comfortable talking about sex, how to take a sex history, how to know whether a patient's a good candidate for medical intervention or better suited for therapy—

things they should be taught in medical school. I also encourage doctors to visit our Web site, because it is intended not only for laypeople, but for doctors and professionals, too. This is working very well for us because it gives doctors a place to sort of pawn it off and not have to deal with it.

SS: How long can a woman remain sexual?

LB: Forever. There's no reason a woman should not be able to remain sexual; plus, sex will keep her healthy. Sex is one of the major things that keep us connected to ourselves. A woman who has a happy, healthy sex life feels happier in general, feels more feminine, more attractive and aware and connected to her body, which will allow her to be more aware when things go wrong with her body. You can be physically intimate and physically connected and even orgasmic until you die. I have a patient who is ninety-three years old. About five or six years ago I mentioned something about masturbation, and she said, "Oh, I never do that!" And I said, "Why not?" Her husband had died when she was in her sixties, and she hadn't been with another man since. "Oh, I wouldn't even know what to do," she said. So I said, "All right, I'm going to send you some stuff." I sent her a tiny purple vibrator (her favorite color is purple), and I included some diagrams showing her how to use it. A few weeks later she said to me, "You know that thing you sent me? It was a little small, don't you think?" So I gave her a bigger one. A couple of months later, she mentioned that she had a second vacation home that she was going to and she asked if I could send one to her there also.

SS: So she's liking it, she's having fun. But for most people, buying a vibrator must be a very embarrassing thing. Where does one buy one?

LB: That's a good point. There are lots of options online. There's one site called www.grandopening.com and another one called www.goodvibes.com. Both of them are oriented toward women. Good Vibes, which is really Good Vibrations, is in San Francisco, and the cool thing is that they send orders in an unmarked package. It just says "Open Enterprises" or something. If you don't order from them for a couple of months, they drop you from their mailing list. The top site right now is www.drugstore.com.

SS: What role can a vibrator play?

LB: It plays more of a role than people imagine. As we start to age, sex gets harder for women, and they think of it as some sort of failure, as do men. My job is to ask or encourage them to include a vibrator in their sex life. It can be very beneficial. There's a whole range of vibrators that are very small. Some can actually fit between people and can be incorporated into sex, or a woman can have her clitoris stimulated to get things going, and those women who complain of feeling numb are able to jump-start their sexual feelings with clitoral stimulation from a vibrator. Even with testosterone cream or capsules or some of these other vasodilators or blood flow–enhancing agents, a vibrator can also help. Sometimes we need more sensation and more stimulation than when we were younger.

SS: So do you give a prescription for a vibrator?

LB: I do. When I am with a woman, we go over everything that's gone wrong and everything that's working and not working. Then I divide the treatment plan, which includes Kegels. But along with the other treatments, I will write down what vibrator I think would work for her, and what books and videos.

SS: Which videos and which books?

LB: There's a range. It depends upon what her issues are. If it's that her partner doesn't know how to stimulate her, and she doesn't quite know how to tell him, then we talk about books on sexual technique. If she feels sort of awkward because she was a virgin when she got married and doesn't really know how to pump things up, I may introduce her to books and videos on erotic massage or on spicing up her love life or things like that. If she's never tried self-stimulation, I might introduce her to a standard plug-in vibrator. If she can have an orgasm on her own but needs extra clitoral stimulation and can't have it during intercourse, then I recommed a smaller vibrator. There are different brands.

SS: Is there a G-spot?

LB: I certainly think so. There's a lot of controversy about what the G-spot actually is.

SS: It's on the inside wall directly behind the clitoris, isn't it?

LB: Yes, and many believe that the two are intricately connected. Many people don't realize it, but the clitoris goes up 10 cm inside. It branches out to where the pubic bone is located. So it actually has two arms that go way back inside the body. It's not only that external button you see. Often the G-spot is where the Skene's glands are in a woman, which is analogous to the prostate gland in the man.

SS: So are there vaginal orgasms as well?

LB: Definitely. Most women will report that vaginal orgasms are much more intense. They include pelvic floor and uterine contractions, and they feel much deeper than a clitoral orgasm. But what I tell people is that an orgasm is an orgasm is an orgasm. It doesn't matter. The majority of women do not reach G-spot orgasm. But I think Kegel strength has a lot to do with it.

SS: What part does a religious upbringing play in all of this?

LB: Religious interpretation is so often sex-negative, that sex is bad. A lot of women (and men) have been raised in an environment where their religious leaders told them they had to wait to be married before they had sex. This communicated that sex was wrong, or bad, or dirty. Masturbation was wrong, as was anything that could lead to a sexual energy or motivation because it might make you want to have sex before marriage. So these women have grown up with all these negative messages about touching themselves, about sexual pleasure, and about exploring sexuality, even with themselves. Then it's expected that on their wedding night they are just going to turn on a light switch and become a sexual being. Those messages, which basically have been the entire nature of their sexual development, are really difficult to turn off.

SS: What about childhood abuse? And I don't mean just sexual abuse.

LB: Anything that interferes with our development—our sense of being in control, our pride in our bodies, our pride in our accomplishments—or anything that interferes with the development of positive self-esteem and our ability to trust and make ourselves vulnerable can negatively impact our sexual lives. So if there is emotional abuse, physical abuse, sexual abuse of any sort, it will interfere with a child's sense of self, self-esteem, and body image and her sense of control and sexual development. Without that sense of self, she doesn't have the ability to enjoy sex and respond sexually.

SS: Do you think sex should be taught?

LB: Absolutely. I create sex education programs, not only for kids, but for parents, too, to teach them how to raise their children to be sexually healthy. In reality, sex education starts at birth, just with touch and sensuality. There are so many things you can do for your children: massaging your babies and helping them develop a sense of sensory awareness by encouraging them throughout their lives; praising them and encouraging them to have a sense of pride and joy in their bodies; allowing and not repressing their desire to explore themselves sexually; not slapping their hands and telling them that masturbation is bad. You may need to guide them to where it's okay to masturbate. You know, if you have company, then it's a good time to tell them, "I know it feels good, and it's fine to do, but it's really something you do in private."

SS: Where would you like to see people's

attitudes about sexual therapists, about women and sexuality, go?

LB: I think women need a stronger sense of entitlement so that they feel they deserve a sexual response. It's worth seeking answers for. It has to be okay to seek help. In fact, seeking help has to become a good thing. Women have to realize they deserve to enjoy sex, and it doesn't mean you are a harlot or that something is wrong with you. It has to be okay to admit that sexual enjoyment is missing from your life and you want to do something about it. In the beginning when we first started this treatment, women would be cringing when they came in: "I can't believe I'm coming to a doctor's office about this." They were embarrassed that they were placing so much importance on their sexuality that they were actually seeing a specialist about it. But I'm starting to see a shift. Women are coming in now and saying, "You know what? There's help available and I'm going to take advantage of it." I would like to see more and more women feeling entitled to their sexual response and acknowledging that sexual response is a basic part of their general health and wellness. They have to stick to their guns when their doctors shuffle them around, or when somebody tells them that this is all in their head, or that this is not a big deal. I would like to see women hold on to themselves and find themselves. In order to do that, you need to keep yourself grounded against all the other pressures. Women have to be motivated and proactive right now, but in the future I'd like to see it come to a place where women don't have to be so intensely tenacious and motivated in order to get help.

SS: I guess at this moment it is necessary for women to be highly motivated. Motivation can save a marriage.

LB: Right.

SS: I believe the work you are doing will save marriages and families.

LB: I believe that it already has. It's very rewarding. If this center proves successful, we plan to open more in other major cities. But right now women have to be proactive—they have to do research, fight with their doctors, and keep asking the same questions again and again and again.

SS: This has been very enlightening. I always thought that sexual dysfunction was the domain of menopausal women. I had no idea how pervasive it is. But this generation is an amazing group of women. We were the women who came into our young adulthood in the sixties, the baby boomers. We are the first generation who wanted better communication than our parents had—we went to therapy, and we got to the bottom of the things that tried to keep us from being all that we could be. And now we've hit a new wall: a lack of understanding about menopause and its ramifications and effects. But the sky is still blue and hopeful because there are professionals like you to guide us and help us through.

LB: And I love what I do.

Perks of being over forty: In a hostage situation you are likely to be released first.

11
KAREN: A FORTY-YEAR-OLD EXPERIENCE

I wanted to talk with younger women, those still considering the possibility of having more children, those for whom menopause is a long, long way down the road, who are burned out because of the "superwoman" complex. They understandably want it all, but it appears there is a price. To be the perfect wife, the perfect mother, the supersuccessful businesswoman, to have the perfect house, give the perfect dinner parties, volunteer at school, bake cookies for the bake sale, give the perfect business presentations, and on top of all this be a sex pistol in the sack with her husband at the end of the day is exhausting, to say the least. There is not enough time in the day, month, or year to be all of the above. As a result, it seems thirty- and forty-year-old superwomen are exhausted. It is taking its toll physically and hormonally. Remember that hormone production is blunted by stress. The superwoman's life is so stressful that at the end of the day there is little to no energy left for sex. I suspect a good night's sleep is the most desirable item on the agenda.

Karen's story appears to be typical of what is going on in this age group with women who are superachievers. The surprising information is that the drive and the desire for sex are blunted by exhaustion and the resultant low testosterone and low estrogen that stem from the stress of this overactive lifestyle. Add to that the lists that occupy the superwoman's mind and it is understandable that something will have gotten off track. Of course, reprioritizing is essential, but in most cases that is not going to happen. What if hormone replacement could be the magic pill to get these women through this stressful and difficult time? This is Karen's story. I was exalted and exhausted after I finished speaking with her. She is bright and intelligent and has so much going for her, but the quality of her life is impaired by her body's physical inability to keep up, and it is working against her.

I am thirty-nine years old; by the time this book is published I will be forty. I had never given hormones much thought. Like most women, hormones were a mystery to be dealt with down the line—it was all about menopause, which didn't concern me and did not appear to be a particularly pleasant passage, so I thought it was better not to think about it until I had to.

The first time hormones became a living, breathing factor in my life was during pregnancy and nursing. It was the first time I realized that I was not in control of my body. It was as though I had lost part of my brain. I've always been so good at math; when out with my girlfriends, I was always the one who could instantly figure the bill, who owed what, factoring in that this one had to fly down so she shouldn't have to pay as much. This would take my brain an instant to decipher. But while pregnant, I couldn't remember a phone number. It was the first time I realized the powerful influence hormones had on my life.

When I was pregnant, I had an acute sense of smell. If my husband ate garlic, I had a difficult time sleeping with him. The smell nauseated me, made me really sick to my stomach. It was only in retrospect that I was able to put it all together, that it was hormonal and that the hormones were in control of my body.

Then there was the weight gain that hung around as a new layer, like another whole me, after the baby and throughout the entire four years that I nursed both my children. When I was going through it, I just presumed it was environmental, but as soon as I stopped nursing, everything came back into balance.

My personality changed during pregnancy also. I became very quiet. My husband would constantly ask if anything was wrong, but I just wasn't aware until looking back on it how inward I had become. It wasn't until afterward that I would think to myself, Ohhh, that's what it was. Once again, another awareness of hormones and that they were not just the concern of menopausal women.

There were the physical changes also. After four years of nursing, my breasts flattened out. In fact, my four-year-old started saying, "Mommy, your boobies look like socks." That was pretty depressing, but after about six months they puffed up again. Hmmm, another hormonal change; my hormonal balance was on a roller coaster. I was beginning to realize that hormones were in charge of me physically, mentally, and emotionally.

I experienced a severe drop in my sex drive. I had a hormone panel done by my doctor to find out that my lack of libido was due to a complete absence of testosterone. Frankly, I was relieved. I had been so distraught at my lack of desire, and now I knew it was physiological. My husband would come to me, but it was as though I were looking through a window. I wanted to have those feelings, but they just didn't seem attainable.

All of this is so difficult for me. I am a perfectionist—I want to be the best wife and create the best home for my family; I want to be the best cook and make crafts by hand; I want to be the best mother and prepare pure food for my children and make sure they feel loved and nurtured. When it comes to work, I am very task oriented. I can get it all done. Next! Bring it on! I love the challenge of watching the business we started grow into something so exciting and successful.

Around this same time, my husband and I spent two years remodeling our home while living out of boxes in a rental in which we had no interest. It was temporary, and we put our lives on hold while building our dream house.

The stress of remodeling, being the perfect mother, starting a new business, running to school with cupcakes for the class (homemade and decorated, of course), and giving the perfect dinner parties was taking its toll. Something didn't feel right. Never did I factor in that I was out of whack hormonally. I just assumed the anxiety was a normal part of everyday existence.

One day I went to the doctor (I have a great cutting-edge doctor), who did another hormone panel on me and thought there must have been some mistake because my adrenals were so high. "With numbers this high you must be a crazy person—you must be bouncing off the walls," he said. "I know it must feel great to be able to race through your day and accomplish so much, but it's going to catch up with you and you are headed for a big crash."

It was a wake-up call, but one I didn't take all that seriously. I had a strange sense of pride that I could do it all. . . . But could I?

One evening my husband asked me for something, and I just blew up at him. It was irrational and emotional, and afterward I felt so bad because I love him so much. I felt terribly guilty that my need for perfection did not leave time for me to be the perfect wife for him. I mean, after my typical frenzied day, how am I supposed to jump in the sack and be the perfect lover? Something's got to give, and it was here that it was caving in.

My husband is very understanding. I don't have the same complaints I hear from my other girlfriends. My husband does pitch in. He shares responsibility for the children, he cleans up after dinner, and he is there for me whenever I need something. I began to think, How long will he wait for me to come around? My husband is the picture of health—he is an athlete, so he is in peak physical condition, and on top of that he is a hunk. How long can my excuses of being overworked and overtired and having too much on my mind remain viable? It makes me feel so sad. I don't know how to fix it. I know it's physiological, but for some reason I can't seem to accept the fact that I have to make some changes. I know I have to get my health on track, I know my hormones are out of whack, yet it's hard to make the connection that I might need hormone replacement in my life at this time. Somehow I feel as though I've failed if I have to supplement my hormones at this early age.

This scenario is no different from those of any of my girlfriends. They are all complaining that at the end of their busy, frenzied, hectic, overachieving days the last thing they feel like doing is having sex. One girlfriend refers to it as "the dirty little chore," like taking out the garbage. In fact, just yesterday she talked about how she "had to take out the garbage last night, ha ha ha." Twice a week she lets him have his way with her, to get it over with so that she can finally get some rest.

We're all working too much, we all have too much stress and anxiety, and we all have low libido. My sister said to me recently, "It's the ones who make their whole lives about their children who end up alone with their children." I don't want that, but I can see how easily it can happen. I feel so guilty. I know I am not meeting the needs of my mate.

I make feeble attempts to fix it. I went back to my doctor, and he gave me testosterone cream, but it made my skin rough and my face break out. I thought, Well, how sexy are pimples, so I stopped using it. My doctor said that obviously the dosage was wrong, but for some reason I didn't pursue getting the right dosage.

I know that I am not eating great. I grab food on the run during the day and take a bite here and a bite there. I know psychologically I am doing it because I can stay really thin this way. Being thin seems to be overly important, but when you are thin you look as though everything in your life is going right. I guess I want the outward appearance of my life to look perfect. Thinness does that.

Lately I have started to pad up a little bit. Not a lot, just five pounds, but it has me nervous. How can I be gaining weight when I haven't changed my eating? I'm sure at the bottom of it is some other hormonal change. Deep in my heart I feel that that little perimenopause is peeking its head out of the ground. I know I am not taking care of myself, and my excuse is that I don't have time. I have started exercising a little, and at the same time I am putting on a little weight. I can't figure out the connection between the two. I can just feel that my body is beginning to betray me.

I need to go to a spa. I need to go away with my husband so that we can just love each other and take care of each other. My husband is so great. He will do anything to get me in the mood. He'll give me a massage, he'll tell me I am so hot. He just loves me and my body. He thinks I am so juicy and great. But I find there just aren't enough hours in the day. It's so important for me to please everybody. I get depressed when I think I am slipping. I feel guilty when my husband and I go out for the evening, but I also feel guilty if we don't go out for a date. If the kids start acting out, then I feel that I am letting them down also.

Work can overtake my life. I could work 24/7 if I didn't have kids. I had my children later in life. I was in my mid-thirties, and the toll on me mentally and emotionally is exhausting. I look at other women who are in their late forties with children my age, and I think, How do they do it? It is a harder job the older you get. There is only so much energy. It puts the body through so much.

When my husband and I do make time for sex, it's so great. It creates a connection between us that lasts throughout the next day. It's the little looks we give each other—that knowing of the intimacy we shared. I want that with my husband, always. But life gets in the way; the stresses begin again, my mind gets full of noise, my anxiety increases, and then my hormone production goes wacky again. I am beginning to understand the connection.

I think it's classic with women my age. We have so much to prove, and we want to have it all. It's the superwoman complex, but it is taking its toll on our health and our relationships. I realize that my own self-maintenance is not high on my list. I know I need to get back to my doctor, but this time I am going to follow his program. He has been offering it to me, but I have been too busy to hear. It's a big commitment. I have to make some serious changes in my life to protect all that I value. I don't know why I am not at the top of my list. I don't know what drives me. It's such a cliché, but we all need to clone ourselves. The other day was so classic me. I had to go to a mother-daughter tea at two o'clock, and at one-thirty I was at a boutique hurriedly buying an outfit. I pulled it off, and I looked rather nice, but when I looked down at my feet in my new open-toed shoes, my toes were in bad need of a pedicure. I wanted to curl those things into my shoes, because now all I could see were my feet, which were in such need of some tender loving care. Instead of giving myself credit for getting to the tea at all with my schedule, I obsessed about my toes. That's my perfectionism driving me again.

I get depressed because it's all too much. I am aware that the stress is damaging me physically. I know I am not there for my beautiful husband. It's as though I am watching him go somewhere, and I'm not on that train with him. I have to get back on that pace with him. I don't want to end up this old haggard wife with the hot husband. My marriage and my relationship with my husband are so important. I have to start making us a priority. I am going back to my doctor. I'm gonna do it this time. I'm hearing myself talk, and it's clear to me that I am the problem. It's me, and it's my hormones. I need my doctor to help me get my life back on track. It's a lot of work, but if I don't do it and something happens to me, this whole thing I've worked so hard to create will crumble. What good is the perfect house, with the perfect children, and the fabulous business, without the stuff of life: contentment, relaxation, fun? I have forgotten about fun. I'm so busy being perfect that I have forgotten that life is to be enjoyed and to have fun.

I have to work on the addiction of work. I am addicted to adrenaline. I love being busy; I am stimulated when I have a hundred things going at once, but at what price?

If ever anything were to happen to my marriage, I would look back and remember when it started. The bitchy times, the short-tempered times, those "fly off the handle" moments. These are the destructive things that break down the best of things. I used to look at my sister and think, What's wrong with you? She was such a perfectionist. Now I've become her. I have to work at this.

I hope my story helps women in the same position. I never realized how serious this whole scenario had become until I started talking about it. We have to help one another. It will take a shift in my thinking, a reevaluation of my priorities, a realistic look at what I want and how can I have it all without sacrificing that which means the most to me. I want to get my life back on track. We women are mirrors for one another. Maybe by seeing my "chicken with her head cut off" existence, someone else will realize how crazy it all is. To think, it all might start coming together with a dose of testosterone.

KAREN: A FOLLOW-UP

I'm happy to report that before this book went to print I spoke with Karen again. She called to let me know that she really had made getting well a priority in her life. She went back to her doctor and had a full hormone panel run. Not only was she practically zeroed out on testosterone, but her estrogen was at half the level it should be for her age, and her progesterone was also low.

Her doctor prescribed natural bioidentical hormones in the form of creams. She's been on a low dose for the last three months and has this to report.

I can't tell you the difference this has made in my life. Within a couple of weeks I could see and feel the difference. Those extra few pounds I had started to carry began melting off. Finally, my body was responding when I was eating right and exercising. There is such frustration when you're doing what you're supposed to be doing and you're still not getting results. The hormones did the trick. But perhaps the greatest improvement is my mood! I am better able to handle the normal everyday stressors that come my way. My temper is much better and I don't sweat the small stuff. Before getting my hormones balanced, you could have told me all day, "Don't worry about it!" but my feelings were real and could not be discounted.

My husband and I started seeing a counselor just to protect what we have created. We made some headway, but once I started the hormones, we ran out of things to discuss! Our sex life has also improved. It's not yet back to full speed, but I've even initiated it a couple of times! My doctor told me that he has a therapist who sends patients his way from time to time. Once he balances their hormones, they usually stop the therapy! That's how powerful our hormones are to our everyday lives.

Thank you, Suzanne, from the bottom of my heart, for encouraging me to seek out these answers for myself. I have such a leg up on the next passage that will come my way. I plan to stay balanced and follow your lead. I love my cream! It's my happy cream, and I can't thank you enough for helping me to see that taking care of myself is the best way to take care of my husband, my children, and even my business. With much love, from a not-quite-cured perfectionist, but at least a much happier one!

Perks of being over forty:
Your investment in health insurance is finally
beginning to pay off.

12

DR. JENNIFER BERMAN: FEMALE SEXUAL DYSFUNCTION

Dr. Jennifer Berman is one of the few female urologists in the United States with specialized training in female urology and female sexual dysfunction. Sexual dysfunction is an embarrassing and uncomfortable condition, and there are very few places a woman can go to find answers. Dr. Berman provides a great service in a comfortable and safe environment. She has also written a book with her sister, Dr. Laura Berman (see chapter 10), called For Women Only.

At some point, most women will experience some sort of sexual dysfunction, usually because of hormonal imbalance, but until recently it has never been given any importance because women are still able to function even if they don't feel anything. I asked her, "What percentage of women in this country are unfulfilled sexually, and why?"

JB: I guess that would really depend upon what range you are talking about, but overall anywhere between 30 to 50 percent of

American women have complained of sexual dysfunction at some time in their lives.

SS: What are the reasons?

JB: The reasons are multifaceted and can range from emotional, relational, and psychological issues all the way to hormonal, medical, and surgical.

SS: What are the most common complaints?

JB: The most common complaint that women relate to their sexual dysfunction is low desire. Again, the reasons for that can be medical and/or physical, but often it is a combination of the two. Even if the original problem is physical, emotional and relational problems can result. And vice versa. If a women comes in because her relationship is in crisis and she is not satisfied with her marriage, frequently we will find that there is also a hormonal problem or some medication that she is on or has been on in her medical history.

SS: What is the average age of your patients?

JB: The average age of the women I see in my practice is forty-five, so they are perimenopausal; but I also see older women and menopausal women. Problems begin around the age of forty-five, but some women will start to notice changes about themselves in their late thirties and early forties. My mission is to inform and educate women about the potential changes that can happen so they can be in tune with their bodies.

SS: How does a woman know when she is in menopause? A lot of the same symptoms are present when a woman experiences PMS or perhaps is just having a bad day.

JB: Very often, women will start to experience changes in their hormones, whether it's irritability, or not sleeping as well, or that their memory is not quite what it used to be. They may experience vaginal dryness, low libido, lack of sexual response, and a lack of feeling in the genital area.

Most often, the problems are due to subtle, if not dramatic, changes in hormones, but I cannot say 100 percent that is the reason all women experience problems. There can be other emotional relationship factors; and a woman will say, "I feel tired, I feel like I have low desire, I feel like I don't respond very well." Yet when she is on vacation in the Caribbean without the kids, just she and her husband, everything is fine. For her problem to be defined as hormonal, it has to cross through all situations and be persistent and pervasive.

SS: Is stress a major factor?

JB: Stress is a major factor affecting women and their sexual lives and, for that matter, their emotional and physical lives also. Stress affects hormones. Stress in women can lower testosterone levels and cause libido problems and sleep problems. But sexual problems can also be caused by surgeries that result in nerve damage, such as in a tubal ligation. There is very little data in the medical literature to support this theory, but women would tell me that after they had their tubal ligation, they noticed their libido and their orgasms changed. I am not saying there is any science to support this, but we are definitely hearing this repeatedly from women.

SS: Are women experiencing lack of libido only in the case of tubal ligations, or would other surgeries cause the same thing?

JB: Any pelvic surgeries that impact blood flow and nerve supply to the genital area can affect a woman's sexual drive, including hysterectomy, removal of the uterus and/or ovaries, bladder surgery, or colon surgery.

SS: That is frightening. I've never given a thought to the fact that any type of pelvic or uterine surgery would have an impact on my sex drive.

JB: Many doctors still do not understand the dangers inherent to nerve and blood flow to the genital area during an episiotomy, which is a "taken for granted" procedure in childbirth.

There are now different philosophies on the benefit of this procedure. Is it better to have a natural tear, or is it better to have a surgical straight tear? An episiotomy incision can definitely cause pain problems that will affect women throughout their lives. They come in and need revisions of their episiotomy scars or other surgical repairs, so it is important for women to know that these procedures can cause pain and nerve damage down the road.

SS: Did you start out wanting to specialize in women's sexual dysfunction?

JB: Yes, but when I first started my practice I thought sexual problems would primarily be the domain of aging and menopausal women. Now that I am immersed in this field, I am finding that younger women are experiencing sexual problems as well, and it is most often due to hormones. Even very young women in their twenties who are on birth control pills will and can experience libido problems and vaginal dryness, and they have no idea what is wrong with them. They go to their doctors and are told it's all in their heads. The birth control pills alter their hormones, and this is where the difficulty occurs.

Often in their mid- to late thirties, women experience testosterone deficiency syndrome, especially after having babies. It happens sometimes after the first baby, but more often after the second baby. Women will come in and say, "Life is great—I've got health, the kids are in school—but I still have this loss of desire and a dramatic change in feeling sexual. It just does not make sense that it is all because I am stressed and tired." In testing, I have found that they do in fact have low testosterone levels and do respond to testosterone. Some young women also have changes in their estrogen levels, so we now realize that after a first or second child, a woman's testosterone levels can drop so much that they need testosterone re-placement forever. There is also a drop in progesterone levels, but that is temporary. There are dramatic fluctuations in a woman's hormones after delivery. But then, in theory, you are supposed to come back to normal and reequilibrate. Now, granted, normally estrogen and progesterone come back, and women do begin to menstruate again and start having normal regular periods and get pregnant again, but testosterone does not return in all women.

SS: How does a woman find out?

JB: I test through blood work. This is defi-nitely not "one dose fits all." Some women do better with topical creams, some with oral sub-lingual delivery, and some with a gel. Each woman absorbs differently and responds differ-ently. Right now, unfortunately, there is not an

FDA-approved treatment plan or delivery system for testosterone in women.

Research is still ongoing, but doctors are now prescribing testosterone off-label and compounding. But one thing to bear in mind is that each compounding pharmacy is different. Doctors need to analyze which ones are better and which compounds work better.

SS: Most women would not think to go to a urologist for sexual problems. The natural choice would be their gynecologists.

JB: The doctors who have the greatest grasp on hormones are endocrinologists or reproductive endocrinologists. As a urologist, I had to learn about it myself. I went to meetings, I read, I talked to everybody, listened to everyone's opinion. I read the medical literature, I read the package inserts, I tried different ones and came up with what I felt comfortable doing. But there is no consensus on what every woman needs, nor, for that matter, should there be, because every woman is different and every woman metabolizes hormones differently and everyone responds to hormones differently.

SS: So you're saying that women have to seek out the right doctor for themselves, and that doctor has to be a self-starter and interested in the newest thinking relative to sexuality and hormones?

JB: Absolutely. When it comes to the correct doctor, women have to be on the prowl, because unfortunately, sexual dysfunction and hormones are not given much attention in medical school. Hormones are very complex. There is a lot to understanding them. You treat full-blown menopause one way, but women in perimenopause—say, in their forties, who are still getting a period and still have some estrogen levels—have to be treated differently, and this brings up a whole other issue. When do we start? Do you start when you are already there and having hot flashes, or is it better to start it earlier?

SS: No wonder women are so confused.

JB: Right, but women have to take charge of their bodies. Maybe they are trying but are not getting answers from their doctors. Women need to feel entitled and valued, to feel that their sexual health is important and that sexual dysfunction is not normal.

SS: So what do we do? Is there Viagra for women?

JB: There is no female Viagra at the moment. They are developing it, but in reality it will be the same for women as it is for men, just packaged differently. Viagra doesn't put you in the mood; but if you are in the mood, it works great. In women it induces warmth, tingling, and a pleasant feeling in the genital area. Women have reported that it does make it easier for them to have an orgasm and improves the intensity of orgasm, but it is not a libido pill. When I prescribe Viagra for a woman, I tell her that it requires stimulation either with themselves or with their partner. It takes thirty to forty-five minutes to work, and during that time, it's important to force stimulation through foreplay, kissing, or whatever it is that they do.

SS: Is Viagra the only way for a woman to jump-start her sexuality while she is working at getting her hormones balanced?

JB: There is also a device called Eros–CTD developed by a company with the intention of improving genital blood flow. It is basically a sucking vibrator, so it's an erotic aid as well as a physical stimulator, the premise being that if you can improve genital blood flow, you can improve sexual pleasure. The same principle applies to women as to men: Use it or lose it. The more sexually active men are, the more blood flows to the penis, and the fewer vascular changes and fibrosis that occur. It's the same for women. It begs the question, do you need an Eros or can you just have a healthy sexual life and/or vibrator to achieve the same effect? The Eros works best if you use it every day. I don't sell the machine in my office, but the erotica shops have done the $30 knockoff. Eros is made by a company called UroMetrics. But most women are uncomfortable with the idea of buying a device, so I have found that giving permission and a prescription to buy a vibrator has been very liberating. But if this does not help, medications and exams are crucial to be sure that damage has not been done to the blood flow to the area.

SS: Does intensity of feeling change as you age?

JB: As you get older, orgasms diminish in intensity, but this is hormone related. It is crucial to get blood levels to rectify this matter. Some women are able to have multiple orgasms, and others cannot. I don't have an anatomic or medical explanation of why this is so. But in theory all women have the capacity to learn to have multiple orgasms and also to ejaculate.

SS: Is it simply "doing what comes naturally"?

JB: Unfortunately, there is no school to teach sexual technique. It is very important for women to know what pleases them and how to stimulate themselves and what they like and what they don't like in order to communicate that to a partner. Men intrinsically don't know what to do. They learn from the women they have been with, but it is up to us to know what feels good and what doesn't and to communicate that.

Doctors can do only so much, so often doctors ignore women's sexual complaints for a variety of reasons. Perhaps it is because their education in medical school was lacking in that regard, or they are uncomfortable talking about these issues, or perhaps they don't have a treatment for it. Doctors like to be able to fix and treat problems. Unless they have a treatment or a solution in hand, they don't want to go there.

I do feel that doctors who use antidepressants as a remedy are doing so basically to shut the woman up. But then the woman's sexual dysfunction gets worse and she gains weight and then (usually) thyroid problems arise.

SS: What else is out there to help with sexual dysfunction?

JB: There is an herbal remedy called yohimbine, which has been out for a long time for men with erection problems, and it's just recently been looked at as a potential remedy for women. A lot of women have had some success with that. There is also a product called Xcite that has three herbs in it. I was approached to help design a placebo control

study, and the study found that it was really effective. Since then I have prescribed it to a lot
of different women, including my mother,
who has breast cancer and doesn't want to take
hormones. She said that for the first time in
twenty-five years, she's having regular sexual
dreams, she's having orgasms in her dreams,
she's lubricated, and everything else.

SS: So what's in the future? Is there light at
the end of the tunnel?

JB: Hopefully, the future will bring height-
ened awareness relative to sexual dysfunction.
Women need to become aware of these problems and demand they get the care they deserve. This generation of women is different
from my mother's and her mother's. They
don't just sit back and take it and say, "This is
what happens when you get old, so you'd better get used to it." I think there will be some
sort of grassroots movement of women forcing
the health care field and health care professionals to address these problems, to research
these issues, and to develop appropriate therapies, both hormonal and nonhormonal.
Women need to be proactive about their
health, especially their sexual health, because
it's not likely that their doctor is going to say,
"By the way, how are you doing in that respect?"

SS: This has been very enlightening. Thank you so much.

JB: Thank you for doing this. A book like yours is going to help women through their confusion.

Perks of being over forty:
You quit trying to hold in your stomach,
no matter who walks in.

13

PATRICIA: A FIFTY-YEAR-OLD EXPERIENCE

Patricia is experiencing menopause and is not taking hormones. She did not want to take synthetic hormones because she has read of the problems that accompany taking these drugs. She would like to take natural hormones, but she is not able to afford them. Because your average gynecologist is not well versed in hormones, there is a lot of guessing going on in doctors' offices. When a menopausal woman comes in visit after visit, complaining about the symptoms, the doctor doesn't know what to do. Patricia's doctor prescribed what has now become a commonplace and accepted remedy. Instead of replacing the lost hormones with natural bioidentical hormones as determined by blood work, her doctor put her on an antidepressant. This is a Band-Aid that temporarily makes the woman feel better because her mood is elevated and the symptoms are more tolerable; but because the hormones are not being replaced, she is experiencing hormonal imbalance, which is accompanied by considerable weight gain. Patricia is a small person by nature, and the weight that is part of this passage is very depressing for her. In addition, the antidepressant she is taking brings with it a lack of zest and lethargy that is part and parcel of the strong drug. The combination of her lack of hormones and the effects of this drug is not making for an enjoyable passage. Her story is one of the more common for the average woman.

I am fifty-one years old as of next week. I am in menopause, but I am not taking hormones. I take isoflavones and phytoestrogens every day. They help a lot with the hot flashes. I also use progesterone cream to help me get through this difficult time. It's a cruel time of life. I mean, you are dealing with the empty nest syndrome, and then all these changes start happening to your body. When I entered menopause, I felt the whole thing was very unfair, but now I am getting used to it. I first realized something was changing when my periods became irregular. Coupled with that, I started experiencing a lot of anxiety—I had a racing heart and palpitations. I was really frightened that I was having a heart attack. It was an irrational fear, but I was feeling irrational pretty much all the time. The hot flashes were awful. I couldn't sleep because of them, and I felt depressed and very tired. Then I started gaining weight, and that was very distressing. Weight can really make you feel awful. On top of all this, I lost all interest in sex. The vaginal dryness made sex painful even if I had wanted it. I didn't want to complain because I had been avoiding sex for so long, but there was nothing I could do but yell, "Ouch!" I missed the closeness together. I worked all day, and I wanted to be with my husband in the evening, but with my moodiness, depression, vaginal dryness, and lack of interest in sex, I was not the most pleasant person to be around.

To make matters worse, my husband is also going through something neither of us understands. He's depressed about the empty nest, he doesn't like his job anymore, and he's tired all the time. His doctor recently put him on an antipsychotic drug. Between the two of us, it's pretty sad. What's difficult is that we really love each other. We are committed to sharing our lives together, but I want a better quality of life. When he's on the antipsychotic, he might as well not be home. He's just not "there." Maybe it has to do with low testosterone, I don't know—our HMOs do not pay for psychological or any kind of hormonal panel to be done, so we just guess at it and anesthetize the depression with prescription drugs.

I keep asking myself, Why does it have to be

this way at this time in our lives? We've raised our kids—why do we have to put up with this crap now? This is a very hard time to get through together.

I am interested in natural hormones (real hormones), and I visited a pharmacist at a compounding pharmacy in my area, and he was wonderful. He sat with me for a full hour and explained about real hormones. My HMO will not pay for an endocrinologist, so I went to my gynecologist, and he put me on an antidepressant, Paxil, so I could handle the symptoms better. Believe me, I feel a lot better on the antidepressant, but I also feel angry that I am denied access to real hormones because I can't afford them.

I am still gaining weight. My body is so foreign to me at this time. I miss being thin. I still feel healthy and strong, but now my thyroid is acting up, so my doctor put me on thyroid medicine. At first I tried kelp because I had read about it, but I had a bad reaction, so I resigned myself to taking the thyroid drug. Add to this the absentmindedness and the joint pain, and some days I want to scream. I take Premarin vaginal cream, and that seems to help with the other uncomfortable symptoms, so I'm doing the best that I can.

I've been in menopause for a year and a half.

Things are better now than they were—they would have to be, given how horrible menopause was when it first started—I can't say this is the best time for me. I want all of this to be over. I want my old life back: the zest, the fun.

There are some good things about this time also. I feel the empowerment of this age. I went out and bought myself a new car. It may not seem like a big thing, but it was for me. I bought it with my own money, and I handled the entire transaction by myself. My husband usually does things like that, but I needed to do this on my own. I am no longer tied to my children. I see them, we are close, but I don't need to chart out each and every moment of their day any longer. I know there is an energy about this age, and if we women could harness it, I know it would be very potent. It's just that the hormones make it very confusing. At times my mind goes completely blank.

I've taken the attitude that I will get through this. One of the things about us baby boomers is that we are helped by one another. We will be very useful to our daughters and grand-daughters. I want to be open with my daughters, and I want to tell them that everything is going to be okay. I want to share my knowledge, but this passage is a tough one. I hope they will have it figured out by the time they are going through this. It upsets lives, it upsets the balance, and it forces a change upon you that I wish would go away, but it won't, so we just have to get through it.

Perks of being over forty:
Your eyes won't get much worse.

14

ATHENA: A SIXTY-YEAR-OLD EXPERIENCE

Athena is a dear friend of mine. She has chosen not to take hormones of any kind, but because she is conscious of and proactive about her health, she is having an easier time of it than some of the other women who have gone the same route. She is happy and upbeat all the time. Hormones are a personal choice, and here is how she is coping with this passage. I ask you to decide for yourself if her way is the direction you would choose. She is enjoying a quality life, but she is experiencing symptoms. We talked on the phone, and here is her take on life at this age.

Actually, I'm fifty-nine, but who's counting? Fifty-nine, sixty—it's all great. Besides, what choice do you have? I love sex. I have always loved sex; and even at my busiest, sex was never my problem. It was always my destressor. So I guess I have been blessed with a healthy libido. I never thought it was unusual; it was just the way it was. I never had a problem with orgasms; in fact, I am the queen of multiple orgasms. My body has always been a willing participant. I used to hear women saying that lubrication was a problem. Well, it had never been a problem for me, but now it's a problem. In fact, I keep yelling when I am with my boyfriend of seventeen years, "My pussy is broken!" You get older, things change. . . . not my sexual desire, just my body's willingness to take part the way it used to.

I have chosen not to take hormones for two key reasons. One, I am generally a naturalist. My instinct is to let nature take its course. I realize at this age things are changing, but because I have enjoyed a great sex life thus far, I don't want to interfere. I understand that we are living longer and all that, but it doesn't feel right to me to try to alter things.

A few years ago, when I was fifty, I did try natural hormones: DHEA, estrogen, and progesterone. I hadn't yet stopped my period, but I was going to a "new thinking" kind of doctor who was of the mind-set that taking hormones was preventative, and I wouldn't have to entertain any of the nasty effects of menopause. I was on these natural hormones for a year and a half (my doctor never ordered a blood test), but it activated a regrowth of my fibroid tumors, which is why I had originally contacted this doctor in the first place. So now I have a mistrust of tampering with nature.

Second, I realize my decision is a trade-off. I know the great good feelings that come with balanced hormones, in particular the well-being that comes with natural hormones, but I don't want to have a period. It's just not a price I am willing to pay.

I am now in menopause. It came late for me, when I was fifty-eight, and my body is experiencing it, that's for sure. But the most upsetting aspect for me is lubrication. The well has run dry. I once was like Bahrain, an oil-rich country, but now I have to use vaginal lubricants, and I'm not crazy about this part.

I experience night sweats on a semiregular basis, but it doesn't drive me up a wall. I haven't lost my breasts as some women do, because I never had any. When God was passing out breasts, I was in the cafeteria eating lasagna. I do exercise. I have been going to an exercise class three times a week for ten years now. So my muscle tone is good, my weight is good, and my energy is good. I take very good care of myself, and I think this is the payoff. I'm in a good mood most of the time; in fact, I would say my mood is wonderful.

I started my period early in life, when I was

twelve years old, and I went into menopause late. I think this has been an advantage. In total I have had more than my share of estrogen— according to my doctors, more than most women—but on the negative side I think this also explains my fibroid situation, which has plagued me. Because of this wealth of estrogen, I don't really relate to most women's complaints. I have had good fortune, but I have also been extremely proactive about my health all my life. I believe fully in the mind-body connection, so I also take very good care of my thoughts. I have always kept a good attitude, I do spiritual work by reading books that inspire me to be a better person, and I have wonderful friends. I am loving my life.

Do I feel fifty-nine? Yeah, I have muscle aches I never had before, and there is that vaginal lubrication situation, but I still love sex with my boyfriend. It's just a little more difficult at point of entry. My gynecologist has prescribed some kind of Pennzoil for the pussy, some kind of vaginal cream, and it's actually pretty good. Let me put it this way: I travel with it. I pack my toothbrush, my pajamas, and my v-cream.

As far as other symptoms, I think I may be a little more jittery and nervous. I have to watch that jumpiness because I just found out I have high blood pressure. I don't like that.

I have always slept well, like a baby, and now I find I get up at least once in the night to pee, but I go right back to sleep. It's a blessing to sleep soundly; in fact, it's a marvelous experience. I'm feeling really good, especially since my doctor had forecast that I was going to have an awful menopause because I was so estrogen rich. I'm glad to say he was wrong, although this is only my first year.

I think it's genetic. My mother did not have a traumatic menopause. She's eighty-nine and still full of energy. According to her, it occurred with no fanfare. It just wasn't a big deal.

When you reach this age, it's hard to know if it's just natural aging or hormonal deficiencies. Now, if I had lost my sexual feelings, as so many women report, I would probably rethink it with someone like Dr. Schwarzbein. You see, I spent years having heavy (and I mean heavy) periods. I had an arsenal of Kotex pads. Tampax couldn't hold the river that flowed from me each month. My periods had been a whole piece of my life, and it was burdensome. So that's why it's difficult for me to entertain the idea of starting up again with the whole period thing.

My skin is drier now, I am using a lot more moisturizing cream on all parts of my body, especially my arms and legs, but I'm not irritable, so it's an okay trade-off.

I am very sensitive to anything artificial. I am careful as to what I put in my body. I don't take over-the-counter drugs if I don't have to, and prescribed drugs are often difficult on my system. When I was on hormones, I got fatter and bloated, and I hated the feeling. I have been blessed with a healthy body, and I value that. I listen to my body and am vigilant about listening to the inner talk. I have friends who take sleeping pills and Prozac, and I wouldn't be interested in anything like that.

My big problem is constipation, but it's been that way since I was thirty years old. I know it's strictly from stress, but I have recently found an interesting acupuncturist/herbalist who is a naturalist, so now we are working on my "inner landscape" through herbs. I am taking enzymes along with the herbs, which help to absorb all the nutrients.

I am distressed about my high blood pressure. I think it's from my stock market losses, even though I am told it's genetic; but nonetheless I am on drugs, and I am not happy about that. I take beta-blockers, atenolol and Norvasc, for blood pressure, and a diuretic, hydrochlorothiazide. My bone density is still good; I mean, there is some loss, but not an alarming amount. I take a potassium enzyme for my bones, along with magnesium, potassium complex, vitamin C, something called Digest, and protease, which cleans the body of plaque.

I am paying attention to the high blood pressure because my dad had it, and so does my sister. It's impossible to discern how our earlier years affected us. I grew up in a very upset household. My father was a frustrated, angry man. He was yelling all the time; so today, when things go wrong, I have this feeling that the sky is falling. I have relearned; I have tried to accept the flaws and then fix them. I am into biofeedback as a result. I realize I can change my inner terrain, as well as help my body retrain itself to be calm. I am learning not to sweat the small stuff. My boyfriend has quiet confidence. He is a calm person, and he has been so good for me in so many ways. Over the years we have grown in intimacy. We are great companions, and we are very loving.

I believe women need to participate in their wellness at all levels. This passage takes managing, and those who do manage it have a better quality of life. If your life is not working, do something about it. I have an ex-mother-in-law who has hated her marriage all her life. She just can't stand being in the same house with her husband. And guess what? Her back is riddled with pain. But she is driven by "what would people say?" Also, she's of a generation of women who didn't drive, so there is no independence. I think that is why so many women my age are managing their pain with Prozac—they'll take anything to deaden the pain.

I'd like to say to women my age that we are in charge of our lives. I believe we have the power within us to alter our thinking, our outlook, and our habits. I also know that what we eat or drink has everything to do with our bodies and our wellness. We are far more in charge of our lives than we suspect. No matter how out of control or hopeless your life may seem, it is not out of reach for anyone to become increasingly happy and healthy.

At fifty-nine, I'm not only flying high, but I'm getting ready to fly higher. I have made a list of goals for the coming year. My business coach told me to write it down. My goal for this year is to become a sensational sixty! You cannot wait for other people to give you your kudos. You've got to say it yourself, kind of a verbal high five. Stop saying those things you constantly say to yourself on a daily basis—you know, the I can'ts. Start acknowledging the good things of each day, even if it's "I made a great poached egg this morning," and then say, "Atta girl."

PART III

LIFE
on your
own terms

Perks of being over forty: You can sing
along with the elevator music.

———

15
QUALITY OF LIFE

Now that you are beginning to understand the importance of balancing your hormones for your physical health, let's look at the emotional and psychological benefits, too. When you are balanced, you are better equipped to take an honest look at your life and determine if you are living your life on your terms. This is the last chance to make changes. These can be tough issues to tackle. When your hormones are out of whack, taking on emotional issues can be devastating. We all know that the PMS-y time of the month is no time to deal with those things that have been on your mind and bothering you. Being chemically altered by PMS clouds your thinking and judgment. There is a tendency to overreact emotionally. Factor in hormone imbalance and life problems as we get older, and forget it. You will get emotional and never be able to make your point because your reaction will be so over the top.

But you are entering the second half of your
life, and I mean the second half. Do you want
fifty more years of the same? Are you happy
with the choices you've made for yourself? Are
you in good health? If not, what are you going
to do about it? You have a whole life ahead of
you. You're not "too old." If life hasn't brought
you all that you've wanted, this is your opportunity to make changes. This is your chance to
reinvent yourself. I've had to do this several
times in my personal and professional life.

I remember the most blatant "opportunity"
came after being fired from *Three's Company,* a
television show I starred in during the 1970s.
My five-year contract was up, and I went in to
renegotiate (which is customary in the industry) and asked to be paid what they were paying the popular men on television. For
instance, Alan Alda, who was starring on
*M*A*S*H,* which was number ten in the rat-
ings, was earning eight times more than I was.
My show was number one, so I figured that
my demands were not unreasonable. Little did
I know that the network had decided to make
an example of the next actress who asked for a
pay raise, so that other women wouldn't get
the same idea that they could be paid the same
as men. Suddenly I went from starring on the
number one show in the country to being un-

employed and persona non grata in the television industry. I was labeled "trouble," so no one wanted to work with me. I became depressed and wasted my days flogging myself for having been stupid enough to ask for such a pay increase. I moped and felt sorry for myself for the better part of the year until one day a little voice inside my head said, *Why are you focusing on what you don't have? Why don't you focus on what it is you have?*

Suddenly I had an awakening. What I had was enormous visibility; everyone in the country knew my name. That was valuable. What could I do with that? That's when I decided to become multidimensional. I took my well-known name and put together a nightclub act. I worked night and day learning to dance, sing, and work on material. I tried out the act for the first time in Denver, and it was pretty dismal. The reviews were devastating. One reviewer said, "Then she sang 'I Don't Know Why,' and I still don't know why." But I had bookings at other places, so I was unable to give up. It didn't take long, though, before the reviews were filled with "charming" and "refreshing" and "engaging." I had reinvented myself as a nightclub performer. I stayed on the road for most of the 1980s.

That's when I started writing books. I had

nothing to do during my days because I worked at night, so I decided it was finally time to explore the effects of living my entire childhood with my violent, abusive, alcoholic father. As I wrote I was amazed at what I remembered: the sounds, the smells, the weather, what we ate, what we wore. I remembered my mother's anguished cries; I remembered the fear I felt at the anticipation of the coming night's events. Who would be "it" tonight? Who was going to be the object of his rage? I remembered hoping it wouldn't be me, then the guilt I felt when it was my mother or my brother or my sister. I worked on the book every day for a year. One day I came to the end of the story. I had done it. I was now a writer. I had reinvented myself again. Now I had two careers.

The book, *Keeping Secrets,* came out and was a nationwide best-seller. My secrets divulged were no longer a source of pain and shame for me; rather, they became a connecting force with the people of this nation. I wasn't alone with my secrets, as I had always thought. I now knew that others had lived similar lives because my book prompted them to write to me and share their own secrets. Most of the letters started with "You've written my life story." So many letters came into our office that we could have filled a small room from floor to ceiling. As a result, offers for lectures came pouring in.

"I can't speak before people," I told my husband.

He booked me anyway. "I know you, you'll figure it out," he said.

My first lecture was dismal. I came equipped with fifty or so notecards, and people were literally falling asleep. I had been afraid to speak extemporaneously, so I relied heavily upon my notes, lost my place several times, and in general was pretty awful.

"I never want to do this again," I said to my husband, feeling humiliated.

"Well, we've already got three bookings that are not cancelable; so you'll have to do these, and then I won't take any more bookings," he said.

I was overwhelmed with fear. I didn't want to bomb again. Then the little voice inside my head spoke to me once more: *The notes didn't serve you well. Why don't you just tell the truth and speak from your heart?* After all, I had lived this story—why couldn't I just tell it as it happened? I had nothing to lose. It couldn't be any worse than this last experience.

Wow! What a difference. The audience was rapt. They listened to every word, and I received a standing ovation. That's when I realized that the truth is mesmerizing. You can't fail when you are telling the truth. There's no way you can get tripped up. Now I had a third career. The offers for lectures came pouring in.

In 1986 I was named Female Entertainer of the Year in Las Vegas along with Frank Sinatra, the Male Entertainer of the Year. I felt pretty good about that. I had reinvented myself. One night my husband and I were coming home from one of my shows in Las Vegas, and I found myself imagining our lives down the road, twenty or thirty years or so. It was clear that singing, dancing, and entertaining night after night was going to be an exhausting way to make a living if it continued to be full-time.

I said to Alan, my husband and manager, "We have to find a way to make a living where I don't have to show up."

"You mean passive income?" he asked.

"Whatever."

Shortly after that he found the ThighMaster, which went on to become one of the highest-grossing fitness products in America. Passive income and a new career. I began to be introduced on talk shows as a "fitness guru." Once again, I was reinvented. Now I had four careers.

As we reach this incredible transition from the first part of our lives to the second half, it's important to truly examine our patterns of behavior and our ability to grow and adapt to change. Are you in the right frame of mind to be open to new experiences, to challenge how you did things in the past, and to look for ways to improve your life? If not, you are wasting your second chance. Look at people around you and see them continue to create the same cycles over and over again. They aren't reinventing, they are re-creating and not realizing that they are in a rut that isn't working. For example, look at a marriage that may have grown old (as I call it when both parties stop paying attention); divorce is not always the answer. So many people leave one partner and marry the exact same person again. It's important to truly look at reality. Ask yourself, What would I ideally like to have in a partner? Perhaps you need to find a completely different type of person—someone who shares your sensibilities, someone who lives your rhythms, someone who likes to do the same things you do. It's sad, but there is no crime in having grown apart over the years. But first you have to see the part you are playing in this drama called your life. Maybe what needs changing is not your partner, but you.

As I am out and about on the lecture circuit, I often speak to large groups of people about the effects of addictions on the family. I cannot tell you how many times, after one of my lectures, a woman will come up to me and tell me that she has married three alcoholics in a row. She's just had "bad luck in choosing husbands," she usually tells me. But what these women really need to do is understand their patterns of behavior. A different person has more than different hair color and size. The big question is *why* she keeps choosing the same person over and over. It's because this type of person is familiar. She knows who to be and how to be with this type of person.

If I hadn't had the good fortune to find myself in intense therapy in my early twenties, I'm sure I, too, would have married alcoholic after alcoholic. Why? Because I was raised by a violent alcoholic! Being with an alcoholic was familiar and, in its sick way, comfortable. As a child I became codependent before I had ever even heard of the word. Codependency is living someone else's life and not your own. I was owned by my father's moods. If he was happy, I was happy; if he was upset, I was upset. Everything revolved around his moods in our family. The family is as strong as its weakest link. The first question I would ask my mother each morning was "What mood is Daddy in today?" It had nothing to do with my feelings; I needed to know what I needed to do that day to be able to adapt to him.

And adaptable I became. I knew that I liked him during the first couple of hours of his drinking each evening. That's when he thought I was cute and smart and funny. I became his court jester during this period. It's also when I began my life as a "pleaser." I would do anything to keep him happy. What I never understood was that I was not in charge of him. Inevitably, each evening he would pass into the next phase of drunkenness. This was when he got "the means and the hates." He was frightening during this phase. I knew not to say anything to make him volatile. I would readjust my personality to be someone who would fit into his miserable and ugly mood. I would work like a dog around the house. I would polish and clean so he couldn't call me a "lazy asshole." I would make sure he didn't run out of beer. He didn't like it when his can of beer was empty. I figured if I could just keep his beer can from running empty, he might forget about his beloved whiskey chasers. Whiskey made him mean and violent. That was usually when one of us would get hurt, or worse. So many nights the police had to come to our house; so many nights we had to take one of us to the hospital emergency room.

Today this would be called spousal abuse or child abuse; but at that time my father was always able to lie and cajole, convincing the officers that things just "got a little out of hand, ha, ha, ha." They would leave, and then we would experience incredible violence. It was an utterly sad and powerless experience for all of us. I was already too "sick" to understand that the figurative tap dancing we all did trying to please him would not and could not change the outcome of events. Each night was a pattern of the prior night. Hiding the whiskey would just enrage him. If we hadn't been so emotionally controlled by him, we might have realized that the choices he was making for himself were his. And he owned those choices. If he wanted to drink himself to death, that was his choice. I look back and see it was inevitable that beer would never be strong enough to numb the feelings he was trying to push away—that it was merely his "gateway" potion to what he really wanted each night. Inevitably and always, the time would come when he retreated to his whiskey bottle. That was when I knew I had lost the battle for the evening. Now fortified with enough whiskey, he would go after one of us. We never knew who it would be, and we never knew when it was coming. The anticipation was terrifying. I would pray it wouldn't be me, and then I was filled with shame and guilt when it was someone else in the family.

Do you see what was happening to me? I was a little girl with no sense of any right to my own feelings. I had no sense that I had any right to have joy or happiness on my own terms. I could only experience the feelings he was experiencing. As I said, if he was happy, I was happy; if he was upset, I was upset.

Now, you ask, what does this have to do with the subject of this book, which is examining the thrills of aging and making this phase the best your life has ever been? Does it not make sense that if I had not had the opportunity to be "found" in therapy in my early twenties, my patterns of behavior learned from earliest childhood would have seriously affected the choices I made later on as an adult? It is so important to work to undo damage that has been done to you in your life, whether it is caused by poor choices you have made or by circumstances in your life that have created behavioral patterns that do not serve you well.

So when a person comes up to me after a lecture and tells me, "I have married three alcoholics in my life; I guess I'm just unlucky with husbands," I think to myself, You have to go back and find the source of your behavioral patterns. If you have reached this stage of life and have not done this, now is the time. If you haven't been able to put your finger on happiness by this time in your life, then surely something in your past is holding you back. Don't be afraid. Freeing yourself of the shadows of life allows you to be open and receptive to all the good things that want to come your way but have never been able to "get inside" because you have emotional blockages. Going back and correcting the things that need fixing in your emotional self is a gift you give yourself.

Until recently, the general consensus was that women raised the children, dabbled in a career or two, and by the time they reached their mid-fifties it was pretty much over. Today it is quite the contrary. Now, at middle age we have a full half of life left. Thank God we all burned our bras in our twenties to fight for equality and were the first generation that wanted to have relationships that were not like those of our parents. We wanted more and we got it. We wanted to have a real relationship with our kids and husbands. We didn't want to be afraid of our husbands as our mothers were. We wanted our kids to be able to discuss what they were going through without fear. We wanted our kids to know that they were safe with their secrets and that we would help them through the painful times without judgment. We also were the first generation of mothers who had to cope with children using drugs and the sadness and powerlessness of the situation. But we did it and we learned. Through our children, many of us found ourselves in therapy, which became life changing. As with all addictions, those who make it out seem to emerge better and stronger. We learned and adapted, but we have come to another passage. We know our greatest lessons are learned from the dark times in our lives.

Now we are faced with a new challenge. We have half a life left. We have a little money, some even have their houses paid for, our children are raised, and many of us have our darling grandchildren. We are figuring out the hormone mystery. We have cleared every obstacle out of the way, and now we are ready. But for what? To have the most glorious time of our lives! We also have something else, the greatest gift: wisdom. At this time in our lives, we can continue to learn and grow with the advantage of wisdom and make the second half the best that life has ever been.

It takes courage to self-examine. Socrates said, "The unexamined life is not worth living." I have lived my adult life like that. I have chosen to really look at the truth about myself. I don't like what I see sometimes. Sometimes I have to admit things to myself about myself that make me feel ashamed or embarrassed or guilty or remorseful. But to allow myself to know the truth about who I believe I am gives me the tools to change. As I confront these feelings, it becomes painfully clear that I do not want to be owned by any negative choices I have either consciously or subconsciously made. This forces me to start changing myself, and I believe this has been the key to my happiness. Later in this book, I talk more about the importance of reinventing yourself. I have forced myself to do this several times, and because I wasn't afraid to try new things, I have been able to realize incredible dreams for myself after age fifty. These new dreams are based upon recognizing exactly what it is that I now want out of life.

Anyone can do this—it just requires being honest with yourself. So let me ask you once again. You have reached the halfway point. Do you want more of the same, which may already be good; or, if it is not, are you going to take charge of your life and change those things that are not working? It's your life.

As my friend Barry Manilow says: "I believe we are who we choose to be. Nobody is going to come and save you. You've got to save yourself. Nobody is going to give you anything. You've got to go out and fight for it. Nobody knows what you want except you; and nobody will be as sorry as you if you don't get it, so don't give up on your dreams."

Perks of being over forty: No one expects you to run into a burning building.

16
WISDOM

There are clichés about women being competitive with one another, and I think this is true when we are younger because we are full of insecurities and aren't able to take comfort in our relationships with other women. I recall such angst being in the company of mature women when I was younger. These women seemed to have it all together. With young women the competition is mostly about men. It's subliminal, for if women really thought about it, we would realize how ridiculous this unconscious vying for attention truly is. As we age, we realize the importance of friendship with other women. We seem to enjoy comparing wrinkles and laughing about it—kind of a "misery loves company."

It seems as though one morning you wake up and your skin is like an ill-fitting suit. What can you do? There is no plastic surgeon who can pick up the slack on your overall body. Face lifts, collagen, and Botox are all temporary Band-Aids that can indeed make you look better. Collagen can fill in lines on the face, Botox can temporarily lift eyebrows, foreheads, the eye area, and even zap the veins in your neck to appear less obvious. But the skin continues to age and sag. Skin deterioration is helped tremendously by replacing lost hormones, but gravity does exist and some things are going to happen no matter what you do.

This is where girlfriends come into play. It's comforting to be able to share the startling effects of aging with a good friend. It creates a bond of loyalty and trust, which over time allows you to open up to one another without judgment. Isn't it great how, with age, we acquire the wisdom to see that women are our friends, not our competitors? Just think what we would have been like if we'd had this kind of confidence and devil-may-care attitude when we were younger. As we approach middle age, we gain a whole new perspective on who we are in the world. We may not be the youngest, hottest babes in the room anymore, but what we have lost in this area we have gained in wisdom and confidence. This is a great trade-off. By this age it is necessary to get over being the prettiest, curviest, or most attractive. Instead, be the most fabulous, interesting, intelligent, charming, and funny woman in the room. That's where the real sexiness clicks in. Once you figure this out, you'll start having more fun than ever before.

Recently, while in New York, I had lunch at a hip, trendy restaurant with a female editor in chief of a very popular magazine. I'd guess she is either in her late fifties or early sixties, but it doesn't matter because she looks great for any age. She is a mother, a grandmother, happily married, and successful in her business. She wore her thick, naturally silver hair at a fabulous shoulder length, had on a beautiful business suit, a little makeup, and confidence galore. Ours was a fabulous table at which to be seated because she held court to some of the most exciting, interesting, and successful men in the entertainment and journalism world. One by one they came to our table to talk with her. She looked great, but it was her confidence that made her stunning. Because of this great self-assuredness, she was sexy. The men joked with her, flirted with her, wanted to do business with her, were not threatened by her, and respected her and her accomplishments. Her sexy femininity attracted them like a magnet. She was in tune with herself, her age, her success, and her attractiveness, and she radiated a wisdom about who she was and what she wanted out of life that was very appealing.

This is how it works for the woman who is comfortable with herself and her age. For the first time in your life, everyone in the room is now taking you seriously. You have reached an age where you have formed your opinions. They are not the opinions of others; instead, at this age you have enough perspective to have formed your own ideas. You carry your own at any dinner party. People who in your younger years dismissed your theories are now interested in your point of view. It's fantastic. People who once would have intimidated you are now seen by you as just "people." As you get older, you realize that there are no big shots. I've watched the most powerful be knocked down. Everyone is vulnerable. Wisdom allows you to realize that.

You finally understand that money does not define a person; only integrity and decency matter. There are wealthy people who are amazing, but it is never about their wealth. It's about who they are and what they think and feel. It's about being caring and compassionate. This is an amazing time of life, but only if you have done the work that leads up to it. There is no room for dysfunction at this age. It's time to get over it, and that requires taking a good look at yourself. Those things from your past or your childhood must stop running your life. If you haven't been able to face the demons of your past, what are you waiting for? That alcoholic father is going to win if you are still

being run by the voices within you that res-
onate the mocking and ridicule he used to dish
out. It's time to look at the situation from another angle: What was his need to badger you
so? Was it his way of coping with his own
sense of inadequacy?

In my life, I allowed my father to convince
me that I was "stupid, hopeless, worthless,
nothin', and a big zero," just as he had always
said to me in his drunken rages. It never
dawned on me as a child that this was really
what he thought about himself. It never
dawned on me that this was his tactic to keep
me under his control. As long as I was emotionally handicapped by his badgering, I
wouldn't leave him, and that was what he
wanted. Without us, he knew he would eventually have to look at the reality of what he had
done with his life. That picture of himself was
too painful, so he kept himself anesthetized
with booze, and the liquor gave him the emotional mustering to hold us in his reign of ter-
ror.

The greatest thing I ever did for myself was
get professional help. It was through therapy
that I was finally able to realize that what happened to me as a child was not my fault. That
was revelatory because I had always assumed I
had been born bad. Why would I think anything else when I had been told over and over

since infancy that I was stupid and hopeless? As adults we forget the impact we have on children. To understand the world from a child's point of view, lie on the floor and look up. Look at how big we appear to be. Children are shaped by those in charge of raising them; everything we are, good and bad, is a result of the input of those who raised us. As adults, it is our job to keep the good parts of us and correct those things in our person that need fixing. If those corrections are not made, the negative influences of our past win. At this point it's your fault.

You have the opportunity in life to overcome and make changes, to shape yourself into the person you want to be. Few of us realize that we are in control of our lives. We must decide what we want from life and then go after it. It takes shaping and tending, much like a beautiful garden. The garden may start out as a barren patch of scruffy earth, but with toil and lots of work it turns into a thing of beauty and joy. Life works the same way. If you haven't started doing the work at this point, then you have a lot of catching up to do, but it's not impossible. It will require total honesty on your part. You have to really look at why you haven't wanted to face the reality of who you have become. It is usually fear and emotional pain that drive us. It's also agitating to dig up those things you'd rather forget from your past, but the fact that you don't want to face them reveals that the issue is still bringing you pain. Take the chance. Face the pain. It will be the most important thing you have ever done for yourself, as important as balancing your hormones.

You cannot imagine how much these old issues hold you down. Coming to terms and then to true forgiveness releases that part of you that has never had a chance to develop because you have been so busy, so clever and cunning, in avoiding the realities. Holding on to old pain can make you sick. It is a proven fact that stress is a major factor in causing disease. You cannot escape from old issues; you can only bury them—but they don't go away. Pay attention to the things in life that make you emotional. What makes you cry? What triggers your emotions? These emotions are you talking to yourself. This is you trying to release old pain. Pay attention to what triggers your feelings, because feelings are our truth. In fact, the smartest part of us is our feelings. They never lie.

If you find yourself crying, figure out what released the flood of emotions. I have a friend who cries every time someone in the family leaves for a trip. She still aches from losing her mother at a young age. Her mother went into the hospital and never came out, so that has left her with abandonment issues. At some point in her life, she will have to do the work to go back and relive the painful time in her childhood when she lost the most important person in the world to her. It will be upsetting. Perhaps she will discover hidden anger. At that time, in order to protect them, children were never told what was truly going on. Maybe she is still angry about not being properly informed of the reason her mother left and not being able to say good-bye in the way she would have wanted.

Maybe the child in her has anger that her mother left her. This has nothing to do with the fact that her mother had no choice; we are talking about the pain of that moment in her childhood, which remains hidden inside her with a child's intensity. You grow up, but the pain does not. The things we don't want to face don't mature. We mature, but the pain is the pain of our child self, pure and without logic or adult understanding. It is the leftover stuff from our past that keeps us from being all that we can be. If this resonates in any way with you, find yourself a group or a good therapist and get it out of you. You can't imagine how freeing it is.

People always comment that I seem so happy, and it's because I am. You know why . . . because I got to the bottom of it. All the books I have written have mostly been about trying to find out why I am the way I am and what I can do to change those things about myself that are in my way. My feelings about my alcoholic father kept me in a choke-hold all of my life. My insecurity overwhelmed my life. I never felt I was good enough for anything. After years of searching, I was finally able to crawl out from under these feelings and see the light. Once I could see, life became easier, more enjoyable, more successful, sexier! Had I not done the work, I don't know where I would be today. There is not a room I walk into where I don't feel I belong. The agitation, the sadness, and the anger I felt during my years of therapy seem so insignificant now. Doing the work was worth it. It changed me and allowed me to become a person I enjoy being.

Once you have taken the big step to make the necessary corrections within yourself, you are prepared to receive your new wisdom. When your thinking is not clouded with negatives and old unresolved issues, the wise part of you takes over. Wisdom is your ability to assess situations. Wise people "get it." Wise people don't overreact. Wise people listen to all sides and make informed decisions. Wise people are easy to be around because you know you are going to be treated fairly. There is a sense of balance and serenity associated with wisdom. You feel and appear peaceful (as long as your hormones are balanced).

Wisdom gives you an inner sense that you can handle any situation. This is no small thing. Acquired wisdom allows you to know that you can handle whatever curve is thrown your way. Wisdom leaves the girl behind, and the woman who emerges is so much more attractive. So much energy is spent at this age trying to capture lost youth, instead of putting emphasis and focus on the new passages. It is the calm of this age that makes you attractive. Calm is cool. Cool is sexy. Wisdom rocks!

Perks of being over forty:
There is nothing else to learn the hard way.

17

TAKING CHARGE OF YOUR LIFE

Middle age really is a wonderful opportunity to reinvent yourself. I talked about the importance of reinvention a bit in chapter 15 and how we need to reinvent ourselves throughout our whole lives. Don't despair—it's never too late to do other things with your life, and now is the best time to be open to new opportunities. Your kids are out of the house, your husband may be slowing down in his career. Now it's time to ask yourself what passions you have always had. It is the best time possible to fulfill dreams or create new ones. I have found that it has been helpful in my life, when trying to figure out what my dreams are, to ask myself what it was that I did when I was a child that totally engaged me. In what activities did I lose myself? Ask yourself the same question: What were the activities that engaged you so deeply that time passed without noticing? These activities are clues to remembering what it is that you love to do and think about.

Maturity is remembering the revelation that all along we have been trying to get back to where we started. I used to play house. Not surprisingly, I am now heavily involved with creating a homewares division on Home Shopping Network (HSN), including appliances, kitchenware, and bedding. In addition, I recently contracted with my publisher to write a book on lifestyle. My hugely successful Somersize line of books came out of my love of cooking, not just a desire to lose weight. I have always loved being in the kitchen, and I became consumed with trying to find delicious dishes that would keep me and my family healthy. It's essential to continue redefining your life from passage to passage. If I hadn't done this, I might be one of those "has-beens" or features on one of those "whatever happened to" shows on television.

I realize that not everyone has the opportunity to sell satin bedding, housewares, and jewelry on television, but look realistically at what it is that you can do within the arena of your interests. The redefining of my life seems to have no connection with the passage that preceded it, yet there is a thread of continuity. Each new endeavor has to do with growth and strength and a yearning to find out who I am and what makes me tick. I'm not ready to sit by the fire and stare. One day that will be nice, but right now I have too much energy and excitement. In ways I feel younger now than ever before, because I have nothing to prove to anyone, not even to myself. I am now driven by my interests.

You can do this, too. I go to many farmers' markets to buy fresh produce, and I see women of all ages setting up little boutique stands and selling wonderful items that they have made themselves. It is very empowering as a woman to make your own money. Even if it's money to spend just on yourself or the house, it puts you in control and allows you the freedom to make choices for yourself. We still live in a world where men are better paid and have better opportunities than women. But things are changing. By being proactive about your life and finances, not only are you making it easier for women of the next generation, but you are also teaching your children about the resiliency and creativity of women.

So many of the woman I talked with in this book referred to this incredible burst of energy, and I believe it's because for the first time they realize they are finally in control of their own lives and can pursue them in any way they'd like. When you are turned on by life, you are sexy. Tune in to your feelings: is there an inner calling you've put on hold for so long that you have forgotten about it? When my mother died, I came across some beautiful watercolor drawings that she had done when she attended the Lux School of Design in San Francisco. I can remember her speaking about Lux, but my father would always make fun of her and put her down. Because of his reaction, we children would join in what I now realize was ridicule. But when my sister and brother and I were cleaning out her house after her death, I cried when I saw those drawings. They were good, really good. In fact, I now have them beautifully framed and kept in one of her favorite guestrooms in my home. I go to that room often to look at them. They make me feel happy and sad simultaneously.

Women of my mother's age put aside their dreams to raise their families. That's the way it used to be. Women of my mother's generation were not supposed to "have it all," and I'm sure frustration was inherent in that role. Today most women have found a way to have it all, but few have found balance. We are still learning how to juggle gracefully. My mother was angry and bitter for many years because of my father's violent alcoholism, but after seeing these drawings, I now believe that some of that frustration was also a result of not being able to express herself creatively. She was always so supportive of my endeavors, I'm sure through me she was able to fulfill some of her dreams.

But the lesson is clear: Life is short, and if you don't get out of it what you want, it's your loss! It's a waste of time to sit around talking about how unfair things are. No one's future turns out the way it was expected to. Life changes for everyone, and it's important to adjust and find another way—that's true creativity.

As we get older, achievement is still important, but we are driven more by personal fulfillment than by what others think. That's why I find this age to be so exciting. I finally feel it's my time. I am now the captain of my ship. It's a waste of time to care what others think. If you do, you are owned by them. Instead, we have to ask what we can do each day to fulfill our dreams. It's exciting to change your life. But change brings risk, and it does get harder as we get older because we become set in our ways. It's frightening to start all over, but change brings a new burst of energy. At middle age, my sister and her husband lost their entire fortune. She had never worked, and after a period of grief and mourning, she rolled up her sleeves and got her real estate license. It wasn't easy. She began by knocking on doors and going from house to house to get listings. She encountered many of the people with whom she used to attend all the fancy parties. She held her head up high, and today she is one of the leading real estate salespeople in the country. She took the risk, put aside her fear, and changed her life. Whenever I am having a bad day, I always call my sister because I know just hearing the excitement in her voice will cheer me up.

These are the kinds of things we can do as women to grow and move forward. Women today are taking more risks because tomorrow appears hopeful. Women have made tremendous progress; the doors of opportunity have opened wider than ever before. We are being heard, and we have rights, although we still have to fight for them, but that is part of the challenge and excitement. There are many women today who are opening their own businesses. Women are redefining the concept of "old." Women in their fifties and sixties are looking hot. Women are achieving great things in areas formerly closed to them. Madeleine Albright became secretary of state at the age of fifty-nine! Women are running studios and corporations; they are exercising, they are proactive about their health, they are having affairs with younger and younger men. Frankly, for me, I enjoy the fact that my husband is ten years older; this way I always get to be the young one. But my girlfriends with young boyfriends seem pretty darned happy, and I have to say there is a glow to their skin.

We women of this generation are exceptional beings. We have rewritten the rules. We are the first generation of women to use therapy as a tool for being happier people. We didn't want to have relationships like those of our parents. We didn't want to have a divide between us and our children, we wanted to talk to them; we wanted them to be comfortable coming to us with any problem. That has made for true intimacy with our children and our spouses. This is a remarkable breakthrough. And we are now experiencing the payoff. Our children are our best friends. There is no one I would rather be with than my son, Bruce, and his family. Bruce is my confidant and I am his. There is no subject too uncomfortable; we are able to talk about anything. Because of this I never feel excluded from his life, nor he from mine. Therapy allowed me to be this way. I certainly didn't learn this in my parents' home. My mother had one personality when she was with us and another when my father was around. If he walked into the room, we stopped talking. When my mother was with her friends, she was relaxed and comfortable; when my father was with her, she sat stiff and uncomfortable.

Therapy allows you to understand the buried anxieties and rages. You can't grow and be able to change if you don't recognize what has made you angry for so long. If you are to have a long and happy life, you have to get to the bottom of all buried pain so you can understand it, forgive, and move forward. Once it is understood, you can let it go and find forgiveness not only for those who caused you pain, but also for the part you played in the drama of your life. If you didn't have a perfect relationship with either or both of your parents, do the work and then get over it. You are an adult now, and you don't need your mommy or daddy to have a happy life. If you didn't "get" what you wanted or thought you wanted, do the work to discover what that was (usually it's love) and then find that love in your own life. Get rid of old jealousies and resentments. If you don't, these emotions will pull you down. You will be the loser. Stay clear of people who are jealous of you. They too will pull you down. Envy is something you aspire to, jealousy is not wanting others to have what they have. Envy is a positive emotion, as in "I want to be like you"; jealousy is a negative emotion, as in "I don't want you to have what you have." Nothing good comes from jealousy. It's destructive, mean-spirited, and petty. Run, don't walk, away from it.

I know a middle-aged man who has everything going for him—great looks, great physique, intelligence, creativity, humor, and energy—except he is jealous of everyone. He is constantly looking over his shoulder and at who is ahead of him, and he wonders why he can't get his life on track. His jealousy is holding him back. It's impossible for him to be all that he can be because so much of his time is wasted on not wanting others to have what they have.

You have worked too hard your whole life to get mired now in petty emotions like jealousy. These negative emotions will hold you back and prevent you from realizing your dreams. You have to be a self-starter. You have got to figure out what you want from this next phase of your life and then decide how to get it. An optimist sees opportunity in every difficulty, and a pessimist sees difficulty in every opportunity. Be an optimist. Look at everything that has happened to you, good and bad, as an opportunity to grow and learn spiritually and emotionally. Turn your lemons into lemonade. Make your greatest problems your greatest opportunity. Take charge of your life and make it exactly what you want it to be. We all have made mistakes, and we will continue to do so, but at this age we realize it's the problems and mistakes that are our greatest opportunities, if we choose to look at them that way. We learn from our past, but the challenge is to not repeat patterns of behavior that are not serving us well.

Perks of being over forty:
Your husband jokes that instead of
buying a woodstove, he is using you
to heat the family room this winter.
Rather than just saying you are
not amused, you shoot him..

18
STAYING COOL

The surest way to guess somebody's age is by their "cool" factor. Staying cool is being comfortable in your skin. It's about liking your age. I remember listening to an interview with Steve Allen one day, and the interviewer said, "You were always one of the really cool guys." And Steve Allen replied, "If you're cool, you're always cool. Just because I'm an old guy now doesn't mean I'm not cool anymore." He was right: just because you get older doesn't mean you suddenly change your take on things. For instance, how old is Jack Nicholson? You never really think about his age, do you? It's because Jack is just a cool guy. So it doesn't matter if he's fifty, eighty, or one hundred, he's still this sexy, impish, mischievous guy. He seems as if he'd be fun to hang around with, and all because he's cool!

Frank Sinatra was cool. It was never about his age. We didn't care if he was getting older; if fact, as he got older he seemed to get sexier.

It's because he always stayed cool. He was the type of guy you could still fantasize about sleeping with even when he was eighty years old. What about Sting or Rod Stewart? They're cool guys because they have created their own style and don't care what people think. They have the right to express themselves in any way they want. You never think about their age; they are just these two sexy guys.

"Cool" is ageless. It's your take on things. It's about not being judgmental. It's about acceptance. If your girlfriend has decided to dye her hair pink and pierce her nose or other body parts, you are okay with it because that's the way she has decided to decorate herself. Don't we earn the right to be, dress, pierce, or adorn ourselves in any way we want? It really doesn't matter how it ends up looking, it's all about expressing ourselves in any way we want because we have earned the right to be whoever we choose to be. It's our life. We are finally in control of ourselves at this age. We've spent a lifetime trying to do what's right and appropriate, and now we can stop being governed by what the rest of the community is doing or what the magazines tell us we should be doing or how we should be dressing. The women who write those articles are all in their twenties anyway.

I think by now we know what's best for us without a twenty-year-old advising us, yet being cool is about being open to what a twenty-year-old has to say, or anyone of any age, for that matter. Some twenty-year-olds are very wise and old souls, and it might just be that they are telling us exactly what we need to hear at that moment. Always be open to the messages, because you never know where they might be coming from. Some of my greatest messages have come from the mouths of my grandchildren.

When I was a child, I always heard that at a certain age (forty was the cutoff), a woman should cut her hair short. All my life I have had long hair; I find it the most versatile. I can braid it, put it on top of my head, wear a ponytail, or style it straight or curly. With long hair I have options. Today it's not about what's appropriate, it's about what looks best, without looking desperate. It's a matter of taste. You have to look in the mirror and decide what looks best. This is where your good taste and wisdom come in. If you are more comfortable with your hair long, then by all means that's how you should wear it. It's up to you to know if it looks great or stupid. Wearing clothes that make you look desperate makes you look stupid. You have to know who you are. What's right for Cher (one of the really cool chicks) may or may not be right for you. Personally, I wouldn't look good in any of her getups. A bare midriff is not my style, but you have to admit, Cher looks great all the time, always has, probably always will. She's always been cool. It's not forced; it's her personal style and expression. That's the goal. Wear what you feel comfortable wearing and be who you want to be.

Now is the time to step out of the box. Buy yourself a black leather skirt if that is something you would feel comfortable in. Recently, I saw Maria Shriver wearing a long black leather skirt, black stiletto boots, a black turtleneck sweater, and a strand of pearls. She looked great. It was her personal style. It was hip, edgy, not desperate; yet she still maintained a ladylike demeanor, because that is who she is. She is someone who is comfortable in her own skin. She's a great mother, has a fabulous marriage and a career of her own invention. She seems to work when it is convenient for her. With four children and as wife of the governor she obviously has taken the time to invent her life so she can have it all.

We look at someone like Maria Shriver and think she was born with a silver spoon in her mouth. Granted, she was born into privilege; but Maria had a lot of disadvantages to overcome. Because she was a Kennedy, the pressure to succeed was enormous. No other member of her family had ever ventured into television. I'm sure there was disapproval within the family, but Maria started at the bottom and worked her way up. I remember in the early eighties, I used to run into her in the back rooms of television studios doing intern work, while I was waiting to go on *The Charlie Rose Show*. She had determination and a desire to have it all. We've seen her hosting the *Today* show while pregnant, then we'll spot her at a premiere with her husband, Arnold Schwarzenegger, looking very fancy, then we'll see a candid shot of her walking around Santa Monica without makeup looking very unglamorous, pushing a baby carriage. She's cool because she doesn't care what anyone thinks of her. She's doing it her way, dressing her way, having her marriage her way, establishing a career her way.

A very important aspect of aging is taking a good look at yourself and assessing your look. The surest way to date yourself is by wearing the same makeup you wore in your twenties or thirties. Most of us do that. Imagine how I would look if I were still wearing the makeup that served me so well when I was playing Chrissy Snow on *Three's Company*. I wore thick black eyeliner all the way around the eye, lots of white highlight under the eye, cotton candy pink blush in big pink rounds on my cheeks, and big pink glossy lips. Top that with pure white-blond hair pulled into two pony-tails on either side of my head, and you have my look of the 1980s. It was real cute then, but today, at fifty-six, I would look quite desper-ate . . . kind of like *Whatever Happened to Baby Jane.*

I remember the day I looked in the mirror and realized that that look of the eighties was no longer serving me well. It had outlived its purpose. Instead of looking cute and perky, I looked old and overly made-up. Suddenly, what once worked now looked unattractive. I scrubbed my face and made the decision to change the color of my hair. White-blond hair is great when you are in your twenties, but in my early forties it drained me of my color and forced me to wear a lot of makeup to fill in the color. I changed my hair to a more natural blond with gold highlights and my makeup to softer, more natural colors. It was an amazing transformation for me. Suddenly people were telling me I looked younger, softer, prettier.

We need to change and update our looks from passage to passage. It says something about ourselves. It says that we are not stuck in a time warp, that we are not holding on to what was, or to "the good old days." Change looks fresh and shows forward motion. If you think you've lost all that was remarkable and valuable about your youth, then you really have to think about why that time in your life was better for you than now. But here's the point: Youth is gone. Today is what is important, so examine why "today" is not bringing you contentment and satisfaction.

Perks of being over forty: You enjoy
hearing about other people's operations.

19

MAUREEN: A SIXTY-THREE-YEAR-OLD EXPERIENCE

Maureen is my sister, sixty-three years old and a real estate supersalesperson. Like me, she is a breast cancer survivor and is on natural bioidentical hormone replacement therapy. As you will read in this chapter, she is enjoying her life to the fullest. She does not want to turn back the clock. Her energy, vitality, and libido are operating at optimum. In speaking to her, I kept trying to find any negatives associated with taking natural bioidentical hormones, but I wasn't able to pull any out of her. She even went so far as to say that she thinks the quality of her life is so spectacular that even if bioidentical hormones were to shorten her life, it would be worth it. That's quite an endorsement.

You've heard from me and my fifty-year-old (ish) point of view relative to replacing lost hormones with real hormones, but listen to my sister talk about hormones from her perspective as a sixty-three-year-old. Maureen is honest to a fault and has graciously shared her point of view.

Before I took bioidentical hormones, I felt dead. The lights were out, my spirit felt dead. I remember wishing a lot, for anything . . . a windfall, winning the lottery, getting back what I had lost. It was a terrible time in my life. I think menopause is a very difficult time for women because a lot of things are going on. For instance, you've had your animals for a long time and they start dying around this age. It's sad and hard. Both my dogs died, my birds died, I lost both of my houses because of the real estate crash of the 1980s, so we lost all our money. For the first time in my life, I realized I had to get a job, but how do you get into the workforce at this age after never having been in the workforce to begin with? I was scared and intimidated, and on top of all of this I had no hormones.

I had no libido. Nothing. I slept in the fetal position for three years, and I wouldn't let my husband touch me. I felt like the frozen chicken in the freezer, packed real tight with clamps on my legs holding them together. Believe me, I made sure that no one reaching in there to get at that package was going to find anything. I was fifty-two then and kept thinking, This can't be happening to me. I was never a complainer. I never complained about my period or cramps. I would be annoyed at the women who complained, and I would think, Oh, grow up, or, Get over it, as I listened to them.

Then I got breast cancer, so I took myself off the prescribed drug hormones I was taking. I went without them for three years. Evidently, one night I was acting so badly that the next day a girlfriend took me out to lunch and put a patch (drug hormones) on me. I realized my mood had been awful, and I did feel some relief from the patch. But then I started gaining weight. I just blew up. I gained so much weight when I started on the patch that I went off them also.

My sexless, angry, depressed life went on like this until I felt that I'd rather not be alive anymore. My days were not bringing me any joy, and I am a happy person by nature. People have always told me how great it is to be around me because I am so "up," but not anymore. I didn't even recognize myself. Everything made me angry, and I was ready to blame my husband at every turn. (No wonder men leave their wives at this age.)

I went to see Dr. Schwarzbein because my sister, Suzanne, seemed to be so pleased with her progress. After all, she had breast cancer also and was enjoying her life on a hormonal basis, so I decided I'd give it a try. As soon as I was on real bioidentical hormones, I was a different girl. Suddenly I couldn't get enough sex.

I was in my prime again, and I was actually wearing out my husband (well, maybe not). I thought, Wow, this is fantastic. Yippee! An "E" ticket. But I soon realized there is more to it than getting your sex drive back (although I must say this alone makes all the rest you have to go through more tolerable).

It's not been easy to find balance. On real hormones I also gained weight. This was depressing. I went up to 150 pounds. My normal weight is 127. My metabolism was so out of whack from the drug hormones and the carbohydrates I had been eating. At the time we were struggling financially, so we went out to dinner a lot because of our work overload, and I had started eating bread. It was inexpensive, and it was always sitting on the table while we waited for our dinner, and it would fill me up so we didn't have to spend so much money. All these carbohydrates threw my hormone levels further out of whack, and now I was insulin resistant, and I didn't even know what that was. All I knew was that I had these two "hams" on either side of my hips, right at the top below your waist, where it makes everything you wear look terrible, and for the first time in my life I had a big ass. The weight made me feel terrible about myself, but the hormones were giving me a renewed zest about life. I had a big ole butt, but my husband and I were having nightly romps of great sex.

My doctor told me that hormonal balance takes patience. I had damaged my metabolism from years of incorrect eating, plus the damage done earlier in my life when I was drinking alcohol (I have been sober for twenty-five years); also, all that time without taking any kind of hormone replacement had left me at zero. I had no hormones. No wonder I felt dead. No wonder I had no will to live. No wonder I was taking it all out on my dear husband. Dr. Schwarzbein said that it would take a few years for everything to find its balance and that eventually the weight would come off, but I had to eat properly to heal my damaged metabolism. Initially, she said, this food would put on weight while it was doing its good work of rebuilding. We also found out that I had plaque in my arteries and I had seriously high blood pressure. All the things you hear about old people were happening to me. But in spite of all of this information, the real hormones were giving me a renewed zest.

I was starting a new career, I was recovering from the shock of having had breast cancer, I was gaining weight, but I was still happier than I had been in a long time, and it had to be because of the hormones. I could feel myself getting stronger, and because of this I made a commitment to myself to become my doctor's best patient. I decided to approach this in the same way I had tackled my alcoholism. I was going to do everything she said and really give this a try. I realized I couldn't do this thing half-assed. The struggle was softened, however, because of the real hormone replacement.

I remembered a story that my mother used to read to me as a child, about "the little train that could," so I used that as a metaphor—"I think I can, I think I can." I started lifting weights, all the while saying to myself, "I can do this." I began meditating and started reading a lot of spiritual books that allowed me to see this not as a time of despair, but as an opportunity to grow and change. I knew I needed to change my life, and these books were giving me the tools to do so. At times I still wanted to hide in the freezer like that chicken, and I didn't want to face my children, but I hung in and continued to do the work physically and emotionally.

It's been hard, that's for sure, but it's becoming worth it. There is no magic pill. Real hormones definitely are the answer, but you've got to be willing to do the work that accompanies this balance. You can't think, now that you are replacing your lost hormones with real hormones, that this is the beginning and the end. If you continue to eat sugar (I ate mine in the form of carbohydrates), you will keep getting fat. The real hormones work by improving your overall well-being; but if you are eating badly, all that sugar is going to interfere with your body's ability to keep your hormones balanced.

Taking real hormones has made me healthier in every way. I realize that if I want a sex life this satisfying, I have to obey the rules. I have to be rigorously honest with myself and my doctors. You can't lie to your doctors; it defeats the purpose. You have to tell them if you are sneaking sugar, otherwise they won't be able to help you properly. They aren't going to sit there and tell you that you are a liar. It's not up to them. If you want to get better, you have to be accountable to yourself. Just as I approached alcoholism, I now do this "one day at a time." If that gets too difficult, I do it one hour at a time or one moment at a time. I want this to work. But I am driving that little train.

Today I am feeling great. My weight is 129. I still have a few more pounds to get rid of. It's taken me four years. That's a lot of patience. But I am eating fantastic meals. Because of my high blood pressure and the fact that I am still insulin resistant to a small degree, I am also watching my fat intake until my levels are acceptable. I visualize that all this great food I am eating is slowly cleaning out my arteries. When my insulin levels are normal, and my blood pressure is normal, and I drive away the plaque through visualization and a healthy lifestyle and diet, I get to incorporate real fats again with more frequency. I do love butter and cream.

I believe I will stay on real hormones forever. If I die because of it (which I don't think will happen), it will have been worth it. I can't describe the well-being you get from replacing lost hormones with the real ones. Frankly, life wasn't worth living the other way.

I have taken those kinds of chances to afford me a better quality of life. I took birth control pills for a long time (almost two decades). I am very fertile, and after having four children, three of them in three successive years, I found that birth control pills gave me a better quality of life at that time. I didn't have to say no to my husband, and it was the one time of the day just for us. With four kids, there is not much time in the day for meaningful conversation. I feel the same way about hormone replacement. I am willing to take the risk. I am really living these days; before I started on real hormones, I felt like the walking dead.

I am accountable for my health. I realized the power we have within when I went through breast cancer. I worked with a healer who truly taught me that we were body, mind, and spirit. This whole passage of life is completely up to me. I absolutely have to be honest with my doctors and the people who are helping me through this period, and keep them informed so they can do their best work. It's stupid to BS your doctors. I have made my choices. It's not going to be anyone's fault, regardless of the outcome. I am not mad at the medical profession. Doctors today are so busy that it is almost impossible for them to keep up with recent studies. Therefore, it is up to me. I am accountable for my health, my spirit, my body. I am accountable for myself in the financial world; because of that I have a coach I work with once a week to improve my business and my relationships with my working team, who happen to be my family.

I am grateful for the new integrated medicine. It's truly interactive, and there is a new respect between doctor and patient in terms of getting to the bottom of what ails you. No longer is medicine a Band-Aid to slap on till the symptoms clear up. Now we are able to go deeper—holistic, if you will—to find out not only what it is, but also what caused it.

When my hormones are balanced, I am turned on about practically everything. I feel great about everything. I love my age. It's a good age. When I meet my contemporaries, I notice that many of them are really getting old. I know the difference between them and me is hormones. I think the big difference is that I have sex regularly. I talk about it. I love it. I never hear any of my girlfriends talking about it. In fact, in your sixties, there is a lot of laughter about the fact that you are not having sex anymore.

I think for me the big difference is sex, not only having sex, but also wanting it. It's a great time of life—there are no interruptions, the kids are gone, there is no right or wrong, just pleasure.

To other women my age who haven't got a handle on things, I would like to say: Take yourself on—be accountable. Find out who you are in every way, and find out all that you can be. Be sure to take care of yourself. Go to the doctor. Try a new one. Switch around. When you hear about a doctor who has a new approach, get an appointment and find out what he or she is up to. Get X-rays, take the latest tests. Take hold of your life. When you start menopause, everything is going to change. This passage requires absolute, rigorous honesty and lots of work, but take it from me, I feel enthusiastic about absolutely every-thing.

I owe my life to these hormones. Without them I felt and behaved badly. Am I ever glad to leave that part of me behind.

"Old" is when . . . a sexy babe catches your man's fancy and his pacemaker opens the garage door.

———

20
RELATIONSHIPS

Hormones are a wonderful component of who we are. They give us life and balance. They make our systems work properly; they make our skin glow, our hair shiny and healthy, our nails strong; and they radiate on the outside the balance within. But hormones can also be responsible for conflict that we have with our partners. Sometimes what seems real, like a relationship problem, might be caused by a chemical imbalance. Think PMS! Remember that time of the month when your chemicals were wonky and you found yourself wondering what ever attracted you to your husband in the first place? Then as soon as you were back in balance, the angry and negative thoughts from a few days ago seemed laughable? Menopause can make you feel like that all the time, so it seems real that your husband is a jerk. I wonder how many marriages break up because of menopause? I wonder how many families could have remained intact if there had been a better understanding of the chemical imbalance that accompanies menopause? It is so important to understand this passage. Everything can be brought into balance through a blood test and a qualified endocrinologist or doctor "in the know."

So don't make any rash decisions or accusations until you have found balance. But if after achieving this balance you still are not happy with your mate and the life you are living, then you can make real decisions for yourself that are not the result of hormonal imbalance. Take a good, hard look at your life. Is your partner boring you? Remember, you have another whole half of your life to spend with this person. Is it worth it? Have the two of you forgotten to notice each other over the years? Is life without your kids empty and void? Do you hate your work? Is sex a distant memory? Do you pine over the body you once had? Have you given up on joy? If your answer is yes to any one of these, it's time to do some emotional work.

Here's the thing: you can change every one of these components, but you are going to have to commit to some hard work. If that puts you off, then you have to ask yourself why you are not willing to put out the effort to change yourself and your life. I agree it's no easy task to revive a marriage that has lost its glow. It's even harder to admit that you no longer have any interest in trying to put the glow back into your marriage. If that is so, it requires a huge change on your part. Divorce could change your financial situation, you might have to go to work for the first time in your life, it might make you feel frightened, and with good reason—but look at the alternative. If you are going to live for another fifty years (and you are, barring some kind of accident), is it worth it to give the second half to a situation that is hopeless or, worse, loveless?

Don't live a loveless life. To be trapped in a situation that has no love is to feel dead inside. You will never find your inner glow living a loveless life. Perhaps you can learn to enjoy your partner as a friend or companion, someone you like to take drives with or to share a home with; but you have to acknowledge this new way of thinking to yourself so you can turn the page and realize that what you once had together no longer exists—it's dead. Your relationship can be reshaped to be something other than what it once was. This is workable, because this person is obviously someone who has qualities that are important to you. How can this relationship be salvaged? By understanding that now it will be on different terms that the two of you find mutually agreeable. In other words, the two of you need to agree to new terms of living together. If your husband (or wife) still interests you as a person with whom sharing a house and occasional social events is enough, then that can bring you happiness.

It is important to address the changes in your relationship to avoid becoming bitter and angry because things are no longer the way they were. In a scenario like this, it is important to establish a life of your own. Make friends of your own, plan lunches and dinners without your mate. Have your own life, but accept the new arrangement responsibly. You want him, but not the way you once wanted him. Accept that this arrangement works both ways. He will want to hang out with his own friends, have lunches and dinners also. You can't be angry with him for having a life without you, because this is what you have both chosen.

I am grateful to be very happily married, so this scenario would not work with my marriage, but for some couples this is a way of holding on to all that the two of them have created. It is easier on your grown kids, your family is whole, and the two of you are no longer frustrated, angry, and bitter. When you do share an evening together or an occasional sexual romp, you can enjoy each other without all the residual resentment that used to ruin your evenings. Who knows, maybe this way you will fall in love with each other all over again. Maybe when the two of you rearrange your present life, each of you might notice how cool your partner has become. But don't count on it, or you will have expectations that could set you up for disappointment.

No matter what path you take with your partner, this is your chance to have the life you want. Take responsibility for your life and your relationships and how they have turned out. And if you don't like what you see, then start doing the work necessary to create the life you want.

"Old" is when . . . your friends compliment you on your new alligator shoes and you're barefoot.

21
MAKING SENSE OF IT

In comparing the points of view of women taking natural bioidentical hormones with those of women who are not, it's apparent to me that the ones who are replacing their lost hormones with real hormones are enjoying the best quality of life. Maureen, my sister, went so far as to say that even if taking bioidentical HRT shortened her life, it will have been worth it because of the difference it's made in how much she enjoys each day.

Life is better on real hormones. Without them we start slowly to fade away. At one time we expected to be like this as we got older, but today it doesn't have to happen. Bioidentical hormone replacement allows you to enjoy a fabulous quality of life, filled with energy and the zest for living. Your health will be better, too, because taking bioidentical hormones helps prevent the onset of the diseases of aging.

My sister experienced terrible mood swings when she first entered menopause. It was a terrible time for both of us, because neither of us knew what was going on. She went on drug hormones and her mood got better, but then things started going wrong metabolically. She started gaining weight, and then because of breast cancer she stopped taking the drug hormones, so her hormone levels zeroed out.

During the three years without hormones she became a person I didn't recognize. She spoke in a flat voice, her enthusiasm was gone, and she said things like "I feel dead." The sister I grew up with, the sister I aspired to be when I was growing up, the sister with the enthusiasm, energy, laughter, and sharp thinking, was gone, replaced by a depressed, unenthusiastic, unhappy person who spoke of things in negative terms. After reading her chapter, you can plainly see that she now has boundless energy, enthusiasm, and a lust for life, all because she has been taking real hormones for ten years. I am so thrilled to have her back again.

One of my husband's dearest friends is also going through the same thing. He was one of the guys my husband used to hang out with in London in the sixties; they partied hard, played hard, and played around (I'm glad I wasn't in the picture at that time). They were two good-looking guys with the world at their feet. Now, though, the differences between them are startling. While Alan has, of course, become more mature as he has aged, with the friend you actually see an old man. Alan couldn't be any healthier or happier—he just glows. The difference between the two men is hormones: my husband is on bioidentical HRT, the testosterone patch and DHEA, and the friend is not. As you will read in chapter 23, Alan cannot say enough about the way he feels on hormones versus the way he felt before them. It has had such a positive effect on our marriage. Between the two of us, we have unbelievable energy and a zest for life.

There is so much confusion out there about this time of life and taking hormones. All I can say is, what have you got to lose? If you take real hormones under a doctor's supervision and find balance through blood tests, it's like getting a second chance at life. To go through the second half with the acquired wisdom and perspective, *and* balanced hormones, is a pretty wonderful experience. If you add to that mix a true change in your thinking about eating properly to keep your hormones balanced, exercising daily, and getting proper rest, you can change your second half of life to be the best it's ever been.

I am asked all the time what I do to look so healthy, and I always explain that I have found the fountain of youth in real hormones. Most people turn off immediately. Everyone has preconceived notions about hormones and aging. There have been so many conflicting stories, and flawed incomplete studies, no wonder everyone is scared and confused. It is difficult to find the right doctor. But after reading this, you are better prepared to ask the right questions. You never know where you will get your information. I found my doctor through my manicurist. I was complaining to her about my problems and she mentioned that she had heard of this doctor in Santa Barbara—one little mention that changed my life. This passage of life takes work, but hasn't everything you've struggled for in your life? Getting on track hormonally is worth the effort. The great thing about endocrinology is that you really have to go to the doctor's office only the first time. Since everything is assessed through blood tests, your relationship with your doctor can be maintained mostly by phone. This is a good thing, because after your hormones are balanced you will have so much energy, you will have trouble fitting another appointment into your busy schedule.

PART IV

THE
MALE
menopause

"Old" is when . . . getting a little
action means you don't have
to take any fiber today.

22

TESTOSTERONE AND MEN

So you think you are in this alone? Well, ladies, your men are going through male menopause, called andropause. It's real, and men truly suffer in silence. It is not a subject discussed in men's magazines. No man wants to talk about declining testosterone levels because it is so tied up in who they are. Without testosterone they aren't "manly."

It's unfortunate that people equate testosterone levels with the ability to have erections. Yes, testosterone levels do indeed affect the quality of erections, but that's the last thing to go; the real issue is loss of general vitality. I noticed this with my husband. His energy was gone—he was wilting like a tulip without water. He'd fall asleep midmorning, then again after lunch, and then again after dinner. I began to worry about him. We went to our internist in Los Angeles, who is a Western, Eastern, and holistically trained doctor. He has turned many people's health around, including mine, and I have great respect for him as a professional. He is of the new ilk of cutting-edge doctors who use Western medicine as a last resort. When an antibiotic is warranted, as with an infection, he is right there for you, but with a virus he prefers to use vitamins and supplements to build up the body's immune system so that you can fight the virus on your own. When I am overworked, he adds to or increases the supplements I take to give me more of a frontline defense.

We asked our doctor why Alan was running on empty. He explained that because of our high-stress lifestyle, overwork, environmental pollution, damaged water, and damaged food supplies, including the damage that has been done to the soil that grows our food, it is necessary to supplement with herbs, vitamins, amino acids, and phytonutrients to make up for the poor-quality air, food, and water we now ingest.

Then we went to see Dr. Schwarzbein. After talking with Alan, she suspected that his hormonal production levels had dropped off. She had Alan take a blood test to review his hormone levels.

Well, lo and behold! My husband was almost out of testosterone. No wonder he couldn't stay awake. Testosterone is vitality, and without it one will not have the energy and zest to get through the day. Dr. Eugene Shippen says in his book *The Testosterone Syndrome* that loss of testosterone is at the core of male menopause (and a key element in female menopause as well). The two sexes have a different experience of midlife menopausal change. In women, there is an explosion of in-your-face symptoms, while in men very similar symptoms sneak in the back door. Most often, men's symptoms, such as loss of energy, ambition, and sexual drive, are written off as burnout or depression. Often, sexual virility is the last to go, so men don't think this "male menopause" applies to them—meanwhile they are drooping and sleeping the day away as my husband had been. Men feel as long as they can still "get it up" everything is okay, and put off going to a doctor. I look at this procrastination at getting help as precious time lost when they could be feeling their best. Because we women are barraged with uncomfortable symptoms, we go on the hunt for relief; because andropause happens to men over a ten- to twelve-year period, they usually chalk it up to natural aging.

Male menopause creeps up on them until finally they can't help but notice that their muscles are shrinking, their energy withering, their self-confidence crumbling, and their virility dropping off. The first sign that a man's hormones levels are dropping significantly is a subtle loss of strength and energy. There is also a depressive change in personality noticed by the wife and friends. There is often a loss of athletic ability, dynamic executive capabilities, self-confidence, eagerness, and aggressive energy, combined with a total unawareness of what they are undergoing. We all know men like this: those once high-spirited, energetic men who seem to have given up on life. A lethargy sets in. They are no longer interested in learning anything new, no longer want to join in the fun.

According to Dr. Shippen, "Men enter a gray zone, a time they neither understand nor wish to talk about." Male menopause is one of the most dynamic and significant events man ever experiences. His testosterone levels fall steadily decade by decade. Very few men have testosterone levels that stay at or near youthful heights right into old age. Dr. Shippen says, "I have never seen an older male in excellent mental and physical health whose testosterone levels were not well within the normal range. And the healthiest, most vital individuals are always in the high-normal ranges."

The changes that men are experiencing at this time are consistent with the hormonal depletion of aging. The optimal function of every cell in our bodies requires optimal hormonal input. Once we all had it, but as our hormone production declines, the result is suboptimal cellular activity. That is the beginning of trouble. It is subtle at first and usually thought of as natural aging, but long-term hormonal decline leads toward illness, fatigue, malaise, and further aging. Any doctor who looks for hormonal decline will find it in middle-aged women or men. Most of the major hormone systems drop significantly and steadily from year to year and decade to decade. It is one of the most important parts of the steady downward spiral into old age and debility. But now these lost hormones can be replaced in men's and women's bodies through bioidentical natural hormones, which results in rapid improvement in physical function.

Dr. Shippen writes, "The major controversy among physicians is whether gradual hormonal decline is a normal, healthy part of aging or is a pathologic, diseaselike state." According to Dr. Shippen, "This controversy sets up a false dichotomy. Hormonal decline is, of course, normal, but so is heart disease. They are also, and equally, disease states and will, in the end, prove fatal to any human being who allows either one to run its course unhindered."

There are many reasons why men, and women, too, should be wary of declining levels of testosterone. Testosterone is more than just a sex hormone—it is an anabolic steroid, which means that along with its unique chemical structure, it has the capacity to promote the formation of bone and muscle in the body. It travels to every part of the body. There are receptors for it from your brain to your toes. Testosterone is vitally involved in the making of protein, which in turn forms muscle. Testosterone is key in the formation of bone, and it improves oxygen uptake throughout the body, vitalizing all tissues. It helps control blood sugar, helps regulate cholesterol, helps maintain a powerful immune system. Testosterone appears to help in mental concentration and improves mood. It is also one of the key components in protecting your brain against Alzheimer's disease.

According to Dr. Shippen, "Without testosterone the muscle, nerve, and vascular systems that a man's sexual organs depend upon grow weak. Testosterone is also one of the most essential guardians of a healthy male heart. Testosterone is a muscle-building hormone, and the heart is the largest muscle in the body. In the human heart there are more cellular sites for receiving testosterone than in any other muscle of the body. Testosterone is also a stimulator of arterial dilation and increases production of nitric oxide, a natural form of nitroglycerin, the tablets heart patients take to open up the coronary arteries when angina pains arise. The pumping power of the heart decreases when testosterone declines, and angina pains begin when nitric oxide production declines. *When testosterone is administered in appropriate doses, most of the major risk factors for heart disease diminish.*" Dr. Shippen also says, "I find it puzzling that testosterone has not been given a prominent role in the treatment of heart disease. When testosterone decreases, cholesterol and triglycerides go up, coronary artery and major artery dilation diminish, blood pressure goes up, insulin levels rise, abdominal fat increases, estrogen levels go up, lipoprotein goes up, fibrinogen goes up, human growth hormones decrease, and energy and strength decrease, leading to a sedentary lifestyle and decreased physical activity. No other single factor in the male body is associated with more risk factors for heart disease than a lack of testosterone. Testosterone works protectively in men just as estrogen does in women."

Speaking of estrogen, men have to worry about their estrogen levels just as women have to monitor their testosterone levels. What? you ask. Here's the science, according to Dr. Shippen. The male body actually manufactures its own supply of the female hormone estrogen. It makes it out of its supply of testosterone. An enzyme called aromatase is widely present in the body and converts a certain portion of the male hormone into the female. The human body is expert at such processes, and actually the two hormones are chemically quite similar. This conversation is necessary for the healthy functioning of estrogen-sensitive tissues in a man's body. Estrogen is powerfully beneficial to the male brain. Too little estrogen will neuter a man just as effectively as too little testosterone. The areas of the male brain that control sexual function are plentifully supplied with the aromatase enzyme and thus have no difficulty converting testosterone to estrogen for its special purposes in those specific locations. Estrogen converted by aromatase can actually unlock or displace testosterone at its various cellular receptor sites. Too much estrogen will switch off activities. The body depends upon various on/off switches to regulate the force of its actions. Since testosterone is a powerful stimulant and energizer, estrogen may logically be a complementary "off" switch to turn down the male libido, as unbridled sexual energy can be totally disruptive to life. Whew! Enough with the science! But here's more . . .

Dr. Shippen says, "In older men, estrogens that rise out of their window of normal function become not a counterbalance, but a nearly permanent condition stuck almost always on 'off.' This is when effects on sexuality and a host of other male complaints become active." In many men, high estrogen levels cause a slow-down in testosterone levels. High estrogen levels can alter liver function, lead to zinc deficiency and obesity, and trigger alcohol abuse. High levels also increase aromatase activity. As a man grows older, he produces larger quantities of aromatase, the testosterone converter. Because of this, he converts higher levels of estrogen. Higher levels of estrogen can produce that "off" switch relative to sexuality. The liver eliminates chemicals, hormones, drugs, and metabolic wastes. Also among its duties is excreting excess estrogen from the body. Because too much estrogen in the male body has negative effects, it is important that the liver work at optimum. Zinc deficiency will adversely affect the male/female hormone ratio. Zinc is also important for normal pituitary function, without which the proper hormonal signals will not be sent to the testicles to stimulate the production of testosterone.

Both men and women require individualized quantities of both estrogen and testosterone to activate their sexuality and create all the other health benefits just mentioned. The good news is that now doctors in the know monitor this situation with HRT. As we age,

hormonal changes are the single most important transforming factor for men and women.
By replacing those hormones as you lose them,
you can gain a reprieve from aging. They truly
are the fountain of youth. This is what we have
all been looking for: the magic potion, the secret elixir. And it's been right under our noses
all along.

Having the means available to reinstate
prime quality of life is an incredible breakthrough in today's medicine. I know that our
mothers and our fathers, who pooh-pooh-ed
this phase of their lives as nothing or hardly
noticed, were just minimizing their experiences. The previous generation did not discuss
their aches, pains, and complaints. It was partly
pride, the "I will suffer in silence" syndrome of
that era; also, there was nothing any doctor
could do to give relief because so little was
known about the endocrine system.

Now, not only are we beginning to understand a woman's need for hormone replacement and the incredible benefits relative to
quality of life and health, but also for the first
time men can find relief for a problem that has
been in the closet for so long. If life is not full
of the usual zest you once enjoyed, perhaps
testosterone may be the missing component.
Every day I watch my husband, full of energy,
taking two steps at a time on the stairs, leaping

out of bed to start his day, on the phone, laughing, enjoying life, and running our businesses with a vigor I haven't seen in quite a few years. He is sold on the stuff. It has improved the quality of his life and therefore, in turn, mine. It all starts with a blood test to determine your levels; then read Alan's experiences in the next chapter to see how he is able to use this information to create a regimen with his doctor that works for him.

"Old" is when . . . "getting lucky" means
you find your car in the parking lot.

23

ALAN: A SIXTY-SEVEN-YEAR-OLD MALE EXPERIENCE

My husband, Alan Hamel, is on bioidentical hormone replacement therapy, and I can vouch for the difference it has made in the quality of his life. It is like getting the "old Alan" back again. He has vitality, strength, and vigor. His mood is wonderful, he is mellow and in general all-around wonderful. He is so excited about the change in his personality and his sense of well-being that he would like to shout from the rooftops that he is on HRT. He has been on hormones for almost a year. Here are his feelings on the subject.

Before hormone replacement therapy, I was missing my usual energy and vitality. I was sleeping more than usual; and even after working out with weights regularly, I noticed my muscles were shrinking. I felt hollow. Also, my libido wasn't where I like it to be.

I have been on HRT for almost a year, and the results are amazing. My muscles are growing again, my vitality and energy are back. I don't feel exhausted by four o'clock in the afternoon, and I sleep more soundly. My mood is more upbeat and alert. My libido is once again my best friend [SS: "I'll vouch for that!"]. My brain is functioning and sharp again, and my general body functions have improved.

What I'd like to say to men is that they are looking for real trouble down the road by neglecting to look into the hormonal system relative to themselves. By not being proactive, they are turning their backs on a wonderful technology available for men. I don't look at HRT any differently from taking vitamins and supplements. Because medical technology is now keeping us alive much longer, nature needs a little assist. When I see my male friends not doing this, I feel sad for them as I watch them shrinking and becoming grumpy. I believe most men reject the concept of testosterone and HRT because they think it is an admission that they are not the "man" they used to be. They consider it a direct attack on their ability to perform sexually. I also believe that my HRT will help me to maintain a much better quality of life as I head down that lonesome road.

On a daily basis I slap on a patch that contains the prescribed correct amount of testosterone that my body needs. I also include a prescribed dosage, which at the moment is 20 mg once a day, of DHEA in capsule form along with my twice-daily ingestion of vitamins and supplements.

Because I am a firm believer in the mind/body connection, I am convinced that on this therapy my mind tells my body that it should be feeling great, and it always is.

"Old" is when . . . an "all-nighter" means not getting up to pee.

24

DR. EUGENE SHIPPEN:
ENDOCRINOLOGY AND
ANDROPAUSE

Dr. Eugene Shippen, one of our country's leading endocrinologists, is the author of The Testosterone Syndrome. *Dr. Shippen is another of the cutting-edge doctors who are making a difference in the lives of thousands of patients who come to him as a last resort and leave after treatment with a renewed vigor for life. My husband devoured his information and was convinced that hormone replacement for men was also a valuable "edge" relative to longevity and vitality. Dr. Shippen is a great proponent of natural hormones and offers a fascinating viewpoint toward aging and how we can improve the quality of our lives.*

SS: Thank you for speaking with me, Dr. Shippen.

ES: Call me Gene.

SS: I loved your book, and I am particularly intrigued with your ideas of reversing the aging process.

ES: I'd rather say modifying it. "Reversing

it" is a tough term, because part of the aging
process is loss of cells. We lose so many brain
cells, renal cells, so there is a decline that comes
with the attrition of aging that we can't really
stop. But we can certainly reverse the loss or
decline of cellular dysfunction due to deficiency, and we can maintain optimal function.
I look at it as though we are optimizing cellular integrity by maintaining signals to those
cells, which in turn enables those cells to remain healthy. Hormones are the signals that
tell those cells to burn insulin or do the million
other things they do. So I look at it as a new
way to maintain optimal cellular function
through the aging process.

I don't particularly like the term *antiaging*
because I think that people then assume we can
live forever just by pumping in a bunch of hormones and turning our hormone levels back to
what they were in our youth. That is too sim-
plistic. My work is to optimize cellular function during the aging process before the aging
changes have occurred. That way we create a
much better environment for those cells so that
they can regenerate and optimize the functional integrity of our body's systems.

SS: What is the biggest complaint you get
from the men who walk into your office?

ES: Energy. And that's pervasive. It's an energy for life, energy for the things you used to

like to do. It's energy in your brain to think clearly and be positively modified. It's energy for an upbeat mood and sense of joie de vivre. It's energy toward your mate. It's pervasive energy, not just fatigue. And it hits every part of the body because there are androgen receptors and estrogen receptors in every tissue. So your muscles are weaker, your joints are achier, your brain is not as sharp, your cardiovascular system is not as responsive, you're more breathless at tasks that didn't used to make you breathless.

SS: But I imagine that most men are not in tune with their lack of vitality; it's too vulnerable. So how do you pull this information out of them?

ES: I have a checklist, which basically looks at energy in every system of the body. For instance, mental, moods, musculoskeletal system, energy toward sex and sexuality, the prostate. A lot of the BPH (benign prostatic hypertrophy) symptoms that we get are due to a loss of energy of the prostate muscles that open and close the doors and allow flow to be maximized. A lot of the BPH symptoms don't correlate at all with the size of the prostate. They correlate with the testosterone. Once we make that link, men don't have to get up to urinate three times a night. There is a misconception among urologists that BHP is really due to enlargement of the prostate. Half of the men don't have an enlarged prostate, and the missing link is testosterone.

SS: So as men lose their hormones, testosterone in this case, they lose their muscle tone not only outwardly, but internally as well?

ES: Correct. Bladder function, prostate function, sexual function, and tone in the muscles of the pelvis are all related to declining testosterone levels and atrophy. They literally lose the athleticism of those muscles.

SS: I would think the biggest complaint that would get men to come to your office would be loss of erections.

ES: That's not the most common. But if you ask them, they'll say, "I'm doing fine." Then I say, "Well, how are you doing compared to when you were thirty-five?" I don't talk about when they were twenty-five. Those were crazy years. But think back to thirty-five, what was your frequency? If they were once- or twice-a-week guys, now they are once or twice a month. They say it's still working all right, so they don't necessarily see it as a problem. They are just more tired, or they are busier, or their mate is not as receptive, or one hundred other things. But when a man's hormones are in balance, meaning our libido is also in balance, we are always looking for windows of opportunity. Libido's a subtle thing and it's vulnerable, so frequently they won't complain of that.

SS: What are the other complaints?

ES: Things are happening that didn't. They will complain that "I'm failing when I didn't use to." So libido and sexual function are highly variable, something that you can't rely on as primary indicators. But pervasive energy changes. If somebody comes in not feeling up to par, you start to explore every part of the energies of life and you will find that low testosterone explains declines in all the energies.

SS: Do you find that men and women don't realize how bad they are feeling until they experience hormonal balance and it makes them feel better?

ES: Yes, because unless you know it's broken, you sort of accept the changes of aging as, "Okay, I'm over fifty, I shouldn't be running up and down the mountains in the same way. I can accept that." But when you fix them, and they start running up and down the steps and so on, and they get their zest for life back, and their energy systems are working again, it's like turning on all the healthy switches that you are familiar with.

SS: I see it in some of my friends—it's about their vitality. I see them slowing down measurably. . . . My husband gave one of his friends your book and he was offended. He said, "What's the matter? I don't have any problems." Is getting help difficult for men because it's all wrapped up in their maleness?

ES: You have no idea how truly bad it is. It's all wrapped up in our cultural expectations; the way in which aging men are portrayed is the way in which doctors have been telling their patients what to expect. I have patients I have put on testosterone, they feel better, they're doing better, and then they see their doctor back home, who tells them only about the dangers. So they stop taking it. And then they feel bad again, but now they are frightened, that to feel better now, they are going to have to pay some kind of price down the road.

SS: Is that true?

ES: Nothing could be further from the truth. It's the healthiest thing they could do. All you are doing is restoring back to normal what is no longer being produced.

SS: It must be terribly frustrating for you.

ES: It is. Men either reject the idea that this is really what they need, or they find another doctor who gives them the fear of prostate cancer, or the unknown. We don't have long-term double-blind studies to show that it is healthy, but my answer to that is if we used that same filter for everything, we might as well stop practicing medicine. No drugs have those kinds of documented benefits for over ten years—where double-blind randomized control studies show that they are safe and efficacious for treatment. Even with statins, the drugs that lower cholesterol, we don't have ten-, twenty-year studies.

SS: You mean like Lipitor and Pravachol?

ES: Right. These drugs may lower your testosterone at high doses. So from my standpoint, these people are running a grave risk of actually decreasing their health in the long term. In the short term they may have fewer events for unknown reasons, but there's no improvement in long-term mortality with these drugs.

SS: As a female I take bioidentical hormones. Is that what you use for men?

ES: Absolutely. I would never use a substitute. All the substituted forms are the ones where we've had bad effects. There's a good reason for that. When you substitute a hormone, it is not metabolized into other hormones the same way. I give testosterone in its natural form. Our body can then convert it into estrogen. As we age and get chubbier, our bodies may produce too much estrogen, and estrogen in men is one of the most important by-products of testosterone. A substitute form of testosterone, like methyltestosterone, cannot be converted like natural testosterone. Only bioidentical hormones will be handled by the body in a natural way, allowing it to balance these secondary hormones in a healthy pattern.

SS: So many women are automatically put on synthetic pharmaceutical hormones at their first complaint. If they are antisynthetic, then the next remedy is black cohosh or eating a lot of yams. Initially this happened to me, and I was in such of state of zeroed-out hormones that I wanted to tell my doctor where to shove those yams, because yams and black cohosh were not giving me any relief.

ES: I say black cohosh is great if you're a geranium, but if you are truly deficient it won't help if you are human. It doesn't provide you with the estrogen benefits on bone and cardio-vascular. There's no proof that it does any of this. In fact, there is growing evidence that black cohosh and other herbs are so weak, they're only covering up some of the subtle symptoms to make women more comfortable.

SS: Then there's soy. Women are downing those soybeans like jelly beans. They're eating tofu (soy is the new buzzword in health food stores), and they are shoving so much soy into their systems, but it makes you think, doesn't soy promote estrogen production?

ES: It has some activating effects.

SS: If so, isn't it a little dangerous to activate

estrogen, because you are creating an imbalance?

ES: Well, yes, that's true. Let's go back to the estrogen receptors. There are two different kinds of estrogen receptors, maybe more. It's well known that there are estrogen alpha and beta receptors. One receptor activates the other. In other words, phytoestrogens can be used for one effect, but the other effect is having some benefits and some side effects. We don't know whether the phytoestrogens activate or block. In small doses soy may activate the receptors in one way and in large doses may end up blocking them. The way I approach it is to consume small amounts of foods to provide the phytoestrogens that have always been in the food chain.

SS: What other foods have estrogenic capacity?

ES: How about clover? You can look at all of the different plants and they all have estrogen to some degree. To overload one type, to kind of force-feed the body to take a very high concentration of soy estrogen, is going down uncharted waters, and it's not a substitute for the natural bioidentical estrogens that are metabolized and balanced in the body.

I try to take a balanced approach. The Japanese get somewhere around 50 mg of phytoestrogens daily from the food they ingest, and I wouldn't take any more than that. But I will tell you this: If I could change something in my book, it would be soy for men. When I had men taking soy, I found it to be helpful.

When we are young, our liver can clear estrogen very efficiently. As we age, lean body mass goes down, fat cell mass goes up, and the circulating testosterone gets converted in greater amounts into estrogen in our fat cells because of enzyme activity in fat cells. If you look at individuals, you'll find that chubby guys who have central obesity (thick through the midsection) are high in estrogen. You'll find the greater the obesity, the greater the number of fat cells, the greater the conversion of testosterone. Where there is a greater conversion of testosterone to estrogen (and men hate to hear this), estrogen proves to be a more powerful hormone to them than testosterone. Estrogen is highly regulated in a man's body. So the estrogen says to the pituitary, "Hey, we've got a lot of estrogen here, so let's turn down the production of testosterone."

SS: But does this extra estrogen provide protection for the man's heart?

ES: On the one hand, it might provide protection for the heart, but as estrogen gets too high, the blood has an increased tendency to clot. One of the studies on heart disease shows that men who have heart attacks have higher estrogen levels and lower testosterone levels. The ratio gets reversed, and the thinking is that maybe increased estrogen increases the likelihood of forming a thrombosis in the coronary arteries.

SS: Is balance the key?

ES: Balance is the key. There are guys who want to get rid of every bit of estrogen. They want to be pure male. I tell them the ying yang is alive and well. Without estrogen there is no libido. There was a study that showed that men who did not produce estrogen had osteoporosis, heart disease, and low libido, yet they had testosterone levels that were two to three times normal.

SS: Why do they do movies called *Grumpy Old Men*?

ES: The studies on mood are so highly variable that it's hard to draw broad conclusions, but I will tell you this: If somebody has never been depressed, and at middle age starts to become depressed, measure his testosterone levels, because the depression won't go away until you correct his testosterone.

The number of men I treat with depression almost always get better with testosterone replacement. Many of them had been on antidepressants and did not get better.

SS: So a man might go to a psychiatrist for

his depression when, in fact, all he needed was to restore his testosterone level?

ES: In a lot of cases, yes. The problem is that once they get on antidepressants they're married to them forever. They feel they can't live without their antidepressants, but antidepressants further depress their testosterone and they don't really get better. So now they are constantly in treatment. But when you ask how they were when they were thirty-five, they could slay a dragon.

SS: Do you feel that testosterone is a means of staving off disease?

ES: Absolutely. The linkage between disease and testosterone has been totally overlooked. It is well documented in literature. Almost every disease drives testosterone down. Testosterone is anti-inflammatory, it's rebuilding, it's anabolic, it's good for insulin. It's good for maintaining all the things that get suppressed in most common diseases—inflammatory disorders, arthritis, asthma, heart disease. The information on heart disease relative to testosterone is absolutely astounding, and it's totally ignored. You can give a shot of testosterone to a man who has coronary artery disease and he'll last a minute longer on a treadmill without changes in the cardiogram. It has an immediate vasodilating effect on the coronary.

SS: Does it have any effect on lungs, or people with emphysema?

ES: Absolutely, yes. And here's another thing: Colitis gets better when testosterone levels are checked and testosterone is administered. Colitis is treated with steroids; as soon as you start taking steroids for colitis (corticosteroids, prednisone), testosterone just drops dramatically. Then a man starts losing muscle mass, he gets weaker and weaker. He loses his insulin sensitivity, he starts to gain weight. Steroids knock you down physically, and testosterone will actually reverse and protect you.

SS: What about DHEA?

ES: I don't give DHEA to anyone who doesn't need it. One of the problems is that they never do double-blind long-term studies looking at this kind of medicine that fixes two, three, or four things at once. So if you just do a study on testosterone and that person is low on DHEA and low in growth hormone, and his thyroid is out of balance, he is not going to have the same benefit from testosterone as another person. You have to look at every one of those parameters and fix them. When you do you'll find that the person responds to testosterone with renewed zest for life and will get his energy back.

Diet is crucial and essential for good health. All the HRT in the world will not do the good it wants to do if you are eating badly. Dietary patterns make a huge difference in our likelihood of getting cancer. There's a supplement that helps the metabolism even more, and it's called omega-3 fatty acids.

SS: Yes, I take that two times a day.

ES: The Japanese get high amounts of DIM (diiodomethane) in their vegetables and a high amount of fish oil in their fish. Yet it's amazing: if they move to our country, they get the same breast cancer or prostate cancer, because they begin to eat our diet, which doesn't have enough omega-3s, and we do not eat the same amount of cruciferous vegetables.

There are other things . . . minerals. Selenium is very important. There are three well-documented things that I look at for modifying the risk of cancer. One is indole-3-carbinol, or I3C, which comes from cruciferous vegetables, and the omega fatty acids help with that. The other is vitamin D, which has been shown to have an effect on estrogen metabolism in a different way. It turns estradiol back into estrone, which is the weak estrogen. When that system is working, the body has the ability to regulate estrogen according to its needs, instead of being overdriven toward the more powerful estrogen, estradiol.

SS: I didn't realize vitamin D had that effect.

ES: Yes, it also has the ability to induce cells that are becoming cancerous to self-destruct, plus it has some anti-inflammatory effect. Vitamin D in adequate doses protects bone from osteoporosis. So vitamin D is helpful in lots of wonderful ways—its anticancer effects, its benefit as an anti-inflammatory, its influence on estrogen metabolism, and its ability to induce cancer cells to self-destruct.

The other important supplement is selenium. Selenium is now being studied in a test with fifty thousand men for its ability to prevent prostate cancer. But selenium has already been established as a useful supplement against breast cancer and colon cancer. In animal testing, selenium reduced tumor replication and had a variety of therapeutic effects on different kinds of tumors. So I put all my patients on selenium. Women should be taking selenium because of the risk of colon cancer as much as breast cancer.

SS: What about antioxidants?

ES: Despite what the cardiologists say about antioxidants (which is that they are not good for anything), I do believe antioxidants are important, along with folic acid and the natural antioxidants.

SS: There's a lot of controversy about HGH [human growth hormone].

ES: I'm very careful with HGH. I test for IgF1, growth factor. If it's low, I test for output. I always do a challenge test. I never give HGH just as an antiaging supplement just because theoretically it's useful. But endocrinology brings in people who have been everywhere else and haven't found relief.

SS: I believe in today's world your endocrinologist is your most important doctor.

ES: Some of them are like frightened sheep unless they're on the cutting edge. Most endocrinologists are very conservative, and they're waiting for the world to move them. I like to live on the cutting edge. I love science.

SS: Me too. I never knew I would be fascinated by physiology.

ES: Well, it's the creative application of science. When people say, "What do you practice, complementary or alternative medicine?" I say, "No, I practice innovative medicine." The only new patients I take are those who are interested in innovative therapy.

For instance, from the standpoint of my research, if you have breast cancer, and you go on hormone replacement, you are no more likely to have a recurrence than a woman who doesn't take it.

SS: Where were you when I was being chastised by the press for taking hormones with my cancer? *People* magazine did a cover story asking, "Is she risking her life?"

ES: If you do get a recurrence or a new tumor, it will most likely be estrogen-receptor positive, which is far less aggressive. So you'll have a better chance of surviving it. Additionally, if you are on bioidentical HRT, your colon cancer risk will drop by 30 to 35 percent, and that's a bigger killer for women. Colon cancer is more likely to kill you. It's the hidden cancer, whereas breast cancer is out front. Breast cancer is 90 percent curable if caught early, and colon is only 45 percent curable; it depends upon the stage, but you are much more likely to die from it. There is a 30 percent reduction of colon cancer risk if you are on bioidentical HRT.

SS: Well, that's great news. Please tell the media, so they can stop scaring women to death about HRT. The reported studies are terribly flawed because they are done with synthetic, pharmaceutical hormones.

Now what do you tell men about bioidentical HRT?

ES: I tell men there's no connection between maintaining normal testosterone levels and prostate cancer, and this has been well supported in literature. The difference between getting cancer in men is diet and lifestyle, as evidenced by Japanese men having less prostate cancer than we do. So they are doing something that doesn't make colon cancer grow and gobble us up. Some of the things that are healthy for us, relative to the study of men and prostate cancer, will in the future be far more beneficial than doing PSA tests and biopsies on men.

SS: What's the future? Where are we going?

ES: In the future, I hope that scientists realize that the complexity of the human organism doesn't always lend itself to long-term double-blind randomized studies. It's time doctors started treating people as individuals. In doing so, there will be massive reductions in all the major degenerative diseases as we normalize hormones, normalize nutrients, and key in on lifestyle, diet, and environmental factors.

I think our capability for living out our normal genetic life span will be greatly enhanced through bioidentical hormone replacement, by keeping all of our functions reasonably intact: our brain, our motor system, our ability to get up and do the things that keep us self-sustaining late into life.

SS: So you're talking quality of life.

ES: Yes, maintaining that general quality of life and maintaining all the functions that we hold dear, sex included. I have some ninety-year-olds who are enjoying that side of life. It's just our perception that sex is no longer important when you are old. We can't envision our grandparents making love, but it's a perception. Balanced hormones give you vitality, and sexual vitality is part of it . . . that is, if science doesn't bog us down with fear over the lack of these long-term studies.

SS: Thank you, this was enlightening. And keep doing the good work. Ever since my husband got on bioidentical HRT, his vitality has returned. I've got my old (young) guy back.

beating
THE
clock

"Old" is when . . . going braless pulls all
the wrinkles out of your face.

25
PHYSICAL AGING

Okay, this is the crummy part. Who likes to wake up each day and find that another part of their body has dropped? You already know I think the best way to fight physical aging is getting your hormones balanced. Finding balance for me has been like finding the fountain of youth. It has allowed me to forget all those symptoms that were beginning to plague me before I started balancing my hormones. But no doubt about it, the body shows its wear and tear around this age. I have become philosophical about it. I have decided to change my take on it. I focus on how great I am looking for my age. I never expected to look this youthful at age fifty-six. Really, when I think about the women of my mother's era, we have great advantages today that were not available to them. One of the first big advantages is that we now know how to take better care of ourselves. We are the first generation of women who have really embraced exercise. We understand nutrition better than ever before; yet, even armed with this knowledge, many still choose to eat foods laden with chemicals and preservatives. Nothing will age you faster than ingesting chemicals. Simply put, aging results when our bodies break down more cells than they build up, and chemicals will certainly break down your cells.

My friend Dr. Schwarzbein says that as a society we are on a frightening accelerated metabolic aging path. If you have read any of my Somersize books, you know what I'm talking about. Bad eating habits, stress, caffeine, alcohol abuse, and inactivity can lead to extended periods of high insulin levels, which prematurely ages our bodies on a cellular level. This aging process leads to disease. Additionally, when the hormone insulin is present in increased levels, it can disrupt every other hormone system in the body, which can lead not only to excessive body fat, but also to degenerative diseases of aging such as different types of cancer, cholesterol abnormalities, coronary artery disease, high blood pressure, osteoporosis, stroke, and type 2 diabetes. Most people do not realize that hormone imbalances always lead to disease. Furthermore, women who are already going through menopause are at extreme risk of disease.

As women age, we naturally become more

insulin resistant, which explains why it gets harder to stay slim as we get older. Adopting a high-carbohydrate diet exacerbates the problem because all those carbohydrates increase insulin resistance. The elevated amount of insulin in the blood increases testosterone levels, which further blunts the production of estrogen and progesterone, the female sex hormones. Compound the problem with a low-fat diet and you have even less hormone production, because we must consume real dietary fat to create hormones. Besides the uncomfortable side effects of hot flashes, cramping, and mood swings, an imbalance of these sex hormones means we cannot produce healthy cells! It is at this critical stage that women become vulnerable to disease.

This is the connection among nutrition, health, and aging. Everything we put into our mouths, good or bad, has a direct effect on our health and, thus, our ability to stay youthful. We all know eating junk food is bad for us, yet I don't think we consider the consequences of the bad food choices we make. Years of poor eating habits cumulatively add up to damaged cells and our bodies' inability to produce new, healthy cells. When we eat poorly, we age faster, not only externally, but internally as well. This accelerated metabolic aging process leaves us vulnerable to disease at an earlier age.

Eating right isn't just about weight loss, it's about total health that determines how well we age. Most important, we can control our bodies' ability to combat the diseases of aging when we understand the connection between the intake of real and healthy foods. It doesn't matter what you have achieved or how much you have earned or what titles you have held. If you don't have your health, you have nothing! (Oh, God, did I just say that? I hear my grandfather's voice in my ear.)

In my Somersize books, I constantly drive home the importance of eating real foods to lose weight; but we need to stay away from processed foods and trans fats for another important health reason. Processed foods introduce free radicals into our systems. It is important to understand the consequences of free radicals.

Free radicals are molecules that carry an extra electron. Since electrons need to be paired off, these free radicals roam through our systems like little home wreckers, trying to steal electrons from healthy cells. This process damages our systems on the cellular level. Antioxidants, such as vitamin E, vitamin A, and vitamin C, help to neutralize free radicals. But when we replace real food (which includes natural vitamins) with processed food, we are not supplying our bodies with the natural antioxidants we need to fight the free radicals; instead, we are introducing more free radicals into our systems! The damage that results over time accelerates the metabolic aging process and leads to insulin resistance, then disease and possible early death. Ironically, two of the most powerful antioxidants, vitamin A and vitamin E, are found in foods that contain real fats. Unfortunately, the fat most people consume is unhealthy fat, like trans fats that come in bags of potato chips and corn chips, or processed foods with ingredients that no one can pronounce.

Processed foods and trans fats aren't the only things compromising our health. Consider that the average American consumes forty-three gallons of sugary soft drinks every year! We are literally killing ourselves with sugar and chemicals that break down our bodies on the cellular level. The sugar and caffeine in one cola wreak havoc on the body by spiking insulin levels. Think about that every time you consider having a can of soda. The average can of soda contains one-quarter cup of sugar. Imagine eating one-quarter cup of sugar in its dry form—you would gag. Yet most of us drink several cans of these sodas every day without even thinking of the amount of sugar we are ingesting and the effect it's having on our insulin levels.

Imagine the insulin in your body looking unsuccessfully for places to store the abundance of glucose from all the sugar we ingest, whether it's in the form of cakes and cookies or high-starch vegetables or white-flour pastas or white breads. Then visualize how the sugar gets converted into fat because your cells just cannot accept any more sugar. Visualize the free radicals sweeping through your system and damaging your cells.

With diet drinks you don't have the sugar to contend with, but you have the additional free radicals from the artificial sweeteners. The most recent studies on the effects of aspartame (NutraSweet, Equal) are frightening. Lab studies have proven irreversible brain damage in laboratory animals. In fact, one can of soda can raise the levels of toxins in the brain of an infant higher than levels that caused brain damage in immature animals.

I apologize for laying all this physiology on you, but I think it is important to understand the effects of food on our bodies, especially at a time in our lives when we are no longer producing a full complement of hormones, which as I have said leaves us vulnerable to disease. Part of looking good and feeling good is internal health. I also want you to understand the importance of healthy cell reproduction.

This is why, when I was diagnosed with

breast cancer, I was so adamant about continuing hormone replacement therapy and did not want to take chemotherapy if there was any way I could avoid it. I knew that chemo would destroy my healthy cells along with the unhealthy ones, and I felt it was a greater risk for me. I know already that as I get older, some of my cells will die off; and there is nothing I can do about that. But I also know that if I am not giving my body the proper combination of nutritious foods, my cells will die off at a more rapid rate. When I feed my body properly, my cells thrive; and I feel empowered knowing I can stave off disease and aging for as long as possible. Healthy cells will keep you young, slim, and looking great.

We are going to age physically, no matter what we do; but we do have control over how we age and how well we age. Look around at the seniors you know. Which ones are in the best health? It's those who have always exercised and eaten properly. I'm not talking fanatics, just those who kept a check on themselves. There is no free lunch. You get out of life what you put into it. That's just the way it goes. The reason some people look better than others is that they work at it. That's the reason celebrities look so extraordinary. They are constantly thinking about their appearance because it is their livelihood. They are in the business of making pictures, whether it's on television, in magazines, or in the movies. Celebrities know that they have to stay fit and healthy if they are to make a living. Eating real foods instead of processed foods, avoiding chemicals, exercising daily, drinking lots of water, getting plenty of rest, watching the consumption of alcohol, and avoiding smoking all add up to looking great. Granted, it's easier to pull into Jack in the Box and order a burger, fries, and a milkshake; but it will show on your hips, in your skin tone, and in your overall general health.

It takes more work and discipline to look good as you age, but you are the beneficiary. When you look around you, it is easy to see those who have given up. It happens to both men and women. First comes the weight gain that accompanies middle age. Weight will keep piling on if no thought is given to controlling it. I know many once thin women who let it get out of hand or did not understand the effects of insulin resistance during this passage. After the weight has taken hold come the various diseases associated with aging.

Most people simply expect that disease is part of aging and have no understanding of the effects of elevated insulin levels (eating too much sugar). Aging and disease do not go hand in hand. Bad lifestyle habits are the culprits in aging. If we could truly grasp that we are in control of our health, that it is not necessary to spend our last years in hospitals or with oxygen tanks or with limbs that can no longer hold us up, we would make the necessary changes immediately. Being ill is a terrible way to spend the second half of your life, and it isn't necessary. You have the power to change the course of your life. It's a choice, but it starts now. If you wait much longer, you will have gone past the point of no return. As they say, this isn't a dress rehearsal, this is the show! We can have life and vigor right up to the end, but it's up to each one of us to choose. And that's what it is—a choice. Have your cake now or choose to beat the odds.

Here is what it takes—*commitment!* It requires that you say to yourself, "Today I am going to change my habits." Then you have to mean it. Once you have truly made a commitment, it gets easier. When the alarm goes off in the morning, don't lie there all cozy and warm. Designate how many days a week you have decided to exercise and then do it. Try doing something that you enjoy. It is not necessary to join a gym and commit all your time and money to exercising. Just find a way to get moving. Physical activity releases stored sugar from your cells. As soon as that stored sugar is released, your body starts burning off its fat reserves. That's when you will start losing weight and your beautiful body will start revealing it-self.

You don't have to be a fanatic. I exercise every other day (every day when I am in train-ing for a tour), and I do this at home. I spend twenty minutes doing cardio. I like to walk up and down my outdoor steps ten times (about twenty steps). That really gets my heart rate up.

Then I use free weights for another twenty minutes, and then I do mat exercises—squats, leg lifts, pushups—and waist exercises. I do use several of my own exercise products (ThighMaster, Bodyrow, UltraTrack), but you can get the same results by stretching and do-ing situps (it just takes a little more effort). Machines force you to be in the right posi-tions, which can make exercise easier and more focused; an improperly performed exer-cise has little to no benefits other than cardio. And with the timers that are often on ma-chines, you get motivated.

Take the stairs instead of elevators, walk to the store rather than drive, play tag with your kids, swim, jog: all of these are easy and enjoy-able ways to get fresh air and exercise. Notice that the older people who are fit and in good health are always the ones who have eaten good food in moderation and were conscious of doing some kind of exercise every day. Exercise feels good, it puts pure oxygen into your bloodstream, it promotes good health and fitness, and it's good for your bones.

Rethink how you eat, too. For breakfast, instead of having a bagel or a muffin (cake in a muffin cup), have a fruit smoothie and fresh eggs and sausages or a healthy and great-tasting breakfast cereal with nonfat milk. Drink decaffeinated coffee; caffeine lowers your serotonin levels, which then makes you crave comfort foods, usually carbohydrates or something sugary. The body accepts carbohydrates, particularly refined white flours, as sugar; so drinking caffeine eventually will make you fat. Besides, caffeine blocks estrogen production, which eventually leads to insulin resistance, which also makes you fat (and bitchy, I might add) and will lead to disease . . . all for a cup of coffee? Try Starbucks' Guatemalan decaf. It's delicious and strong, and you'll suffer no adverse effects.

It's these simple first changes that will set you on a path of healing and good health. Watch and see how quickly you are pleased with what you see in the mirror. As I said, the choice is yours.

Perks of aging: Your joints are more accurate meteorologists than the National Weather Service.

26
BONES

As we age, we hear over and over to take calcium to protect our bones, and for the most part we are pretty good about remembering to take those capsules every day. But have you ever considered how diet affects your bones? What would we be without our skeletons? A pile of jelly! The food we consume from childhood throughout our lives will directly affect our bone structure. At menopausal age, we women start to worry about our bones. Our doctors tell us to have a bone density test. Most of us have already experienced bone loss. We accept this; in fact, we expect this to be the case. But hear this: Bone loss is not a condition that has to accompany middle to old age. Osteoporosis is insidious because you can't see or feel it happening. Most people who have the disease don't know it. And then a bone breaks or fractures.

Each year 430,000 Americans wind up in the hospital because of fractures related to osteoporosis. Hip fractures, which represent about 300,000 of that total, are devastating. One victim in five dies within a year, and half are never able to live independently again. Most of us know someone who has suffered a hip fracture, but you may be surprised to learn that complications of the injury kill even more women every year than breast cancer. Preventing osteoporosis is really a life-and-death matter, like preventing cancer and heart disease.

Hip fractures are just the most obvious part of the problem. Millions of women suffer distressing symptoms that they don't connect to fragile bones. A woman may not realize that her chronic back pain comes from crush fractures in her spine. Fragile vertebrae may have crumbled under the ordinary stresses of everyday life. Osteoporosis can make a woman look old before her time, but she may have no idea that her slumped posture and protruding tummy are caused by fractures in her spine. As a woman you have one-in-three odds of suffering from osteoporosis in your lifetime. You can beat those odds. Medical experts now consider osteoporosis a preventable disease. Osteoporosis is treatable thanks to new findings about nutrition and exercise, as well as new medications and hormone replacement therapy.

Even women in their twenties and thirties can get osteoporosis. Fortunately, this doesn't happen often, since most early victims of the disease have significant risk factors such as prolonged use of steroid medications or lengthy periods of eating disorders. Ironically, many of these women are dancers or athletes who look healthy and fit. The bones we have later in life reflect what we did as kids, teens, and young adults. So in a very real sense, osteoporosis is a disease that starts in childhood. Consider this when you hear of a teenager who is struggling with anorexia. The immediate and long-term effects are devastating. This is why it is so important that our children eat healthy right from the start. What they put into their mouths now will affect not only whether they are overweight or obese later in life, but also how healthy and strong their bones are. If a woman is menopausal or premenopausal, extra calcium can help build strong bones. But simply upping calcium consumption has never been shown to increase bone density or prevent fractures in older women. Add vitamin D to that calcium and the effects are dramatic: bone density increases significantly, and fractures are reduced by 50 percent. That's because vitamin D is needed to absorb calcium and turn it into bone, and many postmenopausal women don't get enough.

Going on HRT using bioidentical hormones can also help build bone strength.
Estrogen replacement has been shown to help
prevent osteoporosis, and you get this benefit
from taking estriol as part of HRT.

Here's something you probably didn't realize: Men also are prone to osteoporosis. An es-
timated two million men have this disease. In
fact, a man is far more likely to suffer an
osteoporosis-related fracture during his lifetime than he is to get prostate cancer; yet men,
and even their doctors, are largely unaware of
this problem. Hormonal stimulation is just as
important for men's bones as it is for women's.
Low testosterone levels are responsible for
about half the cases of osteoporosis in men.
Usually, low testosterone is a consequence of
aging, but certain medical conditions can lead
to more rapid loss. Signs of low testosterone in
men include the following: reduced libido or
impotence, decreased facial and body hair (for
a woman it is increased facial and body hair),
and enlarged breasts (although many men have
low testosterone levels without any symptoms
at all). A blood test can measure testosterone
levels. If you are low in testosterone, ask your
doctor about a bone density test.

Men with a light frame and low body
weight and also men with eating disorders

are particularly at risk for osteoporosis. Competitive athletes in sports with weight classifications especially suffer from the problem. Anyone who has been a yo-yo dieter or had anorexia or bulimia is at a higher risk for osteoporosis. Other risk factors for men and women are inactivity, a diet low in calcium and vitamin D, high alcohol consumption, and smoking (current or past).

Here's what you can do to restore your body and your bones to good health:

1. **NUTRITION:** *Eat real foods, and enough of them. Remember, food is fuel, which you need for energy, and real foods promote healthy cell reproduction. In addition, real foods promote strong healthy bones.*

2. **PHYSICAL ACTIVITY:** *Be active. Weight training in particular promotes bone growth. Here's how. When you do weight training, the muscles tug against the bone, promoting and stimulating bone growth. The outward physical benefits are also apparent. Nothing is more beautiful than toned, defined, cut muscles. Your clothes will look better on you, but the inward effects are the most exciting benefit. You will be building bone or, in the case of bone loss, restoring bone.*

3. **SUPPLEMENTS:** *Take calcium, vitamin D, and Fosamax (if necessary, depending upon your bone loss). This, of course, should be discussed with your doctor.*

4. **HRT:** *Continue to take estriol as part of hormone replacement therapy under your doctor's supervision.*

Perks of aging: People no longer view
you as a hypochondriac.

27

SUPPLEMENTS

Here is the next big thing regarding antiaging: supplements. What a difference it makes to supplement your diet with all the nutrients, herbs, vitamins, phytonutrients, and amino acids that our body needs for survival but in general most of us are missing; they are absolutely life changing. I used to wander into health food stores and gaze at all the vitamins stacked in their neat little rows and wonder what they were all for. At times I would make a feeble attempt to take a "one a day" vitamin, but aside from that I was pretty unaware as to their benefits. I think it is vitally important to find yourself a cutting-edge doctor who is interested in the antiaging approach to life and health.

I never knew anything about this approach to health until after my mother passed away. I experienced terrible grief upon losing her, but my work schedule left me no time to grieve. In fact, the day after I buried my mother, I was on the Home Shopping Network for nineteen hours over the weekend, and my work continued at that pace for several months. Before long, I began to have health problems. I felt as if I were wilting. I couldn't stay awake. I would fall asleep in the car on the way to meetings or work, struggle through whatever it was that I was required to do, and then sleep all the way home. I would walk into the house (it was multileveled, with many stairs), and whereas I used to bound and leap, two stairs at a time, now I had to sit and rest before I could contemplate heading up to the bedroom. If I awakened to go to the bathroom in the middle of the night, I would have to sit and rest halfway to the toilet (and my bedroom was not so big). I felt as if I were slowly running out of gas. I had no energy, I was overly tired for my age, and I couldn't understand because I was on bioidentical HRT and eating properly.

What I hadn't factored in was stress. Stress causes most of our problems. For sure stress blunts hormone production, so even if you are still making a full complement of hormones, acute stress is going to affect your levels. How could I have thought that the loss of my mother, who is the reason I am sane today, was something I could "get over in time"? This stress, along with a lack of nutrients because our food supply is damaged, as well as contaminated water and air, plus my body's inability to operate properly because I was still so upset from my mother's death, coupled with being run-down from overwork . . . and *duh!* No wonder my body was shutting down! I was ignorant of the fact that grief is a process and must be dealt with just like any emotional problem—and will not go away until it has been. I wrongly figured that my sadness would go away "in time."

Soon it was becoming intolerable, and I felt my abilities to work were being compromised. I went to see my internist, who, as I mentioned before, is a Western, Eastern, and holistically trained doctor. He did some tests and confirmed to me what I already inherently knew, that my adrenal and cortisol levels were completely burned out. Besides that, I had developed something called "leaky gut," a precursor to Crohn's disease. This meant that I had developed little leaks in my upper intestine from stress and that the toxins from my intestines were leaking into my bloodstream, which was literally causing me to break down and wilt. I had never felt so fatigued—just walking to the doctor's office exhausted me. We talked for a long while, and after I explained about my mother and my workload and my inability to take any time to come to terms with my grief, he figured that I had gotten this ill because I had not dealt with the pain of losing her. He lectured me about balance, and I felt embarrassed because I know these things; but, of course, the messenger does not always live the message.

Every test he took came up low or depleted. It was this doctor who started me on a regimen of vitamins and herbs. I began with a pharmaceutical-grade multivitamin, calcium and magnesium, folic acid, coenzyme Q_{10} (which carries oxygen to all the glands, including the adrenals), glucosamine (because I complained about joint pain), vitamin C (1,000 mg), Eskimo-3 fish oil and omega-3 fatty acids for the heart, Flora Source to fight yeast, and Adrenal 180 (because my adrenals were blown out).

Throughout the year, he continually changed the amounts depending upon my workload and stress level. When called for, sometimes he added extras, sometimes he took away. It all depended upon my strength and energy. I must say, since taking all these supplements I rarely get sick anymore, and I feel an inner strength I never had before. Even though I am in glorious health today, I continue a regimen of supplements and vitamins as a first guard against illness and as a means of building up my body's strength.

In addition, Dr. Schwarzbein has put me on

more supplements and amino acids: Sam-e, St.-John's-wort, and L-tryptophan for depression, irritability, PMS, and carbohydrate cravings; evening primrose oil and L-glutamine for additional help with carbohydrate cravings; carnitine to decrease carbohydrate cravings and mobilize fat; L-tyrosine, which relieves stress on the adrenal glands (tyrosine converts to adrenaline and aids in the functioning of the adrenals); L-taurine as a diuretic, along with vitamin B_6 for salt and water retention; and lecithin, glycine, and phosphatidylserine for irritability and anxiety.

My friend and master herbalist, Paul Schulick, who produces high-quality herbs and supplements for his company, New Chapter of Vermont, sends me the following: Smoke Shield for smoke exposure, air pollution, and exhaust fumes; Rhodiola, which improves mental, immune, adrenal, and cardiovascular performance; green and white tea capsules for longevity, heart, and immune system function (these contain health-promoting antioxidants); Host Defense, which enhances human natural killer cell activity up to 300 percent; Zyflamend, which reduces inflammation; Holy Basil to deliver nutrients to the mind; and Turmeric Force (turmeric is one of the world's most important healing herbs).

On my own, through a lot of reading, research over the Internet, and talking with several cutting-edge doctors, including my own internist, I found Iscador, to fight the cancer that has already invaded my body. Currently I am NED, no evidence of disease, but I was looking for the most palatable way to fight against the return of this cancer. Iscador is an anthroposophical medicine made from plant extracts, developed by the famed homeopath Dr. Rudolph Steiner in the early 1920s in Europe. It has been used at the Steiner clinics in Europe in place of chemotherapy, and they have had the same results, with no side effects. Iscador is not an FDA-approved drug in this country, so I am not suggesting that you go the same route. I will not know for another two years if Iscador has done all that the manufacturer, Weleda, said it would. I will keep you posted. I inject this extract, made from mistletoe that is grown on special types of trees (it's unlikely that the one you hang above your doorway at Christmas is what they are talking about), every other day, and I will continue to do so for the next two years, while I am still in the danger zone. I so believe in its healing effects that I am considering taking Iscador for the rest of my life. The manufacturer claims that it will build up the immune system, protecting it from invaders such as cancers, which of course is very exciting to me.

I know this seems like a lot of supplements to take, and maybe I am going overboard, but it does show that working with doctors who are "in the know" allows you to get as involved in supplements as you care to be. You should create your own program, but I thought you'd like to see my regimen as a means of comparison. As I said, this particular passage takes more work if we want to have a great quality of life. With the environment as damaged as it is, we have to be proactive about our health. We are not getting the proper nutrients from our food anymore because of the damage that has been done to our soil, air, and water. We ingest chemicals most of the time without even knowing it. Our food supply is contaminated with chemicals and toxins. What are we to do? We can sit idly by and talk ourselves into thinking we are impervious to such things, but I have already had my first scare, which I now consider to be one of the many blessings of cancer. I can't fight the damage done thus far to the environment, so I am taking the first line of defense, by making my body "war ready." At least if I get polluted with chemicals and free radicals by unintentionally ingesting foods that have been contaminated (and face it, when you have to eat in as many restaurants as I do, I am bound to be getting some polluted food without knowing it), at least I can fight back by building up my immune system through supplements, vitamins, herbs, and Iscador. It's all I know how to do.

Do I like taking this many pills in a day—no. But I do care about living a long, healthy life, and I don't know any other way to do it. I am not alone in this. All my doctors concur, and so many doctors who are up on things are turning to supplements as a first line of defense. The new cutting-edge doctors understand that our lives today are not as they were when older doctors were in medical school. We have reached contamination levels of unprecedented proportions in the last several decades.

Recently, I hemorrhaged my vocal cords by overusing them in rehearsal. I went to my throat doctor in a panic, because I would be doing previews for my new Broadway show in four days. He shook his head and said that normally it takes ten to fourteen days for vocal cords to heal, but if I rested my voice completely until then (not a single word), perhaps I had a chance. I returned to him four days later, quite anxious, as you might expect. He looked at my vocal cords on X-ray and said, "This is a miracle. I have never seen such a fast recovery; it must be all the supplements you take." I was able to do the previews in perfect voice. It's little things like this that give me the incentive to take all these ingestibles each day.

If you feel that supplements would benefit your health, start asking around. Get the names of the most advanced or cutting-edge doctors in your town or city. Recent med school graduates have accepted integrated medicine as a normal part of health care. You might find out from one of them where to go for help. Having a Western doctor is a must—in the end, we need to rely on drugs in an emergency—but check around to find out if there is a doctor in your city who also heals through supplements and herbs. A doctor trained in Eastern and holistic medicine along with Western is best of all. Often that doctor has an office on the same floor with an acupuncturist or a massage therapist. This approach to medicine is deliberately integrated and collaborative. You may be asked to turn off your cell phone, to keep the waiting room calm and serene. As a result, this may turn out to be the one time in the day when you can get that quiet. What better way to walk into your doctor's office? Your calm demeanor allows him or her to get to work right away. You've had time to think about why you're there. You can develop a meaningful relationship with your doctor this way.

Perks of aging:
You can eat dinner at four P.M.

———

28

RITA: A SEVENTY-YEAR-OLD EXPERIENCE

Rita is another inspiring woman, full of life and energy and good feelings. It's truly remarkable to talk with a woman of seventy years who is so progressive, because she comes from an era (as my mother did) that accepted doctors' advice as dogma. To go against the grain and partake in something as cutting-edge as natural bioidentical hormone replacement is not only forward thinking but courageous. After talking with Rita, I became more convinced than ever that natural hormone replacement is the way to go. This is a woman who is enjoying her life, and she is as sharp as a tack. Read for yourself. . . .

SS: Good morning, Rita, and thank you for speaking with me. I know you are a patient of Dr. Schwarzbein's, and I was very interested in knowing how you feel, having been on natural hormones for such a long time.

R: I feel great! I entered menopause at age fifty-five. At first I was on synthetic hormones for a few years, and I felt awful. I was depressed, tired, I had constant headaches, my breasts were always swollen and tender, and I was puffy all over because of the water retention, so I just stopped taking the hormones because I thought, I can't feel any worse.

SS: Then what happened?

R: I started to feel as if I were living in someone else's body. I couldn't relate to myself anymore. You know what I mean? My body just didn't behave or react as it had for all the years before menopause. I was pretty discouraged.

Then I heard about this young endocrinologist in my area who was prescribing natural hormones, and everyone who was taking them was talking about how great they were feeling. So I thought, It can't get any worse than this, and I decided to make an appointment.

SS: How long did it take after you started on natural hormones before you began to feel any difference?

R: Almost immediately. I felt more energetic, and my depression was gone. Life was beautiful again.

SS: Tell me about your typical day.

R: Well, I wake up early, around four o'clock, but I wake up so happy I just like to lie there and think good thoughts. Then usually around six A.M., I get up and get ready for work. I teach Spanish at the university. I have worked all my life, since I was seventeen years old. My students all think I am young, and I like it that way. They guess at my age, and usually they say that I am fifty or sixty years old. But I think it's because I have a youthful energy. It's been this way ever since I have been on natural hormones. They make me feel more energetic. I take care of my two grandchildren quite often, and what's great is that I have the energy to be with them. I've always had a lot of energy, I have always been very active; but when I was on synthetic hormones, I just lost my zest for life.

SS: So what is your teaching schedule like?

R: I schedule classes from eight A.M. until noon every day. Two days a week I give two classes in the afternoon from four until seven.

I try to exercise as often as I can. I walk every day and on the weekends. I have a stationary bike that I use quite often, and I move constantly.

On weekends, my husband and I do a lot of things together. We enjoy each other's company. We go to restaurants, or the beach, or we take a lot of drives.

SS: What about sex, if you don't mind my asking?

R: We are still enjoying sex from time to time. It's not the way it once was, but I think ever since I have been on natural hormones, my feelings have come back. When I was on the other hormones, there was a lot of vaginal dryness. That does not make it fun. But now that is gone and sex feels good again. I think my husband should be on natural hormones. He is in his seventies also.

SS: Do you still have a period?

R: Yes, I do. I had a lot of bleeding last year because I had fibroid tumors. So I stopped taking the natural hormones, and then I started to feel awful again. The biggest thing I notice is that my brain stops functioning well when I am not on the natural hormones. So I went back on them, had the fibroids taken care of, and now things seem back to normal.

SS: But doesn't it bother you to have a period at this age? Isn't it just a hassle?

R: No, it really doesn't bother me. It's worth the trade-off. I feel so much better when my hormones are balanced. It's the difference between really living and just existing. So what! I have a period. I also have a brain, and that is more exciting to me than worrying about having a period each month. Besides, when Dr. Schwarzbein explained to me that having a period is the most natural way to go through this passage, it made sense. We are mimicking my normal physiology. That seems right.

SS: Do you take vitamins and supplements?

R: Yes, I do. I think they are very important. My body is working well. I am not stiff and I don't feel old, so I assume that all these things I am doing are making me feel that way.

SS: Are your friends taking natural hormones, or synthetic hormones, or nothing at all?

R: Some of them take nothing, some of them are on synthetic, and I can see the difference between them and me. None of my friends work, they can't think, they forget everything, and they are slow. Whenever I am around my friends, I am thankful that I have a brain that is together. Good brain function is the best part of all of this. I am seventy years old, and I am enjoying my life. I don't want it to be over. I think taking natural hormones gives women a second chance. My life is so good, I can't really remember what it was like before. I am so involved in my present circumstances. I went from being depressed, crying, and miserable to having energy, vitality, and clear thinking, and my zest for life and my work is back.

SS: How long will you continue to take these hormones?

R: Forever. These hormones have changed my life. If my doctor told me that I had to stop them, I'd say, No, no, no! And again, the greatest advantage of taking these hormones and supplements is my clear, sharp, functioning brain. I remember things. My brain is working great, and that is a huge thing.

SS: So you are enjoying this second half?

R: Enjoying it? It's better than the first half was. My relationship with my husband is better, my entire situation is better. When I was young, I had too many problems. Even my husband and I had reached a point where we had just gotten used to each other, but now . . . Wow! We're having a ball!

SS: How great. Is there anything else you would like to say to women?

R: Don't be afraid. Find a good cutting-edge doctor who really knows what he's doing. If you don't, you are the one who will suffer.

SS: Thanks so much. You are wonderful and an inspiration.

Perks of aging:
Kidnappers are not very interested in you.

29

DR. MICHAEL GALITZER: NATURAL HORMONES AND ANTIAGING

I have probably sent more than one hundred people to Dr. Galitzer, and without exception everyone loves him. A girlfriend who was on a series at the same time I was starring in Three's Company *has had chronic medical problems and she finally found relief through Dr. Galitzer. He found that everything troubling her medically was hormonally driven. Dr. Galitzer believes in natural bioidentical hormone replacement; he believes in approaching health holistically, using the best of Eastern, Western, and holistic medicine. Dr. Galitzer's enthusiasm is catching. He takes the mystery out of aging; through instruction, and working together as patient and doctor, the second half of life becomes the enjoyable passage it was designed to be. You will enjoy what he has to say.*

SS: Antiaging medicine is very exciting. Would you explain exactly what it is?

MG: Antiaging is about maximizing energy. I would equate lack of energy with accelerated aging and maximizing energy with slowing down the aging process. If I had to assess someone quickly, more than blood tests, I would tell them optimize your nutrition and optimize your emotional state. By doing those things, you will ultimately optimize your energy and feel younger.

SS: I believe natural bioidentical hormones are the fountain of youth we've all been looking for. What importance do you place on hormones relative to aging?

MG: When patients come to me and complain about lethargy, that they just don't have the same energy or the same sex drive, I try to explain it to them from a hormonal point of view, because I think that puts everything into perspective. The key hormones to start to work on are the adrenals; they sit on top of the kidneys and are most affected by stress.

SS: Stress blunts hormone production, so you would first check the adrenals and then the sex hormones?

MG: Right. In the body the adrenals represent survival, whereas the sex hormones—progesterone, estrogen, and testosterone—basically represent reproduction. To the body, survival is always more important than reproduction. So the body will do whatever it takes to maximize adrenal hormone output and survival. With that in mind, the body will convert the sex hormones into adrenal hormones to maintain survival at any cost, which is why when you are stressed and tired, your sex drive goes down. So you really can't go straight to the progesterone, testosterone, and estrogen before you look at the adrenals. You've got to maximize the adrenal.

SS: How do you do that?

MG: There are lots of ways these days that you can evaluate adrenals—with a blood test, with saliva, or with something called heart rate variability.

SS: What is heart rate variability?

MG: Essentially, the more variable your heart, the more each beat is slightly different in length from the preceding beat, the greater the variability, the healthier the autonomic nervous system. The autonomic is the subconscious nervous system, the autopilot of the body that controls things we don't have to think of, like blood pressure, pulse, and breathing. When you do a good history, you find out that people with weak adrenals get tired around four o'clock in the afternoon. They sometimes get a little dizzy when they stand up, and they also might crave sweets. Most people have weak adrenals, and in some people it is more important than in others.

SS: That's interesting. I was experiencing dizziness for a period of time when I got out of bed in the morning. My doctor had me go to an ear, nose, and throat specialist, but at the same time he said my adrenals were blown out and gave me supplements to rectify the matter. I thought the ENT doctor made the dizziness go away, but now I am realizing that it must have been the adrenal supplements.

MG: Right, there is something new called metabolic typing. There are four basic metabolic types: the slow oxidizer, the fast oxidizer, the parasympathetic dominant, and the sympathetic dominant. What this basically says is that there is one system that helps maximize energy in each person. So if you are a parasympathetic dominant, your adrenals are the key system. If you are a sympathetic dominant, your thyroid is your key system. If you are a slow oxidizer, it is your pancreas.

SS: I think you will have to explain that one.

MG: Okay, say you are a parasympathetic dominant, which means your adrenals are key for maximizing energy and processing energy in your body. If you have weak adrenals you are in big trouble, because basically that is your key system and your key system is out.

This happens in pregnancy. For example, when a woman is pregnant and she is stressed in, say, the sixth month, she will start converting her own progesterone (of which she is making lots during pregnancy) to the adrenal hormones. In month seven, the baby's adrenals kick in, and the woman starts stealing from the baby's adrenals; so the baby's adrenals start revving up to supply the excess adrenal hormones that she needs. Then at birth they cut the cord, so the lady loses her fix and suddenly goes into postpartum depression. The child may then become hyperactive and get colic and all those other things. It is part of the process.

SS: Tell me about cortisol.

MG: Cortisol and DHEA are the two hormones made by the adrenals. Initially when you are stressed, cortisol levels go up, and if you are the kind of person who takes stress home, you take that stress back to the family and have a hard time sleeping. The reason you have a hard time sleeping is that cortisol levels are very high at midnight, and that turns off melatonin and also turns off growth hormones. Growth hormone is secreted in the first two hours of sleep, which really allows for the physiological regeneration in the first half of your sleep. If your cortisol levels are high at midnight, you are not going to sleep very well, and you will wake up not feeling well. So it's important to get the adrenals under control because so much is affected by them.

SS: Yet because of a lack of understanding, most people in this situation would be prescribed sleeping pills when in fact, they might have an endocrinological problem having to do with the hormone cortisol.

MG: Yes, but more important, we have to look at the adrenals first. The adrenal cortex, which is the outer part of the gland, makes cortisol and DHEA. If a person has already gone into first-degree, second-degree, or third-degree stress (massive stress being fourth-degree), when the next stressor comes on, there is no third-degree cortisol or DHEA to be released because the adrenals are shot. So what does the body do? It goes to the adrenaline. The adrenaline is not where you want to be.

The body does not have enzymes to break down the adrenaline. Adrenaline is your last-ditch effort. This can cause people to get very anxious and feel palpitations. Adrenaline also has a real affinity for the joints, so people will have weakness or stiffness in their joints, all triggered by blown-out adrenals.

SS: Women are confused about menopause and they don't know where to go. There are conflicting reports on HRT, but all the studies are done on synthetic hormones. How are you taking care of menopausal women?

MG: First of all, very tenderly. But it is science, and I get to work finding out all that I can about her history. When a menopausal woman comes to me, I take it that her progesterone and estrogen are not very high, so I do a complete hormone check, but I would also like to know the status of her adrenals. The other thing I do is a BTA—blood, urine, and saliva. We look for pH and redux; most people have acidic tissue, which is reflected in an alkaline blood pH. So the higher the pH is over 7.35, the more acidic the tissues are. I usually see 7.55, 7.58, 7.60, which generally represents an enormously acidic body.

What occurs is that the liver is out to lunch. The liver is the major cleansing organ of the body. The danger with an acidic body is osteoporosis. When the tissues become acidic and the body has to neutralize acidity, it steals calcium and magnesium from the bone, which is the greatest reservoir to neutralize cellular acidity. So if you have an acidic body with a liver that is not working as efficiently as possible and estrogen starts to accumulate in the body, you have a woman who is set up for estrogen dominance. Normally people are acidic because of a very sluggish liver, or a poorly functioning lymph system, or it could be they are not drinking enough water. Many of the foods we eat are full of estrogen, pesticides, and insecticides. And let's not forget those mercury-silver dental fillings.

SS: What would mercury fillings have to do with a woman in menopause?

MG: The mercury behaves as estrogen in the body, so you get a kind of setup where you have a sluggish liver and an estrogen level that's too high relative to progesterone. Mercury is one of the biggest problems. The older the fillings the more they leak, and they leak to a certain threshold point over years, and that is when symptoms occur. The mercury the dentist puts in your teeth must be put away in a special container that says "Poison" on it. That should tell you something. Root canals are in a different category and one of the few areas in medicine where dead tissue is retained within the body. You can cut out a person's gallbladder or appendix, but with a root canal, the nerve root is dead but there are so many tiny canals in one single nerve root that it is almost impossible to keep all the canals completely free from infection. So the thinking is that some of these canals are still infected and the infection is able to seep through the bloodstream to other areas. Plus, each tooth is connected to an organ, if you are using the meridian system. So frequently a root canal tooth—say, the upper molar—would connect to the stomach meridian, which connects to the thyroid and the breast. Are you still following me?

SS: Yes, and I am fascinated.

MG: Progesterone usually sinks first in a woman. It can start at age thirty-five. So if you have a person in her forties with not enough progesterone, who is affected by the toxic environment and has mercury fillings, plus too much estrogen, and if the woman is overweight at this point (fat cells make estrogen), what happens is estrogen dominance, which I think is the major player in both breast cancer and prostate cancer.

SS: But innovative integrated antiaging is more than a medical workup, isn't it? New medicine treats body, mind, and spirit.

MG: You are right. So when a woman comes to me, I do testing, but I also ask many questions such as, Do you drink coffee, alcohol, Coke, tea? Do you eat pork, bacon, ham, breakfast sausage? Do you smoke cigarettes? What kinds of medication are you on? Do you ingest sweeteners like Sweet'N Low or Equal? Do you eat lots of fruits, do you eat lots of vegetables? Do you eat a lot of sugar, and do you crave salt? Do you have PMS, do you exercise, do you drink enough water, do you take supplements? Do you have any root canals, and do you have silver fillings?

Then I go a little deeper: Do you meditate? How is your relationship with your significant other? Do you like your work? What is your purpose in life? Why are you on planet Earth? Do you feel connected to God or a higher power? What is your support system like with family and friends? Are you having enough fun in your life? What we put into our bodies, what we think, how we live our lives, the relationships we have, all have a major effect on our health. When someone says to me, "I am not happy in my life," I try to find out what makes her or him happy. What turns you on, what excites you? If I had to look at it, I would say the three major areas are to be happy, to be of service, and to experience who you really are. Certain people may have a different order of what is most important, but the big question is, where does one find joy? I think most people don't really realize that the main purpose in their life is to be happy.

SS: If this person has not been able to find joy in her life, do you recommend counseling?

MG: Yes, we have so many wonderful tools at hand today. Therapy can turn people's lives around. The people who are not happy are really not clear about their purpose. I think you have to look at whom you are spending your time with. Most people spend time with their significant other or with the people at work. If both of those are not working, I think it's going to be pretty hard for a person who isn't that conscious to get out. Antiaging medicine is full-service to mind, body, and spirit. I don't think you can slow down the aging process if you are not balanced emotionally. When these questions are answered, I am better equipped to treat this person because I have all the information. Joy in one's life is nature's best healing antidote. Today we can work together as doctor and patient for maximum results. We are living longer than ever before, and the second half, as you call it, can be the best if we appreciate and value the incredible machine we have been given to house our mind and spirit. But it all works together and cannot be discounted as irrelevant.

SS: What are your feelings about natural bioidentical hormones?

MG: I think natural bioidentical hormones are essential. I think they are essential in creating longevity and slowing the aging process. Obviously reducing toxins and reducing tissue acidity are also important, but the endocrine or hormonal system is the one that most connects with how we feel. The hormonal system is what most correlates to the emotional person; it is not the liver or the kidneys. Basically, the hormonal system is most affected by our emotional state, and it is clear that the hormonal system responds to our outlook on the world.

SS: Wonderful information. Thank you so much.

MG: My pleasure.

Perks of aging:
Things you buy now won't wear out.

30

EVE: AN EIGHTY-YEAR-OLD EXPERIENCE

As much as I enjoy the quality of life I am experiencing on natural bioidentical hormones, I have wondered (a lot) what it is going to be like to have my period when I am in my eighties, and is it worth it? Well, here is a woman in her eighties, still having her period and a full, rich, vital life. I was very anxious to talk with her and found her to be the most inspiring role model. She verified for me that it's a small price to pay for the zest and vitality that she is enjoying. I loved talking with her and learned a lot about the important things in life.

I am eighty years old and feel great, but it wasn't always this way. I was married most of my adult life and have two beautiful children. They give me such joy. I am a recovering alcoholic, sober for thirty-nine years, and at age sixty-five I fractured my back. As I lay in bed for weeks, I felt scared to death that I would never be able to work again. I didn't want to end up bed-ridden, like my daddy. At the time,

I had already been through menopause and had not taken hormones because my Tulsa doctor at that time told me I didn't need them. There was no incidence of heart problems or stroke in my family history, just TB and pneumonia; so my doctor said that hormones were not important for me. After I fractured my back, my doctor told me it was because I had lost so much bone, so maybe now I should take Premarin, a synthetic hormone. I had heard negative things about synthetic hormones from my friends, so I did not want to take them; but after a year in physical therapy, I realized I had to do something. My osteoporosis got worse and I panicked. I decided that I was going to really look into alternative medicines. I felt as if I were starting to fall apart; looking back, I now realize I was. I gave up coloring my hair and wearing nail polish. I tried to avoid chemicals wherever I could, thinking that these things might be contributing to my poor health.

Everyone in Santa Barbara was talking about this endocrinologist Dr. Schwarzbein; some thought she was fantastic, and some thought her theories were crazy, but I heard she was doing natural hormones and I went to see her. I was impressed from the start. Here was this tall, vivacious, good-looking woman with shiny, clear eyes. All I could think of was that I wanted some of what she had. She put me on natural hormones, and I began to notice a difference right away. I felt the urge to be active again. I believe that energy begets energy, so I started to walk every day. I also got into meditation. In my meditation I have rituals: Father, I greet you; I am a radiant, healthy woman. And then I would visualize myself as that woman. I would visualize myself as tall, erect, with good posture. I think good posture is so important; if you've ever fractured your back, you'll understand how desirable it is to have good posture.

My internist was distressed that I was taking these hormones at my age, but I believed in my new doctor and trusted her. To look the way she does, she must be doing something right. And on top of that, I was feeling so much better than I had in years. I began to exercise. I could feel that my bones were strengthening, and my energy was so different. My thinking was back in focus. I felt sharp and in tune.

My friends thought I was crazy because I was having my period again, but I didn't care. I figured it comes with the territory. I was growing bone again, and I was feeling so great. Some months I would bleed more heavily and I would call Dr. S. and say, "Is this for real?" Then we would do another blood panel to find that my hormones needed some adjusting. At my age, things are changing so fast that we need to pay careful attention. I don't use tampons. I don't know, I just can't get used to the idea. My daughters keep trying to encourage me to use them, but I am more comfortable with Kotex.

Today, fifteen years later, I feel great. I have so much energy and joy. I wake up early every day, but I lie in bed until around seven A.M. The first thing I do is make my bed. Once you reach your seventies and eighties, it's easy to fall in love with your bed. So I get up right away and I dance while I am making my bed. I usually listen to Roy Orbison or the Beatles. I do facial exercises for my neck and chin, and I make a promise to my body that I will take good care of it today. Happiness is what this is all about. Since I started with natural hormones, I feel happy most of the time.

I go to exercise classes three days a week. Some of my girlfriends go to these classes for social reasons, but not me. I have a purpose. I am taking care of myself. Exercise is so important; you know, if you don't use it, you will lose it. It all has to do with energy.

After I make my bed and dance, I have coffee (real coffee)—it's my only cup of the day; then while I am making my breakfast, I watch David Letterman. I tape him every night and watch him in the morning because he makes me laugh. For breakfast I usually have yogurt, half of a bran muffin, one-quarter of a Fuji apple, and shredded wheat with milk. Then I either go out or I sit at my computer and go to my Web page. No one reads the stuff I write, but I don't care, I enjoy getting my thoughts down. Once a week I go to line dancing. I love it. There are a lot of nice men there, and we have a lot of fun.

My girlfriends my same age don't have the kind of energy I have. When I walk, I bend and stretch. It feels good. I believe we have a healer within us, and I also believe that exercise is vital. I promised my body that I was going to take good care of it, and that's what I am doing. I lie down for a nap at two o'clock, but I never go to sleep. I just rest. Then I get up and watch Dr. Phil. I really like him. There's something vicarious in watching him. He forces you to really look at the truth about yourself.

I admire Dr. Schwarzbein because she is a front-runner. She has courage and is willing to step out and dare to be different. She gets a lot of criticism, because she is cutting-edge. She has made this her specialty.

I don't have a sex life. I carried a torch for my husband for a long time. But I do still have sexual feelings. I just learned my testosterone is low, so we're going to adjust that. Not so that I can have a stronger libido, but for hormonal balance. It's a good thing my testosterone is low; otherwise, I might be out there walking the streets [laughing]. Regarding men, I do love to hug them and kiss them. I don't care if they are bald or if they are good-looking, I just want them to have good, clear eyes.

I drink about six glasses of water a day, plus one more at night when I take my Metamucil. Yes, as you get older you do have that problem, but I find dancing and exercise really help. For lunch I always have protein and some carbohydrates. I usually have raw vegetables also. Dinner is salmon, a little pasta, and a salad. Right before I go to bed, I have hard rye crackers and maybe some herbed cream cheese and part of an apple.

I am not stiff, I do not have aches and pains, and if aches do come, I refuse to entertain them. If I miss a day of walking, I feel things stiffen up a little. I enjoy laughing. I think we have to laugh at ourselves. I do three Kegel exercises three times a day. It's funny. I have a cat and he is my pal. I talk to him as though he's a person. I never liked cats before. I grew up on a farm and was one of twenty-three kids, so we never had room for any pets. My cat keeps me calm. He's part of my ritual. I never was a *Leave It to Beaver* kind of mom, but I find myself saying, "Hi, I'm home," to him when I come in the door, and it is a nice feeling.

I feel so much of my well-being is because of these hormones. I stopped taking them at one point because they are expensive and when you are a senior every cent counts (it's about $65 a month plus), but after three months I couldn't stand it anymore and I went to the doctor to put me back on hormones.

I plan to continue taking these hormones. It's the sense of well-being—I have to attribute it to that. My body is different from those of other people my age. My thinking is sharp, I read a lot, I'm happy, and I'm satisfied. I have a lot of zest and energy. I look forward to each day. I would say to other women, Try it for six months. What have you got to lose? Don't knock it till you've tried it. I think the mind-set is very important. I feel that I am a well person. Another part of my ritual is that I read anything about being well or staying well. I have a happy attitude, I feel fortunate, I have beautiful children, and I feel each day that God blesses me.

living an

AUTHENTIC

LIFE

Approximately 85 percent of all American
adults are walking around with
burnt-out adrenals, and they deal with it
with Prozac and coffee!

—

31
WHAT YOU DIDN'T GET

The other day I was observing someone I know very well and thinking about the difficult time she was having in her adulthood. It is clear from my vantage point that at the bottom of her trouble is what she "didn't get" in her childhood. I think that is what runs all of us. From outward appearances she had an idyllic childhood, yet upon close examination, was it really? She lived in a beautiful home with a swimming pool, a nanny, and all the creature comforts. But these things will never make up for the unhappiness that pervaded her childhood home. Her parents had a loveless relationship, and when that relationship exploded and they succumbed to divorce, she was left without a proper explanation from either parent and spent the rest of her formative years living with a very angry mother who took shots at her father at every opportunity (a classic situation, by the way). Her mother's anger became her own, and they lived in angry harmony for the rest of the years spent together.

This is a typical scenario in today's modern world. Divorce is the inheritance of this new generation. In my younger years, I was the first person I knew of in my little hometown who was divorced. It was quite a scandal; so much so that I finally had to leave town and move away to escape the whispers and the gossip. Today, divorce is a normal, albeit unhappy, occurrence, something that is more accepted, and the child of divorce does not stand out as he or she once did. Nonetheless, it is not any easier to cope with.

When childhood anger goes unchecked, the result is a chaotic adulthood. As I said in an earlier chapter, the pain you experience as a child does not grow up and mature, even though you do. When the anger or pain of your childhood is not dealt with, it remains locked in your soul and becomes a driving force inside you. One of the most important things you can do for yourself as an adult is confront the pain of your childhood. I grew up with the notion that "the past is the past; let it go." Ah, that it could be so easy! You can move on, but the pain will not. It stays and smolders and is the basis behind your short fuse, or those unexplained moments when you weep for no reason, or the bitterness you feel in general toward life, or the jealousy you can't seem to keep in check. You don't want to be this way, but these feelings are the motivating force behind everything you do. It's embarrassing and difficult to admit even to yourself, because it manifests from something that happened so long ago.

Until you deal with them, these feelings will sit, lying in wait, to ooze out of you at the strangest moments. A good way to discover the driving force behind your unexplained moods is to pay attention to the times when you "lose it." What is it that made you so angry with your husband this morning? (Of course, if your hormones are not balanced, that could explain everything.) I know my buttons are pushed whenever I feel that control over my life is being taken away from me, even a little bit. If my husband makes a plan without consulting me, and it hits me at the perfect hormonal moment of the month, I can get irrationally mad. Why? Obviously I still have more emotional work to do relative to the complete control my alcoholic father had over my life.

So control issues still push my buttons. What are your issues? What makes you emotional? What is the line in the song that your heart responds to? What is the part of the movie when the tears come rolling down your face? Pay attention to these things. These feelings are you talking to yourself. Feelings are how we teach ourselves. Feelings are ourselves trying to let go and release, yet rarely do we pay attention. We just chalk it up to external circumstances—the movie was a tearjerker, or the song was very emotional. But our messages come to us in mysterious ways, through the lyric of a song, a scene in a movie, or a sentence in a book.

Next time it happens, ask yourself, What feeling does that trigger? Take a few moments to think about it. This is not a trivial exercise. These are our opportunities for clarity. We are run by our past until we have dealt with every part of it. You don't need to have been an abused child, as I was; everyone has people and events from the past that are life defining, and often these events are precisely the parts of our lives that have undermined us and made us feel inadequate or unworthy.

What didn't you get in your childhood? Ask yourself this question, and be honest with yourself. After all, this *is* for you! You are old enough to handle it now. Did you not get enough attention? Did you feel you were taking up space in your childhood home? Did you have siblings who taunted you? Did your parents divorce without explanation, and somehow you thought that if only you had been a better child, you could have saved the marriage? Do you feel responsible for some traumatic event that happened in your past? Did someone in your family become very ill and you thought somehow you were responsible? Was one (or both) of your parents abusive, or alcoholic, or a drug abuser? Did you have parents who didn't seem to notice your existence? Do you feel that your parents didn't want you or need you in their lives? Have your relationships not worked out? Were you abandoned? Did your parents not accept you as you are? Do you not have satisfactory relationships with your grown children? There are hundreds of reasons for our unhappiness or our inability to put our finger on happiness. What it eventually comes down to in almost every situation, after peeling away layer after layer (and this can take years or a lifetime), is that you didn't get the love you wanted or thought you should get.

So much of why I am a happy person today has to do with the emotional work I have done in my life to undo the damage of my childhood. I never got the love I wanted or thought I should get from my father. He loved his bottle of booze more than any of us—addiction does that. It took me years to find forgiveness for my father. I spent three years in intense therapy, trying to understand why I had such low self-esteem, why I didn't feel good about myself, and why I was insecure in the presence of just about everyone. Because of this intense therapy, I finally got to the bottom of this force that drove me and had shaped my personality. It was difficult and agitating work. At times I wanted to run from it because it brought back all those buried feelings with full intensity; but I stayed with it, and it is clear to me today that this is the single most important thing I have ever done for myself. Without having done the "work," my life never could have taken the turn that it did. I never would have had the self-esteem to pursue my career, never would have felt worthy of my wonderful husband, never would have learned to love my father for being one of my most important teachers. Through his disease, I was forced to either make a life for myself in spite of the disadvantages of being raised by him and his alcoholism or become a victim of it. I chose not to be a victim, and then I went to work. What a great choice. Because of this choice, I was able to turn his disease around to my advantage. Had I not chosen this path, life as I now know it would not exist. In fact, my self-esteem was so damaged that I question if I would even be alive today.

If this rings any kind of bell with you, think about those things in your life that are in your way. Think about what you didn't get in your life. Generally, we are embarrassed to hearken back so long ago, to times and events that to-day seem like nothing. For many of us, there are obstacles in our lives (some big, some small) that can trigger years of buried feelings that have been in our way. The object of this glorious age, these fabulous forties, fifties, six-ties, seventies, and eighties, is to get the most out of this second half. Finally we have time for ourselves to figure out who we are and what we want. These are big questions and won't be answered easily. It has taken half a lifetime to develop into the person you have become, and if, at this age, you are not happy with that person, it's going to take some time to change into someone else. But it is so worth it! The next fifty years await you, and how glo-rious they can be if you let go of the negative times and events that have been running your life. There is such freedom in looking the past in the eye and choosing to fix those parts of yourself that have been damaged as a result of a past you haven't wanted to remember. The result is an authentic life. When you are living an authentic life, the only person you are ac-countable to is yourself; the only goal is to do the right thing for yourself. It is hard work, and will require focus and attention until your very last day, but what graceful work it is.

Perks of aging: Your supply of brain cells is finally down to a manageable size.

———

32
CONCLUSIONS

By now, I hope I have convinced you not to be afraid of this passage and not to dread it. I stated at the beginning of this book that this is the best I have ever felt and that I have never been happier, menopause and all.

No doubt about it, this passage requires management and handling, but the rewards are worth it. Bioidentical hormones give you an edge over aging never before experienced, if for no other reason than to retain optimal brain function. I don't know about you, but I never want to lose my abilities to think and dream. A great functioning brain is a true gift as we head toward old age. But as you know from reading this book, replacing lost hormones with natural bioidentical ones gives you an edge in almost every area of your life. Hormones are life!

Thank you for going on this journey with me. This is the book I was looking for when I first entered menopause, but it did not exist.

Everything I read pointed out the negatives. I dreaded menopause, and in my first year of this passage the quality of my life was drastically altered. I went on this search for myself, and after going through hundreds of books and studies and talking with many doctors, I was finally able to figure it out. There is no perfect doctor out there; the field is too new. There is too little understanding among doctors. That is why you have to be proactive and get this information for yourselves. We are the pioneers in managing menopause, and our daughters will have an easier time of it because of us. It makes sense, because we are the first generation to live long enough to see menopause all the way through. If you do nothing, you will be the loser. I am enjoying every day because my balance is back and my brain is in perfect working order. I am passionate about understanding not only this time of life, but also what this passage can bring to us emotionally, physically, and spiritually.

This is a tremendous time to be alive. Menopause does not have to be the shameful, icky experience we have all anticipated. Once again we baby boomers have decided not to take this thing sitting down. We have never done this before, and now is not the time to quit. We are still vital and energetic, but coming to terms with the hormone mystery allows us to go out and truly enjoy this age. Balanced hormones coupled with wisdom is a lethal combination. The only obstacle to experiencing all of our potential has been a lack of understanding of the effects of hormone loss.

I do not in any way claim to know everything about hormones; it is too big a subject, and new information comes out every week. But I have opened the door. I have spent hundreds of hours researching and meeting with professionals on the cutting edge. I can hold my own with any doctor regarding this subject. Often I am more informed, and that makes sense, because I have decided to get to the bottom of my own hormonal mysteries. It has been very empowering to understand the inner workings of my body. It has helped me realize that there is cause and effect. If I choose to ingest harmful foods, substances, and chemicals, I know there are consequences. My body is so cleaned out of sugar that when I do decide to indulge, I experience immediate consequences. My mood changes, often I will get a yeast infection, and my energy drops. I also know that it shoots my insulin levels way up, and that, in turn, creates imbalances throughout my entire hormonal system.

One of the many blessings that has come from having lived with cancer in my body is an appreciation of this complex and highly sophisticated house in which I live and the thrill of being alive each day. I wake up grateful. Every day is a borrowed one for me. It doesn't matter if I live to be 105, my cancer taught me to be thankful for all that is. I now treat my body with a tremendous amount of respect. Our bodies need to be well fed with delicious, beautifully prepared, *real* food. Our bodies need nourishment and proper rest. It took me a long time to understand the need to give my body a balanced amount of time out. It is something I am still working on; the workaholic in me is alive and well, but why wouldn't such a finely tuned machine need cooling out?

I used to take a weird kind of pleasure in outworking everyone. I am sure that the drive to push myself as hard as I have at times in my life comes from the child of the alcoholic in me, still trying to please that father. I now know that I am not invincible. In my frustration at not getting satisfactory medical answers to questions about the changes I was going through—physically, hormonally, and emotionally—I realized that it was up to me to do the work and learn how best to take care of myself. I couldn't find anyone to make sense of it for me, and this forced me to be proactive. This is what we all need to do. No one is going to do it for you! The women who look the best and feel the best are the ones who have pushed for more information. We're not at the top of the researchers' list. Only by yelling and screaming are they going to focus on our medical issues.

I know that in the coming years new and cutting-edge information on the hormonal system will become available, and I am going to be right there listening with an open mind, questioning and evaluating. I want to know what's new, and in turn I will pass on everything I learn about this subject to you. I love that I no longer sit in my doctor's office taking every answer and explanation at face value. I now question. I don't give up. Without this passion I would be a very unhappy woman right now. My menopausal symptoms were severe. My life had lost its quality, and for a time I thought that this was the way I was going to be—itchy, bitchy, sweaty, sleepy, bloated, forgetful, and all dried up: those seven miserable little menopause dwarfs. Add to that high insulin levels, and I was on a fast track to disease because of the departure of my hormones.

What a relief to understand that I am in control and have enough information to know and feel when my finely tuned machine is out of whack. I can tell when it's even the tiniest bit off base. How empowering. When it's all working in concert, I feel like a living symphony. I experience joy and happiness that seem to want to burst out of me. I also feel proud to have this knowledge, so that I am not dependent upon anyone or anything telling me what I should do about my body. I know it's entirely up to me to care and protect this magnificent house I get to live in as if it were the most exquisite piece of art.

Hormones *are* the least understood medical mystery. We were never expected to live this long, so generations before us didn't get too worked up over this passage. With the loss of hormones, women contracted the diseases of aging and then died early. In those days, sixty, fifty, even forty was not considered too young to die. Aren't you shocked these days when someone that "young" dies? Medical technology has made tremendous strides. They have figured out how to keep us alive longer than ever before. We are going to live to be ninety or a hundred. But technology has not figured out how to ensure that these extra twenty or twenty-five years are quality ones. I don't know about you, but I want to be dancing on my one-hundredth birthday. Why not? With the new understanding of our hormones, it is possible to stay vital right up to the end. It is hard work, but once you understand, it becomes second nature. Unless I was starving to death, I would rather not eat than ingest fake food loaded with chemicals and preservatives.

But there is more to it. We are, as stated by the professionals and the wonderful, generous people I have talked with for this book, body, mind, and spirit. It's the whole package. Our job in life is to work on ourselves to become the best that we can be. Respecting our bodies is a vital component in our evolution, but evolving and growing emotionally and spiritually completes this trilogy. It is easy to become bitter and angry at what we didn't get; it is easy to blame others for what didn't work out in this life. True growth comes from seeing the part each of us has played in the drama of our individual lives. When we are able to see how we have contributed to those things that have brought us unhappiness or dissatisfaction, we can become accountable. Accountability is taking responsibility for the situation. Accountability is maturity as well as growth, and through this growth we can find resolution. It allows the situation to be rectified. Then each of us will be able to make corrections, or fix what is broken in our selves or our relationships, or make amends, or humble ourselves to do our part in reversing any negative energy that circles around us. It's an opportunity to apologize, to end all disagreements. Doing these things can free you and allow you to have the happiness you want at this age.

And then there is accountability to yourself.

Are you pleased with who you are? If not, you can change. This is the spirit. Every day ask yourself, How can I become a better person? If you ask for it, it will come to you. We already have the answers within; it is up to each one of us to find them. It is my hope that this book has assisted you in your search. Just remember, you are a beautiful and magnificent person. This passage is your opportunity; this search for knowledge will open doors to rooms you never thought of entering. This is your time to soar, not those angst-filled years of youth. The time is now. The world is yours. You are at the top of your game. You have wisdom and perspective. Use it well, and pass it on to the next generation. We are here to help one another become all that we are capable of being. Turn on your personal light as bright as you can make it. The knowledge and wisdom you have gained will make you sexier. Because after all, we now know that these are *"the sexy years."*

RESOURCES

NATURAL HORMONE REPLACEMENT THERAPY

American Academy of Anti-Aging Medicine
1510 West Montana Street
Chicago, IL 60614
(773) 528-4333
www.worldhealth.net

Contact the academy to learn more about natural hormone replacement therapy. It is the leading organization of its kind, dedicated to the advancement of all therapeutic approaches that play a role in antiaging medicine, including natural bioidentical HRT.

Jennifer Berman, M.D.
Female Sexual Medicine Center at UCLA
924 Westwood Boulevard, Suite 515
Los Angeles, CA 90024
(310) 794-3030
(866) 439-2835
www.urology.medsch.ucla.edu/fsmc-jberman.html

Laura Berman, Ph.D.
Berman Center
211 East Ontario Street
Chicago, IL 60611
(800) 709-4709
www.bermancenter.com

Network for Excellence in Women's Sexual Health
www.newshe.com

Newshe is the official Web site of Drs. Laura and Jennifer Berman.

Michael Galitzer, M.D.
12381 Wilshire Boulevard, Suite 102
Los Angeles, CA 90025
(310) 820-6042
www.ahealth.com

Dr. Galitzer specializes in antiaging and natural bioidentical hormone replacement therapy.

Robert Greene, M.D.
1255 East Street, Suite 201
Redding, CA 96001
(530) 244-9052
www.specialtycare4women.com

Dr. Greene specializes in natural bioidentical hormone replacement therapy.

Uzzi Reiss, M.D.
414 North Camden Drive, Suite 750
Beverly Hills, CA 90210
(310) 247-1300
www.uzzireissmd.com

Dr. Reiss, an ob/gyn, specializes in natural bioidentical hormone replacement therapy.

Dr. Diana Schwarzbein
5901 Encina Road, Suite A
Goleta, CA 93117
(805) 681-0003
www.drhormone.com

Dr. Schwarzbein is an endocrinologist who specializes in menopause and a pioneer in natural bioidentical hormone replacement therapy.

Eugene Shippen, M.D.
9 East Lancaster Avenue
Shillington, PA 19607
(610) 777-7896

Dr. Shippen specializes in male menopause (andropause).

www.suzannesomers.com

My Web site has a link to information on bioidentical hormone replacement, including a reprint of the Women's Health Initiative Study.

American College for Advancement in Medicine (ACAM)
23121 Verdugo Drive, Suite 204
Laguna Hills, CA 92653
(800) 532-3688
www.acam.org

ACAM is dedicated to establishing certification and standards of practice or preventive medicine and the ACAM protocol.

American Health Institute
12381 Wilshire Boulevard
Los Angeles, CA 90025
(800) 392-2623
www.ahealth.com

Cofounded by Dr. Michael Galitzer, the institute is a pioneering research organization in the field of longevity medicine and the use of natural hormone replacement therapy.

WEB SITES FOR SEXUAL AIDS

www.goodvibes.com
www.grandopening.com

TESTING HORMONE LEVELS

Aeron LifeCycles
1933 Davis Street, Suite 310
San Leandro, CA 94577
(800) 631-7900
www.aeron.com

Sabre Sciences, Inc.
910 Hampshire Road, Suite P
Westlake Village, CA 91361
(888) 490-7300
www.sabresciences.com

COMPOUNDING PHARMACIES

ApothéCure, Inc.
4001 McEwen Road, Suite 100
Dallas, TX 75244
(972) 960-6601
(800) 969-6601
www.apothecure.com

The Compounding Pharmacy of Beverly Hills
9629 West Olympic Boulevard
Beverly Hills, CA 90212
(310) 284-8675
(888) 799-0212
www.compounding-expert.com

Health Pharmacies
2809 Fish Hatchery Road, Suite 103
Madison, WI 51713
(800) 373-6704

International Academy of Compounding Pharmacists
P.O. Box 1365
Sugar Land, TX 77487
(800) 927-4227
www.iacprx.org

You may call them or go to their Web site and enter your zip code for a referral to the closest compounding pharmacy in your area.

Medical Center Pharmacy
3675 South Rainbow Boulevard
Las Vegas, NV 89103
(800) 723-7455

Solutions Pharmacy
4632 Highway 58 North
Chattanooga, TN 37416
(423) 894-3222
(800) 523-1486
www.lakesidepharmacy.com/index2.ivnu

Steven's Pharmacy
1525 Mesa Verde Drive East
Costa Mesa, CA 92626
(800) 352-3786
www.stevensrx.com

Town Center Drugs and Compounding Pharmacy
72840 Highway 111
Westfield Shopping Town
Palm Desert, CA 92260
(760) 341-3984
(877) 340-5922

Women's International Pharmacy
13925 West Meeker Boulevard, Suite 13
Sun City West, AZ 85375
(800) 279-5708

RECOMMENDED READING

These books have assisted me in my journey to understand this difficult and complex passage and helped me in putting together *The Sexy Years*.

Berman, Jennifer, M.D., and Laura Berman, Ph.D. *For Women Only: A Revolutionary Guide to Overcoming Sexual Dysfunction and Reclaiming Your Sex Life.* New York: Holt, 2001.

Colgan, Michael. *Hormonal Health.* Vancouver, B.C.: Apple Publishing, 1996.

Collins, Joseph, N.D. *What's Your Menopause Type?* Roseville, Calif.: Prima Health, 2000.

Gershon, Michael D., M.D. *The Second Brain.* New York: HarperCollins, 1998.

Hanley, Jesse Lynn, M.D., and Nancy Deville. *Tired of Being Tired.* New York: Putnam, 2001.

Lee, John R., M.D., with Virginia Hopkins.

What Your Doctor May Not Tell You About Menopause. New York: Warner Books, 1996.

Lee, John R., M.D., with Jesse Hanley, M.D., and Virginia Hopkins. *What Your Doctor May Not Tell You About Premenopause.* New York: Warner Books, 1999.

Nelson, Miriam E., Ph.D., with Sarah Wernick, Ph.D. *Strong Women, Strong Bones.* New York: Perigee, 2000.

Regelson, William, M.D., and Carol Colman. *The Super-Hormone Promise: Nature's Antidote to Aging.* New York: Simon & Schuster, 1996.

Reiss, Uzzi, M.D., with Martin Zucker. *Natural Hormone Balance for Women.* New York: Pocket Books Health, 2001.

Sapolsky, Robert M. *The Trouble with Testosterone.* New York: Scribner, 1997.

Schwarzbein, Diana, M.D., and Nancy Deville. *The Schwarzbein Principle.* Health Communications, 1999.

Schwarzbein, Diana, M.D., with Marilyn Brown. *The Schwarzbein Principle II.* Health Communications, 2002.

Shippen, Eugene, M.D., and William Fryer. *The Testosterone Syndrome.* New York: M. Evans, 1998.

INDEX

Suzanne Somers is the author of eleven books, including the *New York Times* best-sellers *Keeping Secrets*; *Suzanne Somers' Eat Great, Lose Weight*; *Suzanne Somers' Get Skinny on Fabulous Food*; *Suzanne Somers' Eat, Cheat, and Melt the Fat Away*; and *Suzanne Somers' Fast and Easy*. The former star of the hit television programs *Three's Company* and *Step by Step*, Suzanne is one of the most respected and trusted brand names in the world, representing cosmetics and skin care products, apparel, jewelry, a computerized facial fitness system, fitness products, and an extensive food line called SomerSweet.